An Introduction to Auditory Processing Disorders in Children

An Introduction to Auditory Processing Disorders in Children

Edited by

Teralandur K. Parthasarathy
Southern Illinois University Edwardsville

LEA

LAWRENCE ERLBAUM ASSOCIATES, PUBLISHERS

2006   Mahwah, New Jersey   London

Acquisitions Editor:	Cathleen Petree
Cover Design:	Tomai Maridou
Textbook Production Manager:	Paul Smolenski
Full-Service Compositor:	TechBooks
Text and Cover Printer:	Hamilton Printing Company
Cover:	APD Management Tripod. (See Chapter 9, p. 163.)

This book was typeset in 10/12 pt. Palatino, Italic, Bold, and Bold Italic.
The heads were typeset in Palatino and Berling.

Lawrence Erlbaum Associates, Inc., Publishers
10 Industrial Avenue
Mahwah, New Jersey 07430
www.erlbaum.com

Library of Congress Cataloging-in-Publication Data

An introduction to auditory processing disorders in children / edited by Teralandur K. Parthasarathy.
   p. ; cm.
  Includes bibliographical references and index.
  ISBN 0-8058-5392-8 (cloth : alk. paper)—ISBN 0-8058-5393-6 (pbk. : alk. paper)
 1. Word deafness in children.   I. Parthasarathy, Teralandur K.
  [DNLM: 1. Auditory Perceptual Disorders—diagnosis—Child.   2. Auditory Perceptual Disorder—
physiopathology—Child.   3. Auditory Perceptual Disorders—therapy—Child.   4. Attention Deficit
Disorder with Hyperactivity—Child.   5. Needs Assessment—Child.   WV 272 I62   2006]
RF291.5.C45I58   2006
618.92′855—dc22

2005018304

Books published by Lawrence Erlbaum Associates are printed on
acid-free paper, and their bindings are chosen for strength and durability.

Printed in the United States of America
10 9 8 7 6 5 4 3 2 1

To my mother and my brother Dr. T. K. Raghunath
for their unrelenting help and support

and

To my wife Dr. Gita Malur, my daugther Shilpa, and my son Shrikanth
for their love, understanding, and support

Contents

Preface

Auditory processing disorder (often called central auditory processing disorder) is not a new entity. Over the past 10 years, numerous advances have been made in the area of assessment and management of auditory processing disorders (APD). Advances in brain imaging technology and electrophysiogic techniques have helped us significantly in our understanding of the brain mechanisms that process auditory information.

In recent years, APD has become an important clinical entity within the field of communication disorders. More and more children are being diagnosed with APD or, in some cases, are described with behavioral manifestations that are compatible with the symptoms of APD.

The purpose of this book is to assist audiologists, speech-language pathologists, and other related professionals in gaining knowledge and understanding in the three major areas related to APD: basic science, assessment, and management.

Many specialists have a keen interest in various aspects of APD. However, there is a tendency for these groups to communicate primarily within their own defined disciplines. Thus, the significant contributions of each group are often not shared with the others. This potentially reduces both our understanding and effectiveness in dealing with APD. It is the purpose of this book to bring together the knowledge base of different professional groups that all too often do not work together and to improve the prospects for a better quality of life for children with a diagnosis of APD. The strength of this book lies in the skill and breadth of knowledge of its contributing authors. They are not only highly regarded clinicians and researchers, but they are also dedicated professionals who have tried to explain, clarify, and demystify APD.

This book will not be the final word on APD. It is, however, a highly positive step in the direction of collating the most recent evidence from all the relevant fields.

With time, assessment and management of APD have taken on a multidisciplinary approach. Taken together, the chapters in this book are an extraordinary compendium of the status of APD in children today. It is the hope of all contributing authors that this information will serve students in audiology and speech-language pathology, practicing audiologists, speech-language pathologists, and members of related professions, notably psychologists, special educators, and physicians.

Contributors

Teri James Bellis   Department of Communication Disorder, The University of South Dakota, Vermillion, South Dakota

Subhash C. Bhatnagar   Marquette University, Milwaukee, Wisconsin

Anthony T. Cacace   Albany Medical College, Albany, New York

David Duesenberg   St. John's Mercy Medical Center, St. Louis, Missouri

Jeanane M. Ferre   Audiology Private Practice, Oak Park, Illinois

Cheryl Deconde Johnson   Colorado Department of Education, Greeley, Colorado

Dorothy A. Kelly   St. Joseph's College, Patchogue, New York

Edward W. Korabic   Marquette University, Milwaukee, Wisconsin

Stephanie McAndrews   Southern Illinois University Edwardsville, Edwardsville, Illinois

Dennis J. McFarland   New York State Health Department, Albany, New York

Teralandur K. Parthasarathy   Southern Illinois University Edwardsville, Edwardsville, Illinois

Gail J. Richard   Eastern Illinois University, Charleston, Illinois

Gail M. Whitelaw   The Ohio State University, Columbus, Ohio

Krista Yuskow   The Ohio State University, Columbus, Ohio

An Introduction to Auditory Processing Disorders in Children

Neuroanatomy and Neurophysiology of the Central Auditory Pathways

Subhash C. Bhatnagar
Edward W. Korabic
Marquette University

HEARING SENSITIVITY

Normal hearing is essential to the acquisition of oral language and effective verbal communication. Any impairment of the auditory system, either congenitally or adventitiously acquired, that affects the transmission and/or perception of sound is likely to have a profound effect on one's ability to hear and comprehend spoken language. The human ear is sensitive to acoustic events within the frequency range of 20 to 18,000 Hertz (Hz). However, the human ear is not equally sensitive to all frequencies within this range. The ear is most sensitive to sound frequencies between 500 and 4,000 Hz—the frequency range most important for speech reception. In terms of intensity, the human auditory system is sensitive to a range of 0 to 140 dB Sound Pressure Level (SPL). Normal conversational speech falls within the range of approximately 50 to 77 dB SPL. Repeated and prolonged exposure to intensity levels above 85 dB SPL can cause permanent structural damage to the inner ear. Sound pressure levels above 140 dB SPL can cause pain sensation and instantaneous structural damage to the hearing mechanism.

OVERVIEW OF AUDITION

The process of audition (hearing) begins when sound waves enter the external auditory meatus and impinge on the tympanic membrane. The subsequent movement of the tympanic membrane serves to convert sound energy into mechanical energy. The motion (vibration) of the tympanic membrane causes the middle ear bones—malleus, incus, and stapes—to be set into motion. This mechanical energy is transmitted to the cochlear fluids of the inner ear via stapes movement in and out of the oval window of the inner ear, thus converting mechanical energy into hydraulic energy. The resulting movement of the fluids causes patterned membrane movement in the cochlea.

Movement of the membranes in the cochlea stimulate the cilia of the hair cells, which in turn causes depolarization of the hair cells. Depolarization activates chemical channels, triggering the release of neurotransmitters, across the synapse between the hair cells and auditory nerve fibers. The neurotransmitter depolarizes the terminals of the auditory nerve fiber and a nerve action potential is generated. The action potential discharges are transmitted by the fibers of the auditory nerve to the cochlear nuclei in the brain stem, which project these nerve impulses to multiple synaptic points in the brain stem as well as the thalamus. The combined signals from both ears are analyzed in the brain stem by their intensity and frequency to localize sound. Auditory impulses finally travel to the primary auditory cortex located on the superior surface of the temporal lobe in the gyri of Heschl, which are involved with sound perception. The auditory impulses further travel to Wernicke's (associational language) area, where the auditory signals are analyzed and interpreted into language-specific meaningful messages and the comprehension of spoken language occurs.

This chapter provides a functional description of the neural circuitry and physiology of hearing from the inner ear to the primary auditory cortex. Each intersecting level of the brain stem is listed and functionally discussed in terms of its significance to the transmission of auditory information.

INNER EAR MECHANISM

The inner ear contains the sensory organs of balance and hearing. The sensory organ for balance is called the vestibular system and includes the utricle, saccule, and three semicircular canals. The sensory organ for hearing is called the acoustic or auditory system. The auditory portion of the inner ear is a snail-shaped structure called the cochlear. Both the vestibular and auditory systems are encased in the same bony capsule, contain the same fluid systems, and share the same cranial nerve—Cranial nerve VIII (Fig. 1.1).

There are two labyrinths in the inner ear: the osseous (bony) labyrinth and the membranous labyrinth. The osseous labyrinth is a bony capsule covering a series of irregular cavities in the petrous portion of the temporal bone. Inside the osseous labyrinth is the membranous labyrinth, which includes the cochlear duct (scala media) and the vestibular apparatus of saccule, utricle, and three semicircular canals. The inner ear fluid perilymph protects the membranous labyrinth from the bony labyrinth. Endolymph is a closed fluid system within the membranous labyrinth of the cochlear and vestibular portions of the inner ear.

COCHLEAR ANATOMY

The cochlea resembles a snail-shaped structure winding two and a half times around a bony, central core called the modiolus. A cross-section of the cochlea is depicted in Fig. 1.2.

With a length of approximately 35 mm, the cochlea is comprised of three fluid-filled chambers or canals: scala vestibuli, scala media, and scala tympani. Scala vestibuli is the uppermost chamber and follows the inner contour of the cochlea. Scala tympani lies at the bottom and follows the outer contour of the cochlea. Scala vestibuli communicates with scala tympani through a small aperture at the apex of the cochlea called the helicotrema.

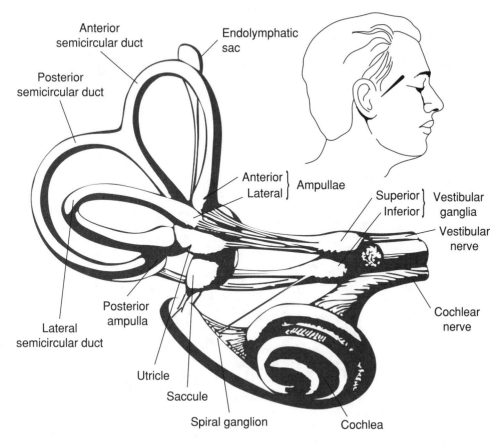

FIG. 1.1. Inner ear labyrinth composed of the semicircular ducts, vestibule, and cochlea along with vestibular and cochlear nerves. From *Neuroscience for the Study of Communicative Disorders*, 2nd. ed. by Subhash C. Bhatnagar, 2001. Copyright 2001 by Lippincott, Williams and Wilkins.

Reisner's membrane, or vestibular ligament, separates scala vestibuli from scala media. The basilar membrane separates scala media from scala tympani. The end organ of hearing—the organ of Corti—is supported by the basilar membrane. Both membranes extend from the osseous (bony) spiral lamina, a bony shell that extends from the modiolus, and attach to the spiral ligament located on the wall of the bony labyrinth.

Scala vestibuli and scala tympani are filled with perilymph, which is secreted by the periosteal lining of the scalae. Scala media is filled with endolymph, which is secreted by stria vascularis, a highly vascularized band of cells on the internal surface of the spiral ligament within scala media. Both of these fluids are marked by different concentrations of sodium and potassium ions. The higher sodium (Na+) relative to the lower potassium (K+) concentration of perilymph makes it similar to cerebrospinal fluid (CSF) or extracellular fluid. The ionic composition of endolymph, which has a higher concentration of K+ relative to Na+, is similar to the intracellular fluid (Haines, 2002).

The organ of Corti, which is located in the scala media on the basilar membrane, contains the sensory cells of hearing—the hair cells. The hair cells are equipped with specialized stereocilia on their tips. There are two types of hair cells: inner and outer (Fig. 1.2). In humans, these sensory cells run in parallel rows from the base of the

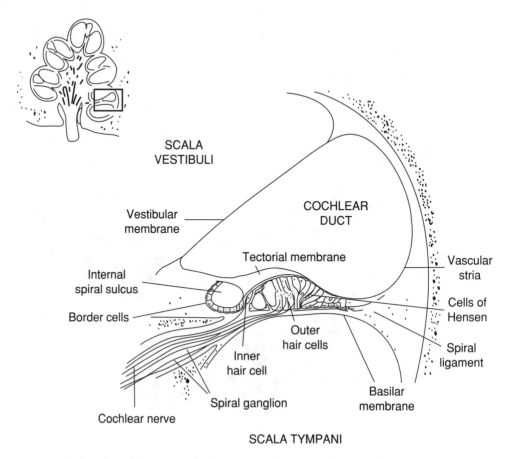

FIG. 1.2. A diagrammatic illustration of the cochlear duct on a radial section of the
cochlea. From *Neuroscience for the Study of Communicative Disorders*, 2nd. ed. by Subhash
C. Bhatnagar, 2001. Copyright 2001 by Lippincott, Williams and Wilkins.

cochlea to the apex of the cochlea. Inner hair cells (IHC) run in a single row, outer
hair cells (OHC) in rows of three or four. The arch of Corti separates the row of IHC
from the rows of OHC. There are approximately 12,000 OHCs and 3,000 IHCs. Fifty to
70 stereocilia project from each IHC, forming a "V" pattern. Forty to 150 stereocilia
project from each OHC, forming a "W" pattern. The cilia of the OHCs fit into inden-
tations on the underside of the overlying gelatinous tectorial membrane. The cilia of
the IHC do not directly insert into the tectorial membrane.

IHC and OHC differ in terms of their innervations: IHC are predominantly innervated by ascending auditory nerve fibers, whereas the OHC are predominantly
innervated by projections from the descending auditory pathways including the olivocochlear bundle (OCB).

COCHLEAR FUNCTION

The cochlea converts the mechanical energy received from the middle ear ossicles into
hydraulic mechanical energy and initiates neural activity. As the stapes moves into the
oval window, it displaces perilymph toward scala tympani through the helicotrema.

Due to the incompressibility of fluids of the cochlea because of the surrounding bony labyrinth, the resulting fluid pressure is relieved by the outward movement of the round window in the scala tympani. As the stapes moves out of the oval window, perilymph is displaced toward the scala vestibuli with a corresponding inward movement of the round window. Because the basilar membrane (BM) is structurally flexible, it responds to this pressure by its own displacement. As the basilar membrane is displaced beginning at its base, the deformation moves toward the apex of the cochlea as a traveling wave. As the wave moves toward the apex of the cochlea, its velocity slows but the amplitude increases. Amplitude of basilar membrane displacement reaches a maximum at a specific point along the membrane before gradually attenuating. The point of maximum amplitude of basilar membrane displacement corresponds to the frequency of the stimulus. Thus, different sound frequencies produce different traveling wave patterns, forming peak amplitudes at different regions of the cochlea. Maximum amplitude of the basilar membrane traveling wave occurs near the base of the cochlea for high-frequency sounds. As the frequency of the stimulus decreases, the peak amplitude of the traveling wave moves toward the apex of the cochlea. A signal consisting of many frequencies will cause a traveling wave with multiple peaks along the basilar membrane.

The hair cells located at the point of the maximum basilar membrane movement are the most stimulated, suggesting that cochlear frequency selectivity is initially related to the mechanical properties of the basilar membrane. However, the frequency selectivity also may be related to structural and electrical properties of hair cells. This relationship between the maximum cochlear response and characteristic frequency is the basis of the place theory of hearing, and this tonotopic organization is preserved throughout the auditory system.

The deformation of the basilar membrane results in the mechanical displacement of the cilia of the hair cells by the overlying tectorial membrane. The mechanical displacement of the cilia—or shearing action—leads to the depolarization of the hair cells. The depolarization triggers the release of neurotransmitters from the synaptic vesicles at the base of the hair cells. The neurotransmitters have a depolarizing effect on the terminals of the auditory nerve fibers that results in the generation of action potentials which travel to the brain stem.

ELECTRIC TRANSDUCTION

The cilia of the hair cells are embedded in the endolymph, which has an electrical potential of +80 mV. This endolymphatic potential is supplied by stria vascularis. Stimulation of the cilia of the hair cells allows this potential to flow through the hair cell, initiating neural activity in the cochlea. Genetic or acquired structural pathology of stria vascularis is likely to alter the biochemical process for nerve impulses (Haines, 2002).

Specifically, the initiation of neural activity in the cochlea is a result of the ionic properties of the hair cells and the transmission of charged particles through the hair cell membranes. The presence of a -70 mV intracellular environment and $+80$ mV endolymphatic potential in scala media results in a 150 mV gradient difference across the apical ends of the cilia. This difference serves to regulate the electrical response of hair cells to mechanical deformation.

Basilar membrane movement deforms the stereocilia against the tectorial membrane, and this results in a graded depolarization of the hair cells. Deformation of the stereocilia of hair cells increases potassium (K+) permeability and opens K+ sensitive pores in the tips of cilia. The inward K+ current enters the hair cells through the cilia and depolarizes the hair cells. This depolarization also opens the voltage-sensitive calcium (Ca_2+) channels at the base of these hair cells (Castro et al., 2003). This triggers an inward movement of calcium into the hair cells, which in turn initiates the release of glutamate (a fast excitatory neurotransmitter) from the synaptic vessels. The cochlear nerve terminals pick up the neurotransmitter and generate action potentials that travel to the cochlear nuclear complex located at the pontomedullary junction.

COCHLEAR AMPLIFIER

Basilar membrane movement provides passive analysis of sound. The OHC help provide active analysis. In other words, OHC serve to alter cochlear mechanics—that is, basilar membrane movement.

OHC have been found to contain contractile proteins. Stimulation of the cilia of the OHC (shearing action of the cilia) allows the endolymphic potential to pass through and cause the OHCs to contract or oscillate. The stimulated OHCs oscillate at the same frequency of the stimulus. This oscillation produces a receptor potential called the cochlear microphonic. This potential mimics the waveform of the stimulus. Because the cilia of the OHC make direct contact with the tectorial membrane, the contractile property of the OHC causes BM movement to be more finely tuned. The contractile properties of the OHC also serve to increase the sensitivity of the ear as a cochlear amplifier. OHC oscillation increases the motion in the cochlea, allowing the tectorial membrane to stimulate (or shear) the cilia of the IHC—the true sensory cells of hearing. OHC contraction (and thus amplification) is dependent on the intensity of the stimulus. OHC participation is greater at low intensities and less at high intensities.

NEURAL CODING OF AUDITORY INFORMATION

The transmission of auditory information from the cochlea to the central auditory nervous system is coded so that all its elements—timing, intensity, frequency, and others—are fully retained. The exact mechanism and format for coding acoustic information are not completely understood. However, it is likely that this information is coded in a variety of ways to ensure a degree of redundancy. For example, cochlear representation of frequency is based on the stimulation of hair cells at a specific region along the basilar membrane. Although cochlea neural units can be stimulated by a wide variety of sound frequencies, they respond maximally only to a specific frequency with a low threshold for that frequency. Thus, the place of stimulation along the basilar membrane may be the way frequency is initially coded in the auditory system. Sound intensity also could be coded by the number of related neural units stimulated along the basilar membrane or by the rate of neural discharge. Furthermore, the location of nerve fibers in the auditory nerve bundle may dictate their role in transmitting information about the auditory signal. For example, the fibers traveling centrally within the ascending tract may mediate specific tonotopic frequency attributes, whereas the fibers that are tertiary and located in the outer edge of the auditory pathway may be responsible for mediating additional coded properties of sound, such as timing, intensity, and information related to binaural or monaural interactions (Kingsley, 1999).

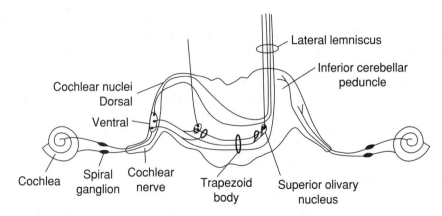

FIG. 1.3. A diagrammatic illustration of the retrocochlear neural mechanism. From *Neuroscience for the Study of Communicative Disorders*, 2nd. ed. by Subhash C. Bhatnagar, 2001. Copyright 2001 by Lippincott, Williams and Wilkins.

RETROCOCHLEAR AUDITORY MECHANISM

The retrocochlear portion of the auditory system (Fig. 1.3) consists of the distal/ peripheral (unmyelinated) and proximal (myelinated) processes of the bipolar spiral ganglion cells. Also referred to as the auditory or cochlear nerve, the unmyelinated peripheral process of the spiral ganglion cells enter the basilar membrane to connect with the hair cells. They pick up the neurotransmitter from the synaptic transmission of the hair cells and generate nerve impulses, which are then transmitted through the proximal fibers of the spiral ganglion cells to the cochlear nuclei in the brain stem. There are about 30,000 spiral ganglion cells, made up of two types of neurons: Types I and II. Amounting to about 90% of the total spiral ganglion cells, Type I cells respond to a narrow range of frequency by being connected to only a few selective hair cells in the cochlea. On the other hand, the axonal processes, originating from Type II cells in the spiral ganglion, are known to synapse with 10 or more hair cells—suggesting their sensitivity to a wider range of frequencies with less precision.

The central processes of these spiral ganglion cells form the acoustic branch of cranial nerve VIII and pass along with facial cranial nerve through the internal acoustic meatus, a canal in the petrous portion of the temporal bone, before synapsing on the cochlear nuclei at the ponto-medullary junction. This explains why a pathology in the acoustic meatus may result in an impairment of both audition and facial functions.

CENTRAL AUDITORY PATHWAYS

The auditory cortical projections, unlike the projections of other sensory systems like somatosensation, are perhaps the most complex because of their multiple synaptic relays at many levels between the cochlear nuclei (second-order neurons) and the thalamus (third-order neurons). The transmission of auditory information to the cortex is regulated by a simple rule that relates to the preservation of the tonotopic code from the cochlear hair cells to the primary auditory cortex. Other aspects of the audition that also are preserved involve the contralaterality of projections and the incorporation of monaural and binaural information. Contralaterality refers to the projections that originate in one ear and travel to the auditory cortex on the opposite side. Some of this information also is transmitted to the auditory cortex on the same side (ipsilateral). Interaural time difference in processing binaural (related to both ears) auditory information is used to identify the direction and source of sound (Bhatnagar, 2001; Kingsley, 1999; Haines, 2002).

The auditory pathway contains two types of fibers: centrally located core fibers and peripherally located belt fibers (Kingsley, 1999). The core fibers are organized tonotopically and maintain tonal representation throughout their course. The belt fibers are less organized in terms of their frequency representation and may be sensitive to timing and spatial aspects of sound patterns.

The central auditory pathway (Fig. 1.3) extends from the cochlear nuclear complex to the primary auditory cortex in the temporal lobe. The myelinated, proximal fibers of the auditory nerve enter the brain stem laterally at the pontomedullary junction and synapse upon the cochlear nuclear complex. Hierarchically organized structures in the central auditory pathway include the cochlear nuclei, fibers of the acoustic stria, trapezoid body, superior olivary nucleus, lateral lemniscus, and inferior colliculus. The auditory pathway from the midbrain to the cortex includes the brachium of inferior colliculus, the medial geniculate body, the auditory radiations (geniculocortical fibers), and the primary auditory cortex located in the transverse gyri of Heschl.

COCHLEAR NUCLEAR COMPLEX

Fibers of the auditory nerve enter the brain stem at the pontomedullary junction dorsolateral to the inferior cerebellar peduncle (restiform body). They terminate in the cochlear nuclear complex, which contains dorsal (posterior) and ventral (anterior) groups of nuclei (Fig. 1.4). The dorsal cochlear nucleus is located dorsal–lateral to the restiform body, whereas the ventral cochlear nucleus is located ventral–lateral to the restiform body. The entering fibers of the auditory nerve divide into dorsal and ventral bundles (stria) in order to synapse onto the cochlear nuclei. Each of the afferent fibers makes specialized synaptic contacts with multiple cell types in the cochlear nuclear complex. These synaptic contracts are orderly distributed in rows in order to maintain discrete tonotopic representation. The cochlear nuclear complex is also known to contain different specialized cells like bushy and multiform (Kingsley, 1999). Some of these cells may provide a sustained response to tones mediating important sound attributes like phase and timing, while the other cells may respond to changes in sound pressure level.

An important principle governing the functional representation at the cochlear nuclear complex and through the ascending auditory pathway is the preservation of precise tonotopic organization. The frequency-related projections from the hair cells in the cochlea synapse ipsilaterally on the specialized cells in the cochlear nuclear complex so that a discrete tonal representation is retained. The fibers from the apex of the cochlea, which represent lower frequencies, terminate at the superficial layers of the cochlear nucleus. The fibers from the base of the cochlea, which represent higher frequencies, penetrate deeper in the nucleus and thereby preserve the tonal correspondence. This discrete tonotopic representation is retained throughout the ascending fibers of the central auditory pathway and all its nuclei up to the auditory cortex.

ASCENDING PROJECTIONS FROM COCHLEAR NUCLEAR COMPLEX

The cochlear nuclear complex gives rise to parallel pathways that carry coded auditory information like intensity as well as monaural and binaural aspects of sounds. These projections, called the lateral lemniscus, ascend in both the ipsilateral and/or contralateral auditory pathways. The exact path taken by these ascending fibers is not as clear as it seems to be in the commonly illustrated diagrams of the brain stem auditory pathways. Most auditory fibers are known to cross the midline and project to the contralateral auditory system, although a small amount of fibers do not cross the midline and instead ascend ipsilaterally (Fig. 1.4).

The cochlear projections that cross the midline travel in three bundles: the dorsal acoustic stria, the intermediate stria, and the trapezoid body. There is a functional

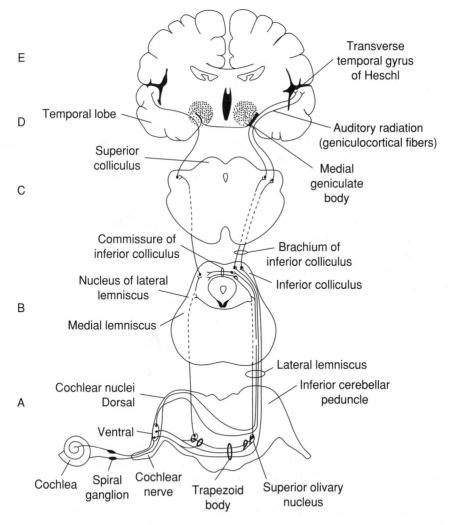

FIG. 1.4.   A diagrammatic illustration of the central auditory pathway. From *Neuroscience for the Study of Communicative Disorders,* 2nd. ed. by Subhash C. Bhatnagar, 2001. Copyright 2001 by Lippincott, Williams and Wilkins.

purpose for each of these axonal channels in terms of mediating specific signal attributes; however, our knowledge of this coding as well as the encoded ones remains incomplete. The cells along the crossing fibers form the nucleus and the trapezoid body. The fibers of the dorsal acoustic stria cross the midline and ascend in the contralateral lateral lemniscus without sending projections to any of the superior olivary nuclei (SON). Some collaterals from the fibers of the intermediate acoustic stria may project to the ipsilateral and/or contralateral superior olivary nucleus while the main body of fibers joins the contralateral lateral lemniscus. The fibers of the trapezoid body, the largest stria of the three bundles, cross the midline to terminate in the SON, which is located laterally in the dorsal pons next to the nucleus of the trapezoid body. Some of the auditory fibers that cross the midline may bypass the SON on their way to the contralateral lateral lemniscus.

SUPERIOR OLIVARY NUCLEUS

The superior olivary nucleus (SON), a collection of nuclei in the pons, is located adjacent to the facial motor nucleus and the facial cranial nerve fibers. This nucleus plays a significant role in localizing sound and is found to be highly developed in animals. Known to be an important auditory relay nucleus, it is the first nucleus to receive inputs from both the ipsilateral and contralateral cochlear nuclei.

The SON contains binaural cells: the lateral superior olive and medial superior olive, which are surrounded by small peri-olivary nuclei. The cell bodies in the SON contain two large dendrites extending in opposite sides from the soma. The medial dendrite receives crossed projections from the contralateral cochlear nuclei, whereas the lateral dendrite receives projections that are from the ipsilateral cochlear nuclei. This anatomical arrangement allows the SON to use interaural difference in sound intensity in addition to the difference in time of sound arrival to calculate the direction and determine the location of sound. Even a slight time difference of as little as 400 msec is considered functionally significant. This ability to localize sound is remarkable, as the path difference between both ears is only approximately 5–6 inches or so.

In addition to receiving binaural afferents, the SON also sends massive inhibitory efferents in olivocochlear fibers to the cochlear hair cells, particularly the OHC. This allows the olivary nucleus to not only regulate the responsiveness of the hair cells to stimuli, but also suppress background noise to improve speech perception in noise.

LATERAL LEMNISCUS

The lateral lemniscus (LL), the primary ascending auditory pathway, extends from the cochlear and superior olivary nuclei to the inferior colliculus of the midbrain (Fig. 1.4). Its fibers climb laterally in the tegmentum (central area) of the pons toward the midbrain. The cell bodies located along the ascending fibers form the nucleus of the LL. Receiving most of its crossed afferents from the ipsilateral superior olivary nucleus and uncrossed afferents from the ipsilateral cochlear nuclear complex, the LL retains bilateral representation with added and stronger representation from the opposite ear. This bilaterality of representation explains why pathology of the central auditory pathway at any point does not always lead to reduced hearing sensitivity in only one ear. The fibers of the LL ascend adjacent to the fibers of the medial lemniscus that mediate fine discriminative touch in the brain stem toward the inferior colliculus in the midbrain (Fig. 1.4). On their way to the midbrain, the fibers of the lateral lemniscus pass dorsolaterally in the tegmentum of the pons, potentially making numerous connections.

INFERIOR COLLICULUS

The fibers of the LL, containing projections from contralateral and ipsilateral ear, ascend through to the inferior colliculus (IC), the round egg-shaped structure in the lower midbrain (Fig. 1.4). Virtually all of the LL fibers are actually known to synapse upon the central cells in the IC; the remaining fibers bypass the nuclei of the IC. Both IC are connected through the bidirectional commissural fibers of the IC, traversing through the pericentral nuclei and connecting with the ascending fibers bilaterally. This anatomical organization permits crossing and further integration of monaural and binaural auditory input, which has additional implications for the sound localization and for determining its other attributes.

The cellular organization in the IC is known to contain frequency-specific regions. However, with increased neuroanatomical complexity and projectional diversity, the central and pericentral cells of the IC are likely to respond to complex patterns of auditory stimuli indicating a higher level of information processing.

With its projections to the deeper cellular layers of the adjacent tectum and superior colliculus (the midbrain structure that mediates visual reflexes), the IC is likely to be concerned with auditory–visual and auditory–motor reflexes. Part of the auditory information from the IC is projected to the cerebellum and adjacently located reticular formation. The information received about the angular location of the sound source is integrated by the cerebellum with visual and other sensory inputs. This integrated information is projected on different ascending and descending pathways to coordinate reflexive movements of the eye, head, and body toward the sound source. With projections to the midbrain reticular formation, the cells in the IC are also likely to be involved with attentional processes and screening of auditory information.

The primary output of the inferior colliculus is to the medial geniculate body of the thalamus. The projections to the thalamus intersect central/external nuclei of the IC and travel through its brachium (Fig. 1.4).

MEDIAL GENICULATE BODY

The medial geniculate body (MGB) is the thalamic relay center for the transmission of auditory information. Shaped like a small protruding ball, it is located in the lateral–caudal portion of the thalamus between the lateral geniculate body and pulvinar (the posteriormost thalamic nucleus) and receives its input from the IC in the midbrain (Fig. 1.4). There is no known crossing of fibers directly at the level of the MGB, but nonetheless the possibility remains for some information to cross to the other side through the thalamic commissural fibers known as the massa intermedia and/or through the corpus callosum. The anterior portion of the MGB, with afferents from the central cells of the IC, projects the frequency representation to the primary auditory cortex in transverse gyri of Heschl, Brodmann area 41. The middle and posterior MGB regions, with afferents from the central and pericentral cells in the IC, project to the primary and secondary auditory cortex, Brodmann areas 41 and 42.

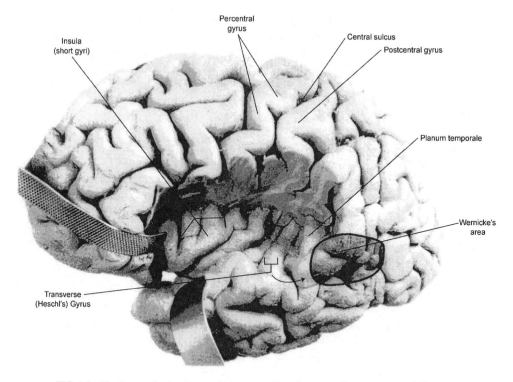

FIG. 1.5. The human brain dissected to expose the primary auditory cortex and the temporal planus in the dominant left hemisphere. From *Neuroscience for the Study of Communicative Disorders*, 2nd. ed. by Subhash C. Bhatnagar, 2001. Copyright 2001 by Lippincott, Williams and Wilkins.

Functionally, this region may be responsible for additional distinctive attributes of the sound.

It is anatomically plausible that with multiple but diverse projections to the adjacent putamen (basal ganglia), amygdaloid nucleus (limbic lobe), and to the tertiary regions of the temporal and parietal cortex, the MGB, with afferents from the brain stem reticular activating system, may participate in regulating attention, activated visceral functions, emotional expression, and integration with pain mechanism.

The projections of the MGB (auditory radiations or geniculo-cortical) pass ventrally (sublenticular) and caudally (retrolenticular) to the lenticular portion of the internal capsule. They terminate in the ipsilateral primary auditory cortex, the gyri of Heschl, which are located in the superior temporal lobe (Fig. 1.5).

AUDITORY CORTEX

The primary auditory cortex (Brodmann area 41) is located on the superior surface of the temporal lobe and is formed by two transversely oriented gyri: anterior gyrus and the portion of the posterior transverse gyrus of Heschl (Fig. 1.5). This area of primary auditory cortex is surrounded by the secondary auditory cortex (Brodmann area 42), which extends onto the lateral surface of the temporal lobe, representing the structural property of the koniocortex with a well-developed inner granular layer similar to the visual cortex and somatic sensory cortex.

The primary auditory cortex receives afferents from the MGB representing crossed and uncrossed fibers from both ears and is known to retain the cochlear tonotopic representation (Fig. 1.4). The geniculo-cortical fibers mediating higher frequencies terminate in the posteromedial region of the gyrus of Heschl and the fibers transmitting lower frequencies synapse in the anterolateral region. The area in between these two regions receives fibers carrying the middle range of frequencies. This tonal representation is based on experiential studies on mammal brains and has not yet been demonstrated on the human brain (Bhatnagar et al., 1989). The secondary auditory cortex along with the primary auditory cortex also represents other essential properties of audition such as timing patterns and spatial attributes, which characterize human speech.

Research carried out on the brains of cats suggests that the primary auditory cortex is not absolutely essential for frequency discrimination; rather, it is of vital importance in recognition and discrimination of sound patterns that are based on the timing and spatial patterns. These timing and spatial attributes of sound patterns play a significant role in the perception of human speech. This has been supported by the observations of unimpaired frequency discriminations and near-normal hearing thresholds in patients with unilateral and bilateral cortical lesions. However, individuals with cortical lesions also are found to exhibit an impaired ability to perceive and discriminate speech. A somewhat similar observation has been made on cats trained to discriminate low–high–low pitch tone sequence from high–low–high pitch patterns. After the cortical ablation, these trained cats could no longer discriminate such temporally based sound patterns.

Located posterior to the auditory cortical region is the planum temporale (temporal planum) area, which is hidden by the overlying operculum of the temporal, parietal, and frontal lobes (Fig. 1.5). In most individuals, the left planum temporal area has been found to be larger in the right brain, a fact that has been related to cerebral dominance by Geschwind and Levitsky (1968).

The primary auditory cortex and surrounding area are the site of auditory sensation and perception. An extensive axonal bundle connects the primary auditory cortex to Wernicke's area (Brodmann area 22), the language cortex, which includes part of the planum temporale and posterior–superior first temporal gyrus. It is concerned with recognizing language stimuli, interpreting their meanings with respect to auditory memories and linguistic experiences, and comprehending spoken language. Wernicke's area, as part of the larger language interpretative cortex, also receives visual and somesthetic information and may contribute as well to language formulation. An injury confined to Brodmann area 22 results in Wernicke's aphasia, a language syndrome characterized by impaired auditory comprehension and fluently produced copious speech marked with a severe word-finding deficit and the verbal output carrying little meaning. Similar linguistic errors are noted in reading and writing. Wernicke's area also extends to the inferior parietal lobule that contains supramarginal (Brodmann area 40) and angular (Brodmann area 39) gyri, the structures that are known to play an important role in reading and writing functions.

DESCENDING AUDITORY PROJECTIONS

Descending fibers, which run parallel to the auditory ascending afferents projections, are known to exist along the entire course of the auditory pathway, with conduction of impulses traveling in the reverse direction (Fig. 1.4). These synaptic connections of the ascending and descending fibers not only regulate the functioning of all the auditory relay nuclei, but they also serve as feedback circuits to refine the perception of pitch and loudness properties and to sharpen the reception of specific frequencies through the process of lateral inhibition. The recurring connections of the descending fibers begin from the primary auditory cortex and make synaptic relays to the thalamus, brain stem (inferior colliculus), and superior olivary nucleus before terminating in the cochlear hair cells. The descending connections, consisting of cortico-geniculate, cortico-collicular, colliculo-olivary, and olivary-cochlear fibers, serve to modulate responsiveness of hair cells and improve the signal-to-noise ratio. They also are known to enhance cues for sound localization and contribute to the quality of the perceived sound by suppressing competing signals. Furthermore, the descending pathways also help us differentiate between sounds generated externally from ones generated internally. This ability to differentiate sound sources explains why the auditory nuclei are inhibited during self-vocalization. Gamma aminobutyric acid (GABA) and a glycine are the neurotransmitters that are known to work on inhibitory interneurons involved with the descending auditory pathway.

Originating from the SON, the olivo-cochlear bundle (OCB) is composed of two tracts: lateral and medial. The lateral tract is an uncrossed fiber tract that originates from the lateral superior olivary complex (SOC). The fibers composing this tract are unmyelinated and connect with afferent auditory fibers at the base of the IHC. The medial tract is mostly a cross-fiber tract that originates from the medial SOC. Fibers of this tract are myelinated and are fewer in number than those composing the lateral OCB. These fibers connect directly to the base of the OHC. It has been suggested that the OCB functions as a feedback loop that causes some type of regulation or inhibition in the cochlea. The OCB may play a role in suppressing background noise to help people hear in noise. Specially, the OCB may serve to attenuate the transduction of certain sound frequencies by regulating the contractile properties of the OHCs (e.g., cochlear amplifier). By changing the OHC length, it lifts the tectorial membrane and alters the responsiveness of the stereocilia of the selective IHCs by reducing their bend subsequent to a movement of the basilar membrane. It is known that reflexive activity of the olivary-cochlear projections can reduce hearing sensitivity by over 20–25 dB (Kingsley, 1999).

AUDITORY REFLEXES

Auditory reflexes integrate sensorimotor information to coordinate head and eye movements and direct attention toward the sound, control the middle ear ossiculare movements, and also influence vestibular functions. This sound-triggered reflex mechanism involves four anatomical pathways.

The first pathway includes the projections from the inferior colliculus to the deep cellular layers of the superior colliculus and tectum (midbrain region responsible for ocular reflexes), which integrates auditory and visual systems. This information is transmitted through the visceral fibers of the oculomotor cranial nerve for controlling intraocular movements in the startle reflex.

The second pathway involves the integrated auditory efferents that travel through the superior olivary nucleus in the brain stem to the medial longitudinal fasciculus, which projects bilaterally to the motor nucleus of ocular (oculomotor, abducens, and trochlear) cranial nerves. Part of the information is also relayed to the neck muscles. Neural impulses traveling on these two pathways regulate ocular movements and head coordination, and startle response in response to auditory stimuli.

The third pathway includes the auditory projections to the adjacent vestibular nuclei and the brain stem reticular area, which project to cervical and spinal motor neurons through the tectospinal projections. This participates in body equilibrium and controlling head position. It also regulates the whole body movement in response to a loud sound.

The fourth pathway involves regulating the ossicular movements by controlling the muscles of stapedius and tensor tympani. The motor nuclei of the facial and trigeminal cranial nerves are connected with the superior olivary nucleus. Serving as the sensory path of the reflex, the input from the cochlear and superior olivary nuclei activates the facial and trigeminal nerves that contract the stapedius and tensor tympani muscles in the middle ear. This contraction dampens the ossicular movements to protect it from being overdriven, causing damage at the ossicular joints or beyond in the cochlea in response to high intensity stimuli.

CLINICAL CONSIDERATIONS

Disorders of hearing result from unilateral and/or bilateral damage to the peripheral auditory system (outer ear, middle ear, inner ear, auditory nerve fibers) and/or the central auditory nervous system (cochlear nuclear complex to the primary auditory cortex). The specific nature of a hearing impairment is determined by the anatomical location of the lesion rather than its etiology.

The symptoms of any peripheral auditory system lesion, in general, include reduced hearing sensitivity and difficultly hearing and/or understanding speech. These symptoms can be measured using conventional audiometric procedures. Lesions involving the central auditory nervous system (CANS) affect the transmission of information and are associated with signal processing impairments, many times without a significant loss of hearing sensitivity. Pathologies of the CANS predominantly produce symptoms in the ear contralateral to the site of the lesion.

SENSORINEURAL HEARING LOSS

Sensorineural hearing loss (SNHL) is an impairment of hearing that results when there is damage to the neural units within the cochlea and/or the neural structures that lie beyond. SNHL results from neural unit damage—either to the hair cells in the cochlea or to the auditory nerve fibers. In most cases, a SNHL is permanent/irreversible.

COCHLEAR PATHOLOGY

SNHL due to cochlear pathology is an impairment of hearing that results from damage to the hair cells in the cochlea. Symptomatology of a SNHL due to cochlear pathology includes:

Poor word recognition ability. Patients can hear speech but are unable to understand it. They frequently complain that "people mumble when speaking." This poor word recognition ability may still be present even when the intensity of speech increases above normal conversational level.

Greater difficulty hearing in noise. Patients frequently complain that they have much more difficulty hearing in noise. They may state that they have little or no difficulty hearing in quiet, but if there is any background noise present (e.g., microwave oven, dishwasher, running water, television, etc.) they have extreme difficulty understanding speech.

Tinnitus. Patients frequently complain of tinnitus (sensation of ringing or other sound in the head without external cause), which may take a variety of forms. The most common form is a high-pitched ringing sensation.

Speaking more loudly. Patients have difficulty self-monitoring the loudness of their voice due to the hearing loss. To compensate, they tend to speak at a higher than normal conversational level.

Recruitment. Recruitment is defined as the abnormally rapid growth of loudness. In other words, once the individual's threshold of hearing is reached, any further increase in the intensity of sound will be perceived as being uncomfortably loud. Patients with recruitment complain that they have difficulty understanding speech at the normal conversational level. However, if the speaker raises the intensity of his or her voice above normal conversational level, it appears to the patient that the speaker is shouting. Recruitment is consistent with outer hair cell damage.

AUDITORY NERVE PATHOLOGY

Impairment of hearing also can result from disease, irritation, or pressure on the nerve trunk of the auditory nerve. This lesion typically results in a structural alteration that is visible radiologically. The symptomatology of this SNHL includes hearing but not understanding speech, greater difficulty hearing in noise than in quiet and tinnitus. Typically, a patient with this site of lesion will describe his or her tinnitus in unusual terms—for example, bacon frying, hissing, or buzzing.

AUDITORY NEUROPATHY

Auditory neuropathy is a hearing impairment marked by abnormal functioning at the level of the auditory nerve with no visible structural alteration. Possible sites of auditory neuropathy include IHC, the synaptic juncture between IHC and the auditory nerve, and the auditory nerve or perhaps auditory pathways of the brain stem (lateral lemnicus). Patients may or may not have other neuropathies outside of the auditory system. Auditory neuropathy also is referred to as auditory dysynchrony because of the dyschronous pattern of neural activity. Symptomology of auditory neuropathy includes hearing but not understanding speech and more difficulty hearing in noise than in quiet. This symptomology may exist even without sensitivity loss.

CLINICAL ASPECTS OF THE CENTRAL AUDITORY NERVOUS SYSTEM

The central auditory nervous system includes the lower brain stem (cochlear nuclei, superior olivary nucleus, and the lateral lemniscus), upper brain stem (inferior colliculus and medial geniculate body), and the primary auditory cortex. Clinically, the most identifying feature of CANS dysfunction is a near-normal sensitivity to auditory stimuli but impaired processing of linguistic signals and their metalinguistic properties.

LOWER BRAIN STEM DYSFUNCTION

Structural and functional impairments involving the structures of the *cochlear nuclear complex, superior olivary nucleus,* and the *lateral lemniscus* are associated with central auditory disorder of the lower brain stem.

With input from the ipsilateral inner ear, a pathological involvement of the cochlear nuclear complex not only alters the hearing sensitivity in the ipsilateral ear and can cause ipsilateral hearing loss, but it also interrupts the cochlear projections to the SON. This serves to localize the source and direction of the sound by binaural summation of information after processing input from both (ipsilateral and contralateral) cochlear nuclei. Thus, a lesion involving the superior olivary nucleus may have only a minimal effect on hearing sensitivity, but it would have a significant, profound effect on the ability to identify and discriminate the source of sound—a skill which is essential for survival.

With crossed and uncrossed projections joining the LL, its unilateral involvement is not likely to cause a severe hearing impairment in either ear. However, the interruption of the ascending fibers of the LL can produce subtle processing symptoms such as impaired ability to process speech in noise, difficulty with the identification of sound source, missing crucial linguistic information in conversational context, inconsistencies in responsiveness, distorted figure–ground differentiation, and so on.

UPPER BRAIN STEM DYSFUNCTION

The cellular organization in the inferior colliculus is known to contain frequency-specific regions. However, with increased neuroanatomical complexity and projectional diversity, the central and pericentral cells of the inferior colliculi are likely to respond to and screen complex patterns of auditory stimuli indicating, a high level of information processing. This collicular level involvement also affects the integration of audition with visual–motor functions for reflexive responses.

With multiple input and diverse projections, the MGB seems to have an important role for integrating complex auditory patterns with the reticular arousal system (Bhatnagar et al., 1989a, b). Its pathology may restrict a subject's ability to regulate attention, screen auditory information, control speed of information processing, and activate audition-triggered visceral functions. These patients, who are similar to others with a pathology anywhere in the central auditory nervous system, may perform at a near-normal level on traditional pure tone tests.

CORTICAL DYSFUNCTION

Even with a bilaterally received tonal representation on the transverse gyri of Heschl's gyri (Brodmann area 41), the primary auditory cortex in humans is not considered to be absolutely essential for the basic frequency discrimination. Rather, it plays a vital role in discriminating complex time-based sound patterns that typify phonemic units of language. A unilateral pathology of the primary auditory cortex either does not or only minimally affects the auditory sensation. However, it can affect the ability to process and perceive complex sound patterns. Cats trained to discriminate low–high–low pitch tone are no longer able to discriminate sound patterns after a cortical lesion involving the primary auditory cortex (Kingsley, 1999). Cortical or cerebral deafness requires a lesion involving the Heschl's gyri bilaterally.

The language association cortex (Brodmann area 22) located adjacent to the primary auditory cortex provides clear evidence of lateralization for linguistic functions, which relates to the auditory analysis of speech sounds. A pathological involvement of the anterior secondary auditory cortex, which is located in the superior temporal region in the left brain, affects the perception of speech and produces acoustic or sensory aphasia. Responding near normal on the test of frequency sensitivity, patients with acoustic aphasia display an impaired ability to discriminate speech sounds/phonemes, a skill essential for learning and understanding language. Luria (1973) noted that the patients with impaired phonemic discriminative skill had also developed a different attitude toward their own language. As the spoken words began to appear as the words of a foreign language, they could not monitor their own verbalization. With impaired phonemic discrimination, the patients also failed to take dictation and write phonemes and words. With the lesion extending posteriorly to the temporal and parietal cortex, these subjects, also called Wernicke's aphasics, exhibit additional linguistic and amnesic symptoms (Bhatnagar, 2001). These consist of an impaired inability to repeat a series of orally presented words, and impaired word finding, where the patient cannot name object or people and find words. The posterior temporal–parietal region, as part of the larger language interpretative cortex, also receives visual and somesthetic information and contributes to language formulation, reading comprehension, and writing. An extensive injury confined to the secondary auditory cortex involving the temporal–parietal cortex results in a full syndrome of Wernicke's aphasia. Its clinical characteristics include severely impaired comprehension for auditory and written stimuli. With poor comprehension, patients fail to self-monitor and often produce inappropriate utterances of which they are unaware. The presence of word-finding deficit results in a verbal confusion, semantic or unrelated paraphasia, and neologisms that renders the verbal output in a disjoined form of speech which is usually referred to as jargon aphasia. With fluently spoken copious speech, marked with lexical blocks and hesitation and lack of semantic precision, individuals with Wernicke's aphasia also display visual-receptive symptoms in terms of impaired reading and writing processes, particularly if the lesion extends to the inferior parietal lobule.

Pure word deafness is an infrequent subtype of Wernicke's aphasia. Its clinical characteristics include the profound loss of auditory comprehension and verbal repetition, while the patients' ability to name, read, write, and use language is preserved. Lesions associated with pure word deafness involve the temporal lobes and separate the primary auditory cortices bilaterally from Wernicke's area. This disconnection prevents the auditory impulses from reaching the level of perception and comprehension while sparing other language functions (Bhatnagar, 2001).

The perception of nonverbal sounds and musical stimuli has been related to right temporal lobe functioning. Research undertaken on patients undergoing temporal lobotomy for medically intractable epilepsy has revealed that the right nondominant hemisphere processes music and prosodic stimuli. Milner (1962) noted that a right temporal lobotomy resulted in impaired ability to process tones, which was not disturbed after a left temporal lobectomy. Kimura (1967) noted that the left ear, with direct projections to the right hemisphere, was superior in comparison to the right ear in processing music and tones. This observation by Kimura of left ear superiority has been reconfirmed by Schuloff and Goodglass (1969) and Sparks et al. (1970), who found that there was a bilateral decrement in auditory recognition with damage to either of the temporal lobes. The exact nature of the decrement depended on the nature of material presented. For example, the left temporal lesion resulted in bilateral deficit in recognizing words, whereas the right temporal lesion produced a deficit in the bilateral processing of tones.

SUMMARY

This chapter provides a functional description of the neural circuitry and physiology of hearing from the inner ear to the primary auditory cortex in the temporal lobe. The anatomy of each intersecting neuroaxial level is discussed in light of its role in the transmission and information processing. In addition to a discussion of clinically pertinent sensory and perceptual functions, neurolinguistic issues such as cerebral dominance, language processing, and linguistic functions of the dominant and non-dominant hemisphere are discussed as they affect an individual's auditory processing ability.

ACKNOWLEDGMENTS

We thank Teresa Schwarz and Maria Fratangelo for help in the preparation of this manuscript. This chapter is based on information covered in *Neuroscience for the Study of Communicative Disorders* (2nd ed. 2001). Baltimore: Lippincott Williams and Wilkins. The illustrations are reproduced with permission.

REFERENCES

Bhatnagar, Subhash C. (2001). *Neuroscience for the study of communicative disorders* (2nd ed.). Baltimore: Lippincott.

Bhatnagar, S. C., Andy, O. J., Korabic, E. W., & Tikofsky, R. S. (1990). Effect of bilateral thalamic stimulation on dichotic verbal processing. *Journal of Neurolinguistics, 5*(4), 407–425.

Bhatnagar, S. C., Andy, O. J. , Korabic, E. W., Tikofsky, R. S., Saxena, V. K., & Collier, B. D. (1989a). The effect of thalamic stimulation in processing of verbal stimuli in dichotic listening tasks: A case study. *Brain and Language, 36*(2), 236–251.

Bhatnagar, S. C., Andy, O. J., & Linville, S. E. (1989b). Tonotypic cortical representation in man. *Pavlovian Journal of Biological Science, 24*(2), 50–53.

Castro, A. J., Merchut, M. P., Neafsey, E. J., & Wurster, R. D. (2003). *Neuroscience: An outline approach.* St Louis: Mosby.

Geschwind, N., & Levitsky, W. (1968). Human brain: Left–right asymmetries in temporal speech region. *Science, 161,* 186–187.

Haines, Duane E. (2002). *Fundamental neuroscience* (2nd ed.). Philadelphia: Churchill-Livingston.

Kimura, D. (1967). Functional asymmetry of the brain in dichotic listening. *Cortex, 3,* 163–178.

Kingsley, R. E. (1999). *Concise text of neuroscience* (2nd ed.). Baltimore: Lippincott.

Luria, A. (1973). *The working brain.* London: Penguin.

Milner, Brenda. (1962). Laterality effects in audition. In V. B. Mountcasle (Ed.), *Interhemispheric relations and cerebral dominance* (ch. 9). Baltimore: Johns Hopkins University Press.

Schulooff, C., & Goodglass, H. (1969). Dichotic listening: Side of brain injury and cerebral dominance. *Neurophychologia, 7,* 149–160.

Sparks, R., Goodglass, H., & Nickel, B. (1970). Ipsilateral versus contralateral extinction in dichotic listening from hemisphere lesions. *Cortex, 6,* 249–260.

Neuromaturation and Neuroplasticity of the Central Auditory System

Gail M. Whitelaw
Krista Yuskow
The Ohio State University

An appreciation of the anatomy and physiology of both the peripheral auditory structures and central auditory nervous system (CANS) is an important foundation for understanding auditory processing and its disorders. However, as noted by Bruer and Greenough (2001), the brain is a dynamic organ that constantly adjusts to the demands placed on it in terms of activity and learning, including the processing of auditory information. In order to explore the dynamic nature of the brain in relation to auditory processing, knowledge of the structure and function of the auditory system, as offered in chapter 1, is critical. Chapter 1 addresses information to enhance understanding of the flexible nature of the brain in terms of neuromaturation and neuroplasticity. The purpose of this chapter is to address key concepts related to the maturation of the CANS, along with the impact of experience and the environment on that system. Just as assessment and management of auditory processing disorders are often framed in terms of an interdisciplinary/multidisciplinary perspective, many disciplines contribute to an understanding of neuromaturation and neuroplasticity. This chapter incorporates concepts from relevant disciplines including hearing science, neuropsychology, and developmental psychology as well as clinical audiology that connect brain development to auditory processing.

A historical view of auditory processing disorders (APD) suggested that the etiology of these disorders was due to a "lesion" in the auditory system. Assessment, therefore, focused on determining the "site of lesion," a classic approach applied to adults. As auditory processing assessment in children was considered in the 1970s, the test schema were based on a similar "site of lesion" philosophy. This philosophy was based on a concept that an abnormal structure or structures in the auditory system was responsible for the deficits, and thus identifying the abnormal structure was part of the assessment. However, this approach did not take into account information about development or individual differences in auditory processing skills and also was an oversimplification of the functions of the auditory system. Unfortunately, this restricted perspective of assessment and treatment of auditory processing disorders continues to permeate practices in the field today. This limited approach has also impacted practical issues, such as third-party reimbursement for assessment of APD, as payers are also looking for the diagnosis of a "lesion" in order to provide coverage.

Current research suggests that the "site of lesion" view accounts for a limited approach to APD assessment and management and does not account for contemporary understanding of the auditory nervous system function and structure based on current research in the neurosciences. Recent advances in understanding neuromaturation and neuroplasticity include developments in technology that allow for expanding the knowledge of auditory structures and function, including the single-photon emission computed tomography (SPECT) procedure and functional magnetic imaging (fMRI), and the discovery and dissemination of cutting-edge information based on research from the "Decade of the Brain" (1990–1999) initiative, an opportunity designed to support neuroscience research and enhance public awareness of the benefits of this research. In addition, animal-based studies and information from clinical populations allow for a clearer understanding of current knowledge, which should drive assessment and management of APD.

NEUROMATURATION

Neuromaturation is defined as the development and growth of the nervous system with regards to processing and understanding language (Mendel, Danhauer, & Singh, 1999). Neuromaturation suggests that instead of being a rigid organ, the brain including the central auditory nervous system, undergoes a long developmental progression over a prolonged time course. For the purposes of this chapter, neuromaturation will be considered in terms of structural and functional development, with behavioral and electrophysiologic findings that support this development presented. As Chugani, Mueller, and Chugani (1996) noted, normal maturation of the brain is characterized by complex anatomical, molecular, and organizational changes that are necessary to "prepare the individual for optimal adaptive behavior" (p. 347). Obviously, the auditory system must prepare for the adaptive demands faced by a listener, including processing variations in the speech of individual speakers, grasping auditory information presented in less than optimal listening environments, and comprehending information of varying degrees of linguistic complexity.

STRUCTURAL MATURATION

In humans, the neuromaturational process begins prenatally and continues well into adolescence. Embryologic and fetal aspects of this development are briefly discussed here. For a comprehensive overview of prenatal development of the auditory system, the reader is referred to a series of articles by Peck (1994a,b 1995).

Both the peripheral auditory structures of the outer, middle, and inner ear and the structures of the central auditory nervous system develop during this same embryonic period. Prenatal development of the peripheral auditory structures is clearly understood and has been well documented. A comprehensive review of development of the peripheral auditory structures is available in Northern and Downs (2002) and Bhatnagar (2002). Maturation of the auditory system proceeds in a centripetal manner—from the periphery to the cortex. Thus, the more peripheral structures, such as the cochlea, are essentially adultlike in terms of structure by the 5th month of gestational age while cortical structures continue to evolve during the postnatal period.

Unlike the peripheral auditory system, understanding of the development of the central auditory nervous system is not as straightforward. As noted by Phillips (2001), the structures and functions of the peripheral auditory system are clearly prescribed; in contrast, the number of contributing elements and functions ascribed to the CANS results in considerable complexity. Thus, prenatal development of the CANS is more intricate, with more information to glean from both structure and function in the postnatal period than for peripheral structures.

The human brain is formed between the 6th week and 5th months of embryonic development, and during that time, 100 billion neurons—or nerve cells—are made. This translates into a quarter to half million nerve cells created each minute during this $3\frac{1}{2}$-month time frame, with no additional nerve cells generated after this time (Rakic, 1996; Cowan, 1979). Embryonic and fetal maturation of brain structures proceeds in a caudal to rostral progression or from brainstem to cortex. The brainstem governs many functions critical to survival, such as respiration, and these structures are completed early in the developmental process. From an auditory perspective, the auditory pathway and brainstem auditory nuclei are identified as areas of early and rapid maturation (Jiang, 1995). Cortical structures that govern communication, although important to quality of life, are not critical to survival, and continue to develop over a much longer time course. Central nervous system structures and connections/pathways between these structures are not completed until well after birth. Structural evidence that the CANS is not adultlike at birth is based on a number of observations, including an indistinct neuronal arrangement of cell bodies and an auditory cortex only half the thickness of that of an adult (Sininger, Doyle, & Moore, 1999).

McCall and Plemons (2001) outlined a sequence of general brain development that is helpful in understanding the neural pathways critical to auditory processing skills. This sequence occurs in both independent and overlapping steps:

1. *Neural proliferation*: This phase includes development of the 100 billion neurons that are necessary for the hardwiring of the brain.

2. *Neural migration*: This is the prenatal period in which nerve cells reach out to different areas of the brain to establish connections.

3. *Synaptogenesis and differentiation*: This phase begins when neural migration is nearly complete. Synaptogenesis refers to neural cells making connections, called synapses, to form networks. This process produces the foundation for the functional capabilities of the brain. As neurons develop during this phase, they send out multiple branches of axons and dendrites, extensions that reach from the cell body and mediate impulses (Bhatnagar, 2002). Axons are efferent motor structures that transmit information away from the cell body to other neurons. Dendrites are afferent or receptive structures that transmit information to the cell body from other cells via synaptic sites. These synaptic connections expand in a pattern of branching and subbranching similar to that observed as a tree grows, a process known as arborization (Bhatnagar, 2002). This synaptogenesis occurs during both the prenatal and postnatal periods, with synaptic contacts increasing in the cerebral cortex from 2,500 to 15,000 per neuron during the first 2 to 3 years of life, about twice that of the average adult brain (Gopnic, Meltzoff, & Kuhl, 1999). Even as infants, humans are active processors of information. This period is characterized in postnatal periods as one of dynamic perception, in which selected behaviors influence the neural development and are thought to be related to a higher proportion of excitatory synapses present in the brain of young children.

At this point, neurons are also becoming differentiated for diverse brain functions, such as for processing of sensory information or for performing motor activities.

This differentiation occurs at different times depending on the area or function of the brain. It has been noted that the peak developmental activity for regions associated with peripheral hearing occurs during the first prenatal month. However, the complex processes that control auditory behaviors and interact with auditory processing skills, including executive functioning and language skills, experience peak development between 1 year of age and adolescence. Changes in neuronal synaptic activity during development are well documented, and there is considerable evidence of widespread synaptic rearrangement occurring in the immature brain (Bear, Connors, & Paradiso, 1996). Specific to the development of neural networks and differentiation for audiology processing, the organization of neuronal systems that govern processing of language and auditory information in children are poorly understood at this time. The results of recent fMRI studies performed on healthy young children suggests that networks for this type of processing are regionally localized and lateralized by age 5 (Ahmad, Balsamo, Sachs, Xu, & Gaillard, 2003).

4. *Neural overproduction*: A greater number of network connections will be developed than will ever be used by the brain. This overabundance of neural connections will compete for a limited amount of neurochemical resources in the brain. Understanding this aspect of neuromaturation necessitates an appreciation of neurotransmitters, the chemical agents released by a nerve cell that permit communication between neuron synapses. As noted previously, a "site of lesion" approach to auditory processing that focuses exclusively on neuroanatomy does not take into account the importance of these neurochemical factors in auditory skills. Recent evidence supports the fact that neurochemicals promote the development and stability of neural circuits and may stimulate growth of higher cognitive centers in the cerebral cortex (Simon, 1999; Stapp, 1999). Thus, from this rich "arbor" of connections discussed previously, only the most viable develop the specific connections from neuron to neuron (Stapp, 1999).

5. *Selective elimination and degeneration*: Brain connections that are not used are eliminated, which helps to fine-tune and differentiate capabilities of the brain. As will be discussed later in this chapter, connections that are strengthened by language experience and exposure to auditory information are maintained and reinforced while weaker connections are eliminated or pruned. This suggests that although auditory exposure and experience influence the normal maturation of auditory behavioral qualities, central auditory synaptic connections are also influenced by the amount and/or pattern of sound the listener encounters during development (Sanes & Walsh, 1998).

6. *Myelination*: In this final stage of brain development, nerve cells become coated with a layer of fatty cells that provide insulation and speed neural conductions. This contributes to the efficiency of brain function. While this myelination process of the CANS begins in the second half of gestation, the brain remains only partially myelinated and diffusely interconnected at birth (Ward, 2001). Myelination occurs at varying rates. Some afferent and efferent axons experience complete Myelination around 11 months of age, with axonal density increasing until 2 or 3 years of age, coinciding with speech production and increased conduction velocity in auditory pathways (Sininger et al., 1999). Other structures related to auditory processing and executive functioning, including the corpus callosum, do not complete the myelination process untill late adolescence or early adulthood.

Much of early auditory processing encompasses skills that are mediated at the brainstem, such as localization of auditory information. The majority of auditory brainstem development persists throughout the first 2 years of life (Huttenlocher, 1979; Sininger et al., 1999). However, recent evidence suggests that although not as efficient in processing auditory information, the brainstem may continue to change through childhood and may be able to develop at least some basic auditory discrimination abilities—it is critical that the impact on children receiving cochlear implants is considered (Moore, 2002).

Early hearing behaviors are considered mostly reflexive, with the human auditory cortex undergoing considerable development during the first 6 months of prenatal development (Trainor et al., 2003). Many of the activities that would be considered as auditory processes are those governed by cortical functions. Change detection is a basic process of the auditory cortex. Change detection skills appear to develop based on exposure, and consequently adults have a greater number of neural networks for these skills than children. Newborn discrimination of sounds appears to be at a subcortical level, as language/auditory-specific categorization does not begin to emerge until after 4 months of age. Cortical development is observed throughout adolescence. During the first phase of postnatal cortical development (birth to age 1 year), there is a rapid decline in neuronal density, an increase in synaptic density and the number of synapses per neuron, along with dendritic growth and expansion in the total volume of the cerebral cortex. During the second phase (age 1 year to adolescence), cortical maturity is characterized by a slow decline in both synaptic and neuronal density (Huttenlocher, 1979). This is a unique type of growth, as generally maturation connotes adding to the organism's development rather than removing or pruning from the system. Recent data on cortical development focuses on the development of specific aspects in the six layers of the cortex. Recent research specifically addresses development of four of these six layers. Moore (2002) noted that layer I is primary level to function through about age 4 months, a finding that is consistent with observations about the reflexive nature of auditory processing until this age. Layers II, III, and IV emerge after age 4 months, with evidence that layers II and III do not fully mature until 5 years of age. This unique approach to understanding development of the auditory cortex is consistent with other findings in relation to the CANS; however, this research approach is in its early stages and certainly warrants additional investigation.

A structure of interest in that it incorporates the concepts of neural pathway development is the corpus callosum, a bundle of fibers that serves as the primary connection between the two hemispheres of the brain. The corpus callosum, as a structure, provides a model for the role of neuromaturation and its role in auditory processing, in addition to an understanding of the need for both analytic and gestalt processing of incoming information. Neuropsychologic literature has well documented the differentiated roles for each hemisphere of the brain: the left hemisphere dominant for speech and language skills and analytic abilities, and the right hemisphere dominant for abstract thinking, temporal and spatial relationships, perception of music, and gestalt abilities. Also well documented is the concept of cerebral dominance, which recognizes that nearly all humans are left brain dominant for auditory and/or language activities. At birth, the corpus callosum is one third of its adult size with myelination continuing through the adolescent years. The transfer of information via the corpus callosum is dependent on the myelination of the axon, which is in turn dependent on sufficient neural maturation. Sufficient maturation of this primary interhemispheric pathway is critical for integration of analytic and gestalt skills necessary to be an effective processor of auditory and language information. The increase in myelination of corpus callosum axons with increases in chronological age is reflected in transcallosal transfer times that decrease with age, reaching minimal values in the teenage years but with some variability among individuals. This maturational process of myelination of the corpus callosum is thought to be related to the developmental finding of right ear advantage (REA), which is discussed later in this chapter.

The normal neuromaturational process discussed here is a precondition for normal development of auditory processing skills, necessary to support perception and production of speech and language. Recent evidence from studies on children with cochlear implants indicates that this development, along with information on neuroplasticity to be presented later in this chapter, support auditory perception and the functional correlates of listening (Sharma et al., 2004). These functional correlates are dependent not only on peripheral hearing acuity and the development of peripheral auditory structures, but also the relationship between these structures and those of the developing CANS.

FUNCTIONAL MATURATION

It is clear that peripheral auditory structures are functional at birth, as the newborn's ability to hear immediately after birth has been well established. In addition, there is considerable behavioral and electrophysiologic evidence to indicate that the infant auditory system is able to process relatively sophisticated aspects of speech and non-speech signals (Dehaene-Lambertz, 2000; Eimas, 1999, Trehub, Schneider, Thorpe, & Judge, 1991). However, infants and children with normal peripheral hearing acuity clearly differ from adults in terms of their ability to process auditory information. For example, children demonstrate poorer abilities when compared to adults in terms of a variety of auditory behaviors and require a more favorable listening environment for performing auditory tasks (Hall, Grose, Buss, & Dev, 2002; Hnath-Chisolm, Laipply, & Boothroyd, 1998; Olsho, Koch, Carter, Halpin, & Spetner, 1988). These differences are greater than would be anticipated by attention and motivation of the listener alone and have been attributed to the ongoing maturation of the central auditory nervous system.

Although the ability of the auditory system to make simple discrimination is established early, development of auditory skills needed to process complex auditory signals is the area of interest in relation to functional maturation. As noted previously, early auditory processing abilities, such as simple discrimination between two auditory signals, are described as mostly reflexive, with newborns ability to discriminate sounds thought to occur on the subcortical level (Trainor et al., 2003). Although structure supports an early ability to detect changes in auditory stimulus, as noted earlier, differentiation for developing specific auditory categorization begins to emerge sometime after 4 months of age. Sufficiently detailed representations of the acoustic signal that can support behavioral detection and discrimination along a number of dimensions (e.g., spectral, spatial, and temporal) must be established in the CANS; the link between neural activity and perceptual activity is very complex (Phillips, 2001).

In order to process an auditory signal, neurons from periphery to cortex are required to manage information about characteristics of the signal, including the frequency, intensity, and temporal aspects of a given stimulus. Considerable research from both behavioral and electrophysiologic protocols indicates that the auditory system of children is less able to cope with certain auditory demands that challenge the CANS. An example of this is the processing of frequency changes in tonal stimuli, with differences noted in child performance when compared to that of adults. This maturational pattern not only affects simple auditory tone processing, but also has implications for the processing of more complex stimuli important for speech perception and oral language development (Martin et al., 2003).

Behavioral techniques for addressing auditory processing skills in humans require the listener to respond to a task thought to be related to a functional auditory process, but are dependent as well on the listener's capability to perform the task and attention and motivation toward the task, independent of the actual ability of the auditory system. Despite these limitations, behavioral testing is the foundation of many current assessment techniques in clinical auditory processing assessment. These techniques can generally be modified for clinical administration and have a direct correlate between the clinical environment and a "real-world" listening situation, such as the less than optimal environment a child may encounter in the classroom. In order to understand abnormal performance, normative data are obtained to determine how a particular auditory processing skill develops in typical children. Based on the limited scope of this chapter, several examples will be provided to support the concept that there is functional maturation of skills related to the neuromaturational processes.

As previously mentioned, a right ear advantage for dichotic types of listening tasks—that is, when different auditory information is presented to each ear simultaneously—is often observed both structurally and functionally in young children. The REA can be defined as a cerebral dominance phenomenon in which normal right-handed listeners have scores for the right ear that are consistently higher than scores for the left ear for dichotically presented signals (Mendel et al., 1999). Clinical and research protocols used to address the development of this type of dichotic listening consistently suggest that this REA is observed through ages 9 to 10 years, although performance varies based on the linguistic complexity of the signal, with development noted for specific types of dichotic skills through adolescence (Fischer & Hartnegg, 2004). The REA is thought to be related to the development and transmission pattern of auditory information through the corpus callosum to the language centers in the left hemisphere of the brain. As a clinical example of right ear advantage, Keith (2000) demonstrated improvement in left ear scores with age until it reaches right ear performance on the Competing Words subtest of the SCAN-C, a test battery for addressing auditory processing performance in children. This improvement is attributed to the maturation of the CANS, specifically thought to be related to the interhemispheric pathways.

Despite a movement away from a "site of lesion" perspective for the assessment of auditory processing, many behavioral test batteries continue to rely on functional auditory behaviors attributed to certain primary structures in the CANS. Binaural listening, or how the two ears work together as a team, is a core skill for auditory processing and generally one aspect of auditory processing assessment. This skill is thought to be mediated at the level of the brainstem, with functional correlates related to localization of sound, a critical skill for listening, particularly in less than optimal listening environments. Masking level difference (MLD) is a highly sensitive clinical technique which uses either tonal or speech stimuli to determine how effectively the ears are able to work together to process information, thought to give insight into the function and development of the areas of the brainstem responsible for dichotic listening. A recent study by Hall and his colleagues (2004) continues to find a developmental improvement in this MLD task for children between the ages of 5 and 10 years of age and between a child population and adult subjects. The results of this study suggest developmental improvement in binaural temporal resolution.

Electrophysiologic measures can provide insight into auditory system functional development, in some cases providing similar findings to those obtained via behavioral measures and in others a unique view of auditory system development. These procedures are used in research studies in animals and humans to gain an understanding of functional auditory behaviors and, to a lesser extent, in clinical assessment of auditory processing disorders. These measures are objective in that the listener is not required to provide a behavioral response to a given task, but listener cooperation is required. The results obtained from electrophysiologic measures are free from the attentional and motivational limitations of behavioral assessment but require a greater leap from research finding to functional listening skill. A thorough description of electophysiologic protocols is beyond the scope of this chapter; however, several types of electrophysiologic protocols that are illustrative in development of auditory function are presented here.

Auditory evoked potentials (AEPs) and event related potentials (ERPs) have been used for many years to assess auditory function, providing a noninvasive method for addressing the structure and development of the auditory system. Results of these potentials are visualized by a series of peaks that are arranged in accordance with locations along the auditory pathway and are categorized as early, middle, or late response according to its latency (2–10 msec, 10–50 msec, or 50–500 msec, respectively). Neural maturation can be observed based on analysis of a number of parameters, including latency (e.g., time of measured response in relation to onset of the auditory stimulation) and morphology (e.g., physical appearance of the waveforms). Maturation of the auditory brainstem response (ABR), an early evoked potential thought to be generated primarily in the auditory brainstem, has been observed to develop over the first year of life, with decreases in response latency observed with increases in chronological age during that year (Gorga, Reiland, Beauchaine, Worthington, & Jesteadt, 1987). Exploration of these types of developmental changes has been conducted in both human and animal subjects. Consistently, a fundamental difference between stimulus processing by central auditory neurons in young versus adult subjects is response efficacy and reliability. Relative to adult responses, the responses from younger subjects exhibit longer response latencies, smaller response amplitudes, and greater response variability (Jiang, 1995; Sanes & Walsh, 1998). These differences are attributed to an increase in synaptic efficiency, dendritic growth, and axonal myelination over time. However, the time frame for this development depends on the structural and functional area of interest and the type of evoked potential used.

Electrophysiologic evidence can support the same types of functional auditory development as observed in behavioral testing. An example is the issue of binaural interaction, a skill that was discussed earlier in relation to the behavioral MLD protocol and as an electrophysiologic measure here in relation to the Auditory Brainstem Response (ABR) protocol. Research results reveal developmental differences in using a binaural interaction component (BIC) derived from the ABR procedure, consistent with improvement in binaural interaction abilities over time. In addition, differences between typical development in normal children and in children identified as having auditory processing disorders have been observed, underlying the differences between development and disorder of the CANS (Gopal & Pierel, 1999). In addition to providing insight into development of the auditory system, a number of cortical evoked potentials have been used to demonstrate changes in neural activity that are associated with auditory training or therapy and will be highlighted later in this chapter in regards to neural plasticity (Tremblay, Kraus, McGee, Ponton, & Otis, 2001).

A proliferation of brain research suggests a greater understanding of auditory development may not be far off. As noted earlier, procedures such as SPECT and fMRI have provided insight into auditory function and development. SPECT allows for imaging both metabolic and physiologic functions via computed tomography with radioactive contrast, fMRI for high-resolution imaging of specific functions and neural activity by representing oxygen level and flow. A recent study using fMRI studies of brains in a small number of typically developing six- to ten-year-old children revealed that binaural stimulation resulted in consistent activation in primary and secondary auditory cortices with no hemispheric dominance. These admittedly preliminary results warrant further research in view of the potential clinical implications of such findings (Ulualp, Biswal, Yetkin, & Kidder, 1998). In addition, a greater interest in the impact of neurochemical aspects of the auditory system is likely to provide further insights into auditory development and function. A recent study found that the neurotransmitter serotonin is involved in early auditory cortical processing, with gender differences noted (Kahkonen et al., 2002). Clearly, these types of studies require additional attention.

The ability for CANS development to support processing of complex auditory signals, such as listening to speech in a room with a variable noise background, has a complicated developmental progression and extends well into adolescence (Sharma, Kraus, McGee, & Nicole, 1997). Based on current clinical research, studies in developmental psychoacoustics, and normative data of current tools for assessment of auditory processing skills in children, adult models of central auditory processing appear not to be appropriate for children, at least for ages 11 years and younger.

DEVELOPMENT OF AUDITORY PROCESSING

One approach that can be used to facilitate understanding of auditory processing is to address the basic processes or skills required to effectively use complex auditory information. As these processes will be used as a framework throughout this book, the neuromaturational aspects of these components are highlighted here, with support from the literature in the area of developmental psychoacoustics. This information may help to direct both understanding of assessment and management of auditory processing disorders. Some of these neurodevelopmental skills have been reviewed previously in this chapter and are summarized here.

Depending on the model used to define auditory processing, various component skills may be considered. For the purposes of this discussion, auditory processes reviewed include localization/lateralization of auditory information, auditory figure ground, binaural interaction, dichotic listening, temporal abilities, and auditory discrimination, with a summary provided in Table 2.1. In considering these isolated skills, it is important to recall that the effective "processing" of auditory information for effective communication and learning is not an isolated event but requires coordination with other sensory information, including processing of language and visual information, in order to develop a gestalt. This type of integration must be considered in terms of executive functioning skills, including attentional skills, memory skills, increase in sophistication of language skills in areas including pragmatics and problem solving, which improve throughout childhood and into early adulthood (Anderson, Anderson, Northam, Jacobs, & Catroppa, 2001; Luciana & Nelson, 2002).

The ability to localize auditory information in space is thought to be important on many fronts, including being able to hear well in a noisy environment and to determine direction of incoming auditory information, which can assist in alerting. The auditory localization skills present at birth are thought to be a reflexive skill rather than an integrated auditory process. A localization or head turn response in

TABLE 2.1
Overview of Development of Selected Auditory Processes

Auditory Process	Neuromaturational Course
Localization	Ability present shortly after birth; however, lacks precision.
	Skill continues to develop through age 5 years, reaching adultlike performance at this age.
Hearing in noise	Depending on the type of listening situation, improvements are noted at least through ages 10–11 years.
Dichotic listening	Improvement noted through at least ages 9–10 years, with performance on specific skills not reaching adultlike ability until adolescence.
Binaural interaction	Reaches adult values between ages 6–8; however, may be task-dependent.
Temporal processing	Appear to reach adultlike performance at 10–12 years of age.
Speech sound discrimination	Discrimination abilities present at birth; however, precision in discrimination noted to improve through 8 years of age.

response to an auditory signal is noted to emerge at 4 months of age, when the central auditory nervous system appears to be able to compare time of arrival differences of an auditory stimulus between the two ears, and dramatic improvements in this skill are noted through the first year of life. Localization abilities do not reach adult-like levels until approximately 5 years of age (Morongiello & Clifton, 1984; Sininger, Doyle, & Moore, 1999).

Listening in less than optimal listening environments is of interest in an assessment profile, as listening in the presence of background noise is often indicated as a concern for a person suspected of having an auditory processing disorder. A number of studies have been conducted to address the development of speech-in-noise skills in typically developing children. The results of these studies demonstrate a developmental trend; however, there is an interaction between task parameters and age that children reach adult-like performance. A study by Johnson (2000) reveals that the more complex the noise introduced (e.g., addition of reverberation, decrease in linguistic redundancy) to stimulus tasks, the longer developmental trend for speech in noise performance. Even in a more optimal task, 6- and 7-year-old subjects demonstrated considerable difficulty listening in somewhat optimal noise listening situations when compared to older subjects. However, for the more challenging listening situations, performance did not mirror that of adults until late adolescence. Developmental improvement in listening in noise skills has been observed through age 11, as reported by Elliot (1979). This trend is also observed in analyzing normative performance on the Bamford-Kowel-Bench-Speech-In-Noise (BKB-SIN) Test, in which children are asked to repeat a sentence in a varying signal-to-noise ratio, with performance improving through age 10 (Valdez, 2004).

Binaural interaction processes allow the listener to team information between the two ears, necessary in most listening situations. As noted previously in this chapter, development of skills such as masking level difference (MLD) matures well into child-hood, through at least age 8 years (Hall et al., 2004). This is consistent with other find-ings and suggests that the ability of the central nervous system to integrate binaural cues increases at least through 6–8 years of age (Boothroyd, 1997).

Dichotic listening skills have been discussed previously, with REA thought to be a measurement of this skill present between ages 9–10. Again, task-specific dif-ferences are noted, with improvements in dichotic listening skills noted through adolescence (Hugdahl, Carlsson, & Eichele, 2001). Improvements in these dichotic listening skills are attributed to improved interhemispheric transfer to increase myeli-nation of the corpus callosum, the structure that connects the two hemispheres of the brain.

The ability to discriminate between and among speech is demonstrated at birth, as infants appear to be able to discriminate between speech sounds at birth. However, in the first year of life, infants demonstrate preferences for sounds present in their own language, with these types of categorizations noted by age 6 months (Gopnic, Meltzoff, & Kuhl, 1999). Thus, developmentally, infants appear to "lose" some discrimination abilities, with preferences for prosodic patterns of native language noted between 9–12 months of age. However, precision in making discriminations among speech sounds of a listener's native language appears to improve through age 8 years (Kraus, Koch, McGee, Nicol, & Cunningham, 1999).

Temporal processing skills have been addressed clinically with several types of psychoacoustic paradigms. One is a gap detection paradigm, a measure of temporal resolution, with research in this area suggesting improvement in skills noted with increases in chronological age. However, differences in age of maturation of skill are noted depending on the skill noted and paradigm used. Gap detection skills improve with increases in chronological age; although adultlike performance is reported as early as age 10, but is observed as late as 16–18 years of age (Fischer & Hartnegg, 2004; Grose, Hall, & Gibbs, 1993). Clinical norms of temporal pattern processing tests are observed to improve with increases in chronological age through about age 12, when performance appears to reach adultlike levels.

NEUROPLASTICITY

One aspect of neuromaturation that deserves in-depth discussion is neuroplasticity. Neuroplasticity is the ability of the nervous system to undergo organizational changes in response to internal and external deviations (Mendel et al., 1999). It is part of the inherent ability of the brain and allows the brain to grow and change in response to the dynamic environment. The ability of neurons to individually and collectively respond to such new information and experience is an expression of neural plasticity (Stapp, 1999). Sur, as cited in Restak (2001), noted that the brain is remarkably plastic, and this is a mutual interaction of nature and nurture. While genes play a role as the "architect" by setting down the structural blueprint for neuromaturation, the environment can be viewed as the creative force behind transforming that structure to an individual brain function.

As has been noted, neuromaturation and neuroplasticity are complementary, but the systems underlying these processes are relatively independent. A traditional view of plasticity was that the process was a means of protecting the developing brain from potential negative impacts of neural insult and accompanying deficits in function. However, as noted in an excellent overview article on neuroplasticity, Stiles (2000) presented a contemporary view that plasticity is a central feature of normal brain development and that plasticity is a basic process that underlies neural and cognitive functions. In addition, although neuroplasticity has traditionally been addressed in terms of the cortex, recent evidence reveals that there is a "layering" of plasticity at all levels of the CANS (Phillips, 2001).

Historically, it has been well accepted that the younger the brain the greater the plasticity, a concept known as the "Kennard effect" (Bear et al., 1996; Chugani et al., 1996). However, newer views regarding functional plasticity in childhood suggest that an age- or stage-based model of plasticity is equivocal and that what might be thought to be critical periods are rarely brief and/or seldom sharply defined (Bruer, 2001; Dennis, 2000). Although most researchers continue to believe that to some degree, brain plasticity varies inversely with age and that the developing brain is capable of reorganizing in ways that a mature brain cannot, age is now considered only one factor in neuroplasticity. The current thought is that critical periods are not necessarily limited to a narrow and rigid time period. To reflect this idea, many neuroscientists now prefer the term "sensitive" phase or period rather than critical period. This view implies longer, less well-defined periods when specific types of experiences can have a significant impact on development or on "repair" of a disorder.

As noted above, age is only one factor in neuroplasticity, with gender, motivation, site and extent of lesion, and related factors also contributing to the process (Thompson, 2000). There is evidence that neural plasticity is part of normal brain development and not simply a reparative process as has been characterized by much of the literature in the past. Deacon (2000) noted that there is considerable evidence to support that adult brains are capable of plastic adaptation to injury including some degree of structural reorganization, contrary to classic theory.

Bruer and Greenough (2001) offered a model of neuroplasticity that may best incorporate current research. This model suggests that neuroplasticity can be viewed as experience-expectant development and experience-dependent development. Experience-expectant development incorporates aspects of brain development that require or expect certain types of experience to occur at specific times during development if normal development is to occur. This approach is thought to incorporate a critical or sensitive period approach. Typically, sensory and motor systems (e.g., vision, auditory, first language learning) develop in part via experience-expectant processes. These experiences are thought to affect the brain by causing chemical changes within cells that influence cell function and structure. The experience-expectant model is related to synaptic elimination development and relies on eliminating synapses as part of the typical neuromaturational process outlined earlier in this chapter. The historical view suggests that if deprived of stimulation or experience during these sensitive periods, necessary neurochemical changes do not take place and development of the auditory system may be incomplete (Stapp, 1999). The experience-expectant model addresses the role of plasticity in specialization of neural networks, again part of the typical neuromaturational process, which is designed to result in the eventual parceling of networks into specialized circuits. This parceling results in optimizing efficiency and performance with increasing development. However, as noted by Restak (2001), this partitioning of the brain into specialized zones is preceded by a long period of plasticity that for some activities, such as learning, continues over a lifetime.

In contrast, Bruer and Greenough (2001) pointed out that experience-dependent development is driven by experiences that are unique to an individual and to the physical, social, and cultural environment of that individual. This type of development allows for learning from personal experiences; information derived from that experience is stored to be used in later problem solving. Experience-dependent development is age-independent and allows for learning throughout life. These types of brain modifications are viewed as a lifetime process, involving both the addition of synapses and increases to the neural vascular system and glial cells that support neurons. This process is observed well into maturity.

There are many positive implications of an experience-expectant/experience-dependent model of neuroplasticity. Clearly, for auditory and language skills to develop, there are sensitive periods for plasticity. However, the experiences that enhance this type of development are considered to be ubiquitous in the typical environment of infants and children. Thus, with the exception of extreme cases of deprivation, auditory processing disorders are deficits inherent in the auditory system. As experience-dependent changes can occur throughout our lifetime and humans can benefit from experiences throughout the lifetime, evidence suggests that this type of plasticity can strengthen old synaptic connections and develop new synaptic connections throughout a lifetime. Understanding of this type of plasticity raises questions regarding what types of environments and/or experiences may maximize auditory learning or development.

The questions raised regarding environment or experience in capitalizing on neuroplasticity to change or improve auditory processing abilities are of considerable clinical value. Management of auditory processing disorders often focuses on "person-centered" or therapeutic approaches applied to the individual and "context-centered" or environmental modifications. In many cases, parents and educators wish for a "quick fix" and devalue environmental modifications as an appropriate therapeutic approach. Current research in neuroplasticity can help to support both of these management strategies as having potential in the remediation process. Clearly, developmentally appropriate auditory stimulation during appropriate sensitive phases is of benefit as Bruer (2001) suggested, for it is during these specific time frames when the nervous system is impressionable. This auditory exposure and experience work in consort with neurochemical and neurobiological sequences to ensure the appropriate development of the auditory neural system.

Many recent studies have focused on how exposure to complex environments influences neuroplasticity in animals. A summary of these studies suggests that rats raised in complex environments experience formation of additional neural synapses. In addition to synaptic formation, supporting vascular formation and glial cell development are also observed, indicating that the brain remains sensitive to complex and challenging experiences well into maturity, and even mature animals exhibit dendritic elaboration to enriched environments (Greenough, 1986). In reviewing recent information from recent studies, Stiles (2000) reported that these animal studies suggest that optimal patterns of brain organization are not necessarily fixed at a specific critical period: Subjects in these studies demonstrated benefits from "enriched environment" throughout their lifetimes. However, it is critical to note that although sensitive phases for neural change occur throughout a lifetime, neural functioning and/or neuroplastic potential during different time periods are not necessarily equal (Stapp, 1999). These animal models are likely to be strong predictors of human auditory development and the role of complex experience, if history is any indicator. Additional implications of these studies and application of both neuromaturation and plasticity are discussed in the next section of this chapter.

As early as 1967, Lennenberg proposed that the neural systems mediate language development according to a maturational blueprint. This raised the idea that "speech and language" are special in the developmental process, a concept that has been supported by research since that time. Different brain regions are genetically prespecified for particular language, and under a typical neuromaturational timetable, specific regions become committed to predesignated functions, a pattern observed via imaging studies in most adults with typical language and auditory function. Considerable data to support the preferential preservation of language over other cognitive functions and complete recovery or "sparing" of auditory processing skills are often noted following injury when far less complete recovery is noted for other functions (such as motor/visual skills), for reasons not clearly understood (Chugani et al., 1996; Stiles, 2000). Further evidence, however, supports a decreased capability for learning language in later childhood. The end of this sensitive phase is marked by an increased need for intense and arousing stimulation if changes in auditory processing skills are to occur (Doupe & Kuhl, 1999).

Recent evidence supports the impact of training on neural plasticity and, in turn, on functional auditory behaviors. Phillips (2001) pointed out that changes in the auditory cortex, representing the neuroplasticity of the system, as a result of behavioral training have been well documented in animal models. Thompson (2000) described how treatment/therapy enhances the "representational plasticity" of the CANS, resulting in the ability to engage new neural networks post-treatment. Some of the best evidence for changes in auditory function related to environmental changes and experiences are manifested by children and adults who have received cochlear implants. Improvements in communicative behaviors following implantation appear to be positively influenced by the rate of plastic changes in central auditory pathways (Sharma et al., 2004). In addition, studies with both normal hearing and subjects with cochlear implants using later evoked potentials demonstrate both longer periods of plasticity in the brainstem and cortex than traditionally believed and the ability to demonstrate neural activity changes associated with training and auditory rehabilitation (Gordon, Papsin, & Harrison, 2003; Tremblay et al., 2001).

All such research, however, points to the need for stimulation or treatment to be varied, challenging, and developmentally appropriate in order to capitalize on the experience-dependent neuroplasticity available in the auditory system (e.g., McCall & Plemons, 2001). This has significant implications for developing auditory processing skills in young children and remediating auditory processing disorders in both children and adults. Historically, many of the therapeutic approaches designed to address auditory processing disorders in children, such as completing preprinted worksheets, have not capitalized on current knowledge of neuromaturation and neuroplasticity. Clearly, a favorable listening/learning environment may help to address experience-expected types of plasticity. Designing auditory training programs to challenge the auditory system and present a varying and progressively difficult task holds great promise in taking advantage of the available plasticity in the CANS. This is the early stages of development of such programs, as is noted with the Fast ForWord program (Tallal et al., 1998) and in dichotic listening therapy (Musiek, Shinn, & Hare, 2002), and these programs will serve as a foundation for future remediation and auditory training programs. In addition, techniques to measure effectiveness of a given program are needed and will continue to be developed (Jirsa, 2002).

CONSIDERATIONS IN ASSESSMENT AND MANAGEMENT OF AUDITORY PROCESSING DISORDERS

Auditory processing develops as a function of required auditory exposure, neural maturation, and neural plasticity. In defining important aspects of auditory processing disorders in children, three areas should be considered: development, disorder, and cerebral morphologic abnormalities. Anything that may interrupt the developmental process has the potential to impact the CANS, and, in turn, the functional skills related to auditory processing. As noted in this chapter, the long developmental time course of the brain certainly opens a door for interference with typical neurodevelopment. In addition, individual variations in development are noted, with greater variations with younger children and less variation noted with increases in chronological age. One of the challenges in clinical audiology is separating children with developmental delays in auditory processing skills from those with true auditory processing disorders at a young age. It is anticipated that some children will "catch up" while others will continue to demonstrate the same degree of deficit year after year or demonstrate minimal levels of improvement as compensatory skills are developed. This challenge requires additional understanding of clinical implications of neurodevelopment and neuroplasticity and incorporating this understanding into the clinical tools. Until that time, many audiologists have opted to assess children when they reach a specific age, such as 5 or 7 years of age. An argument regarding neuroplasticity can be made that the auditory system can continue to benefit from intervention over a long time course, so what might be perceived as "delay" in identification would not appear to be catastrophic based on current knowledge. However, there continues to be evidence that suggests that young children can benefit from early identification of auditory processing disorders, as the type of intervention may differ at an earlier age. Clearly, these issues require further attention and research.

As noted earlier in this chapter, a "site of lesion" approach to the identification of auditory processing disorders is generally not accepted for children, particularly as a clearer understanding of CANS development has emerged. However, a small number of children do experience auditory processing deficits as a result of a "lesion," narrowly defined as an area or region of damaged tissue or an injury to a given area in the CANS. Although rare, auditory processing disorders are observed in children who experience a lesion or disease process such as temporal lobe seizures or demyelinating conditions of the brain. In addition, auditory processing disorders are observed in children with a history of traumatic brain injury or postconcussive syndrome. Knowledge of neuromaturation and neuroplasticity should help to understand the impact of these disorders or lesions on assessment and management of APD in this population. The neural maturation and plasticity of the auditory system ensures the functional processing of auditory information throughout a lifetime, with evidence for improved processing and perception through adolescence. With continued aging into the fifth and sixth decades of life, the integrity of the CANS continues to change and there is often an associated decline in auditory processing abilities.

In understanding neuromaturation and neuroplasticity, the question that is now beginning to be asked comes back to a "site of lesion" question: Where is the location of the disorder in the CANS that results in the auditory processing disorder? For a third category of children, the possible explanation is that of cerebral morphologic abnormalities (CMA), most likely a genetic condition impacting specific areas of the brain (Musiek, Baran, & Pinheiro, 1994). These types of deficits were first identified in postmortem studies of brains of people with known learning disabilities and have been observed in structures essential for auditory processing of information. In addition, it is assumed that abnormal morphology may be related to abnormal auditory functioning and, clearly, a genetic component may be present, as many children identified as having auditory processing disorders have family members who report similar types of behavioral listening difficulties or a similar learning style. With continued increases in knowledge in relation of development of the CANS and techniques to enhance the understanding of the function of the brain, a greater understanding of etiology of auditory processing disorders and the role of CMAs will emerge.

SUMMARY

This chapter provides an overview of neuromaturation and neuroplasticity and a resultant framework within which to understand the development of underlying auditory processes and components of the typical development of these processes. Maturation of the auditory system is addressed in terms of the structural changes noted in the central nervous system over time, but perhaps even more important is the functional development of skills noted with increases in chronological age. These functional processes include binaural hearing and dichotic listening, temporal processing, and listening in noise. The impact of neuroplasticity is addressed, both from a perspective of the negative impact of disease or injury over the long course of development of the central auditory nervous system and from the potential effectiveness of management/intervention approaches in relation to neuroplasticity. A current view of neuroplasticity is offered which supports the concept that the "critical period" theories offered in the past are a restrictive view of neuroplasticity of the auditory system. The current view suggests that changes in the central auditory nervous system may have a much wider time window than previously believed, although the characteristics of the stimulation (e.g., progressively challenging, interesting, etc.) have an impact on potential changes. This view is likely to impact clinical approaches to the management and treatment of auditory processing disorders in the future.

REFERENCES

Ahmad, Z., Balsamo, L. M., Sachs, B. C., Xu, B., & Gaillard, W. D. (2003). Auditory comprehension of language in young children: Neural networks identified with fMRI. *Neurology, 60,* 1598–1605.

Anderson, V. A., Anderson, P., Northam, E., Jacobs, R., & Catroppa., C. (2001). Development of executive functions through late childhood and adolescence in an Australian sample. *Developmental Neuropsychology, 20,* 385–406.

Bear, M. F., Connors, B. W., & Paradiso, M. A. (1996). *Neuroscience: Exploring the brain.* Baltimore: Williams & Wilkins.

Bhatnagar, S. C. (2002). *Neuroscience for the study of communicative disorders* (2nd ed.). Philadelphia: Lippincott.

Boothroyd, A. (1997). Auditory development of the hearing child. *Scandinavian Audiology. Supplementum, 46,* 9–16.

Bruer, J. T. (2001). A critical and sensitive period primer. In D. B. Bailey, Jr., J. Bruer, F. J. Symons, & J. W. Lichtman (Eds.), *Critical thinking about critical periods* (pp. 3–26). Baltimore: Paul Brookes.

Bruer, J. T., & Greenough, W. T. (2001). The subtle science of how experience affects the brain. In D. B. Bailey, Jr., J. Bruer, F. J. Symons, & J. W. Lichtman (Eds.), *Critical thinking about critical periods* (pp. 209–232). Baltimore: Paul Brookes.

Chugani, H. T., Mueller, R., & Chugani, D. C. (1996). Functional brain reorganization in children. *Brain and Development, 18,* 347–356.

Cowan, W. M. (1979). The development of the brain. *Scientific American, 241,* 112–133.

Deacon, T. W. (2000). Evolutionary perspectives on language and brain plasticity. *Journal of Communication Disorders, 33*(4), 273–290.

Dehaene-Lambertz, G. (2000). Cerebral specialization for speech and non-speech stimuli in infants. *Journal of Cognitive Neuroscience, 12*(3), 449–60.

Dennis, M. (2000). Developmental plasticity in children: The role of biological risk, development, time, and reserve. *Journal of Communication Disorders, 33,* 321–332.

Doupe, A., & Kuhl, P. (1999). Birdsong and human speech: Common themes and mechanisms. *Annual Review of Neuroscience, 22,* 567–631.

Eimas, P. D. (1999). Segmental and syllabic representations in the perception of speech by young infants. *Journal of the Acoustical Society of America, 105*(3), 1901–1911.

Elliot, L. L. (1979). Performance of children aged 9 to 17 years on a test of speech intelligibility in noise using sentence material with controlled word predictability. *Journal of the Acoustical Society of America, 66,* 651–653.

Farran, D. C. (2001). Critical periods and early intervention. In D. B. Bailey, Jr., J. Bruer, F. J. Symons, & J. W. Lichtman (Eds.), *Critical thinking about critical periods* (pp. 233–266). Baltimore: Paul Brookes.

Fischer, B., & Hartnegg, K. (2004). On the development of low-level auditory discrimination and deficits in dyslexia. *Dyslexia, 10,* 105–118.

Gopal, K. V., & Pierel, K. (1999). Binaural interaction component in children at risk for central auditory processing disorders. *Scandinavian Audiology, 28,* 77–84.

Gopnic, A., Meltzoff, A., & Kuhl, P. (1999). *The scientist in the crib: What early learning tells us about the mind.* New York: HarperCollins.

Gordon, K. A., Papsin, B. C., & Harrison, R. V. (2003). Activity-dependent developmental plasticity of the auditory brain stem in children who use cochlear implants. *Ear and Hearing, 24,* 485–500.

Gorga, M. P., Reiland, J. K., Beauchaine, K. A., Worthington, D. W., & Jesteadt, W. (1987). Auditory brainstem responses from graduates of an intensive care nursery: Normal patterns of response. *Journal of Speech and Hearing Research, 30,* 311–318.

Greenough, W. T. (1986). What's special about development? Thoughts on the bases of experience-sensitive synaptic plasticity. In W. T. Greenough & J. M. Juraska (Eds.), *Developmental neuropsychobiology* (pp. 387–407). New York: Academic Press.

Grose, J. H., Hall, J. W., & Gibbs, C. (1993). Temporal analysis in children. Journal of Speech and Hearing Research, 36, 351–356.

Hall, J. W., Buss, E., & Dev, M. B. (2004). Developmental effects in the masking-level difference. *Journal of Speech-Language-Hearing Research, 47,* 13–20.

Hall, J. W., Grose, J. H., Buss, E., & Dev, M. B. (2002). Spondee recognition in a two-talker masker and a speech-shaped masker in adults and children. *Ear and Hearing, 23,* 159–165.

Hnath-Chisolm, T. E., Laipply, E., & Boothroyd, A. (1998). Age-related changes on a children's test of sensory-level speech perception capacity. *Journal of Speech, Language, and Hearing Research, 41,* 94–106.

Hugdahl, K., Carlsson, G., & Eichele, T. (2001). Age effects in dichotic listening to consonant-vowel syllables: Interactions with attention. *Developmental Neuropsychology, 20,* 445–457.

Huttenlocher, P. R. (1979). Synaptic density in human frontal cortex—developmental changes and effects of aging. *Brain Research, 163,* 195–205.

Jiang, Z. E. (1995). Maturation of the auditory brainstem in low risk preterm infants: A comparison with age-matched full term infants up to 6 years. *Early Human Development, 42,* 49–65.

Jirsa, R. E. (2002). Clinical efficacy of electrophysiologic measures in auditory processing disorder management programs. *Seminars in Hearing, 23,* 349–356.

Johnson, C. (2000). Children's phoneme identification in reverberation and noise. *Journal of Speech, Language, and Hearing Research, 43,* 144–157.

Kahkonen, S., Ahveninen, J., Pennanen, S., Liesivuori, J., Ilmoniemi, R. J., & Jaaskelainen, I. P. (2002). Serotonin modulates early cortical auditory processing in healthy subjects: Evidence from MEG with acute tryptophan depletion. *Neuropsychopharmacology, 27,* 862–868.

Keith, R. W. (2000). *SCAN-C: A test of auditory processing disorders in children—revised.* San Antonio, TX: Psychological Corporation.

Kraus, N., Koch, D. B., McGee, T. J., Nicol, T. G, & Cunningham, J. (1999). Normal development of speech-sound discrimination in school-age children: Psychophysical and neurophysiologic measures. *Journal of Speech, Language, and Hearing Research, 42,* 1042–1060.

Lennenberg, E. H. (1967). *Biological foundations of language.* New York: Wiley.

Luciana, M., & Nelson, C. A. (2002). Assessment of neuropsychological function through use of Cambridge Neuropsychological Testing automated battery: Performance in 4-to12-year-old children. *Developmental Neuropsychology, 22,* 595–624.

Martin, B. A., Shafer, V. L., Morr, M. L., Kreuzer, J. A., & Kurtzberg, D. (2003). Maturation of mismatch negativity—a scalp current density analysis. *Ear and Hearing, 24,* 463–471.

McCall, R. B., & Plemons, B. W. (2001). The concept of critical periods and their implications for early childhood services. In D. B. Bailey, Jr., J. Bruer, F. J. Symons, & J. W. Lichtman (Eds.), *Critical thinking about critical periods* (pp. 267–287). Baltimore: Paul Brookes.

Mendel, L. L., Danhauer, J. L, & Singh, S. (1999). *Singular's pocket dictionary of audiology.* San Diego, CA: Delmar Learning.

Moore, J. K. (2002). Maturation of the human auditory cortex: Implications for speech perception. *Annals of Otology, Rhinology, and Laryngology. Supplement, 189*, 7–10.

Morongiello, B. A., & Clifton, R. (1984). Effects of sound frequency on behavioral and cardiac orienting in newborn and five-month-infants. *Journal of Experimental Psychology, 38*, 429–446.

Musiek, F. E., Baran, J. A., & Pinheiro, M. L. (1994). *Neuroaudiology: Case studies.* San Diego, CA: Singular.

Musiek, F. E., Shinn, J., & Hare, C. (2002). Plasticity, auditory training, and auditory processing disorders. *Seminars in Hearing, 23*, 263–275.

Northern, J. L., & Downs, M. P. (2002). *Hearing in children* (5th ed.). Baltimore: Lippincott.

Olsho, L. W., Koch, E. G., Carter, E. A., Halpin, C. F., & Spetner, N. B. (1988). Pure-tone sensitivity of human infants. *Journal of the Acoustical Society of America, 84*, 1316–1324.

Peck, J. E. (1994a). Development of hearing. Part I: Phylogeny. *Journal of the American Academy of Audiology, 5*(5), 291–299.

Peck, J. E. (1994b). Development of hearing. Part II: Embryology. *Journal of the American Academy of Audiology, 5*(6), 359–365.

Peck, J. E. (1995). Development of hearing. Part III: Postnatal development. *Journal of the American Academy of Audiology, 6*(2), 113–123.

Phillips, D. P. (2001). Introduction to the central auditory nervous system. In A. F. Jahn & J. Santos-Sacchi (Eds.), *Physiology of the ear* (2nd ed., pp. 613–638). San Diego, CA: Singular Thompson Learning.

Rakic, P. (1996). Development of the cerebral cortex in human and non-human primates. In M. Lewis (Ed.), *Child and adolescent psychiatry* (2nd ed., pp. 9–30). Baltimore: Lippincott.

Restak, R. (2001). *The secret life of the brain.* Washington, D.C.: Joseph Henry Press.

Sanes, D. H., & Walsh, E. J. (1998). The development of central auditory processing. In E. W. Rubel, A. N. Popper, & R. R. Fay (Eds.), *Development of the auditory system* (pp. 271–314). New York: Springer.

Sharma, A., Kraus, N., McGee, T. J., & Nicole, T. G. (1997). Developmental changes in P1 and N1 central auditory responses elicited by consonant-vowel syllables. *Electroencephalography and Clinical Neurophysiology, 104*, 540–5.

Sharma, A., Tobey, E., Dorman, M., Bharadwaj, S., Martin, K., Gilley, P., & Kunkle, F. (2004). Central auditory maturation and babbling development in infants with cochlear implants. *Archives of Otolaryngology—Head and Neck Surgery, 130*, 511–516.

Simon, N. (1999). The auditory system, brain maturation, and development in autistic children. *Journal of Autism and Developmental Disorders, 29*, 94–95.

Sininger, Y. S, Doyle, K. J., & Moore, J. K. (1999). The case for early identification of hearing loss in children. Auditory system development, experimental auditory deprivation, and development of speech perception and hearing. *Pediatric Clinics of North America, 46*, 1–14.

Stapp, Y. (1999). TESL-EJ: Neural plasticity and the issue of mimicry tasks in L2 pronunciation studies. *TESL-EJ, 3*, A–1.

Stiles, J. (2000). Neuroplasticity and cognitive development. *Developmental Neuropsychology, 18*, 237–272.

Tallal, P., Miller, S. L., Bedi, G., Byma, G., Wang, X., Nagarajan, S. S., Schreiner, C., Jenkins, W. M., & Merzenich, M. M. (1998). Language comprehension in language-learning impaired children improved with acoustically modified speech. In M. E. Hertzig & E. A. Farber (Eds.), *Annual progress in child psychiatry and child development: 1997* (pp. 193–200). New York: Brunner-Routledge.

Thompson, C. K. (2000). Neuroplasticity: Evidence from aphasia. *Journal of Communication Disorders, 33*, 357–366.

Trainor, L., McFadden, M., Hodgson, L., Darragh, L., Barlow, J., Matsos, L., & Sonnadara, R. (2003). Changes in auditory cortex and the development of mismatch negativity between 2 and 6 months of age. *International Journal of Psychophysiology, 51*, 5–15.

Trehub. S. E., Schneider, B. A., Thorpe, L. A., & Judge, P. (1991). Observational measures of auditory sensitivity in early infancy. *Developmental Psychology, 27*, 40–49.

Tremblay, K., Kraus, N., McGee, T., Ponton, C., & Otis, B. (2001). Central auditory plasticity: Changes in the N1-P2 complex after speech–sound training. *Ear and Hearing, 22*, 79–90.

Ulualp, S. O., Biswal, B. B, Yetkin, F. Z., & Kidder, T. M. (1998). Functional magnetic resonance imaging of auditory cortex in children. *Laryngoscope, 108*, 1782–1786.

Valdez, C. J. B. (2004). *Establishing children's norms for understanding speech in noise.* Unpublished master's thesis, The Ohio State University.

Ward, L. M. (2001). Human neural plasticity. *Trends in Cognitive Sciences, 5*, 325–327.

Delineating Auditory Processing Disorder (APD) and Attention Deficit Hyperactivity Disorder (ADHD): A Conceptual, Theoretical, and Practical Framework

Anthony T. Cacace
The Neurosciences Institute, Albany Medical College

Dennis J. McFarland
The Wadsworth Labs, New York State Health Department

Individuals from various professions (education, psychology, speech/language pathology, audiology, psychiatry, pediatrics, neurology, etc.) are often called upon to provide a diagnosis for children who have difficulty in developing the skills necessary to succeed in an educational environment. When sensory, motor, cognitive, and medical issues are ruled out, other areas are given consideration. Because information processing through the auditory modality is a major channel for communication and learning, an assessment of auditory perceptual abilities is often made when speech, language, and/or other related academic competencies (reading, spelling, mathematical skills, etc.) are deficient.

A common disorder of childhood, which includes difficulty in focusing attention on tasks, hyperactivity and impulsiveness, is also implicated when academic problems are at issue. This cluster of features, often manifest in educational environments, falls under the rubric of attention deficit hyperactivity disorder (ADHD). This diagnostic amalgam is defined differently by different organizations (American Psychiatric Association [APA], World Health Organization [WHO]) and even within different countries (e.g., Gillberg, 2003). Nevertheless, based on subjective reports from educators and other specialized professionals dealing with communication skills and learning (dis)abilities in childhood, questions have been raised about the association between deficits in auditory perception (also referred to as central auditory processing disorder [CAPD] or auditory processing disorder [APD]) and ADHD. This chapter explores the relationship between CAPD and ADHD and specifically addresses whether these are: (a) separate and distinct entities, (b) part of the same disorder, (c) comorbid disorders, and/or (d) mistakes in diagnosis. In our review, we discuss how these two disorders are defined, and we compare and contrast assessment protocols. We consider whether available approaches are adequate to delineate these conditions and lead to reliable and valid diagnoses. Historical overviews are used for perspective and, when possible, the etiology and biological basis of each condition are provided.

CENTRAL AUDITORY PROCESSING DISORDER (CAPD)

Early attempts to quantify the effects of lesions on the central auditory system made use of stimuli such as filtered speech (Bocca, 1958; Hodgson, 1972) and dichotic presentation of digits (Kimura, 1961). These studies used patients with known brain lesions to identify features that might characterize CAPD (see Jerger, 1973 for relevant historical details). The use of more complex tests was considered necessary because patients did not always show deficits with simple auditory discrimination or detection tasks. The similarity of test scores between subjects with structural lesions and those with functional deficits was subsequently used as a means of validating the use of CAPD tests in subjects without demonstrable lesions (Jerger, Johnson, & Loiselle, 1988).

A recent consensus conference (ASHA, 1996) defined CAPD as a deficit in one or more of the following central auditory processes: sound localization and lateralization, auditory discrimination, auditory pattern recognition, temporal aspects of audition, auditory performance with competing acoustic signals, and auditory performance with degraded acoustic signals. It was also stated that CAPD often coexists with more global dysfunction (i.e., attention or linguistic deficits) that may affect performance across modalities (ASHA, 1996). However, this position has been criticized because it fails to address how the specificity of the deficit is to be determined (Cacace & McFarland, 1998). We have argued elsewhere that perceptual dysfunctions are modality-specific (McFarland & Cacace, 1995). Following this logic, the primary deficit in CAPD should be manifested in tasks that require the processing of acoustic information, whereas it should not be apparent or at least manifest to a lesser extent when similar types of information are presented to other sensory modalities. Therefore, CAPD should be distinguished from cognitive, language-based, and polysensory or supramodal attentional problems (e.g., ADHD) in which modality-specific perceptual dysfunctions are not expected. Based on a critical review of the literature (Cacace & McFarland, 1998), we concluded that the modality-specific nature of auditory-based learning problems has seldom been established. We have also argued that this failure had been due in large part to the "inclusive" framework used in the evaluation of CAPD. The inclusive framework holds that performance on auditory tests alone provides sufficient evidence for diagnosis. The obvious limitation with unimodal inclusive definitions of CAPD is that individuals with problems that are not of a perceptual nature are at risk for misclassification.

This concern is further highlighted by the way in which common tests used in diagnosis have been designed. In the assessment of CAPD, so-called sensitized tests of auditory function are commonly applied, because simpler measures often result in normal performance. The term "sensitized" refers to the fact that certain dimensions of the stimulus have been altered in some way to challenge the processing resources of the auditory system. Sensitization could alter stimuli by filtering, time compression, use of competing messages or noise, simultaneous presentation of different stimuli to separate ears, and so forth (e.g., Berlin & Lowe, 1972; Hodgson, 1972). However, mere indication that stimuli have been sensitized does not specify what processes are affected by these alterations. Consideration must be given to the possibility that sensitized stimuli also render these tasks sensitive to nonperceptual factors. Because tests used to evaluate for CAPD are constructed to limit stimulus redundancy and/or to increase stimulus complexity, they can inadvertently assess other factors or processes, such as sustained or divided attention (Cacace & McFarland, 1998). Indeed, these inadvertent and unwanted side effects can add additional complexity to interpretation of test performance.

We also emphasize that for any area to be studied with precision and rigor, it requires a definition that is clear and straightforward; one that allows for hypotheses to be tested and diagnoses to be made. Our view on CAPD is unambiguous although our concerns are neither original nor novel. We believe that appropriate testing should allow for differentiation between cases with auditory perceptual deficits from those with nonperceptual deficits. In principle, when a child is being tested for auditory perceptual deficits, the optimal protocol should assess similar tasks in multiple sensory modalities, limit cognitive factors in the test design (i.e., memory requirements and attention), and minimize motor requirements during response selection (see McFarland & Cacace, 1997; McFarland, Cacace, & Setzen, 1998; Cacace, McFarland, Ouimet, Schriber, & Marro, 2000 for detailed descriptions of multimodal tasks where adaptive psychophysics or psychometric functions have been applied). Many investigators, across a variety of disciplines, have also been concerned with the validity of the CAPD diagnostic label particularly with respect to children with diverse problems with reading, language, and attention (Burd & Fisher, 1986; Cook et al., 1993; Grundfast, Berkowitz, Connors, & Belman, 1991; Kamhi & Beasley, 1985; Rees, 1973, 1981; Vellutino & Scanlon, 1989; Kamhi, 2004). Therefore, we use the definition of CAPD originally proposed by McFarland and Cacace (1995) and one that was also embraced by the American Academy of Audiology following the Bruton Consensus Conference (see Jerger & Musiek, 2000, p. 468): CAPD is a *modality-specific perceptual dysfunction* not due to peripheral hearing loss. Clearly, with dissatisfaction building and serious questions being raised about the validity of the unimodal inclusive framework, it appears that the field is posed and sufficiently mature to build on past conceptualizations, and evolve toward a more refined definition of CAPD that emphasizes the specificity of the deficit (McFarland & Cacace, 1995; Cacace & McFarland, 1998; Jerger & Musiek, 2000). Whereas the wheels of science are slow to turn when paradigms shifts are advocated (Kuhn, 1996), much can be gained by such a change. Improving the specificity of diagnosis is necessary if we are to minimize overlap between CAPD and other diagnostic categories and if we are avoid misclassification of individuals. These benefits will provide much-needed momentum so that further advancements can be made as we move forward in this area.

ATTENTION DEFICIT HYPERACTIVITY DISORDER (ADHD)

The concept of ADHD has been evolving, both with respect to terminology and underlying theoretical explanations. Like CAPD, ADHD is controversial, not completely understood, considered descriptive in nature, and generally lacking in a strong theoretical foundation and a cohesive theory (Castellanos & Tannock, 2002). Based on the historical record, advances in this area have been slow (see Sandberg & Barton, 1996; Barkley, 1998, for comprehensive details). Below, we provide perspective on this topic and discuss salient aspects of this history.

Descriptions in the form of case reports and anecdotal accounts date back to the mid-1800s when characteristics of inattention and hyperactivity were observed in children recovering from nervous system diseases or injuries. In a series of lectures given to the Royal College of Physicians, British pediatrician George Frederic Still (Murchison Scholar, prolific writer, and first professor of pediatrics at King's College London [1906]) reported on a group of children who were aggressive, defiant, and resistant to discipline, and who also had difficulty in paying attention and in staying on task. Whereas unknown medical or biological causes (either inherited or caused by injury at birth) were thought to underlie these behaviors, they were also attributed to a "defect of moral control" or poor parenting (Still, 1902). Tredgold (1908) was in general agreement with Still, and he speculated that brain damage or mild anoxia at the time of birth could result in behavioral problems and/or learning disabilities manifested later in life, which were often observed in early educational settings. After a worldwide outbreak of encephalitis (1917–1918), many children showed similar symptoms, which led physicians to speculate that the disorder resulted from brain damage. This led to the term "post-encephalitic disorder." These children were also labeled as "incorrigibles"; one expert has suggested that this label is characteristic of a complicated form of ADHD (DSM-IV classification; Denkla, 2003). Subsequently, in cases when brain damage was ruled out, the term "minimal brain dysfunction" was applied. Some historians credit Tredgold with providing the first account of this term.

In 1937, physicians reported evidence that stimulant medication (i.e., amphetamines, methylphenidate) could help to relieve symptoms of hyperactivity and impulsivity in children. These early reports were largely ignored until the 1950s, when there was a rapid increase in the use of drug therapy in psychiatry. By the mid-1960s, stimulant medication had become a common treatment for hyperactivity and impulsive disorder. Chess (1960) is credited with coining the term "hyperactive child syndrome." At that time, controversy focused on biological versus environmental etiologies, which ranged from poor parenting to use of food additives to exposure to environmental toxicants. By 1965, the APA established the diagnostic category "hyperkinetic reaction of childhood". Over the next 15 years, research began to elucidate the neurological origins of these attentional and hyperkinetic behaviors. Subsequently, in a series of research papers, Douglas and colleagues identified four major characteristics of the syndrome, which included: deficits in attention and effort, impulsivity, problems in regulation of arousal levels, and need for immediate reinforcement (e.g., Douglas & Parry, 1983; Douglas, Barr, O'Neill, & Britton, 1986; Douglas & Benezra, 1990). These characteristics continue to be important for the diagnosis of the disorder.

Based on this work, the APA established a new diagnostic category "attention deficit disorder with or without hyperactivity." In 1987, the name was changed to "attention deficit-hyperactivity disorder." With the growing awareness that hyperactivity need not be present for a diagnosis of attention deficit disorder, the APA defined three distinct categories of ADHD: Attention Deficit/Hyperactivity Disorder, predominantly hyperactive-impulsive type; Attention Deficit/Hyperactivity Disorder, predominantly inattentive type; and Attention Deficit/Hyperactivity Disorder, combined type. In the 1990s, evidence that ADHD is heritable led to efforts to identify specific genetic causes. Other work has led to advances in the recognition of its neurobiochemical underpinnings, related to the functioning of the neurotransmitters in the brain, particularly dopamine. The WHO (1992) and the APA (1994) now recognize ADHD as a neuropsychiatric condition. However, conceptualization of and views about this disorder in the scientific community continue to evolve.

For purposes of simplicity, we use the DSM-IV definition of ADHD. Diagnosis is made when developmentally inappropriate behaviors are manifested within three symptom domains: inattention, impulsivity, and hyperactivity with onset of symptoms before 7 years of age and functional impairments occurring across two settings (i.e., home, school, playground, etc.) (see fourth edition of the *Diagnostic and Statistical Manual of Mental Disorders* [DSM-IV]; APA, 1994). The term hyperkinetic disorder (HKD) is used in the 10th revision of the *International Classification of Diseases* (ICD-10; WHO, 1992) to describe similar traits. In Scandinavian countries, a construct characterized by a disorder of attention, motor control, and perception (DAMP) has been used for approximately 2 decades and is now gaining in popularity. This term refers to concomitant ADHD and developmental coordination disorder in children who do not have severe learning disability or cerebral palsy (Gillberg, 2003).

Although the DSM-IV classification is widely used in research and practice, it should be noted that considerable controversy exists concerning the exact nature of ADHD and the theory that best describes this common disorder. For example, Milich, Balentine, and Lynam (2001) proposed that the inattention type and hyperactive-impulsive type are completely different disorders. Likewise, Rasmussen and colleagues (2002) reported evidence that six distinct types of ADHD exist. Sergeant, Geurts, and Oosterlaan (2002) have discussed five current theories concerning the nature of ADHD. Thus, these examples illustrate some of the diversity in thinking about ADHD. We can only speculate that concepts and theories will also continue to evolve as further advancements in this area are made.

RELATIONSHIP BETWEEN CAPD AND ADHD

The root cause of the controversy in the differential diagnosis of CAPD and ADHD can be understood if we consider how these entities are conceptualized or, for that matter, misconceptualized. ADHD is often described in terms of behavioral characteristics that can be captured by direct observation, questionnaire, and/or clinical interviews. However, complicating matters is the fact that there exist *no* objective tests that can be used to diagnose ADHD. Similarly, several authors have described "auditory behaviors" that characterize CAPD (e.g., Willeford, 1977; Keith, 1995; Bellis & Ferre, 1999). For example, Keith (1995, p. 103) described behaviors associated with CAPD as follows: "inconsistent responses to auditory stimuli, exhibition of short attention spans and are easily fatigable, distractible by both auditory and visual stimuli, have difficulty with auditory localization, need information to be repeated, have difficulty remembering information presented verbally, have difficulty counting or reciting the alphabet or remembering the days of the week, months of the year or addresses and phone numbers, can be allergic to various factors in the environment and sometimes have histories of chronic otitis media." Clearly, this list contains a heterogeneous and broad array of characteristics. Some of these are clearly misplaced, given that they are neither behaviors nor specifically auditory in nature (i.e., memory for verbal material; recitation of common facts such as the alphabet, days of the week, and months of the year; remembering addresses or phones number; or being reactive to allergens in the environment). Even for the remaining factors, it is not at all clear that such a collection of behaviors would result from deficits in auditory perception. For example, distractibility to both auditory and visual stimuli is not consistent with modality specificity. What is most striking, however, is the similarity between the conceptualization of CAPD by individuals such as Keith (1995) and descriptions of ADHD commonly found in the literature.

Just as some authors discuss CAPD in terms of auditory behaviors, Breier, Gray, Klass, and Foorman (2002) have discussed the "behavioral deficit" in ADHD as due to problems in response inhibition. We contend that neither sensory (auditory) perceptual processes nor inhibitory processes should be referred to as "behaviors." To understand our concern, consider the following scenario: In a behavioral testing situation, the examiner varies stimuli in a systematic manner and records the behaviors of the individual. The stimuli can be characterized, among other ways, in terms of the sensory modality (e.g., auditory or visual). Likewise, the individual's behavior can be classified as correct or incorrect according to some criterion. If the methodology has been constructed properly, the test stimuli constitute well-defined inputs to the system; the responses constitute the output from the individual. In contrast, terms such as auditory perception and response inhibition represent theoretical constructs that serve to explain the observed variation in behavior that occur in the presence of various stimulus conditions. The distinction between observable behavior and theoretical constructs serves several important functions. First, it emphasizes that the diagnostic process involves hypothesis testing, as internal processes associated with either CAPD or ADHD are not directly observable. Second, this conceptualization allows for the operation of multiple processes to be involved that could influence the observed relationships between input and output (i.e., stimuli and resultant behaviors). Each of these processes should be considered. Thus, there is not a simple one-to-one correspondence between a behavior associated with test performance and a disorder involving some hypothetical process.

The observation that a child performs poorly on a single test is consistent with one of several alternative explanations, each of which is a hypothesis that should be given consideration. If sufficient evidence is not available to decide between alternative hypotheses, then a differential diagnosis is not possible. According to this logic, when the inclusive framework is employed and when test performance is limited to just auditory stimuli, we contend that there is insufficient evidence to make the diagnosis of CAPD. Indeed, most authors acknowledge that modality-specific effects in perception are not expected for ADHD. Yet, in current assessment protocols for CAPD, the unimodal framework continues to be used (e.g., Bellis & Ferre, 1999, among many others). At this juncture, the obvious question to ask is how do we distinguish CAPD from supramodal dysfunction using the "unimodal" approach to testing? Our answer to this question is clear. When testing involves only auditory stimuli, the assessment is incomplete, and therefore the resultant diagnosis is indeterminate. Similarly, hypothetical models resulting from incomplete assessment strategies or therapies that are developed from indeterminate diagnoses are themselves questionable, and caution should be used in their application. To our knowledge, no validated model of CAPD interventions has been published in the peer-reviewed literature.[1] Such models, however, can be found in other sources such as magazine articles, books, and/or book chapters for which critical examination and supporting data are often lacking or not required by the publisher. Additionally, the Internet is another potential source of information about this disorder. However, the rule of thumb about the Internet is best expressed by the phrase "caveat emptor," a Latin expression meaning let the buyer or consumer beware. Indeed, there is no guarantee that information derived from this medium will be either accurate or credible. Consequently, distinguishing the wheat from the chafe can be a difficult task, particularly for vulnerable parents looking for a simple solution to why their child has difficulty learning (Kamhi, 2004).

This distinction between observable behavior and latent internal state can be illustrated by considering what some authors call "listening behavior" (e.g., Keith & Engineer, 1991). A common example that illustrates this problem can be found in a didactic classroom situation in which a child does not respond to a teacher's query such as, "What city is the capital of New York State?" One possibility is that the child was not listening. However, this is only one of several hypotheses that should

---

[1] We recognize that environmental controls are often advocated as a means to manage presumed cases of CAPD; however, this option can be instituted in the absence of any specific diagnosis and for that matter in the absence of specific testing protocol.

be considered. It is equally possible that the child did not understand the question, did not complete or comprehend the reading assignment on which the question was based, became anxious, did not know the answer, is unmotivated or is defiant, and will not answer questions even though he or she knows what the answer is. Although listening is not an observable behavior, it is nonetheless useful to talk about listening as an internal state, because the implications of a child having problems with listening are different from those of the alternative possibilities. However, it is not prudent to merely assume that the problem involves listening without gathering more information. Thus, the inference about listening is different from noting whether or not the child answered the question, and whether or not the answer was correct. The latter are directly observed events. In contrast, problems with listening should be inferred from a consistent pattern of behaviors across situations.

Children described with CAPD are often characterized as having difficulty that includes "hyperactivity, inattentiveness, and short memory span" (Chermak & Musiek, 1992). It has also been suggested that children classified as having CAPD may in fact have some form of attention deficit disorder. Others suggest that it is difficult to differentiate between these classifications, inferring that they coexist (Grundfast et al., 1991; Peck, Gressard, & Hellerman, 1991; Moss & Sheiffe, 1994; Riccio, Hynd, Cohen, Hall, & Molt, 1994; Riccio, Cohen, Hynd, & Keith, 1996). We now consider each of these possibilities in more detail.

CAPD AND ADHD ARE SEPARATE AND DISTINCT CLINICAL ENTITIES

Chermak, Hall, and Musiek (1999) stated that CAPD and ADHD are characterized by different problems related to attention. Furthermore, Chermak, Tucker, and Seikel (2002) reported that the symptoms endorsed by audiologists for CAPD are distinct from those endorsed by pediatricians for ADHD. Likewise, Riccio and coworkers (1996) suggested that these entities are separate and distinct, based on a low correlation between performance on staggered spondaic word (SSW) test and a display of behaviors characteristic of ADHD. Thus, based upon conceptual distinctions, symptoms used in diagnosis, and patterns of correlated test results, it had been proposed that CAPD and ADHD are distinct entities. Also noteworthy in this debate is the observation that both groups reached this conclusion by adopting a unimodal framework in their CAPD assessments.

Chermak and colleagues (1999) stated that ADHD can be characterized by a deficit in sustained or selective attention. This is contrasted with the deficit in focused and divided attention seen in CAPD, as measured, for example, by dichotic listening tests. They suggest that the auditory continuous performance test (CPT) will prove helpful in substantiating this distinction. Although superficially this distinction may appear logical, there are several problems with this position. Chermak and coworkers' characterization of the attention deficit in ADHD differs from that found in the DSM-IV. The DSM-IV lists symptoms of inattention in ADHD as "often fails to give close attention to detail," "has difficulty sustaining attention," "does not seem to listen," and "is easily distracted." This list does not explicitly rule out problems with focused or divided attention.

There is considerable controversy in the literature concerning how best to characterize the nature of the attention problems in ADHD (see Barkley, 1997 for a review). For example, Prior, Sanson, Geffen, and Freethy (1985) have reported that children diagnosed with ADHD show deficits on dichotic listening tasks. These authors characterized the deficit as involving both focused and selective attention. Likewise, Shalev and Tsal (2003) found that children with ADHD are more susceptible than normal children to visual distracters when searching a high-density visual array. They suggest that ADHD is better characterized by problems in orienting than in problems with vigilance. Barkley (2003) suggested that ADHD is not a problem with attention, but rather with intention. It is apparent that there is not a general consensus in the literature on how to best conceptualize ADHD. Indeed, Chermak and coworkers' (1999) distinction is neither generally agreed upon nor empirically supported. In our conceptualization, the critical distinction between the attention deficits in CAPD and in ADHD lies in modality specificity. That is, can deficits in attention that are specific to auditory stimuli and absent from visual stimuli be demonstrated? Deficits in selective, divided, or sustained attention that are specific to the auditory modality should be viewed as CAPDs. In contrast, disorders that involve multiple sensory modalities are not properly characterized as "auditory" perceptual disorders, and should be considered supramodal in nature. We will consider this issue of auditory attention in more detail later.

Whereas CAPD and ADHD can present overlapping symptomology, Chermak et al. (2002) have suggested that professionals use differing behavioral descriptors to characterize these two disorders. They report rankings by audiologists and pediatricians of 58 symptoms associated with CAPD and ADHD of the inattentive type. According to their analysis, none of the four behaviors that ranked 2 standard deviations (SDs) above the grand means were ranked in common. In contrast, when McFarland and Cacace (2003) reexamined all of the data presented in the appendix of the Chermak et al. (2002) study, they found that the two sets of rankings were in fact highly correlated (Pearson's $r = 0.75$, $p < 0.0001$) (see Fig. 3.1). As this example illustrates, limiting data analysis to only a small proportion of the actual sample can lead to erroneous conclusions. Inclusion of all of the data demonstrated that considerable overlap exists in the conceptions of audiologists about CAPD and the

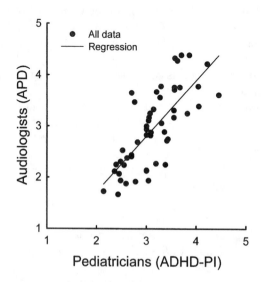

FIG. 3.1. Correlation of audiologists' ratings (APD) and pediatricians' ratings (ADHD-PI; primarily inattentive subtype) from Chermak et al. (2002, appendix data). Correlation of rating between audiologists and pediatricians: $r = 0.75$, $p < 0.0001$, based on linear regression analysis (from McFarland and Cacace, 2003, with permission of the publisher).

conceptions of pediatricians about ADHD. McFarland and Cacace (2003) further noted that data presented by Chermak and colleagues (2002) dealt with *conceptual* overlap and failed to address the issue of *diagnostic* overlap. Diagnostic overlap is the critical issue, as there is neither general conceptual agreement about ADHD (Sergeant, Geurts, Heijbregts, Scheres, & Oosterlaan, 2003) nor conceptual agreement about CAPD.

The contention that ADHD and CAPD are distinct due to a lack of correlation between measures of the two (Riccio et al., 1996) is perhaps the most compelling argument that these two disorders are distinct (notwithstanding the fact that these authors used a unimodal framework). However, other empirical evidence suggests that a considerable degree of overlap exists between CAPD and ADHD. For example, Tillery, Katz, and Keller (2000) reported that 36 of 66 children with ADHD (~55%) failed two or more CAPD tests. Likewise, Keith, Rudy, Donahue, and Katbamna (1989) reported that the SCAN battery is sensitive to deficits in attention.

CAPD AND ADHD ARE INDISTINGUISHABLE

This argument can take two forms. In one form, it is asserted that auditory processing difficulties comprise one of several features that make up ADHD. Thus, ADHD would consist of auditory processing deficits, visual processing deficits, tactile processing deficits, and so on. An alternative assertion is that auditory processing deficits cause ADHD.

The ASHA consensus statement (ASHA, 1996) asserts that CAPD may stem from more a general dysfunction such as attention deficit. Likewise, Chermak and colleagues (2002) stated that "APD is not a label for a unitary disease, but rather a description of functional deficits," and, furthermore that, "auditory processes involve the deployment of nondedicated, global mechanisms of attention and memory in service of acoustic signal processing." This view associates the presence of CAPD with failure on specific tests and is not concerned with underlying mechanisms. Moreover, this view also follows from a definition of CAPD in terms of specific behaviors (i.e., performance on tests of sound localization and lateralization, auditory discrimination, auditory pattern recognition) rather than in terms of auditory perceptual processes. Thus, if a child with ADHD performs poorly on a test involving only auditory stimuli, then that child is held to have an auditory processing deficit.

It is certainly possible to equate a diagnosis of CAPD with poor performance on tests that involve only auditory stimuli. However, a consideration of other cases indicates that the operational approach has not fared well, nor has it withstood the test of time. This approach is similar to logic used in the "early days" of intelligence testing, when it was asserted that intelligence was whatever the intelligence test measured (Boring, 1923). However, this view was subsequently abandoned when the circular nature of this definition was recognized, and when researchers became aware of the difficulties inherent in applying it to the variety of tests that had been developed (Tyler, 1965). As applied to CAPD, the extreme form of an operational view would hold that a specific type of auditory processing deficit is associated with performance on each specific test.

Defining CAPD in terms of whatever the specific tests measure does not provide a definition that can be usefully generalized to practical situations. For example, if the intent is to understand the learning problems of a student, then it is not particularly helpful to describe the problem as involving deficits in the perception of pitch patterns or dichotic digits. Rather, it is useful to describe auditory processing in terms such as auditory pattern perception and auditory stream segregation. These are general constructs that are widely applicable, but they are not associated with test performance in a one-to-one manner. Thus, a dichotic listening test should be viewed as one of many tests that involve auditory stream segregation, as well as other factors such as attention and memory. If a child has problems with auditory stream segregation, then a consistent pattern of test performance would be expected across tests involving this construct. At the same time, similar tests in the visual modality should not show these impairments. In this way, the hypothesis that a child had a deficit in a general process, such as auditory stream segregation, would be supported. Presumably, this deficit would also be manifested in a noisy classroom listening environment.

Testing for CAPD continues to involve tasks such as dichotic listening, as originally designed by Kimura (1961). Dichotic listening tests require perceptual grouping based on somewhat unnatural binaural cues. More recent research has identified additional cues that are relevant to auditory grouping (Darwin, 1997). A shift in the focus to general perceptual processes, rather than performance on specific tests, could provide the basis of new testing strategies. Likewise, equating auditory processing disorders with specific test performance does not provide a means of relating concepts of central auditory processing with developments in auditory neuroscience. Current concepts in this area involve constructs such as sound localization and sound identification (Read, Winer, & Schreiner, 2002). Specific neurophysiological mechanisms are being identified, and these constructs are being associated with distinct auditory processing streams (e.g., Stecker & Middlebrooks, 2003; Schubotz, von Cramon, & Lohmann, 2003). Auditory processes that are operationally defined in terms of specific test performance do not provide theoretical constructs that can be related to these evolving concepts in auditory neuroscience.

Several authors have taken the position that CAPD can be a cause of ADHD. For example, Chermak et al. (1999) stated that "the relationships among CAPD, ADHD, and learning disabilities are complex and not completely understood, and the primacy of any one of these disorders as causal to another remains unclear." Likewise, Keller and Tillery (2002) suggested that CAPD be assessed as a possible cause of ADHD. Although it is possible that CAPD is a cause of ADHD, there is no convincing evidence to support this position. In our view, however, the primary issue here is whether it is possible to demonstrate that there are cases diagnosed as ADHD that can be characterized either by a modality-specific attention deficit or by an auditory modality-specific deficit that is causally related to attention.

CAPD AND ADHD ARE FREQUENTLY COMORBID

It has often been suggested that the overlap found between CAPD and ADHD is due to comorbidity (e.g. Riccio et al., 1994, 1996). This view holds that the two entities are distinct, but that they are frequently present in the same individual. We have previously discussed the issue of comorbidity in CAPD (McFarland & Cacace, 1995). There we suggested that for comorbidity to be a useful concept, the onus would be on the clinician or researcher to demonstrate auditory modality-specific effects in at least some proportion of the population.

Angold, Costello, and Erkanli (1999) provided a detailed review of the topic of comorbidity. They emphasized that comorbidity is a well-established concept within diagnostic medical models whereby two diseases can occur conjointly. Obviously, there is little controversy on this point, because many disease states are often well defined and easily differentiated. However, when disease categories are less well established or when professionals deal with "disorders" (i.e., behavioral or psychiatric syndromes that are deviant from the standard of normality), the determination of comorbidity becomes useful for establishing the prevalence of and relationships among symptoms. Documentation of a comorbid relationship between disorders is important, as it implies that there is a problem with the classification system rather than any meaningful association between underlying diseases. Thus, "rather than being a bothersome problem to be ignored, or an embarrassment to categorical diagnosis, or something to be defined away by use of combined diagnostic categories, co-morbidity has emerged as an opportunity for understanding better the development of psychopathology and as a potential tool for improving nosology" (Angold et al., 1999).

CAPD AND ADHD: MISTAKE IN DIAGNOSIS

It has been suggested that a child with ADHD could be mistakenly diagnosed or misclassified as having CAPD (Grundfast et al., 1991; Cacace & McFarland, 1998). This view follows from the assumption that many tests of central auditory processing require close attention to auditory stimuli. Furthermore, CAPD test batteries do not generally include tests that rule out supramodal effects. Conversely, it has also been suggested that children with CAPD could be mistakenly diagnosed with ADHD (Report on Medical Guidelines and Outcome Research, 2000). In either case, multimodal testing with psychometrically matched tests would help to clarify this issue.

The existence of comorbid features may reflect a shortcoming in the accuracy of differential diagnosis using current procedures and criteria (Riccio et al., 1994). As we have emphasized, if a unimodal inclusive framework is used (as is the case for many studies), delineating modality-specific from supramodal effects cannot be achieved with any degree of confidence.

In keeping with the concept of modality specificity, evaluation of the appropriateness of the CAPD diagnosis in children with so-called listening problems should consider whether the children's inattentiveness is more pronounced with auditory stimuli than with stimuli presented in other sensory modalities. Continuous performance tests are frequently used in assessment when disorders of attention are suspected. Traditionally CPTs were employed using only visual stimuli (Gordan & Mettelman, 1988). However, Bedi, Halperin, and Sharma (1994) found that distractibility could be modality-specific. This group of researchers found that distractibility from visual stimuli was associated with CPT measures of inattention and with teacher ratings of behavior but not with cognitive or academic achievement measures. In contrast, auditory distractibility was associated with cognitive functioning and reading scores but not with CPT inattention or teacher ratings. As more astute professionals come to recognize the importance of modality specificity, CPTs are being developed and marketed to assess both auditory and visual performance (Tinius, 2003; Aylward & Brager, 2002). Although use of multimodal CPTs is a step in the right direction, the operating characteristics of such tests, including test–retest reliability, need to be scrutinized and evaluated in more detail.

AUDITORY ATTENTION AND THE CPT

A number of authors have suggested that the auditory CPT is useful in distinguishing ADHD from CAPD. Chermak and colleagues made this assertion, although they did not indicate how this information was to be used. Medwestsky (2002) suggested that CAPD is characterized by a tendency to miss targets on the auditory CPT (i.e., errors of omission), while ADHD is characterized by a tendency toward false alarms (i.e., errors of commission). The fundamental issue in our view is whether or not there are auditory modality-specific effects involved in CPT performance.

In the original version of the CPT (Rosvold et al., 1956), subjects were required to detect visual target letters embedded in nontarget letters. Variations of this task have been examined with populations of children diagnosed with ADHD. In a meta-analysis of 26 studies, Losier, McGrath, and Klein (1996) found that children with ADHD made more omission errors and more commission errors than controls. Both types of errors were reduced with use of methylphenidate. However, the diagnostic utility of the CPT is controversial. For example, Mayes, Calhoun, and Crowell (2001) reported that the CPT had a high diagnostic accuracy for ADHD. In contrast, McGee, Clark, and Symons (2000) reported that CPT scores were more closely related to reading disorders than to ADHD. Others take issue with the fundamental premise of the CPT (Corkum & Siegel, 1993) and suggest that it is difficult to distinguish arousal deficits from deficits associated with sustained attention.

A number of studies have dealt with comparisons of visual and auditory CPTs. Groups of children with ADHD show decrements in performance relative to controls on both visual and auditory versions of the CPT (Sykes, Douglas, & Morgenstern, 1973; Tinius, 2003). Thus, as a group, children with ADHD do not show modality-specific effects on the CPT.

Aylward and Brager (2002) examined the performance of a large group of children on the Gordon Diagnostic System (Gordon, 1983). This task requires a button to be pressed each time the number 1 is followed by the number 9. Stimulus presentation was either visual or auditory. The 634 subjects were all referred because of concerns with their school performance. When a criterion of performance below the 25th percentile was used, 15.5% of children failed both modalities, 9.6% failed only the visual test, and 15.5% failed only the auditory test. These results suggest that modality-specific effects can be observed with this version of the CPT. However, those authors did not report information on the reliability of these tests. In the evaluation of whether there exist differences in auditory and visual test performance, it is important to consider the consistency of effects within subjects. Test reliability refers, among other things, to the extent to which test results are repeatable at different points in time. If test reliability is low, then it is unlikely that the results of an initial test will be repeated a second time. If test reliability is low, it is also unlikely that two tests measuring the same construct will give the same results.

The reliability of tests can also be improved by modifications in test design. For example, some studies indicate that dichotic listening tests have poor reliability (Bradshaw, Burden, & Nettleton, 1986). Use of a target detection task, rather than the usual recall procedure, dramatically improves test–retest reliability (Voyer, 2003). Use of a detection task also minimizes factors related to response production and strengthens the validity of dichotic listening as a perceptual measure. Reliability is an important issue, and it needs to receive more attention in the CAPD testing literature (Cacace & McFarland, 1995). Therefore, more extensive coverage of this topic can be found in the chapter on controversial issues in CAPD (McFarland and Cacace, chap. 13, this volume).

Another approach to the issue of modality specificity in CPT performance involves examination of intercorrelations between visual and auditory forms of the test. Borgaro and coworkers (2003) were concerned about this aspect of CPT construct validity. Their analysis involved three forms of the CPT test crossed with two modalities of presentation. Rosvold and coworkers (1956) originally used an X design in which each instance of the target had to be reported. The A–X design requires reporting

TABLE 3.1
Comparison of three structural models of confirmatory factor analyses based on the
published data of Borgaro et al. (2003).

Model	AGFI	X^2	p	Delta X^2	p
General + Aud + Vis	0.9332	2.9011 (3)	0.4071	0.2510 (3)	0.9689
General + Aud	0.9680	3.1521 (7)	0.8706	3.2581 (2)	0.1961
1 General	0.9506	6.4102 (9)	0.6983	—	—

Note. These included a model with a single general factor (1 General); a model with a
general factor and an auditory factor (General + Aud); and a model with a general factor, an
auditory factor, and a visual factor (general + Aud + Vis). Column 1 identifies the model,
column 2 contains the adjusted fit index (AGFI), column 3 provides the chi-square residual
and indicates the amount of variance not accounted for by each model, column 4 provides
probability of chi-square values, column 5 shows change in chi-square resulting from the
addition of each new term, and column 6 shows the probability values of the change.

each X that follows an A. This task presumably has greater working memory requirements than does the X design. The X–X design requires the reporting of every instance
of a repeated item, and presumably has still greater working memory requirements.
Borgaro and coworkers (2003) used the metric d-prime (d′) as a measure of performance in a population of 100 heterogeneous psychiatric patients (not including ADHD
cases). They found that correlations among all forms of the CPT were of the same magnitude, and they concluded that all forms of the CPT measured a single construct.

The conclusion reached by Borgaro and colleagues seems reasonable, based on an
inspection of their data. However, in order to characterize their analysis statistically,
we entered their published correlations into a standard statistical program (Statistical
Analysis Systems, SAS) and performed a more formal analysis with structural equation modeling (SEM). Structural equation modeling, also referred to as confirmatory
factor analysis, allows for the comparison of alternative models. We considered a
model with a single general factor, where all tests loaded on the same factor; a model
including a general factor and an auditory factor; and a model including a general
factor; an auditory factor, and a visual factor. These three models are nested, in the
sense that each more complex model includes all terms contained in the previous
simpler model. The models can thus be compared in terms of how much information
is added by each additional level of complexity. The results are shown in Table 3.1.

The first model included a general vigilance factor and two modality-specific factors. The second model was nested within the first, in that it included the same factors
(with the exception that the effect of visual modality is left out). Finally, the third
model was nested within the other two and included only the general factor. The
second column of Table 3.1 contains the adjusted goodness of fit index (AGFI), which
is an index, varying between 0 and 1, which indicated goodness of fit; it is adjusted
for the degrees of freedom in the model. Adjusted goodness of fit index values above
0.90 are generally considered good fits. As can be seen in the table, all of the models
provided good fits of the data. The third column gives the chi-squared (X^2) residual
for each model and indicates the amount of residual variance not accounted for by
each model. Column 4 shows the probability of these X^2 values. None of these are
significant, indicating that none of the models have significant residual error. Column
5 shows the change in X^2 resulting from the addition of each term to the model. None
of the addition of terms causes a significant change, as indicated in column 6.

Several conclusions can be drawn from these data. First of all, removal of either the
auditory or visual term from the full model does not produce a significant reduction

in the variance accounted for by the model. Second, the single general factor does not significantly differ from chance. Thus, the data are readily accounted for by a single vigilance factor, and addition of modality-specific terms does not improve the fit. This is essentially the conclusion that Borgaro and colleagues (2003) reached from inspection of their correlation matrix. The findings from our structural modeling do not support the concept of modality-specific vigilance. However, the population in this study did not include patients with ADHD, so the generality may be limited.

Modality effects with the CPT in ADHD are of interest when we consider what methodology is appropriate for the demonstration of modality-specific effects. Groups of individuals with ADHD show deficits on both auditory and visual forms of the CPT. However, because ADHD is a heterogeneous entity, subgroups may show modality-specific effects. To demonstrate modality specificity in subgroups of this disorder, however, it is necessary either to collect reliable data on individuals or to examine the structure of test intercorrelations in groups.

Vigilance, as measured by the CPT, is the most thoroughly studied aspect of attention in ADHD. In addition, this topic is of interest given the suggestion that the ACPT (Keith, 1994) be added to CAPD test batteries (e.g., Chermak et al., 1999). However, there are many facets to the study of attention. It is possible that auditory-specific mechanisms operate on other aspects of attention such as those involved in feature selection or stream segregation. Furthermore, it is also possible that other supramodal attentional factors influence CAPD test performance.

Children with ADHD are often described as being impulsive. However, their response latencies on the CPT are generally *longer* than those of controls. This fact has led some to question the appropriateness of describing ADHD in terms of impulsivity (Swanson, Castellanos, Murias, LaHoste, & Kennedy, 1998). A popular measure of impulsivity in ADHD is the Matching Familiar Figures Test (MFFT; Kagan, 1965). In this test, the subject is shown a standard picture and six similar pictures. The instruction is to pick the identical matching picture. Children with ADHD show fast, inaccurate responding on the MFFT that has been characterized as impulsive (Barkley, 1997). Thus, children with ADHD show slow reactions during simple detection with the CPT, but faster reaction times when careful scanning of features is required. Such patterns illustrate the complexity of defining the attention deficit in ADHD. They also illustrate some of the possible ways in which the cognitive style of ADHD children can influence their performance on perceptual tasks. The child with ADHD may have particular difficulty with tasks requiring systematic evaluation of multiple stimulus features. Both the CPT and the MFFT use easily discriminable stimuli. The problems that children with ADHD have with these tasks illustrate how factors such as impulsivity or vigilance can affect test performance. This is one basis for the concern that children with ADHD may do poorly on tests purported to measure perceptual functioning.

It is worth noting that some authors have used constructs other than attention to characterize ADHD. For example, Barkley (1997) has argued that the core deficit in ADHD involves executive functioning. In this regard, the study of Sonuga-Barke, Dalen, and Remington (2003) is of interest. These researchers gave young children with ADHD a battery of tests measuring executive functioning and delay aversion. They found that executive deficits and delay aversion made independent contributions to the prediction of ADHD symptoms. Such results suggest that ADHD represents a collection of deficits rather than a single core deficit. Hoza, Pelham, Waschbusch, Kipp, and Owens (2001) have documented decreased persistence of children with ADHD. This result relates to the curious and often underrecognized findings of Silman,

Silverman, and Emmer (2000) that children may perform poorly on CAPD tests due to poor motivation. These authors also highlight the difficulties in distinguishing between an attention deficit and poor motivation.

BIOLOGICAL BASIS

Anatomical tract tracing is a well-established method by which to identify the auditory nervous system. However, the complexity of the ascending auditory system, particularly in the cortex, in large part limits this approach to the lower auditory centers and tracks. The neocortex has traditionally been divided into sensory, association, and motor areas. With electrophysiologic methods, sensory areas are identified by their modality-specific responsiveness (e.g., Thompson, Johnson, & Hoopes, 1963; Wallace, Ramachandran, & Stein, 2004). With the use of this criterion, auditory-specific areas beyond Heschl's gyrus have been identified (e.g., Kaas, Hackett, & Tramo, 1999; Kaas & Hackett, 2000; Romanski et al., 1999a, b; Romanski & Goldman-Rakic, 2002). There has been considerable interest in recent years in these secondary and tertiary auditory areas and the possibility that they are associated with separate streams of processing (Hart, Palmer, & Hall, 2004). One widely proposed scheme holds that there are distinct streams for identification of auditory objects and spatial location (e.g., Kaas & Hackett, 2000), in a manner similar to the processing streams identified in visual cortex (e.g., Baizer, Ungerleider, & Desimone, 1991). These conclusions are based on studies demonstrating modality-specific electrophysiological responses in animals (e.g., Tian, Reser, Durham, Kustov, & Rauschecker, 2001). More recently, similar findings have been reported with modality-specific activations in humans, using various imaging methodologies (positron emission tomography, PET; functional magnetic resonance imaging, fMRI) (e.g., Warren & Griffiths, 2003; see also Arnott, Binns, Grady, & Alain, 2004 for a meta-analysis review). Central auditory processing disorder is presumably a result of pathology in these modality-specific areas, but this has seldom been demonstrated in children receiving this diagnosis.

Research on the biological basis of attention and its deficits does not have as clear-cut a criterion as modality specificity for a guide. Attention deficit hyperactivity disorder is currently diagnosed on the basis of observed symptoms, and attention is identified by theoretical inference. Both of these are controversial and are still evolving. For example, disagreement between parent and teacher reports on symptoms is common (Mitsis, McKay, Schulz, Newcorn, & Halperin, 2000; Wolraich et al., 2004). Likewise, there are a number of competing explanations of ADHD (Sergeant et al., 2003). Cerebral glucose use in hyperactive adolescents and in adults with a history of hyperactivity in childhood shows left frontal lobe dysfunction during an auditory CPT (Zametkin et al., 1990, 1993). Lou, Henriksen, Bruhn, Borner, and Nielsen (1989) also noted reduced blood flow in the anterior striatum in children with ADHD, while occipital and parietal–temporal areas showed increased blood flow. These results indicate that ADHD is related to frontal lobe dysfunction.

The occurrence of dysfunction within the right frontal–striatal system in ADHD patients has led Heilman, Voeller, and Nadeau (1991) to draw parallels between the neurological disturbance of neglect seen in adults following stroke on the right side of the brain and the pathophysiology underlying the attentional component of ADHD found in children. Although (hemispatial) neglect can manifest anywhere along a scale of severity, it is often characterized by the failure to report, respond, or orient to stimuli presented contralateral to the lesion when sensory (i.e., peripheral visual, auditory or tactile loss) and motor deficits are ruled out. Moreover, the neglect phenomenon can be exacerbated by the presence of competing stimuli presented ipsilateral to the lesion. This can lead to complete extinction of stimulus events or motor exploration in contralateral hemispace. In relation to the auditory domain, the observation that localization or recognition deficits are exacerbated by the presence of ipsilateral competing noise is reminiscent of CAPD testing using sensitized stimuli (e.g., dichotic listening and competing message tasks).

Whereas the clinical or bedside evaluation of hemispatial neglect in adults has focused on the use of visual test material, there is mounting evidence that this disturbance is multimodal in nature. Visual neglect is often accompanied by auditory neglect, and their co-occurrence correlates with the severity of the disturbance (see Pavani, Ladavas, & Driver, 2003 for a review). Because neglect falls under the broad rubric of spatial attention, it is highly relevant here, as directing attention toward sensory events in extrapersonal space is an important ability in the initiation and adjustment of adaptive behavior. By combining knowledge gained from subjects with brain damage and more recent work from functional imaging studies, Mesulam (1999) proposed that the allocation of spatial attention is coordinated by a large-scale distributed neural network of interconnected cortical areas within and between posterior parietal cortex, frontal eye fields, and cingulate cortex. Experimental evidence suggests that the parietal component is specialized for the perceptual representation of behavioral relevant extrapersonal events as targets for attentional behaviors. The frontal component is specialized for selecting and executing motor strategies involved in foviations, exploration, and reaching. The cingulate component is specialized for modulating effort and motivation. Damage to any one of the three components can cause neglect. According to the model, "This network coordinates all aspects of spatial attention, regardless of the modality of input or output. It helps to compile a mental representation of extrapersonal events in terms of their motivational salience, and to generate 'kinetic strategies' so that the attentional focus can shift from one target to another" (Mesulam, 1999).

As noted above, the manifestation of neglect can range from a spectrum of difficulties, including subtle asymmetries, to the complete extinction of events occurring in the contralateral hemispace. Whereas anomalous lateralization performances (rightward bias) have been found in children with ADHD using common tasks such as letter cancellation and line bisection (e.g., Adelstein, 1995; Voeller & Heilman, 1988; Sheppard, Bradshaw, Mattingley, & Lee, 1999), such findings are not universal. Klimkeit, Mattingley, Sheppard, Lee, and Bradshaw (2003) suggested that such biases are absent in perceptual tasks that do not require a motor response or active spatial exploration of the environment and/or in paradigms such as dichotic listening using syllables, words, and emotional stimuli (e.g., Davidson & Prior, 1978; Manassis, Tannock, & Barbosa, 2000). These findings are interesting and require further study, as comparison of motor-based exploratory performance with skills on a purely perceptual task may illuminate the locus of dysfunction within the various epicenters of the distributed neural network proposed by Mesulam (1999).

Based on an MRI study of subcortical and cortical brain areas in school-aged boys with ADHD and matched controls, abnormalities were confirmed in right-sided prefrontal striatal systems (Castellanos et al., 1996). Neuroanatomical differences and correlations with behavioral and neurophysiological measures also differentiated adolescents with ADHD from normal controls (Matero, Garcia-Sanchez, Junque, Estevez-Gonzalez, & Pujol, 1997). Thus, functional and structural imaging data have converged on a role for frontal lobe and basal ganglion dysfunction in ADHD. Swanson and colleagues (1998) have reviewed the structural data and have concluded that ADHD is associated with a smaller caudate nucleus, globus palladus, and frontal cortex. They describe these areas as "associative," being interposed between sensory and motor areas. The obvious conclusion from this data is that ADHD is associated with abnormalities in "polysensory" brain areas.

There is considerable interest in the possibility that dopamine plays a key role in the pathology of ADHD. Drugs used in the treatment of this disorder, such as methylphenidate, act primarily on dopamine. Furthermore, the ascending dopaminergic system projects heavily to the frontal and striatal systems that were identified as being disordered in ADHD (Faraone & Biederman, 1998).

Levy, Hay, McStephen, Wood, and Waldman (1997) found evidence for heritability of ADHD based on a large-scale twin study. Their data further suggest that this trait varies along a continuum of severity rather than being categorical in nature (as implied by the current DSM schemata). After reviewing evidence from twin, adoption, family, and association studies, Acosta, Arcos-Burgos, and Muenke (2004) also suggested that ADHD has a genetic basis. Furthermore, they noted that a sizable percentage of schoolchildren with ADHD have been identified across diverse populations. Acosta and coworkers (2004) noted that there have been consistent associations between ADHD and the gene for the dopamine D4 receptor (DRD4) as well as between ADHD and the gene for the dopamine transporter (DAT). Other genes associated with dopamine and serotonin have also been implicated in ADHD. ADHD has been associated with an allele (the 7-repeat allele) of the DRD4 receptor that appears to have a reduced sensitivity for dopamine (Asghari et al., 1995). Because the 7-repeat allele occurs in approximately half of children diagnosed with ADHD, its impact on the symptoms of ADHD can be examined. Swanson and coauthors (2000) reported that in children with ADHD, the absence of the 7-repeat allele was associated with poor performance on tests of attention. Langley and coauthors (2004) reported that in children with ADHD, the 7-repeat allele is associated with poorer performance on the MFFT but not the CPT. Furthermore, this allele did not differentiate children with inattention from children with impulsive-hyperactive symptoms, as determined by ratings. Thus, in laboratory tests, the 7-repeat allele is associated with impulsivity rather than vigilance, but there seems to be no specificity with regard to rated symptoms. There have been inconsistent reports on the possible association of the dopamine D5 receptor (DRD5) with ADHD. Lowe and colleagues (2004) pooled data from 14 groups in order to increase the sensitivity of their analysis. They reported a highly significant association between a DRD5 marker and ADHD. Furthermore, this association was primarily with the inattentive type ADHD.

Genetic studies are rapidly improving our understanding of ADHD. However, neuropsychological testing suffers from problems with specificity, as does unimodal CAPD testing. This is most apparent for tests that attempt to measure executive function (Dodrill, 1997; Sergeant et al., 2002). In order to relate the ADHD phenotype to specific genotypes, tests specific to ADHD but insensitive to other comorbid disorders need to be developed.

The study of genetics in ADHD is one of the first areas in psychiatry where replicable genetic associations have been established. The results suggest a complex genetic etiology with several genes involved in specific traits. Continued study is likely to provide objective measures and clarification of traditionally contentious issues. In addition, the associations seen to date involve the dopamine system, which projects heavily to the polysensory frontal and striatal areas. Other transmitter systems may also be involved in attention and impulsivity. For example, Sarter, Givens, and Bruno

(2001) have reviewed studies that implicate acetylcholine in the regulation of vigilance. Acetylcholine projects widely to the neocortex and is involved in the regulation of receptive fields in sensory areas such as auditory cortex (e.g., Bakin & Weinberger, 1996; Kilgard & Merzenich, 1998). To date, however, no clear associations with this neurotransmitter system and ADHD have been established. Todd, Lobos, Sun, and Neuman (2003) have reported an association of ADHD with the nicotinic acetylcholine receptor, but replication of their findings is necessary.

ADHD appears to involve pathology mainly in polysensory areas in frontal cortex and basal ganglia. Alterations in the dopamine system are also implicated. This neurotransmitter system projects heavily to the same polysensory frontal–striatal areas. Thus, given the neuroanatomical colocalization, it is hard to advocate a perceptual basis for ADHD specific to the encoding of information in the auditory sensory modality.

SUMMARY

When criteria for the diagnosis of both CAPD and ADHD are applied, these two entities are found to co-occur frequently. Indeed, there has been a considerable amount of discussion about the possible reasons for this association. Diagnostic overlap could be due to mistaken diagnosis, comorbidity, or to a causal role of CAPD in ADHD. However, neither debate nor discussion contained within informal groups, state or nationally sponsored committees, or consensus conferences can resolve these issues. Instead, they must be resolved by research designed to evaluate the modality specificity of effects. Such an approach is necessary if we are to establish the perceptual basis and construct validity of CAPD in children with learning/behavioral problems (Cacace & McFarland, 1998).

REFERENCES

Acosta, M., Arcos-Burgos, M., & Muenke, M. (2004). Attention deficit/hyperactivity disorder (ADHD): Complex phenotype, simple genotype? *Genetics in Medicine, 6*, 1–15.

Adelstein, A. (1995). ADHD and attention in the visual-spatial domain. Doctoral dissertation. *Dissertation Abstracts International: Section B: The Sciences & Engineering, 56(2-B)*, 1098.

American Psychiatric Association. (1994). *Diagnostic and Statistical Manual of Mental Disorders* (4th ed.). Washington, DC: American Psychiatric Association.

American Speech-Language-Hearing Association. (1996). Central auditory processing: Current status of research and implications for clinical practice. *American Journal of Audiology, 5*, 41–54.

Angold, A., Costello, E. J., & Erkanli, A. (1999). Comorbidity. *Journal of Child Psychology and Psychiatry, 40*, 57–87.

Arnott, S. R., Binns, M. A., Grady, C. L., & Alain, C. (2004). Assessing the auditory dual-pathway model in humans. *NeuroImage, 22*, 401–408.

Asghari, J., Sanyal, S., Buchwaldt, S., Paterson, A., Jovanovich, V., & Van Tol, H. (1995). Modulation of intracellular cyclic AMP levels by different human dopamine receptor variants. *Journal of Neurochemistry, 65*, 1157–1165.

Aylward, G. P., & Brager, P. (2002). Relations between visual and auditory continuous performance tests in a clinical population: A descriptive study. *Developmental Neuropsychology, 21*, 285–303.

Baizer, J. S., Ungerleider, L. G., & Desimone, R. (1991). Organization of visual inputs to the inferior temporal and posterior parietal cortex in macaques. *Journal of Neuroscience, 11*, 168–190.

Bakin, J., & Weinberger, N. (1996). Induction of a physiological memory in the cerebral cortex by stimulation of the nucleus basalis. *Proceedings of the National Academy of Sciences, 93*, 11219–11224.

Barkley, R. (1997). Behavioral inhibition, sustained attention, and executive functions: Constructing a unifying theory of ADHD. *Psychological Bulletin, 121*, 65–94.

Barkley, R. (1998). History. In R. Barkley (Ed.), *Attention-deficit hyperactivity disorder: A handbook for diagnosis and treatment* (2nd ed., pp. 3–55). New York: Guilford.

Barkley, R. (2003). Issues in the diagnosis of attention-deficit/hyperactivity disorder in children. *Brain and Development, 25,* 77–83.

Bedi, G. C., Halperin, J. M., & Sharma, V. (1994). Investigation of modality-specific distractibility in children. *International Journal of Neuroscience, 74,* 79–85.

Bellis, T., & Ferre, J. M. (1999). Multidimensional approach to the differential diagnosis of central auditory processing disorders in children. *Journal of the American Academy of Audiology, 10,* 319–328.

Berlin, C. I., & Lowe, S. S. (1972). Temporal and dichotic factors in central auditory testing. In J. Katz (Ed.), *Handbook of clinical audiology* (pp. 280–321). Baltimore: Williams & Wilkins.

Bocca, E. C. (1958). Clinical aspects of cortical deafness. *Laryngoscope, 68,* 301–309.

Borgaro, S., Pogge, D. L., DeLuca, V. A., Bilger, L., Stokes, J., & Harvey, P. D. (2003). Convergence of different versions of the continuous performance test: Clinical and scientific implications. *Journal of Clinical and Experimental Neuropsychology, 25,* 283–292.

Boring, E. G. (1923). Intelligence as the tests test it. *New Republic, 35,* 35–37.

Bradshaw, J. L., Burden, V., & Nettleton, N. C. (1986). Dichotic and dihaptic techniques. *Neuropsychologia, 24,* 79–90.

Breier, J. I., Gray, L. C., Klass, P., & Foorman, J. M. (2002). Dissociation of sensitivity and response bias in children with attention deficit/hyperactivity disorder during central auditory masking. *Neuropsychology, 16,* 28–34.

Burd, L., & Fisher, W. (1986). Central auditory processing disorder or attention deficit disorder? *Journal of Developmental and Behavioral Pediatrics, 1,* 215–216.

Cacace, A. T., & McFarland, D. J. (1995). Opening Pandora's box: The reliability of CAPD tests. *American Journal of Audiology, 4,* 61–62.

Cacace, A. T., & McFarland, D. J. (1998). Central auditory processing disorders in school-aged children: A critical review. *Journal of Speech and Hearing Research, 41,* 355–373.

Cacace, A. T., McFarland, D. J., Ouimet, J. R., Schriber, E. J., & Marro, P. (2000). Temporal processing deficits in remediation-resistant reading-impaired children. *Audiology & Neuro-Otology, 5,* 83–97.

Castellanos, F. X., Giedd, J. N., Marsh, W. L., Hamburger, S. D., Vaituzis, A. C., Dickstein, D. P., Sarfatti, S. E., Vauss, Y. C., Snell, J. W., Lange, N., Kaysen, D., Krain, A. L., Ritchie, G. F., Rajapakse, J. C., & Rapoport, J. L. (1996). Quantitative brain magnetic resonance imaging in attention-deficit hyperactivity disorder. *Archives of General Psychiatry, 53,* 607–616.

Castellanos, F. X., & Tannock, R. (2002). Neuroscience of attention-deficit/hyperactivity disorder: The search for endophenotypes. *Nature Reviews Neuroscience, 3,* 617–628.

Chermak, G. D., Hall, J. W., & Musiek, F. E. (1999). Differential diagnosis and management of central auditory processing disorder and attention deficit hyperactivity disorder. *Journal of the American Academy of Audiology, 10,* 289–303.

Chermak, G. D., & Musiek, F. E. (1992). Managing central auditory processing disorders in children and youth. *American Journal of Audiology, 3,* 61–65.

Chermak, G. D., Tucker, E., & Seikel, J. A. (2002). Behavioral characteristics of auditory processing disorder and attention-deficit hyperactivity disorder: Predominantly inattentive type. *Journal of the American Academy of Audiology, 31,* 332–338.

Chess, S. (1960). Diagnosis and treatment of the hyperactive child. *New York State Journal of Medicine, 60,* 2379–2385.

Cook, J. R., Mausbach, T., Burd, L., Gascon, G. G., Slotnick, H. B., Patterson, B., Johnson, R. D., Hankey, B., & Reynolds, B. W. (1993). A preliminary study of the relationship between central auditory processing disorder and attention deficit disorder. *Journal of Psychiatric Neuroscience, 18,* 130–137.

Corkum, P. V., & Siegel, L. S. (1993). Is the continuous performance test a valuable research tool for use with children with attention-deficit-hyperactivity disorder? *Journal of Child Psychology and Psychiatry, 34,* 1217–1239.

Darwin, C. J. (1997). Auditory grouping. *Trends in Cognitive Sciences, 1,* 327–333.

Davidson, E. M., & Prior, M. R. (1978). Laterality and selective attention in hyperactive children. *Journal of Abnormal Child Psychology, 6,* 475–481.

Denkla, M. B. (2003). ADHD: Topic update. *Brain & Development, 25,* 383–389.

Dodrill, C. B. (1997). Myths of neuropsychology. *Clinical Neuropsychologist, 11,* 1–17.

Douglas, V. I., Barr, R. G., O'Neill, M. E., & Britton, B. G. (1986). Short term effects of methylphenidate on the cognitive, learning and academic performance of children with attention deficit disorder in the laboratory and the classroom. *Journal of Child Psychology and Psychology, 27,* 191–211.

Douglas, V. I., & Benezra, E. (1990). Supraspan verbal memory in attention deficit disorder with hyperactivity normal and reading-disabled boys. *Journal of Abnormal Child Psychology, 18,* 617–638.

Douglas, V. I., & Parry, P. A. (1983). Effects of reward on delayed reaction time task performance of hyperactive children. *Journal of Abnormal Child Psychology, 1*, 313–326.

Faraone, S. V., & Biederman, J. (1998). Neurobiology of attention-deficit hyperactivity disorder. *Biological Psychiatry, 44*, 951–958.

Gillberg, C. (2003). Deficits in attention, motor control, and perception: A brief review. *Archives of Disorders of Children, 88*, 904–910.

Gordon, M. (1983). *The Gordon diagnostic system*. DeWitt, NY: Gordon Systems.

Gordan, M., & Mettelman, B. B. (1988). The assessment of attention: I. Standardization and reliability of a behavior-based measure. *Journal of Clinical Psychology, 44*, 682–690.

Grundfast, K. M., Berkowitz, R. G., Connors, C. K., & Belman, P. (1991). Complete evaluation of the child identified as a poor listener. *International Journal of Pediatric Otorhinolaryngology, 21*, 65–78.

Hart, H. C., Palmer, A. R., & Hall, D. A. (2004). Different areas of human non-primary auditory cortex are activated by sounds with spatial and non-spatial properties. *Human Brain Mapping, 21*, 178–190.

Heilman, K. M., Voeller, K. S., & Nadeau, S. E. (1991). A possible pathophysiological substrate of attention deficit hyperactivity disorder. *Journal of Child Neurology, 6*, 74–79.

Hodgson, W. R. (1972). Filtered speech tests. In J. Katz (Ed.), *Handbook of clinical audiology* (pp. 313–324). Baltimore: Williams & Wilkins.

Hoza, B., Pelham, W., Waschbusch, D., Kipp, H., & Owens, J. (2001). Academic task persistence of normal achieving ADHD and control boys: Performance, self-evaluation, and attributions. *Journal of Consulting and Clinical Psychology, 69*, 271–283.

Jerger, J. (1973). Diagnostic audiometry. In J. Jerger (Ed.), *Modern developments in audiology* (2nd ed., pp. 75–112). New York: Academic Press.

Jerger, S., Johnson, K., & Loiselle, I. (1988). Pediatric central auditory dysfunction: Comparison of children with confirmed lesions versus suspected processing disorders. *American Journal of Otolaryngology, 9* (suppl), 63–71.

Jerger, J., & Musiek, F. (2000). Report of the consensus conference on the diagnosis of auditory processing disorders in school-aged children. *Journal of the American Academy of Audiology, 11*, 467–474.

Kaas, J. H., Hackett, T. A., & Tramo, M. J. (1999). Auditory processing in primate cerebral cortex. *Current Opinion in Neuroscience, 9*, 164–170.

Kaas, J. H., & Hackett, T. A. (2000). Subdivisions of auditory cortex and processing streams in primates. *Proceedings of the National Academy of Sciences, 97*, 11793–11799.

Kagan, J. (1965). Reflection-impulsivity and reading ability in primary grade children. *Child Development, 36*, 609–628.

Kamhi, A. G. (2004). A meme's eye view of speech-language pathology. *Language, Speech, and Hearing Services in Schools, 35*, 105–111.

Kamhi, A. G., & Beasley, D. A. (1985). Central auditory processing disorder: Is it a meaningful construct or a twentieth century unicorn? *Journal of Communication Disorders, 9*, 5–13.

Keith, R. W. (1986). *SCAN: A screening test for auditory processing disorders*. San Antonio, TX: Psychological Corporation, Harcourt Brace.

Keith, R. W. (1994). *ACPT: Auditory continuous performance test*. San Antonio, TX: Psychological Corporation, Harcourt Brace.

Keith, R. W. (1995). Tests of central auditory processing. In R. Roeser & M. Downs (Eds.), *Auditory disorders in school children* (3rd ed., pp. 101–116). New York: Thieme Medical Publishers.

Keith, R. W. (1999). Clinical issues in central auditory processing disorders. *Language, Speech, and Hearing Services in the Schools, 30*, 339–344.

Keith, R. W., & Engineer, P. (1991). Effects of methylphenidate on the auditory processing abilities of children with attention deficit-hyperactivity disorder. *Journal of Learning Disabilities, 24*, 630–636.

Keith, R. W., Rudy, J., Donahue, P. A., & Katbamna, B. (1989). Comparison of SCAN results with other auditory and language measures in a clinical population. *Ear and Hearing, 10*, 382–386.

Keller, W. D., & Tillery, K. L. (2002). Reliable differential diagnosis and effective management of auditory processing and attention deficit hyperactivity disorders. *Seminars in Hearing, 23*, 337–347.

Kilgard, M., & Merzenich, M. (1998). Cortical map reorganization enabled by nucleus basalis activity. *Science, 279*, 1714–1718.

Kimura, D. (1961). Some effects of temporal-lobe damage on auditory perception. *Canadian Journal of Psychology, 15*, 156–165.

Klimkeit, E. I., Mattingley, J. B., Sheppard, D. M., Lee, P., & Bradshaw, J. L. (2003). Perceptual asymmetries in normal children and children with attention deficit/hyperactivity disorder. *Brain and Cognition, 52*, 205–215.

Kuhn, T. S. (1996). *The structure of scientific revolutions* (3rd ed.). Chicago: University of Chicago Press.

Langley, K., Marshall, L., Thomas, H., Owen, M., O'Donovan, M., & Thapar, A. (2004). Association of the dopamine D4 receptor gene 7-repeat allele with neuropsychological test performance of children with ADHD. *American Journal of Psychiatry, 161,* 133–138.

Levy, F., Hay, D. A., McStephen, M., Wood, C., & Waldman, I. (1997). Attention-deficit hyperactivity disorder: A category or a continuum? Genetic analysis of a large-scale twin study. *Journal of the American Academy of Child and Adolescent Psychiatry, 36,* 737–744.

Losier, B. J., McGrath, P. J., & Klein, R. M. (1996). Error patterns on the continuous performance test in non-medicated and medicated samples of children with and without ADHD: A meta-analytic review. *Journal of Child Psychology and Psychiatry, 37,* 971–987.

Lou, H. C., Henriksen, L., Bruhn, P., Borner, H., & Nielsen, J. B. (1989). Striatal dysfunction in attention deficit and hyperkinetic disorder. *Archives of Neurology, 46,* 48–52.

Lowe, N., Kirley, A., Hawi, Z., Hawi, Z., Sham, P., Wickham, H., Kratochvil, C. J., Smith, S. D., Lee, S. Y., Levy, F., Kent, L., Middle, F., Rohde, L. A., Roman, T., Tahir, E., Yazgan, Y., Asherson, P., Mill, J., Thapar, A., Payton, A., Todd, R. D., Stephens, T., Ebstein, R. P., Manor, I., Barr, C. L., Wigg, K. G., Sinke, R. J., Buitelaar, J. K., Smalley, S. L., Nelson, S. F., Biederman, J., Faraone, S. V., & Gill, M. (2004). Joint analysis of the DRD5 marker concludes association with attention-deficit/hyperactivity disorder confined to the predominantly inattentive and combined subtypes. *American Journal of Human Genetics, 74,* 348–356.

Manassis, K., Tannock, R., & Barbosa, M. A. (2000). Dichotic listening and response inhibition in children with comorbid anxiety disorder and ADHD. *Journal of the American Academy of Child and Adolescent Psychiatry, 39,* 1152–1159.

Matero, M., Garcia-Sanchez, C., Junque, C., Estevez-Gonzalez, A., & Pujol, J. (1997). Magnetic resonance imaging measurement of the caudate nucleus in adolescents with attention-deficit hyperactivity disorder and its relationship with neuropsychological and behavioral measures. *Archives of Neurology, 54,* 963–968.

Mayes, S. D., Calhoun, S. L., & Crowell, E. W. (2001). Clinical validity and interpretation of the Gordon diagnostic system in ADHD assessment. *Neuropsychology Development and Cognition, Section C: Child Neuropsychology, 7,* 32–41.

McFarland, D. J., & Cacace, A. T. (1995). Modality specificity as a criterion for defining central auditory processing disorder. *American Journal of Audiology, 4,* 32–44.

McFarland, D. J., & Cacace, A. T. (1997). Modality specificity of auditory and visual pattern recognition: Implications for the assessment of central auditory processing disorders. *Audiology, 36,* 249–260.

McFarland, D. J., Cacace, A. T., & Setzen, G. (1998). Temporal order discrimination for selected auditory and visual stimulus dimensions. *Journal of Speech, Language, and Hearing Research, 41,* 300–314.

McFarland, D. J., & Cacace, A. T. (2003). Potential problems in the differential diagnosis of (central) auditory processing disorder (CAPD or APD) and attention-deficit hyperactivity disorder. *Journal of the American Academy of Audiology, 14,* 278–280.

McGee, R. A., Clark, S. E., & Symons, D. K. (2000). Does the Conners' continuous performance test aid in ADHD diagnosis? *Journal of Abnormal Child Psychology, 28,* 415–430.

Medwestsky, L. (2002). Central auditory processing. In J. Katz, R. F. Burkard, & L. Medwetsky (Eds.), *Handbook of clinical audiology* (3rd ed., pp. 510–524). Philadelphia: Lippinott.

Mesulam, M. M. (1999). Spatial attention and neglect: Parietal, frontal and cingulate contributions to the mental representation and attentional targeting of salient extrapersonal events. *Philosophical Transactions of the Royal Society of London B Biological Science, 354,* 1325–1346.

Milich, R., Balentine, A. C., & Lynam, D. R. (2001). ADHD combined type and ADHD predominantly inattentive type are distinct and unrelated disorders. *Clinical Psychology: Science and Practice, 8,* 463–488.

Mitsis, E. M., McKay, K. E., Schulz, K. P., Newcorn, J. H., & Halperin, J. M. (2000). Parent-teacher concordance for DSM-IV attention-deficit/hyperactivity disorder in a clinic-referred sample. *Journal of the American Academy of Adolescent Psychiatry, 39,* 308–316.

Moss, W. L., & Sheiffe, W. A. (1994). Can we differentially diagnose an attention deficit disorder without hyperactivity from a central auditory processing disorder? *Child Psychiatry and Human Development, 25,* 85–96.

Pavani, F., Ladavas, E., & Driver, J. (2003). Auditory and multisensory aspects of visuospatial neglect. *Trends in Cognitive Sciences, 7,* 407–441.

Peck, D. H., Gressard, R. P., & Hellerman, S. P. (1991). Central auditory processing in the school-aged child: Is it clinically relevant? *Developmental and Behavioral Pediatrics, 12,* 324–326.

Prior, M., Sanson, A., Geffen, G. M., & Freethy, C. (1985). Auditory attentional abilities in hyperactive children. *Journal of Child Psychology and Psychiatry, 26,* 289–304.

Rasmussen, E., Neuman, R., Heath, A., Levy, F., Hay, D., & Todd, R. (2002). Replication of the latent class structure of attention-deficit/hyperactive disorder (ADHD) subtypes in a sample of Australian twins. *Journal of Child Psychology and Psychiatry, 43*, 1018–1028.

Read, H. L., Winer, J. A., & Schreiner, C. E. (2002). Functional architecture of auditory cortex. *Current Opinion in Neurobiology, 12*, 443–440.

Rees, N. S. (1973). Auditory processing factors in language disorders: The view from Procrustes' bed. *Journal of Speech and Hearing Disorders, 38*, 304–315.

Rees, N. S. (1981). Saying more than we know: Is auditory processing disorder a useful concept? In R. W. Keith (Ed.), *Central auditory and language disorders in children* (pp. 94–120). San Diego, CA: College Hill Press.

Report on Medical Guidelines and Outcome Research. (2000). *Unlocking the mystery and misdiagnosis of central auditory processing disorder, 11*, 9–10.

Riccio, C. A., Cohen, M. J., Hynd, G. W., & Keith, R. W. (1996). Validity of the auditory continuous performance test in differentiating central auditory processing disorder with and without ADHD. *Journal of Learning Disabilities, 29*, 561–566.

Riccio, C. A., Hynd, G. W., Cohen, M. J., Hall, J., & Molt, L. (1994). Comorbidity of central auditory processing disorder and attention-deficit hyperactivity disorder. *Journal of the American Academy of Child and Adolescent Psychiatry, 33*, 849–857.

Romanski, L. M., Bates, J. F., & Goldman-Rakic, P. S. (1999b). Auditory belt and parabelt projections to the prefrontal cortex in the rhesus monkey. *Journal of Comparative Neurology, 403*, 141–157.

Romanski, L. M., & Goldman-Rakic, P. S. (2002). An auditory domain in primate prefrontal cortex. *Nature Neuroscience, 5*, 15–16.

Romanski, L. M., Tian, B., Fritz, J., Mishkin, M., Goldman-Rakic, P. S., & Rauschecker, J. P. (1999a). Dual streams of auditory afferents target multiple domains in the primate prefrontal cortex. *Nature Neuroscience, 2*, 1131–1136.

Rosvold, H. E., Mirsky, A. E., Sarason, I., Bransome, E. D. J., & Beck, L. H. (1956). A continuous performance test of brain damage. *Journal of Consulting Psychology, 20*, 343–350.

Sandberg, S., & Barton, J. (1996). Historical development. In S. Sandberg (Ed.), *Hyperactivity disorders of childhood* (pp. 1–25). Cambridge, England: Cambridge University Press.

Sarter, M., Givens, B., & Bruno, J. P. (2001). The cognitive neuroscience of sustained attention: Where top-down meets bottom-up. *Brain Research Reviews, 35*, 146–160.

Schmidt, F., & Hunter, J. (1999). Theory testing and measurement error. *Intelligence, 27*, 183–198.

Schubotz, R. I., von Cramon, D. Y., & Lohmann, G. (2003). Auditory what, where, and when: A sensory somatotopy in lateral premotor cortex. *NeuroImage, 20*, 173–185.

Sergeant, J. A., Geurts, H., Heijbregts, S., Scheres, A., & Oosterlaan, J. (2003). The top and bottom of ADHD: A neuropsychological perspective. *Neuroscience and Biobehavioral Reviews, 27*, 583–592.

Sergeant, J. A., Geurts, H., & Oosterlaan, J. (2002). How specific is a deficit of executive functioning for attention-deficit/hyperactivity disorder? *Behavioral Brain Research, 130*, 3–28.

Shalev, L., & Tsal, Y. (2003). The wide attentional window: A major deficit of children with attention difficulties. *Journal of Learning Disabilities, 36*, 517–527.

Sheppard, D. M., Bradshaw, J. L., Mattingley, J. B., & Lee, P. (1999). Effects of stimulant medication on the lateralization of line bisection judgements in children with attention deficit hyperactivity disorder. *Journal of Neurology, Neurosurgery, and Psychiatry, 66*, 57–63.

Silman, S., Silverman, C., & Emmer, M. (2000). Central auditory processing disorders and reduced motivation: Three case studies. *Journal of the American Academy of Audiology, 11*, 57–63.

Sonuga-Barke, E., Dalen, L., & Remington, B. (2003). Do executive deficits and delay aversion make independent contributions to preschool attention-deficit/hyperactivity disorder symptoms? *Journal of the American Academy of Child and Adolescent Psychiatry, 42*, 1335–1343.

Stecker, G. C., & Middlebrooks, J. C. (2003). Distributed coding of sound localization in auditory cortex. *Biological Cybernetics, 89*, 341–349.

Still, G. F. (1902). The Coulstonian Lectures: Some abnormal psychical conditions in children. *Lancet, 1*, 1008–1012, 1077–1082, 1163–1168.

Swanson, J., Castellanos, F. X., Murias, M., LaHoste, G., & Kennedy, J. (1998). Cognitive neuroscience of attention deficit hyperactivity disorder and hyperkinetic disorder. *Current Opinion in Neurobiology, 8*, 263–271.

Swanson, J., Oosterlaan, J., Murias, M., Schuck, S., Flodman, P., Spence, M. A., Wasdell, M., Ding, Y., Chi, H. C., Smith, M., Mann, M., Carlson, C., Kennedy, J. L., Sergeant, J. A., Leung, P., Zhang, Y. P., Sadeh, A., Chen, C., Whalen, C. K., Babb, K. A., Moyzis, R., & Posner, M. I. (2000). Attention deficit/hyperactivity disorder children with a 7-repeat allele of the dopamine receptor D4 gene have extreme behavior but normal performance on critical neuropsychological tests of attention. *Proceedings of the National Academy of Sciences, 97,* 4754–4759.

Sykes, D. H., Douglas, V. I., & Morgenstern, G. (1973). Sustained attention in hyperactive children. *Journal of Child Psychology and Psychiatry, 14,* 213–220.

Thompson, R. F., Johnson, R. H., & Hoopes, J. J. (1963). Organization of auditory, somatic sensory, and visual projection to association fields of the cerebral cortex in the cat. *Journal of Neurophysiology, 26,* 343–364.

Tian, B., Reser, D., Durham, A., Kustov, A., & Rauschecker, J. P. (2001). Functional specialization in rhesus monkey auditory cortex. *Science, 292,* 290–293.

Tillery, K. L., Katz, J., & Keller, W. D. (2000). Effects of methylphenidate (Ritalin) on auditory performance in children with attention and auditory processing disorders. *Journal of Speech, Language, and Hearing Research, 43,* 893–901.

Tinius, T. P. (2003). The intermediate visual and auditory continuous performance test as a neuropsychological measure. *Archives of Clinical Neuropsychology, 18,* 199–214.

Todd, R., Lobos, E., Sun, L., & Neuman, R. (2003). Mutational analysis of the nicotinic acetylcholine receptor alpha 4 subunit gene in attention deficit/hyperactivity disorder: Evidence for association with an intronic polymorphism with attention problems. *Molecular Psychiatry, 8,* 103–108.

Tredgold, C. H. (1908). *Mental deficiency (amentia).* New York: W. Wood.

Tyler, L. E. (1965). *The psychology of individual differences.* New York: Appleton-Century-Crofts.

Vellutino, F. R., & Scanlon, D. M. (1989). Auditory information processing in poor and normal readers. In J. J. Dumont & H. Nakken (Eds.), *Learning disabilities, volume 2: Cognitve, social and remedial aspects* (pp. 19–46). Amsterdam: Swet & Zeitlinger.

Voeller, K. K. S., & Heilman, K. M. (1988). Attention deficit disorder in children: A neglect syndrome? *Neurology, 38,* 806–808.

Voyer, D. (2003). Reliability and magnitude of perceptual asymmetries in a dichotic word recognition task. *Neuropsychology, 17,* 393–401.

Wallace, M. T., Ramachandran, R., & Stein, B. E. (2004). A revised view of sensoky cortical parcellation. *Proceedings of the National Academy of Sciences, 101,* 2167–2172.

Warren, J. D., & Griffiths, T. D. (2003). Distinct mechanisms for processing spatial sequences and pitch sequences in the human brain. *Journal of Neuroscience, 23,* 5799–5804.

Willeford, J. A. (1977). Assessing central auditory behavior in children: A test battery approach. In R. W. Keith (Ed.), *Central auditory dysfunction* (pp. 43–72). New York: Grune & Stratton.

Wolraich, M. L., Lambert, E. W., Bickman, L., Simmons, T., Doffing, M. A., & Worley, K. A. (2004). Assessing the impact of parent and teacher agreement on diagnosing attention-deficit hyperactivity disorder. *Journal of Developmental Behavioral Pediatrics, 25,* 41–47.

World Health Organization. (1992). *The ICD-10 classification of mental and behavioral disorders: Clinical descriptions and diagnostic guidelines, tenth revision.* Geneva: World Health Organization, 1992.

Zametkin, A. J., Liebenauer, L. L., Fitzgerald, G. A., King, A. C., Minkunas, D. V., Herscovitch, P., Yamada, E. M., & Cohen, R. M. (1993). Brain metabolism in teenagers with attention-deficit hyperactivity disorder, *Archives of General Psychiatry, 50,* 333–340.

Zametkin, A. J., Nordahl, T. E., Gross, M., King, A. C., Semple, W. E., Rumsey, J., Hamburger, S., & Cohen, R. M. (1990). Cerebral glucose metabolism in adults with hyperactivity of childhood onset. *New England Journal of Medicine, 323,* 1361–1366.

Audiologic Behavioral Assessment of APD

Teri James Bellis
The University of South Dakota

The overall purpose of assessment is to gather data and evidence about an individual's functional capabilities. Assessment of a child suspected of having APD may include both formal and informal measures, and should be a multidisciplinary endeavor, with input from professionals representing a variety of disciplines. Therefore, audiologists, speech-language pathologists, psychologists, teachers, physicians, and others collaborate in the assessment process. The term *assessment* should be differentiated from that of *diagnosis*, which refers specifically to the categorization of impairment for purposes of determining the nature or cause of a given dysfunction. Because APD is fundamentally an auditory-based deficit, the responsibility for diagnosing APD falls under the scope of practice of the audiologist (ASHA, 2004a, 2005a,b). According to the Preferred Practice Patterns for speech-language pathologists (SLPs; ASHA, 2004b), the SLP's role in APD assessment is in the delineation of cognitive-communication and/or language abilities that may be associated with the APD in a given individual. Nevertheless, a multidisciplinary approach to assessment and treatment/management of APD is critical, given the complex and heterogeneous nature of an APD on the individual. A variety of behavioral and physiologic tools are available to the audiologist for purposes of assessing the child's auditory capabilities and diagnosing APD. This chapter provides an overview of behavioral audiologic measures used in the assessment process. Chapter 8 will discuss how central auditory and related test results are interpreted for APD diagnostic purposes.

GENERAL PRINCIPLES OF AUDIOLOGIC BEHAVIORAL ASSESSMENT OF APD

APD has been defined as a deficit in one or more of the auditory mechanisms that underlie a variety of auditory behaviors, including sound localization and lateralization; auditory discrimination, auditory pattern recognition, temporal (or timing-related) aspects of audition, auditory performance in competing acoustic signals, and auditory performance with degraded acoustic signals; and that cannot be attributed to (or is not the result of) higher-order, more global cognitive or multimodal dysfunction (ASHA, 1996, 2005a,b; Bellis, 1996, 2003; Chermak & Musiek, 1997). As such, no single behavioral test or measure is sufficient to assess fully an individual's auditory capabilities. Instead, the central auditory test battery should focus on a variety of auditory performance areas, and should employ both verbal and nonverbal signals to examine different aspects of auditory processing and levels or loci within the central auditory nervous system (CANS).

The selection of the specific audiologic measures to be used will depend on a variety of factors, and should be individualized for the child in question and his or her presenting complaints and difficulties. Factors such as chronological and mental age, cognitive capacity, linguistic experience (including native language), attention and memory, fatigability, motivation, and others can and will influence how a given individual performs on these measures, and should be taken into account when selecting central auditory test tools.

Because of the impact of these factors and others on behavioral central auditory test performance, these measures have come under criticism in recent years (Jerger, 2000; Silman, Silverman, & Emmer, 2000). As a result, it has been implied by some that these tests are of limited utility or reliability, and that physiologic tests should be relied on for APD assessment and diagnosis. However, it should be remembered that all psychophysical measures are influenced, to some extent, by factors both extrinsic and intrinsic to the individual, including tests of speech and language, psychoeducational tests, and even a standard audiologic test battery. Basic signal detection theory states that attention, motivation, content of instructions, language, presence of reinforcement, and a variety of additional factors will influence an individual's response proclivity. For example, it is well-recognized that something as simple as the instructions provided to a listener can influence the results of standard pure-tone and speech recognition threshold testing. Yet, we would not interpret this finding as evidence that we should discontinue behavioral audiologic evaluation and rely on physiologic measures for hearing testing. Instead, we recognize that, whereas physiologic tests provide information about how anatomical structures in the peripheral and central auditory system respond to auditory signals, only behavioral measures can tell us how the individual in question actually *uses* that information. In this respect, behavioral audiologic tests for APD are no different. Although physiologic tests may provide important information about neurophysiologic representation in the CANS, only behavioral measures can illuminate areas of functional deficit. However, we must make all attempts during testing to be aware of and take steps to minimize additional nonauditory confounds.

The neuromaturational status of the child is of paramount importance. Because of variability in test performance and level of difficulty of the tests, the majority of behavioral audiologic test tools used to assess APD are of questionable validity and utility in children under the age of 7 years. Audiologists should be conscientious in their selection of central auditory test battery components, and should make sure that the tests chosen are appropriate to the child and are administered, scored, and interpreted in a manner consistent with the literature regarding each test. Children who are taking medication for attention-related deficits, seizure disorders, or other potentially confounding conditions should be medicated prior to behavioral central auditory testing so that these additional confounds may be minimized. Other cognitive, social, cultural, linguistic, physiologic, and related factors should be carefully taken into consideration by the examiner and controlled to the greatest extent possible.

Although most tests of central auditory function are best administered and interpreted in the presence of normal peripheral hearing sensitivity, there are some that are relatively resistant to the effects of peripheral auditory dysfunction. For this reason, the peripheral auditory system should be fully evaluated prior to beginning behavioral central auditory assessment, and test selection should be undertaken with caution when peripheral auditory dysfunction is present. Further, strategies such as examination of ear differences and intertest patterns, to be discussed in chapter 8, can assist the audiologist in interpreting test results obtained from individuals with hearing loss.

Another factor to consider when selecting central auditory tests is the purpose of the testing itself. If the purpose is to gain information about a child's listening function under a variety of conditions, then behavioral checklists, functional observation, and various screening tools may be utilized to assist in the assessment process. If, however, the purpose of the testing is to diagnose APD, the audiologist should select those tests that have been shown to have the greatest sensitivity and specificity for disorders of the CANS. That is, tests should be chosen that are best able to identify individuals with APD (*sensitivity*) while, at the same time, correctly identifying those individuals who do not have the disorder (*specificity*). The determination of sensitivity and specificity is reliant on a gold standard; however, because of the heterogeneity of APDs, an absolute gold standard for these disorders has yet to be identified and, quite possibly, never will be. Nevertheless, efficiency measures using individuals with known dysfunction of the CANS provide important information to guide the audiologist in weighing the relative value of behavioral central auditory tests for APD diagnosis (ASHA, 2005a,b). Audiologists should become familiar with the literature regarding sensitivity and specificity of various central auditory test tools, and should use this information in their test battery selection. Screening tools should never be used for diagnostic purposes.

In short, behavioral assessment of central auditory function is a complex endeavor, requiring familiarity with the vast array of tests and measures available and knowledge regarding the influence of auditory and nonauditory confounds on test performance. This process necessarily requires that audiologists engaging in central auditory assessment gain additional knowledge and skills that often are not provided in their educational programs or easily available via test manuals but that, instead, require careful and ongoing perusal of relevant information provided in scholarly journals and textbooks. For a more comprehensive discussion of these topics, readers are referred to Bellis (2003) and Chermak and Musiek (1997). For detailed information regarding administration, scoring, and interpretation of central auditory tests, including normative guidelines, readers are referred to Bellis (2003). Many of the tests to be discussed in this chapter can be obtained through Auditech of St. Louis, or are available on the *Tonal and Speech Materials for Auditory Perceptual Assessment* (1998) compact disc as well as through other sources.

CATEGORIES OF BEHAVIORAL CENTRAL AUDITORY TESTS

As previously stated, the central auditory test battery should consist of measures that are reliant on intact neural processing of auditory stimuli and that assess a variety of auditory abilities and anatomical levels or loci within the CANS. To this end, several categories of behavioral central auditory test measures exist, and audiologists should attempt to include at least one appropriate measure from each category, using the principles discussed in the previous section.

Several schemata have been suggested for categorizing central auditory test measures (e.g., Bellis, 1996, 2003; Bellis & Ferre, 1999; Chermak & Musiek,1997; Jerger & Musiek, 2000). In the vast majority of these, the auditory behaviors identified in the ASHA (1996, 2005a,b) and subsequent definitions of APD serve as guides to the categorization of behavioral test tools that may be utilized for comprehensive central auditory assessment. Recently, Domitz, Schow, and colleagues (Domitz & Schow, 2000; Schow & Chermak,1999; Schow et al., 2000; Schow et al., 2002), on the basis of a series of factor analyses, proposed an extremely useful diagnostic construct in which currently available behavioral central auditory test measures are related directly to the auditory behaviors and processes identified in the ASHA (1996) definition. In their schema, measurable auditory processes (and tests thereof) can be categorized as follows:

Tests of Binaural Separation (BS)

Binaural Separation (BS) is the ability to attend to a signal presented to one ear while, at the same time, ignoring a competing signal presented to the opposite ear (Bellis, 1996, 2003; Chermak & Musiek, 1997). It has also been referred to as *directed auditory attention*; however, because use of the term *attention* inherently refers to a higher-order, more global cognitive skill, the more accurate and precise term *BS* is recommended when discussing this specific measurable auditory process.

Dichotic tests are those in which different auditory signals are presented to each of the two ears simultaneously, and have been used to explore central auditory function for several decades (e.g., Broadbent, 1954; Bryden, 1963; Dirks, 1964; Kimura, 1961; Satz, Achenback, Pattishall, & Fennell, 1965). BS is assessed via the use of dichotic tests that require report of one ear. Virtually any stimuli can be used for dichotic testing, including linguistic stimuli (words, sentences, digits, running discourse) and nonlinguistic stimuli (complex tones, chords).

One of the commercially available dichotic paradigms that is most commonly used to assess BS is the Competing Sentences Test. First described by Willeford (see Willeford & Burleigh, 1994), this test involves the presentation of differing simple sentences to each ear simultaneously, with the target presented at a lower intensity than the competition. The listener is instructed to attend to and report the target sentence and ignore the competing sentence. The test is reported to be sensitive to dysfunction of the cerebral hemispheres and interhemispheric pathways; however, the utility of the test as well as the normative values for listeners ages 7 years through adult appear to rely on the way in which the test is scored (Bellis, 2003). Furthermore, a more recent version of Competing Sentences using different, somewhat more linguistically complex sentences has been made available via Auditech of St. Louis; however, this version appears to yield lower scores and greater variability in adults than does the original version (Hexamer & Bellis, 2000). Therefore, as with all tests of central auditory function, it is necessary to develop material-specific normative values for each version of this test. An additional test using dichotically presented sentences is also available in the SCAN-C Test for Auditory Processing Disorders in Children—Revised (Keith, 2000a) and SCAN-A Adolescent/Adult version (Keith, 1994), discussed below. Readers are cautioned, as with all tests of central auditory processing, to carefully study the literature regarding these tests prior to administering and interpreting them for APD assessment purposes.

A second commercially available dichotic test used to assess BS is the Synthetic Sentence Identification with Contralateral Competing Message (SSI-CCM) test (Jerger &

Jerger, 1974, 1975). The "sentences" used in this test consist of third-order approximations of English sentences which, therefore, resemble "scrambled" or nonsense sentences, thus lightening the linguistic load of the test. The sentences are presented to the target ear while competing continuous discourse is presented to the opposite ear. This is a closed-set test in which listeners are required to choose from a list of printed options which of the 10 possible sentences was presented. This test reportedly has been shown to be instrumental in identifying cortical dysfunction (Jerger & Jerger, 1975).

The Competing Words subtest of the Screening Test of Central Auditory Processing Disorders (SCAN) (Keith, 1986) and its subsequent versions [SCAN-C (Keith, 2000a) and SCAN-A (Keith, 1994)] also requires directed report of dichotically presented stimuli. In this test, monosyllabic words are presented to each ear and the listener is instructed to report the word heard in the target ear. This test has been suggested to be sensitive to neuromaturation of the central auditory system (Keith, 1986) and to be instrumental in identifying dyslexic children (Moncrieff & Musiek, 2002); however, the validity and utility of the SCAN as a diagnostic tool for APD has been called into question in recent years (e.g., Bellis, 2003; Domitz & Schow, 2000; Musiek et al., 1990; Schow et al., 2000).

Although the preceding three tests represent the most commonly used commercially available dichotic tests requiring BS, new measures are on the horizon. For example, Jerger and colleagues have reported on the use of electrophysiologic correlates to both linguistic and nonlinguistic behavioral dichotic paradigms for the identification of children and adults with APD (Greenwald & Jerger, 2001, 2003; Jerger et al., 2002). In addition, it has been suggested that some tests of central auditory processing, such as the Dichotic Digits test (Musiek, 1983a), to be discussed below, may be more sensitive if administered in a directed listening paradigm (Moncrieff & Musiek, 2002).

Tests of Binaural Integration (BI)

In contrast to BS, Binaural Integration (BI) requires report of stimuli presented to both ears during dichotic listening (Bellis, 1996, 2003; Chermak & Musiek, 1997) and, as such, has sometimes been referred to as *divided auditory attention*. Commercially available tests of BI abound, and include tests that span the linguistic continuum from consonant–vowel (CV) syllables to sentences.

One of the most commonly used tests of BI that also has been shown to have excellent sensitivity and specificity for disorders of the cerebral hemispheres, interhemispheric pathways, and brainstem is the Dichotic Digits Test (Musiek, 1983a). In this test, pairs of digits from 1 to 10 (excluding 7) are presented to each ear and the listener is instructed to report all 4 digits heard. Additional advantages to the Dichotic Digits test are that it is easy and quick to administer while being relatively resistant to peripheral hearing loss (Musiek, 1983a; Musiek et al., 1991; Strouse & Wilson, 2000).

Another widely employed dichotic BI test is the Staggered Spondaic Word (SSW) test (Katz, 1962). This test involves the dichotic presentation of spondees in such a manner that the second syllable of the leading word overlaps the first syllable of the lagging word. Both the ear-specific and overlapping spondees form separate words. For example, if *upstairs* is presented to the right ear and *downtown* is presented to the left ear, the word *downstairs* is formed by the overlapping (or competing) segments and the word *uptown* is formed by the noncompeting segments. Thus, four possible conditions may be scored: Right Competing, Left Competing, Right Non-Competing, and Left Non-Competing. Although a rather complex scoring construct has been proposed for the SSW and related to various proposed subtypes of APD (Katz, 1986; Katz, Smith, & Kurpita, 1992; Masters, Stecker, & Katz, 1993), Schow and Chermak (1999) demonstrated that the RC and LC scores of the SSW appear to assess the process of BI, as do other similar dichotic tests requiring report of both ears. In contrast, the non-competing scores (LNC and RNC) of the SSW appear to assess general word recognition in quiet. Therefore, this author recommends that, when used, performance on the competing conditions of the SSW should be viewed in the same manner as results of any other dichotic speech test and the SSW should be considered merely one component of an overall test battery rather than a stand-alone diagnostic test for APD.

The Dichotic CV test (Berlin et al., 1975) is more difficult than either the Dichotic Digits or SSW tests, and may be inappropriate for young children (Bellis, 2003). It consists of the presentation of CV segments (pa, ta, ka, ba, da, ga), one to each ear either simultaneously or with leading-ear lag times ranging from 15 to 90 msec. Listeners are instructed to choose both segments heard from a printed list. The Dichotic CV test has been shown to be sensitive to cortical dysfunction (Berlin et al., 1975); however, it is easily confounded by the presence of peripheral hearing loss (Bellis, 2003). Furthermore, unlike other dichotic listening tests, the Dichotic CV test does not show expected neuromaturational effects in normally hearing children (Roeser, Millay, & Morrow, 1983). Therefore, its utility in diagnosing APD in children is questionable.

The Dichotic Sentence Identification (DSI) test was developed expressly for the purpose of evaluating central auditory function in adults with peripheral hearing loss (Fifer et al.,1983). It involves the presentation of the synthetic sentences developed for the SSI, discussed previously, in a dichotic BI paradigm. Listeners are instructed to choose from a printed list the two sentences that were heard. Normative values for adults with varying degrees of peripheral hearing impairment are available (Fifer et al., 1983); however, the utility of this test in evaluating children is questionable.

When taken together, dichotic tests requiring BI or BS fall under the category of "auditory performance in competing acoustic signals" in the ASHA (1996, 2005a,b) definition of APD. However, by evaluating *both* integration and separation, a more precise and thorough evaluation of auditory functioning with different task demands under conditions of competition can be accomplished, which can ultimately lead to a more functionally relevant, individualized, deficit-specific intervention plan for the child in question. The dichotic tests discussed in the previous two sections are summarized in Table 4.1.

Tests of Monaural Separation/Closure (MSC)

MSC refers to the ability to fill in the missing pieces and achieve auditory closure when the signal is distorted in some manner or is presented in a condition of noise. One of the most common complaints of individuals with APD is problems processing under difficult listening conditions. When evaluated, many of these individuals will do quite well with standard audiologic testing of word recognition in quiet. However, when the signals are distorted or degraded in some manner, they often demonstrate significant difficulties, because some of the instrinsic redundancy of the speech signal has been removed. As such, these tests are often referred to as *monaural low-redundancy speech tests* (Bellis, 1996, 2003; Chermak & Musiek, 1997). Tests requiring MSC fall under

TABLE 4.1
Tests of Binaural Integration (BI) and Binaural Separation (BS) in Order
of Linguistic Loading

Test	Process Assessed
Dichotic Consonant–Vowels (CVs)	BI
Dichotic Digits	BI (BS if directed report)
Staggered Spondaic Word Test (SSW)	BI (competing conditions)
Competing Words subtest of SCAN	BS
Dichotic Sentence Identification	BI
Synthetic Sentence Identification—Contralateral Competing Message (SSI-CCM)	BS
Competing Sentence Test	BS

the category of "auditory performance with degraded acoustic signals" in the ASHA (1996, 2005a,b) definition of APD. There are several means by which acoustic signals may be degraded; this section discusses some of the most common tests of MSC.

One of the earliest means of degrading an auditory signal to assess integrity of the CANS was via low-pass filtering of the speech signal (Bocca, Calearo, & Cassinari, 1954). In low-pass filtering, high-frequency information above a specified frequency cut-off is removed, which, in essence, renders the audibility of the speech signal similar to that of speech in the presence of a high-frequency hearing loss. Since the 1950s, several studies have employed low-pass filtered speech in the detection of CANS dysfunction, and readers are referred to Rintelmann (1985) for a review. In general, low-pass filtered speech tests have been shown to be sensitive to both brain stem and cortical dysfunction. At present, a number of filtered word tests are available commercially using different word lists, low-pass cut-offs, and speakers (male versus female); however, many of them do not have published normative values nor sensitivity/specificity data. Each of these variables will have a significant impact on the appropriateness of the test for a given individual as well as on the normative values for the test.

Possibly the first commercially available low-pass filtered speech test was the Ivey filtered speech test included in the Willeford (1977) test battery. This test consisted of two lists of 50 consonant–nucleus–consonant (CNC) words filtered at 500 Hz. Although this test historically has been one of the most commonly used tests of MSC, its use has been overshadowed by the ready availability of other low-pass filtered word lists through a variety of sources. Wilson and Mueller (1984) investigated the effects of various filtering cut-offs on performance using the Northwestern University (NU)-6 word recognition lists. As a general rule, they found that a 500 Hz cut-off appears to be overly difficult, even for normally hearing adults, when NU-6 word lists are used. Therefore, it is generally recommended that a 1,000 Hz cut-off be selected for NU-6 words. A discussion of normative values for children using NU-6 words low-pass filtered at 1,000 Hz with both male and female speakers is available in Bellis (2003). Additional research remains to be completed using alternative filtering cut-offs and word lists.

A second method of reducing the intrinsic redundancy of speech signals is to alter the temporal characteristics via compression while retaining the frequency or spectral characteristics. These time-compressed speech tests assess an individual's ability to achieve auditory closure when the speech signal occurs very rapidly. As with other tests of monaural low-redundancy speech, normative values will be based on the word lists chosen, the speaker, and the compression ratio. In general, as the degree of compression increases, performance of normally hearing listeners decreases (e.g., Beasley, Forman, & Rintelmann, 1972). For example, 65% time compression of NU-6 words has been shown to be overly difficult even for normal listeners; therefore, when using NU-6 word lists, a 45% compression ratio may be more appropriate for clinical use (Bellis, 2003; Wilson et al.,1994). Time-compressed speech tests may be made even more difficult through the addition of reverberation, which is the echo that occurs when auditory signals are presented in enclosed spaces. Reverberation adds an additional means of reducing the redundancy of a speech signal and challenging the listener's ability to achieve auditory closure.

Perhaps the most common method of reducing redundancy of a speech signal is by imbedding the signal in a background of noise. Speech-in-noise tests may well be the most frequently employed—and most misused—tests of auditory function (Bellis, 2003; Mueller & Bright, 1994). This is because the choice of speech material, type of competing noise, and signal-to-noise (S/N) ratio, among other factors, will significantly impact the normative values obtained on a given speech-in-noise test, yet the vast majority of these tests are administered with little or no attention to the need for material-specific normative values. Moreover, because dysfunction virtually anywhere in the peripheral or central auditory pathways may affect an individual's ability to understand speech in noisy backgrounds, the utility of speech-in-noise tests for APD diagnostic purposes is questionable. Nevertheless, use of speech-in-noise tests may provide a method of confirming and quantifying an individual's reported functional difficulties. In addition, there are a few speech-in-noise tests developed for central auditory assessment that are currently available and that have accompanying normative data, and these are discussed below.

The Synthetic Sentence Identification with Ipsilateral Competing Message (SSI-ICM) (Jerger & Jerger, 1974) is identical to the SSI-CCM, discussed previously, except that the competing signal is routed to the same ear as the target sentence, rendering it a test of monaural separation rather than binaural separation. The SSI-ICM has been reported to be sensitive to dysfunction of the low brainstem, and a comparison of SSI-ICM versus SSI-CCM performance is useful in the differentiation of brainstem versus cortical dysfunction (Jerger & Jerger, 1974, 1975).

Jerger, Jerger, and Abrams (1983) developed the Pediatric Speech Intelligibility (PSI) Test for the purpose of evaluating speech-in-noise abilities of young children. In this test, stimuli of varying linguistic complexity are presented at various S/N ratios, and the children are instructed to point to the picture representing the target message. The PSI is one of the few tests of speech-in-noise with well-developed normative data for the pediatric population. Similarly, the Selective Auditory Attention Test (SAAT) (Cherry, 1980) may be administered in a monaural mode for purposes of assessing MSC (Schow & Chermak, 1999). A final measure of speech-in-noise that has been standardized on young children is the Auditory Figure–Ground subtest of the SCAN (Keith, 1986).

Additional tests of speech-in-noise have been employed for the determination of benefit from amplification for listeners with hearing impairment. However, the utility of these and related measures of speech-in-noise for evaluation of central auditory function remains to be studied. In addition, new measures of speech-in-noise for central auditory assessment are in current development (e.g., Jerger et al., 2000) that may provide important augmentation to the central auditory test battery.

TABLE 4.2
Tests of Monaural Separation/Auditory Closure

Low-Pass Filtered Speech
Time-Compressed Speech
Time-Compressed Speech with Reverberation
Synthetic Sentence Identification with Ipsilateral Competing Message (SSI-ICM)
Pediatric Speech Intelligibility Test (PSI)
Auditory Figure–Ground subtest of SCAN
Selective Auditory Attention Test (SAAT)

In summary, tests of MSC have been shown to be useful in the identification of brainstem and cortical dysfunction. However, a plethora of these types of tests abounds, many without sufficient research basis regarding sensitivity/specificity and normative data. Therefore, audiologists are cautioned, as always, to examine carefully the literature regarding each test prior to use for assessment purposes. The tests discussed in this section are summarized in Table 4.2.

Tests of Auditory Patterning/Temporal Ordering (APTO)

Falling under the category of "auditory pattern recognition" in the ASHA (1996, 2005a,b) definition of APD, APTO refers to the ability to discriminate among and sequence auditory stimuli. At present, there are two primary tests of APTO that are commercially available: Frequency (or Pitch) Patterns (Pinheiro & Ptacek, 1971; Ptacek & Pinheiro, 1971) and Duration Patterns (Pinheiro & Musiek, 1985).

The Frequency Patterns test consists of the presentation of triads of tone bursts that differ in frequency. The frequencies chosen for the original version of this test are 1,122 Hz (high) and 880 Hz (low). These frequencies are close enough to one another to be differentiated by normal listeners but difficult to discriminate by some individuals with APD. Through combining these two frequencies in three-tone patterns, or triads, six patterns are possible: high–low–low, high–high–low, high–low–high, low–high–high, low–high–low, and low–low–high. Following an instruction period that includes both visual and verbal modeling and practice items, 30 test items are administered and the listener is instructed to report verbally each pattern that was presented. If difficulty is noted during this verbal report condition, a second report condition may be employed in which the listener is instructed to hum or provide a motor response to represent the patterns. This condition removes the linguistic labeling component of the test and provides additional diagnostic information. The Frequency Patterns test has been shown to be sensitive to cortical dysfunction, and a comparison of verbal versus nonverbal report conditions is useful in illuminating dysfunction of the interhemispheric pathways, including the corpus callosum (Musiek, Pinheiro, & Wilson, 1980). The test also provides information regarding central auditory neuromaturation in children (Musiek, Gollegly, & Baran, 1984).

The Duration Patterns test (Pinheiro & Musiek, 1985) is identical in form to the Frequency Patterns test, except that 1,000 Hz tone-burst stimuli are presented that differ in duration (i.e., "short," 250 msec and "long," 500 msec). As with Frequency Patterns, both verbal and nonverbal report conditions may be employed for purposes of investigating cortical and interhemispheric central auditory function. Both tests are

TABLE 4.3
Tests of Auditory Patterning/Temporal Ordering

Frequency Patterns
Duration Patterns

relatively resistant to the presence of peripheral hearing loss, as long as the stimuli are audible to the listener (Musiek, Baran, & Pinheiro, 1990). The two tests discussed in this section are summarized in Table 4.3.

The above four measurable auditory processes (BS, BI, MSC, and APTO) were those that were specifically identified via factor analysis in the Domitz, Schow, and colleagues series of articles (Domitz & Schow, 2000; Schow & Chermak, 1999; Schow et al., 2000; Schow et al., 2002). These processes, and the tests that measure them, were related to three of the six auditory behaviors included in the ASHA (1996, 2005a,b) definition of APD: (a) auditory performance with competing acoustic signals (BS and BI), (b) auditory performance with degraded acoustic signals (MSC), and (c) auditory pattern recognition (APTO). The ASHA (1996, 2005a,b) definition of APD also include three additional general auditory behaviors: (a) Auditory discrimination, (b) sound localization and lateralization, and (c) (other) temporal aspects of audition. There are few tests commercially available today that evaluate these behaviors in a manner consistent with recommendations for APD diagnostic testing. Furthermore, Schow et al. (2000) have suggested that these three behaviors likely underlie the four factors discussed in the previous section. A discussion of these three categories follows:

Tests of Auditory Discrimination

The term *auditory discrimination* refers simply to the ability to differentiate between auditory stimuli. Tests of auditory discrimination may employ speech stimuli (i.e., minimal contrast phoneme pairs, consonant–vowel syllables, rhyming words, and so forth) or nonspeech stimuli (i.e., stimuli differing in duration, frequency, intensity, and/or other temporal parameters). With the exception of speech and language tests that assess speech sound discrimination, there are few commercially available tests of auditory discrimination developed expressly for use in APD assessment and diagnosis. Yet the ability to discriminate among similar-sounding auditory stimuli is arguably one of the most important determinants of auditory processing ability.

One test that has been shown to be instrumental in investigating children's ability to make fine-grained auditory discriminations necessary for normal speech perception is the Parameter Estimation by Sequential Tracking (PEST) Auditory Discrimination paradigm described by Kraus and colleagues (1999). In this two-alternative, forced-choice paradigm, listeners are required to discriminate between consonant–vowel syllabi that involve rapid spectro-temporal acoustic changes in the third formant frequency (e.g., /da/ vs /ga/). A just noticeable difference (jnd), or discrimination threshold, is obtained, which can be compared against available normative data for children and adults. This test has been shown to be instrumental in identifying children with auditory-based learning and language difficulties. In addition, difficulties in behavioral discrimination have been shown to be reflected in the neurophysiologic representation of the same stimuli using auditory electrophysiologic measures (Kraus et al., 1996). Although this test appears to represent an exciting and important addition to the central auditory test battery, administration of the test requires specialized equipment not typically found in the audiology clinic. Moreover, it is this author's experience that the currently available and updated version of the hardware specifically recommended by the developers of this test is no longer compatible with the test software. As such, widespread use of this procedure likely will not occur until such time as it can be made more easily available to practicing audiologists.

The psychoacoustics literature is replete with research regarding methods of obtaining difference limens for intensity, frequency, duration, and other auditory parameters. Because fine-grained auditory discrimination is presumed to underlie more complex auditory skills, such as general speech perception; processing of prosodic or emotional aspects of speech, including rhythm, rate, intonation, and stress; and a host of other auditory abilities, assessment of a listener's speech and nonspeech discrimination abilities logically would be a critical addition to any central auditory test battery. However, the vast majority of practicing audiologists have neither the knowledge nor the equipment to conduct these tests. Furthermore, the psychophysical procedures that are traditionally recommended to obtain discrimination thresholds typically take an enormous amount of time, which may preclude their use with children, who often exhibit limited attention or become easily fatigued. Therefore, until such time as commercially produced tests of fundamental auditory discrimination become available, this very important area of central auditory assessment may remain overlooked.

Tests of Sound Localization/Lateralization

Sound localization is the ability to determine the source of an auditory stimulus, whereas lateralization is a term used to refer to the perception within the head of the location of an auditory stimulus (i.e., midline, right ear, left ear). Localization and lateralization ability is determined by a number of factors, including peripheral auditory sensitivity, integrity of auditory nerve and brainstem structures, and function of cortical and interhemispheric regions of the brain. Of these, however, dysfunction of the auditory nerve and brainstem seems to have the greatest impact on localization and lateralization of auditory stimuli, and it appears that the fundamental groundwork for these abilities occurs at the low brainstem level (e.g., Nordlund,1964; Pickles, 1985). In addition, dysfunction of the auditory cortical regions and interhemispheric pathways will also affect adversely an individual's perception of auditory space and, therefore, his or her lateralization and localization abilities (e.g., Lepore et al., 1994; Pinheiro & Tobin, 1969, 1971; Sanchez-Longo et al., 1957).

When taken together, auditory tests that measure the way in which the two ears work together have been referred to as *binaural interaction* tasks (Bellis, 1996, 2003; Chermak & Musiek, 1997). Although a variety of binaural interaction tests are available commercially today, the vast majority of them have been criticized for their poor sensitivity to anything but gross brainstem lesions (e.g., Lynn & Gilroy, 1975). However, one test that has been shown to exhibit good sensitivity to brainstem dysfunction is the masking level difference (MLD).

The MLD paradigm is based on the findings of Licklider (1948), who showed that, when the phase relationship of two signals delivered to the two ears are adjusted so that they are out of phase with one another, listeners' ability to perceive the target signal is improved as compared to conditions in which the signals are in phase. This phenomenon has come to be called *binaural release from masking*. The MLD provides a sensitive measure of (primarily) brainstem auditory function, and can be evaluated using tonal or speech stimuli. At present, MLD procedures that employ speech stimuli are commercially available. In addition, some audiometers include a built-in tonal MLD feature; however, many do not. Therefore, the measurement of tonal MLDs, which have been reported to be more sensitive to brainstem dysfunction, may require additional psychoacoustic equipment.

Another measure of binaural interaction is binaural fusion. Binaural fusion tests involve the presentation of complementary portions of a signal to each of the two ears either simultaneously or in an alternating fashion. For example, the consonant portions of a word may be presented to one ear while the vowels are presented to the other. Conversely, the high-pass and low-pass portions of a word each may be presented to different ears, necessitating fusion at the brainstem level for the complete word to be perceived. There are several binaural fusion tests available today using a variety of separation schemes; however, none of them have been shown to be particularly sensitive to anything but very gross brainstem pathology (e.g., Lynn & Gilroy, 1975; Musiek, 1983b). Because other tests are available that demonstrate significantly better sensitivity for the identification of brainstem dysfunction, including the auditory brainstem response (ABR) and the MLD, the clinical utility of most binaural fusion and related tests for central auditory assessment is highly questionable.

More precise lateralization paradigms have been used for evaluation of central auditory dysfunction, including evaluation of interaural intensity differences (Pinheiro & Tobin, 1969, 1971) and interaural timing and intensity jnds (Levine et al., 1993a, b). In addition, Jerger & Estes (2002; Estes, Jerger, & Jacobson, 2002) examined electrophysiologic correlates to the perception of auditory movement in the horizontal plane in normally hearing children and adults and children suspected of exhibiting APD. These measures and others currently under development, including tests of localization precision in the horizontal and vertical planes, may provide important augmentations to the behavioral central auditory test battery; however, none of them are available in a commercial format at the present time.

Tests of Temporal Processing

The final category of measurable auditory processes is that of temporal processing. The term *temporal* refers to timing-related aspects of the auditory signal and, as such, temporal processing may be thought of as being critical to virtually every aspect of auditory processing, as well as being a component of all of the tests and categories previously discussed in this chapter. In fact, one could argue that every auditory processing disorder has, at its core, some type of temporal processing deficit, whether it be related to relative timing of input between ears, analysis of auditory patterns over time, discrimination of rapidly changing spectral information, or some other timing-related auditory skill. In auditory processing, the old adage that timing is everything is entirely true.

There are several psychoacoustic paradigms that have been used for the discrete evaluation of specific temporal processes. These include, but are not limited to: (a) gap detection, or the measurement of the ability to detect a short silent interval imbedded in an auditory signal; (b) auditory fusion, or the measurement of the silent gap duration needed for an individual to perceive one versus two signals; (c) temporal integration, or the measurement of detection thresholds of brief tones varying in duration; (d) two-tone ordering, or the measurement of the silent gap duration needed for an individual to determine the order of two tones; and (e) backward and forward masking, or the measurement of the effect of noise immediately preceding (forward)

TABLE 4.4
Selected Measures of Other Auditory Processes

Measures of Auditory Discrimination
    Northwestern University PEST Auditory Discrimination Paradigm
    Intensity, Frequency, and Duration Difference Limens
Measures of Sound Localization/Lateralization and Binaural Interaction
    Masking-Level Difference (MLD)
    Binaural Fusion
    Interaural Intensity and Timing Difference Limens
    Localization Precision
Measures of Temporal Processing
    Gap Detection
    Auditory Fusion (including Random Gap Detection Test)
    Temporal Integration
    Two-Tone Ordering
    Backward and Forward Masking

---

or following (backward) on the detection threshold for a target signal. All of these paradigms are in common use in psychoacoustics laboratories, and may be rather easily administered by the enterprising audiologist with a little know-how and the correct equipment. However, with the exception of Frequency and Duration Patterns, discussed previously in the section on APTO, only one test of discrete temporal processing is readily available commercially at the present time: the Random Gap Detection Test (RGDT; Keith, 2000b).

Contrary to what the name of the test would lead one to expect, the RGDT is actually a measure of auditory fusion rather than gap detection. This test measures listeners' ability to detect one versus two stimuli at varying silent gap interval durations. It is easy and quick to administer, and has been standardized on children of various ages. However, the utility of the RGDT for APD diagnosis has yet to be determined.

The development of commercially available tests of discrete temporal processing is arguably one of the greatest needs in APD diagnosis today, and efforts are underway in several laboratories to meet this need. However, until such time as these tests become readily available, this important aspect of auditory processing may continue to be overlooked by most audiologists engaged in central auditory assessment. Measures of auditory discrimination, sound localization and lateralization, and temporal processing are summarized in Table 4.4.

INFORMAL AUDIOLOGIC BEHAVIORAL ASSESSMENT PROCEDURES

Informal methods of assessing a child's auditory function can add invaluable information to the overall diagnostic picture. All too often, clinicians tend to rely solely upon the results of formal tests without giving much attention to the real-life ramifications and implications of a given disorder. As a result, recommendations for management and intervention tend to consist of one-size-fits-all, cookie-cutter programs that may or may not address the individual child's presenting difficulties and complaints. This is especially true with APD, as each individual child's unique confluence of top-down abilities (cognition, language, attention, and related skills) and bottom-up abilities (including the APD itself) results in a significant degree of heterogeneity. Thus, the same central auditory test findings may be accompanied by very different functional difficulties for different children. Informal audiologic behavioral assessment procedures for APD, including functional questionnaires and observation, can assist audiologists in understanding the functional difficulties exhibited by a particular child and, in that way, can aid in the development of a truly individualized, deficit-specific intervention plan.

It cannot be overemphasized, however, that the types of informal measures discussed in this section should never be used for diagnostic purposes. Because many different types of learning, language, and auditory disorders can mimic APD in their auditory behavioral characteristics, information gleaned from informal assessment measures—along with multidisciplinary input from speech-language pathologists, psychologists, educators, and others—should be used solely for screening purposes and to gain insight into areas of functional difficulty for the development and monitoring of ecologically valid intervention plans.

Several published checklists and questionnaires are available that probe auditory behaviors and difficulties in the classroom and at home. Jerger and Musiek (2000) caution that the majority of these, however, include behaviors that are not specific to APD but are, instead, highly influenced by higher-level, more global cognitive, language, and related abilities. Nevertheless, these tools can assist audiologists in examining auditory functioning in a variety of settings for a variety of behaviors that may be consistent with APD, including difficulty hearing in noisy environments, difficulty understanding rapid or distorted speech, difficulty following spoken instructions, difficulty discriminating among speech sounds, and inconsistent responses to auditory information or inconsistent auditory awareness (Jerger & Musiek, 2000). The following auditory checklists and questionnaires are available from the Educational Audiology Association (www.edaud.org):

The Children's Auditory Performance Scale (CHAPS) (Smoski, Brunt, & Tanahill, 1998) is perhaps one of the most commonly used checklists for the evaluation of auditory behaviors. Designed to be completed by parents, teachers, or others who interact with the child, the CHAPS provides a means of comparing a child's auditory abilities across a variety of listening conditions (i.e., in quiet, in noise, in ideal conditions, with multiple inputs, and when sustained attention or memory are required) to those of same-aged peers. The Fisher Auditory Processing Checklist (Fisher, 1985) is a second tool that explores auditory behaviors, specifically in the classroom setting. Shorter and somewhat less comprehensive in scope than the CHAPS, it is designed to be completed by classroom teachers.

Other auditory-based checklists and questionnaires are available that have been developed primarily for purposes of exploring functional difficulties in children with hearing impairment, but that may provide important information about children with other types of auditory dysfunction, including APD. The Children's Home Inventory of Listening Difficulties (CHILD; Anderson & Smaldino, 2000) is unique in that it is a family-centered tool for the exploration of listening problems. It includes questions for both the parents and the child to respond to, is written in easily understandable language, and provides specific examples of listening situations as probe items. This author has found the CHILD to be useful in illuminating the nature of a child's functional listening difficulties and as a guidance tool in the counseling and management process. The Screening Instrument for Targeting Educational Risk (SIFTER) (Anderson & Matkin, 1996) as well as the more recent Secondary SIFTER (Anderson, 2004) is useful in examining educational ramifications of auditory impairment, and includes probe items related to school behavior, class participation, academics, attention, and communication. Similarly, the Listening Inventory for Education (LIFE) (Anderson & Smaldino, 1998) also assesses education-related listening function.

A more formalized approach to behavioral observation of children's listening difficulties in real-world settings has been developed by Johnson (2002; Johnson & VonAlmen, 1997). The purpose of the Functional Listening Evaluation (FLE) is to determine how adverse listening conditions affect a child's auditory abilities in situations that more closely resemble actual listening environments than traditional sound-booth measurements. The FLE provides specific instructions regarding materials, environmental set-up, and administration, and includes an interpretation matrix to assist in evaluating the effects of noise, distance, and presence of visual augmentation on the child's auditory skills.

Questionnaires and checklists that probe attention and related abilities may also provide important information that can assist in the differential diagnosis process. Tools to explore these areas are in common use by psychologists and other professionals, and include but are not limited to the Conners' Rating Scales-Revised (Conners, 1996); the Swanson, Nolan, and Pelham-IV (SNAP-IV) Teacher and Parent Rating Scale (Swanson, 1992); and the Barkley (1998) ADHD Checklists.

SUMMARY

In conclusion, there exist a number of behavioral assessment tools to assist audiologists in evaluating auditory processing abilities; however, test development remains a critical area of further need. Caution should be exercised when selecting diagnostic test tools for APD, and tests should be chosen that exhibit good sensitivity and specificity for disorders of the CANS and that are appropriate for the child in question. Informal methods of assessing auditory function can provide valuable information regarding real-world impact of auditory disorders and can assist in the differential diagnosis process; however, informal assessment measures and screening tools should never be used for APD diagnostic purposes. The evaluation of central auditory function, including selection of test measures and interpretation of test results, requires additional knowledge and skills that are often not addressed in the typical audiologist's educational training. Finally, it is this author's opinion that audiologic evaluation of central auditory function should never be a starting point in the overall assessment process. Instead, a multidisciplinary approach that first examines the child's presenting areas of strengths and weaknesses and higher-level cognitive, language, learning, and attention-related abilities should be employed so that audiologists may enter into the central auditory diagnostic evaluation with an understanding of the whole child and the factors that may impact his or her performance on tests of central auditory function.

REFERENCES

American Speech-Language-Hearing Association. (1996). Central auditory processing disorders: Current status of research and implications for clinical practice. *American Journal of Audiology, 5,* 41–54.

American Speech-Language-Hearing Association. (2004a). Scope of practice in audiology. *ASHA.* Suppl. No. 24.

American Speech-Language-Hearing Association. (2004b). Preferred practice patterns for the profession of speech-language pathology. Available: http://www.asha.org/members/deskref-journals/deskref/default.

American Speech-Language-Hearing Association. (2005a). (Central) auditory processing disorders—The role of the audiologist [Position Statement]. Available: http://www.asha.org/members/deskref-journals/deskref/default.

American Speech-Language-Hearing Association. (2005b). (Central) Auditory Processing Disorders [Technical Report]. Available: http://www.asha.org/members/deskref-journals/deskref/default.

Anderson, K. L. (2004). *Secondary SIFTER*. Tampa: Educational Audiology Association.

Anderson, K. L., & Matkin, N. H. (1996). *Screening Instrument for Targeting Educational Risk (S.I.F.T.E.R.)*. Tampa: Educational Audiology Association.

Anderson, K. L., & Smaldino, J. J. (1998). *Listening Inventory of Education (L.I.F.E.)*. Tampa: Educational Audiology Association.

Anderson, K. L., & Smaldino, J. J. (2000). *Children's Home Inventory of Listening Difficulties (CHILD)*. Tampa: Eduational Audiology Association.

Barkley, R. A. (1998). *Attention deficit hyperactivity disorders: A handbook for diagnosis and treatment*. New York: Guilford.

Beasley, D. S., Forman, B., & Rintelmann, W. F. (1972). Intelligibility of time-compressed CNC monosyllables by normal listeners. *Journal of Auditory Research, 12*, 71–75.

Bellis, T. J. (1996). *Assessment and management of central auditory processing disorders in the educational setting: From science to practice*. San Diego: Singular Publishing Group.

Bellis, T. J. (2003). *Assessment and management of central auditory processing disorders in the educational setting: From science to practice* (2nd ed.). Clifton Park, NY: Thomson Learning.

Bellis, T. J., & Ferre, J. M. (1999). Multidimensional approach to the differential diagnosis of central auditory processing disorders in children. *Journal of the American Academy of Audiology, 10*, 319–328.

Berlin, C. I., Cullen, J. K., Hughes, L. F., Berlin, J. L., Lowe-Bell, S. S., & Thompson, C. L. (1975). Dichotic processing of speech: Acoustic and phonetic variables. In M. D. Sullivan (Ed.), *Central auditory processing disorder* (pp. 36–46). Omaha: University of Nebraska Medical Center Conference.

Bocca, E., Calearo, C., & Cassinari, V. (1954). A new method for testing hearing in temporal lobe tumors. *Acta Otolaryngoloica, Stockholm, 44*, 219–221.

Broadbent, D. E. (1954). The role of auditory localization in attention and memory span. *Journal of Experimental Psychology, 47*, 191–196.

Bryden, M. (1963). Ear preference in auditory perception. *Journal of Experimental Psychology, 16*, 359–360.

Chermak, G. D., & Musiek, F. E. (1997). *Central auditory processing disorders: New perspectives*. San Diego: Singular Publishing Group.

Cherry, R. S. (1980). *Selective auditory attention test*. St. Louis: Auditec.

Conners, C. K. (1996). *Conner's Rating Scales—Revised*. San Antonio: Psychological Corporation.

Dirks, D. (1964). Perception of dichotic and monaural verbal material and cerebral dominance for speech. *Acta Oto-laryngology, 58*, 78–80.

Domitz, D. M., & Schow, R. L. (2000). A new CAPD battery—Multiple auditory processing assessment (MAPA): Factor analysis and comparisons with SCAN. *American Journal of Audiology, 9*, 101–111.

Estes, R. I., Jerger, J., & Jacobson, G. (2002). Reversal of hemispheric asymmetry on auditory tasks in children who are poor listeners. *Journal of the American Academy of Audiology, 13*, 59–71.

Fifer, R., Jerger, J., Berlin, C., Tobey, E., & Campbell, J. (1983). Development of a dichotic sentence identification test for hearing impaired adults. *Ear and Hearing, 4*, 300–305.

Fisher, L. I. (1985). Learning disabilities and auditory processing. In R. J. Van Hattum (Ed.), *Administration of speech-language services in the schools* (pp. 231–292). San Diego: College Hill Press.

Greenwald, R. R., & Jerger, J. (2001). Aging affects hemispheric asymmetry on a competing speech task. *Journal of the American Academy of Audiology, 12*, 167–173.

Greenwald, R. R., & Jerger, J. (2003). Neuroelectric correlates of hemispheric asymmetry: Spectral discrimination and stimulus competition. *Journal of the American Academy of Audiology, 14*, 434–443.

Hexamer, M., & Bellis, T. J. (2000, April). A comparison of dichotic sentence procedures: The Willeford and Auditec versions of the Competing Sentence Test. Poster presented at the South Dakota Speech-Language-Hearing Association Annual Meeting, Sioux Falls, SD.

Jerger, J., (2000). Testing with marshmallows. *Journal of the American Academy of Audiology, 11*, 56.

Jerger, J., & Estes, R. (2002). Asymmetry in event-related potentials to simulated auditory motion in children, young adults, and seniors. *Journal of the American Academy of Audiology, 13*, 1–13.

Jerger, J., & Jerger, S. W. (1974). Auditory findings in brainstem disorders. *Archives of Otolaryngology, 99*, 342–349.

Jerger, J., & Jerger, S. W. (1975). Clinical validity of central auditory tests. *Scandinavian Audiology, 4*, 147–163.

Jerger, S., Jerger, J., & Abrams, S. (1983). Speech audiometry in the young child. *Ear and Hearing, 4*, 56–66.

Jerger, J., Moncrieff, D., Greenwald, R., Wambacq, I., & Seigel, A. (2000). Effect of age on interaural asymmetry of event-related potentials in a dichotic listening task. *Journal of the American Academy of Audiology, 11*, 383–389.

Jerger, J., & Musiek, F. (2000). Report of the consensus conference on the diagnosis of auditory processing disorders in school-aged children. *Journal of the American Academy of Audiology, 11*, 467–474.

Jerger, J., Thibodeau, L., Martin, J., Mehta, J., Tillman, G., Greenwald, R., Britt, L., Scott, J., & Overson, G. (2002). Behavioral and electrophysiologic evidence of auditory processing disorder: A twin study. *Journal of the American Academy of Audiology, 13*, 438–460.

Johnson, C. D. (2002). *Functional listening evaluation.* Tampa: Educational Audiology Association.

Johnson, C. D., & VonAlmen, P. (1997). The functional listening evaluation. In C. D. Johnson, P. V. Benson, & J. Seaton (Eds.), *Educational Audiology Handbook* (pp. 336–339). San Diego: Singular Publishing Group.

Katz, J. (1962). The use of staggered spondaic words for assessing the integrity of the central auditory nervous system. *Journal of Auditory Research, 2*, 327–337.

Katz, J. (1986). *SSW Test User's Manual.* Vancouver, WA: Precision Acoustics.

Katz, J., Smith, P., & Kurpita, B. (1992). Categorizing test findings in children referred for auditory processing deficits. *SSW Reports, 14*, 1–6.

Keith, R. (1986). *SCAN: A screening test for auditory processing disorders.* San Antonio: Psychological Corporation.

Keith, R. (1994). *SCAN-A: A test for auditory processing disorders in adolescents and adults.* San Antonio: Psychological Corporation.

Keith, R. (2000a). *SCAN-C test for auditory processing disorders in children—revised.* San Antonio: Psychological Corporation.

Keith, R. (2000b). Development and standardization of SCAN-C Test for Auditory Processing. *Journal of the American Academy of Audiology, 11*, 438–445.

Kimura, D. (1961). Cerebral dominance and the perception of verbal stimuli. *Canadian Journal of Psychology, 15*, 166–171.

Kraus, N., Koch, D. B., McGee, T. J., Nicol, T. G., & Cunningham, J. (1999). Normal development of speech–sound discrimination in school-age children: Psychophysical and neurophysiologic measures. *Journal of Speech, Language, and Hearing Research, 42*, 1042–1060.

Kraus, N., McGee, T. J., Carrell, T. D., Zecker, S. D., Nicol, T. G., & Koch, D. B. (1996). Auditory neurophysiologic responses and discrimination deficits in children with learning problems. *Science, 273*, 971–973.

Lepore, F., Lassonde, M., Poirier, P., Schiavetto, A., & Veillette, N. (1994). Midline sensory integration in callosal agenesis. In M. Lassonde & M. A. Jeeves (Eds.), *Callosal agenesis: A natural split brain?* (pp. 155–169). New York: Plenum.

Levine, R. A., Gardner, J. C., Stufflebeam, S. M., Fullerton, B. C., Carlisle, E. W., Furst, M., Rosen, B. R., & Kiang, N. Y. S. (1993a). Binaural auditory processing in multiple sclerosis subjects. *Hearing Research, 68*, 59–72.

Levine, R. A., Gardner, J. C., Stufflebeam, S. M., Fullerton, B. C., Carlisle, E. W., Furst, M., Rosen, B. R., & Kiang, N. Y. S. (1993b). Effects of multiple sclerosis brainstem lesions on sound lateralization and brainstem auditory evoked potentials. *Hearing Research, 68*, 73–88.

Licklider, J. C. R. (1948). The influence of interaural phase relations upon the masking of speech by white noise. *Journal of the Acoustical Society of America, 20*, 50–159.

Lynn, F. E., & Gilroy, J. (1975). Effects of brain lesions on the perception of monotic and dichotic speech stimuli. In M. D. Sullivan (Ed.), *Central auditory processing disorders* (pp. 47–83). Omaha: Proceedings of the Conference at University of Nebraska Medical Center.

Masters, M., Stecker, N., & Katz, J. (1993, April). CAP disorders, language difficulty, and academic success: A team approach. Paper presented at the American Speech-Language-Hearing Association Annual Convention, Los Angeles.

Moncrieff, D. W., & Musiek, F. E. (2002). Interaural asymmetries revealed by dichotic listening tests in normal and dyslexic children. *Journal of the American Academy of Audiology, 13*, 428–437.

Mueller, H. G., & Bright, K. E. (1994). Monosyllabic procedures in central testing. In J. Katz (Ed.), *Handbook of audiology* (4th ed., pp. 222–298). Baltimore: Williams & Wilkins.

Musiek, F. E. (1983a). Assessment of central auditory dysfunction: The Dichotic Digits Test revisited. *Ear and Hearing, 4*, 79–83.

Musiek, F. E. (1983b). Assessment of central auditory dysfunction: The Dichotic Digits Test revisited. *Ear and Hearing, 4*, 318–323.

Musiek, F. E., Baran, J. A., & Pinheiro, M. L. (1990). Duration pattern recognition in normal subjects and patients with cerebral and cochlear lesions. *Audiology, 29*, 304–313.

Musiek, F. E., Gollegly, K. M., & Baran, J. A. (1984). Myelination of the corpus callosum and auditory processing problems in children: Theoretical and clinical correlates. *Seminars in Hearing, 5*, 231–241.

Musiek, F. E., Gollegly, K. M., Kibbe, K. S., & Verkest-Lenz, S. B. (1991). Proposed screening test for central auditory disorders: Follow-up on the Dichotic Digits Test. *American Journal of Otology, 12*, 109–113.

Musiek, F. E., Gollegly, K. M., Lamb, L. E., & Lamb, P. (1990). Selected issues in screening for central auditory processing dysfunction. *Seminars in Hearing, 11*, 372–384.

Musiek, F. E., Pinheiro, M. L., & Wilson, D. H. (1980). Auditory pattern perception in "split-brain" patients. *Archives of Otolaryngology, 106*, 610–612.

Nordlund, B. (1964). Directional audiometry. *Acta Oto-laryngology, 57*, 1–18.

Pickles. J. O. (1985). Physiology of the cerebral auditory system. In M. L. Pinheiro & F. E. Musiek (Eds.), *Assessment of central auditory dysfunction: Foundations and clinical correlates* (pp. 67–86). Baltimore: Williams & Wilkins.

Pinherio, M. L., & Musiek, F. E. (1985). Sequencing and temporal ordering in the auditory system. In M. L. Pinheiro & F. E. Musiek (Eds.), *Assessment of central auditory dysfunction: Foundations and clinical correlates* (pp. 219–238). Baltimore: Williams & Wilkins.

Pinheiro, M. L., & Ptacek, P. H. (1971). Reversals in the perception of noise and tone patterns. *Journal of the Acoustical Society of America, 49*, 1778–1782.

Pinheiro, M. L., & Tobin, H. (1969). Interaural intensity difference for intracranial localization. *Journal of the Acoustical Society of America, 46*, 1482–1487.

Pinheiro, M. L., & Tobin, H. (1971). The interaural intensity difference as a diagnostic indicator. *Acta Oto-laryngology, 71*, 326–328.

Ptacek, P. H., & Pinheiro, M. L. (1971). Pattern reversal in auditory perception. *Journal of the Acoustical Society of America, 49*, 439–498.

Rintelmann, W. F. (1985). Monaural speech tests in the detection of central auditory disorders. In M. L. Pinheiro & F. E. Musiek (Eds.), *Assessment of central auditory dysfunction: Foundations and clinical correlates* (pp. 173–200). Baltimore: Williams & Wilkins.

Roeser, R. J., Millay, K. K., & Morrow, J. M. (1983). Dichotic consonant–vowel (CV) perception in normal and learning-impaired children. *Ear and Hearing, 4*, 293–299.

Sanchez-Longo, F., Forster, F., & Auth, T. (1957). A clinical test for sound localization and its applications. *Neurology, 8*, 119–125.

Satz, K., Achenback, E., Pattishall, E., & Fennell, E. (1965). Order of report, ear asymmetry and handedness in dichotic listening. *Cortex, 1*, 377–395.

Schow, R., & Chermak, G. D. (1999). Implications from factor analysis for central auditory processing disorders. *American Journal of Audiology, 8*, 137–142.

Schow, R. L., Seikel, J. A., Chermak, G. D., & Berent, M. (2000). Central auditory processes and test measures: ASHA 1996 revisited. *American Journal of Audiology, 9*, 1–6.

Schow, R. L., Seikel, J. A., Chermak, G. D., Berent, M., & Domitz-Vieira, D. M. (2002). Support for a multiple-factor model of auditory processing. *American Journal of Audiology, 11*, 9–12.

Silman, S., Silverman, C. A., & Emmer, M. B. (2000). Central auditory processing disorders and reduced motivation: Three case studies. *Journal of the American Academy of Audiology, 11*, 57–63.

Smoski, W. J., Brunt, M. A., & Tanahill, J. C. (1998). *Children's Auditory Performance Scale*. Tampa: Educational Audiology Association.

Strouse, A., & Wilson, R. H. (2000). The effect of filtering and inter-digit interval on the recognition of dichotic digits. *Journal of Rehabilitation Research and Development, 37*, 1–9.

Swanson, J. M. (1992). *The SNAP-IV teacher and parent rating scale*. Irvine, CA: University of California.

Tonal and speech materials for auditory perceptual assessment, disc 2.0. (1998). Mountain Home, TN: James H. Quillen VA Medical Center.

Willeford, J. (1977). Assessing central auditory behavior in children: A test battery approach. In R. W. Keith (Ed.), *Central auditory dysfunction* (pp. 43–72). New York: Grune & Stratton.

Willeford, J. A., & Burleigh, J. M. (1994). Sentence procedures in central testing. In J. Katz (Ed.), *Handbook of clinical audiology* (4th ed., pp. 256–268). Baltimore: Williams & Wilkins.

Wilson, L., & Mueller, H. G. (1984). Performance of normal hearing individuals on Auditec filtered speech tests. *Asha, 27*, 189.

Wilson, R. H., Preece, J. P., Salamon, D. L., Sperry, J. L., & Bornstein, S. P. (1994). Effects of time compression and time compression plus reverberation on the intelligibility of the Northwestern University Auditory Test No. 6. *Journal of the American Academy of Audiology, 5*, 269–277.

Electrophysiologic Assessment of APD

Teralandur K. Parthasarathy
Southern Illinois University Edwardsville

Electrophysiologic assessment has assumed an important role in the clinical practice of audiology. Electrophysiologic measures provide objective support in regard to the integrity of the peripheral and central auditory pathways. Auditory processing (AP) is concerned with the efficiency of using the auditory system to deal with incoming and stored auditory information. For example, discriminating speech, suppressing background noise, locating the sound source, and integrating auditory information with other sensory modalities are among many skills we all require to perform effectively in everyday listening situations.

Auditory processing disorders (APD) are one or more deficits in AP that significantly interfere with a person's ability to reach his or her potential. Patients with APD often experience difficulty understanding speech in the presence of competing messages, noise, or reverberation. They frequently require repetition of material, slower pace, or clearer speech production in order to comprehend. In addition, they may appear inattentive or distracted and frequently display an inability to immediately recall information or to access stored auditory information. Metalinguistic aspects of language seem to impact on the individual's AP ability, just as AP ability impacts on the development of metalinguistic skills (ASHA, 1996).

Diagnosis of APD in children for the past 25 years has been mostly based on behavioral measures. However, accumulating evidence in the last few years, especially in children, clearly indicates that such behavioral measures are influenced by nonauditory factors, including motivation, distractibility, language skills, intelligence, and cognitive skills (Cacace & McFarland, 1998). Electrophysiologic measures seem to prove useful in the differential diagnosis of APD in children (Jirsa & Clontz, 1990; Jirsa, 1992, 2001; Jerger et al., 2002). The Bruton Conference at the Callier Center, University of Texas, Dallas (Jerger & Musiek, 2000), emphasized that a minimal test battery for the diagnosis of APDs in school-aged children should include auditory brainstem response (ABR) and middle latency response (MLR) testing. The late latency response

(LLR) was included in the list of optional procedures that are potentially useful for sharpening the diagnosis of APD.

This chapter reviews the most common electrophysiological tests used in the assessment of APD. In addition, acoustic reflex (AR) and otoacoustic emissions (OAEs) measurements are discussed as they provide a physiologic basis of auditory function. The Bruton Conference consensus statement recommended including AR measurements and OAEs as part of the central auditory assessment (Jerger & Musiek, 2000).

The measurement of AR, OAEs, and auditory brainstem response are specific electrophysiologic tests used to evaluate the integrity of the peripheral and brain stem auditory pathways. The middle latency response and late latency response are specific electrophysiologic tests to evaluate the integrity of the cortical and subcortical areas of the brain. Although behavioral tests provide significant information in the evaluation of APD, the electrophysiologic measures provide objective evidence related to the integrity of the peripheral and central auditory pathways.

AR measurements evaluate the automatic response of the stapedial muscle (innervated by the facial nerve) to high-intensity sounds. Again, as a part of a diagnostic test battery, AR measurements can provide valuable information about the status of the middle ear, inner ear–cochlea, VIIIth (auditory) and VIIth (facial) nerves, and the lower auditory brain stem.

OAEs are responses generated by the cochlea's outer hair cells in response to a sound. These "cochlear echoes" travel through the middle ear and tympanic membrane and can be recorded by placing a tiny microphone within the ear canal. As part of a diagnostic test battery, measurements of OAEs can provide valuable information about the integrity of the cochlea's outer hair cells (OHCs) when used in conjunction with other behavioral and electrophysiologic tests. Children with organic-based problems, traumatic brain injury, and syndromes (e.g., fragile X, autism) who demonstrate poor progress with a variety of intervention strategies are considered good candidates for electrophysiological assessment. In addition, confidence in the clinical diagnosis of APD is increased significantly when abnormal test results are shown across both electrophysiologic and behavioral tests.

ACOUSTIC REFLEX TESTING

The stapedial muscle acoustic reflex (AR) is one of the powerful diagnostic techniques available to audiologists. Acoustic reflex threshold and acoustic reflex decay tests have been useful in the assessment of VIIIth nerve and lower brain stem lesions (Hall, 1985; Wilson & Margolis, 1991). The acoustic reflex threshold (ART) refers to the lowest amount of sound intensity at which a minimal change in the mobility of the middle ear at the plane of the eardrum can be measured. The clinical application of AR measurements in detecting lower brain stem lesions has focused on a comparison of ipsilateral and contralateral ARTs. The reflex-eliciting stimuli should not exceed 110 dB HL for any signal, unless there is clear indication of a significant air–bone gap in the ear to which sound is delivered.

The acoustic reflex decay (see Fig. 5.1) refers to the diminution of the stapedial muscle reflex activity in response to a 10-second signal presented at 10 dB above the stapedial acoustic reflex threshold. Results are considered abnormal if amplitude of the stapedial reflex declines to less than half of its maximum amplitude or completely disappears within the first 5 seconds of the stimulus presentation (Jerger & Hayes, 1980).

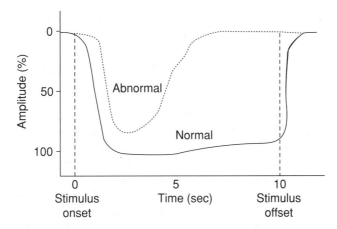

FIG. 5.1. Examples of normal and abnormal acoustic reflex decay. Abnormal reflex decay occurs when the reflex amplitude gradually declines to at least half of its original maximum amplitude within a 5-second period. (From "Electrophysiologic Assessment of CAPD: A review of basics," by T. K. Parthasarathy, 2000, *The Hearing Journal, 53*(4), 52–60. With permission.)

It should be noted that there is a danger that stimulation at 10 dB above the stapedial acoustic reflex threshold for 10 seconds may be upsetting to the patient. Furthermore, several case reports have documented temporary or permanent threshold shifts following the acoustic reflex decay testing. Thus, audiologists should be extra cautious and judicious in using acoustic reflex decay testing in which auditory stimulation is continuous for 5 to 10 seconds in duration.

There have been numerous reports regarding abnormal ART and acoustic reflex decay patterns in different types of central auditory nervous system (CANS) lesions, including head trauma, brain stem vascular disorders, multiple sclerosis, and various types of mass lesions (Hall, 1985; Wilson & Margolis, 1991). In subjects with normal hearing sensitivity or patients with a borderline to mild sensorineural–cochlear hearing impairment, acoustic reflex thresholds are present at 90–95 dB HL or lower for frequencies between 500 Hz and 2,000 Hz. An elevated ART with significant acoustic reflex decay (i.e., 50% or greater amplitude decline) or failure to elicit AR in a patient with no facial nerve involvement or conductive pathology is considered a positive index of auditory nerve/brain stem lesion.

The sensitivity of the AR to central auditory lesions seems to depend on the manner in which AR are measured. Presence or absence of AR is one of the diagnostic measures, but latency and amplitude of AR can be used an index to enhance overall sensitivity (Wilson & Margolis, 1991).

OTOACOUSTIC EMISSIONS

OAEs are low-level, subaudible sounds that are generated in the cochlea, but can be recorded in the external ear using a low-noise microphone (Kemp, 1986). Although the exact mechanism underlying the production of OAEs is not fully understood, they are believed to be manifestations of the motile response of the OHCs (Brownell, 1989).

OAEs can be used to evaluate and confirm normal cochlear function. This can be important in the diagnosis of CANS involvement because OAEs are absent in patients with a hearing loss greater than 30 dB HL (Kemp, Ryan, & Bray, 1990). Therefore, OAEs alone are of little clinical value in the neurodiagnostic application. However, if there is hearing loss greater than 30 dB HL and OAEs are present, it may suggest that the type of hearing loss is neural or retrocochlear (beyond the cochlear level) or the patient may be malingering (Robinett, 1992).

Recently, OAEs have been used to provide an index of the olivocochlear bundle (OCB). The OCB is a part of the efferent auditory pathways that seems to help people hearing in noise. The OCB, first described by Rasmussen (1946), has two systems—the medial (MOCB) and the lateral (LOCB; Warr and Guinan, 1978). Research data suggest that the crossed, myelinated MOCB fibers primarily innervate the OHCs, and that the OHCs contract in the presence of MOCB stimulation (Collet, Veuilett, Bene, & Morgan, 1992). Clinically, the audiologist can evaluate the integrity of the MOCB by simply presenting a noise in the contralateral ear. While normal-hearing subjects clearly show suppression of OAEs close to 3 dB, patients with auditory nerve and/or brain stem lesions show a complete lack of suppression (Berlin, Hood, Secola, Jackson, & Szabo, 1993; Parthasarathy, 2001).

AUDITORY EVOKED POTENTIALS

From the time sound energy reaches the inner ear, what is conducted and transmitted to the brain is a series of tiny electrical potentials. By means of computer averaging, it is possible to extract the tiny electrical potentials. These complex electrical activities can be recorded over a broad time interval after the stimulus presentation and are commonly referred to as the auditory evoked potentials (AEPs).

AEPs are considered objective, electrophysiologic tests to evaluate the integrity of specific portions of the auditory pathways. For audiologic purposes, it is convenient to group the AEPs into categories based on the latency values over which they occur. The term "latency" refers to the time interval between the introduction of a stimulus and the occurrence of the AEPs' waveform peak. The most commonly used AEP is the auditory brainstem response (ABR), which occurs within 10 msec following the stimulus onset. The ABR reflects neural activity from the VIIIth nerve to the midbrain.

The middle latency response (MLR) occurs within the first 50 msec following the stimulus onset and reflects activity at or near the auditory cortex. The late latency response (LLR) occurs between 50 and 300 msec following the stimulus onset and reflects activity of the thalamus and auditory cortex—structures that involve the attentional, integrative, and discriminative functions of the brain. ABR, MLR, and LLR occurring within 200 msec following the stimulus onset are "obligatory" responses that depend on the stimulus characteristics. However, the LLR that occurs around 200 msec and later—such as the mismatch negativity (MMN) and P300—are "discriminative" responses that depend on attentional, integrative, and discriminative functions of the brain.

AUDITORY BRAINSTEM RESPONSE

The ABR occurs within the first 10 msec following the stimulus onset and consists of a series of five major waveform peaks, each identified by a Roman numeral (see Fig. 5.2). Each waveform peak represents neuroelectrical activity at one or more auditory nuclei along the auditory brain stem pathway (Jewett and Williston, 1971; Moller,

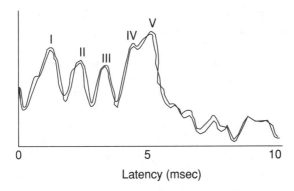

Latency (msec)

FIG. 5.2. A normal auditory brainstem response (ABR) waveform, showing waves I through V. (From "Electrophysiologic Assessment of CAPD: A review of basics," by T. K. Parthasarathy, 2000, *The Hearing Journal, 53*(4), 52–60. With permission.)

Jannetta, & Moller, 1981). These neuroelectrical responses are recorded by placing an active, noninverting electrode on the high forehead or vertex and a reference, inverting electrode on the mastoid or the earlobe. Stimuli with rapid rise times, such as clicks, filtered clicks, or tone pips, are used to generate a synchronous, brain stem neuro-electric response. By using the computer averaging method, a series of five readable major peaks is obtained, stored, and interpreted for later analysis.

While waves I and II of the ABR are generated by the peripheral auditory nerve and wave III by the cochlear nucleus and the trapezoid body, waves IV and V have multiple generator sites. However, the superior olivary complex (SOC) and the nuclei of the lateral lemniscus seem to contribute significantly for the ABR waves IV and V, respectively (Moller et al., 1981).

ABRs can be reliably recorded from premature infants as young as 30 weeks conceptional age. However, published research data suggest that the ABR tends to assume characteristics similar to those obtained from adults by 24 months of age. For this reason, for infants from 30 weeks to 24 months of age, each clinical facility must obtain separate age-specific norms for ABR latencies and amplitudes.

There are numerous audiologic and neurootologic applications of the ABR. The audiologic clinical applications, such as establishing the patient's electrophysiological threshold (i.e., the lowest stimulus intensity level at which the ABR wave V is differentiated from background noise), involve examining changes in ABR wave V latencies with a decrease in stimulus intensity. Because the ABR can be recorded from premature infants as young as 30 weeks conceptional age, the audiologist can use ABR for estimating hearing status regardless of a child's age.

The neurootologic applications involve measuring the ABR relative interpeak latencies (i.e., difference between the absolute latencies of two waveform peaks) for waves I–III, I–V, and III–V. In addition, the ABR waveform morphology (i.e., the overall shape or pattern) and the presence/absence of ABR waveform peaks are considered important variables for all ABR clinical applications (Musiek, Gollegly, Kibbe, & Verkest, 1988; Musiek & Lee, 1995). For example, in cases of VIIIth nerve lesion such as vestibular Schwannoma (acoustic tumor), ABR results may be a delayed wave V latency and an abnormally long interpeak latency interval for ABR waves I–V. Other neurootologic lesions such as brain stem neoplasms and multiple sclerosis may result in poorly formed or absent ABR waveforms because of the lack of synchrony in the neural response. It should be kept in mind that the ABR is more effective in detecting acoustic tumors than brain stem lesions (Musiek et al., 1988). In addition, the ABR absolute amplitude measures are not as reliable as latency measures (Starr and Achor, 1975).

The clinical utility of the binaural interaction component (BIC) in children at risk for APD was investigated by Gopal & Pierel (1999). The BIC was derived by subtracting the summed monaural from the binaural waveforms of the ABR. The derived negative (DN1) peak of the BIC normally occurs in the latency range of peak ABR V. Compared to the control group of nine children, the APD group showed a significant reduction in the amplitude of the BIC. Further research is required, however, before the BIC of the ABR can be regarded as clinical tool for APD diagnostic assessment, due to the small amplitude and high variability of the derived response (Fowler, 2004).

Recently, Jirsa (2001) evaluated the clinical utility of maximum length sequence (MLS) of the ABR in APD children. Statistically significant differences in the MLS–ABR V latency were found between children with audiologically confirmed APDs and an age-matched control group. Additional research is required relating to the sensitivity and specificity of these measures alone and in conjunction with other electrophysiologic and behavioral tests (Jirsa, 2001).

Undoubtedly, the ABR is a valuable electrophysiological test in evaluating the integrity of the auditory brain stem pathway. In some children with APD, the ABR is the test of choice because of their limited speech and language skills. Furthermore, patients with auditory deprivation, head trauma, or neurological disease; and the elderly are all considered good candidates for ABR evaluation.

MIDDLE LATENCY RESPONSE

The middle latency response is a series of waveforms occurring from 10 to 50 msec following stimulus onset (Geisler, Frishkopf, & Rosenblith, 1958) and is characterized by several vertex negative and positive peaks (see Fig. 5.3). The first negative peak (Na) occurs at about 18 to 20 msec and the most prominent first positive peak (Pa) occurs at about 25 to 35 msec. The second positive peak (Pb) occurs at about 40 to 60 msec following the stimulus presentation.

For the audiologic application of MLR to estimate hearing sensitivity, the electrode configuration is essentially similar to that for the ABR. However, for the neurootologic

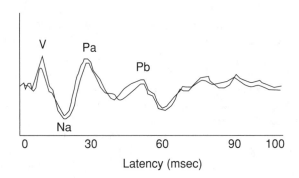

FIG. 5.3.   A normal middle latency response (MLR) waveform. Both positive and negative waveform peaks are denoted as well as the ABR wave V. (From "Electrophysiologic Assessment of CAPD: A review of basics," by T. K. Parthasarathy, 2000, *The Hearing Journal*, 53(4), 52–60. With permission.)

application, the neuroelectric activity is picked up by recording noninverting electrodes placed at the vertex, as well as the right and left temporal lobes and the inverting electrodes at the earlobes. The presumed neural generators involve the interaction of many brain structures including the primary auditory cortex, the thalamo-cortical projections (Kilney, Paccioretti, & Wilson, 1987; Ozdamar and Kraus, 1983), the inferior colliculus, and medial geniculate body in the midbrain (Fisher, Bognar, Turjman, & Lapras, 1995), as well as structures outside the primary auditory pathway such as the reticular formation and multisensory nuclei of the thalamus (Buchwald, Hinman, Norman, Huang, & Brown, 1981; McGee, Kraus, Comperatore, & Nicol, 1991).

Interest in the clinical application of MLR increased significantly after the discovery of the ABR for providing valuable information on the integrity of the central auditory nervous system. In addition, the MLR is a useful test in evaluating for APD due to the location of the neural generators of this neuroelectric response (Purdy, Kelly, & Davies, 2002).

Many variables can influence the MLR waveforms—the repetition rate, arousal level, maturational state. Audiologists with knowledge and experience with the MLR test procedure are able to employ it successfully. In the central auditory assessment, only Na and Pa responses are used. The other waveforms of the MLR—Nb, Pb, Nc, and Pc—are more variable and thus considered unreliable for clinical use. It should be kept in mind that the MLR waveform latencies are not as sensitive as amplitude measures (Scherg & Von Cramon, 1986).

The influence of sleep is an important consideration when performing the MLR. Although some latency and amplitude changes are observed in adults as a function of the stage of sleep (Osterhamel, Shallop, & Terkildsen, 1985), there is a general consensus that sleep does not significantly affect the MLR recording in adults as it does in children. It appears that MLRs in children are consistently present during certain stages of sleep (stage 1 and REM sleep), occasionally detectable during other stages of sleep (stage 2 and stage 3), and rarely detectable during stage 4 of the sleep cycle. Detectability during different sleep stages seems to improve with the maturation of the child's CNS (Kraus, Ozdamar, Hier, & Stein, 1982).

In adults, the thalamo-cortical pathway is fully mature and imparts stability to the MLR response, making the MLR response consistently detectable regardless of sleep stage. In children, however, the thalamo-cortical pathway is only partially developed, not reaching maturity until puberty (Kraus, Smith, Reed, Stein, & Cartee, 1985). Thus, if children are to be tested for MLR while sleeping, the sleep state must be monitored.

In patients with a unilateral lesion in the auditory cortex, the amplitude of Na–Pa for the electrode over the involved hemisphere is either diminished or absent (Kraus et al., 1982; Woods, Clayworth, & Knight, 1985). Because the MLR waveforms can be absent or delayed in latency in normal children younger than 10 years of age, the maturational factor should always be considered when using the MLR test for the assessment of APD in children. In addition, the MLRs obtained from infants and children younger than 10 years of age show poorer waveform morphology, longer response latencies, and significantly greater variability than compared to adults (Suzuki, Hirabayashi, & Kobayashi, 1983). Thus, the minimum age for reliable MLR recording is 10 years and older. Maturational delay is one of the presumed etiological factors in patients with various learning disabilities (LD) including APDs. In patients over 10 years of age with a negative neurologic diagnosis, a significant left ear deficit (LED) for speech and/or nonspeech stimuli in conjunction with a poorly formed or absent MLR may be an objective marker for maturational delay (Musiek & Berge, 1998). Recently, Purdy et al. (2002) found statistically significant differences in the Na latency and Nb amplitude between children with learning disability with a suspicion of APD and an age-matched control group. Compared to the age-matched control group, wave Na of the MLR was significantly prolonged in latency with smaller Nb amplitude in the LD group.

LATE LATENCY RESPONSE

The auditory evoked potentials occurring after 50 msec—the late latency responses— reflect the activity of the thalamus and auditory cortex, structures that involve the attentional, integrative, and discriminative functions of the brain. Thus, LLRs are also called the event related potentials (ERP). LLRs (see Fig. 5.4) are characterized by a negative (N1) peak with an onset latency close to 90 msec followed by a positive (P2) peak at about 180 msec following stimulus onset (Davis, 1939; Picton, Woods, Baribeau-Braun, & Healy, 1977; Purdy et al., 2002). In an awake subject, the N1 and P2 responses can be elicited by presentation of a click or tonal stimuli.

At approximately 300 msec, a large positive wave, which is commonly referred to as the "P300" response, is seen in response to rare or novel stimuli that are embedded in more frequent stimuli with an oddball paradigm (Sutton, Braren, Zubin, & John, 1965). In the oddball paradigm, for example, 1,000-Hz tones may be presented 85% of the time (frequent stimuli) along with 2,000-Hz tones, which are presented 15% of the time (rare stimuli). The subject is asked to attend by simply counting the number of rare stimuli presented. The P300 requires conscious attention to and discrimination of stimulus difference between the frequent and rare stimuli (Sutton et al., 1965, Purdy et al., 2002). Thus, the LLR waveform latencies and amplitudes are significantly affected by subject state and the level of attention to the stimulus (Squires & Hecox, 1983).

Recently, an additional LLR that has received considerable attention is the mis-matched negativity (MMN), a negative wave occurring at approximately 200 msec. The clinical application of MMN is in its infancy. The MMN is a passively elicited response, not requiring attention or behavioral response. Kraus et al. (1994) have shown APD deficits correlated to MMN abnormalities. Preliminary results compar-ing pre and postlistening training measures have shown significant changes in both the magnitude and duration of MMN (Kraus et al., 1995; Tremblay, Kraus, Carrell, & McGee, 1997). The characteristics of the MMN suggest its potential clinical utility with

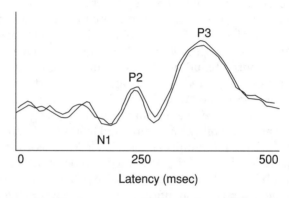

FIG. 5.4. A normal late latency response (LLR) waveform. Both positive and negative waveform peaks are denoted as well as the P3 (event-related) response to rare stimuli in attend condition. (From "Electrophysiologic Assessment of CAPD: A review of basics," by T. K. Parthasarathy, 2000, *The Hearing Journal, 53*(4), 52–60. With permission.)

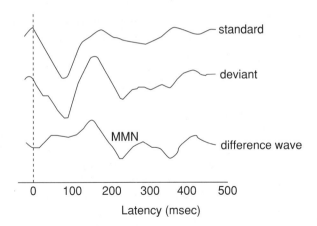

FIG. 5.5. A normal mismatch negativity (MMN) response waveform to standard /ga/ and deviant /da/ synthesized speech stimuli. The difference waveform is obtained by subtracting the standard from the deviant waveform. (From "Electrophysiologic Assessment of CAPD: A review of basics," by T. K. Parthasarathy, 2000, *The Hearing Journal*, 53(4), 52–60. With permission.)

subjects (e.g., children with language or learning disorders, high-risk children, subjects with aphasia or dementia) for whom communication is compromised or difficult and whose auditory memory and discrimination are in question.

The MMN waveform is an event related potential derived by subtracting the evoked response waveform of the "same" stimuli from the evoked response waveform of the different stimuli (see Fig. 5.5). The MMN is also elicited with an oddball-type paradigm, but, unlike with the P300 response, the subject's conscious, overt attention is not required. The subject simply listens to the stimuli. Unlike other LLRs, the MMN appears to be present at birth (Walker et al., 2001). The MMN is considered a preconscious, automatic response to stimulus change (Kraus & McGee, 1994). Particularly interesting is the fact that an MMN can be generated in response to differences in a wide array of stimuli—tones, noise bursts, or natural speech—at a subject's perceptual threshold (Sams et al., 1985; Sams, Aulanko, Aaltonen, & Naatanen, 1990). MMN is not consistently detected in normal hearing subjects; more research is needed to address issues related to method of recording, detectability, and validity of MMN (Dalebout & Stack, 1999).

In order to improve the signal-to-noise ratio of the MMN, recently the median method was evaluated as an alternative way of expressing the MMN to signal averaging (Fox & Dalebout, 2002). Because the median is a more valid measure of central tendency in asymmetric distribution, it was assumed that the median method might enhance the detection of the MMN. However, the median method was unable to improve the detectability of the MMN in the majority of cases (Fox & Dalebout, 2002). Further research is required before MMN can be used clinically (Dalebout & Stack, 1999).

Although precise anatomic generators of the LLRs are not known, N1 and MMN appear to originate from the primary auditory cortex and association auditory cortex, which are located on the superior temporal plane of the brain (Knight, Hillyard, Woods, & Neville, 1980). In addition, the MMN is thought to represent activity from some input from the hippocampus and thalamus (Kraus et al., 1995). The limbic system and the primary auditory cortex appear responsible for the P2 response (Ritter, Simson,

Vaughan, & Macht, 1982). The P300 response seems to be linked to the hippocampus and/or the posterior temporal lobe (Buchwald, 1990; McPherson, 1996).

The complete maturation for N1 and P2 does not occur until adolescence, and the P300 response latency values reach adultlike values during the mid-teenage years (Musiek, Baran, & Pinheiro, 1992). The MMN appears to be robust in school-age children as it occurs at adultlike latency values, although amplitudes are generally larger in children (Kraus & McGee, 1994).

Little research data are available on the specificity and sensitivity of the LLRs for APD. Musiek et al. (1992) reported specificity rates of 70% and sensitivity rates of approximately 80%. The overall clinical effectiveness of the P300 response in evaluating patients with APD was higher than were the N1 and P2 responses. Jirsa and Clonz (1990) measured the P300 response in a population of normal school-aged children and children with APD. The normal group compared to the APD group had significantly shorter latencies, but there was no significant difference in the P300 amplitude between the two groups. However, Purdy et al. (2002) reported significantly prolonged latency with smaller amplitude of the P300 response in the LD group with a suspicion of APD. Results such as these are useful as objective markers to support the clinical utility of P300 response. Because P300 response can be elicited by a variety of stimuli, including speech contrasts and phonemes, the P300 response may be useful in monitoring therapy progress in patients with APD (Jirsa, 1992). The P300 response in conjunction with the MMN may provide an objective method for evaluating the speech perceptual skills of patients diagnosed with APDs, and assist in establishing the most appropriate intervention program.

SUMMARY

Children with organic-based problems, traumatic brain injury, or syndromes (e.g., fragile X, autism); children who demonstrate poor progress with a variety of intervention strategies; children with language or learning disorders; and high-risk children are considered good candidates for electrophysiological assessment. Clinical evaluation of central auditory disorders is often challenging due to the diffuse nature of the CANS. However, electrophysiologic measurement continues to be a powerful method in the diagnosis of audiologic and neurologic disorders.

Careful interpretation of the AR can provide important diagnostic information about the presence or absence of VIIIth nerve and lower brain stem lesions. In-depth analysis of ABR in light of presence or absence of ipsilateral and contralateral acoustic reflexes will help in determining the specific site of brain stem lesions.

Because OAEs can be measured noninvasively and are sensitive to the cochlea's OHCs, they are potentially a valuable addition to APD assessment. Furthermore, OAEs can be helpful in providing information about the efferent auditory pathway.

The ABR is now well established as a valuable clinical tool for use with young and difficult-to-test children. The MLR provides a clinical electrophysiologic tool for assessment that extends beyond the auditory brain stem to the thalamo-cortical auditory pathway. The MLR requires a minimum of three electrodes sites for the neurodiagnostic evaluation. Factors that seem to reduce the clinical effectiveness of MLR are the intersubject variability, maturational effects, and stages of sleep.

Electrophysiologic measures such as ABR and MLR do not replace behavioral measurements, but they provide valuable objective information about the status of the portions of the central auditory pathways. At present, further research is needed to improve the signal-to-noise ratio before the BIC of the ABR can be used clinically for diagnostic APD assessment. Clinical utility of the LLR is not routine, but measures such as P300 and MMN hold the most promise for CANS evaluation because these two tests are able to assess aspects related to hearing and auditory processing. More research is needed to correlate the auditory evoked potential characteristics and patterns with the APD behavioral symptomatology they present.

New techniques, collectively termed *functional neuroimaging*, are gaining popularity in the assessment of APD (Laureys, Salmon, Goldman, & Majerus, 2003). Functional magnetic resonance imaging (fMRI) has been used to visualize and confirm the spatial distribution of brain activation to a variety of auditory stimulation in normal and abnormal subjects (Laureys et al., 2003; Millen, Haughton, & Yetkin, 1995). Brain activity is much more complex for words, and different neuronal networks are recruited when lexical, phonological, and semantic levels of processing are engaged (Laureys et al., 2003). Stimuli that are challenging or interesting produce greater cortical activation. At present, it is unclear whether greater amounts of activation represent greater cognitive ability, tissue health, effort, motivation, or some combination thereof. More research is needed to clarify these important fundamental issues before fMRI can be embraced as a valuable addition to the central auditory assessment battery.

Electrophysiologic measures of auditory function provide objective evidence of APD and should be included in every audiological test battery. Each evaluation procedure has advantages and limitations, so the use of a diagnostic test battery approach is crucial in clearly defining the exact nature of APD and appropriate intervention strategies.

REFERENCES

American Speech-Language-Hearing Association (1996). Task Force on Central Auditory Processing Consensus Development. Central auditory processing: Current status of research and implications for clinical practice. *American Journal of Audiology, 5,* 41–54.

Berlin, C., Hood, L., Secola, P., Jackson, D., & Szabo, P. (1993). Does Type I afferent neuron dysfunction reveal itself through lack of efferent suppression? *Hearing Research, 65,* 40–50.

Brownell, W. E. (1989). Outer hair cell electromotility and otoacoustic emissions. *Ear & Hearing, 11,* 82–92.

Buchwald, J. (1990). Animal models of event-related potentials. In J. Rohrbaugh, J. R. Parasuraman, & R. Johnson (Eds.), *Event related potentials of the brain* (pp. 57–75). New York: Oxford University Press.

Buchwald, J., Hinman, C., Norman, R. S., Huang, C. M., & Brown, K. A. (1981). Middle and long-latency auditory evoked potentials recorded from the vertex of normal and chronically lesioned cats. *Brain Research, 205,* 91–109.

Cacace, A., & McFarland, D. (1998). Central auditory processing disorder. *Journal of Speech Language Hearing Research, 41,* 355–374.

Collet, L., Veuilett, E., Bene, J., & Morgan, A. (1992). Effects of contralateral white noise on click evoked emissions in normal and sensorineural ears: Towards an explanation of the medial olivocochlear system. *Audiology, 31,* 1–7.

Dalebout, S. D., & Stack, J. W. (1999). Mismatch negativity to acoustical differences not differentiated behaviorally. *Journal of the American Academy of Audiology, 10,* 388–399.

Davis, P. A. (1939). Effects of acoustic stimuli on the waking human brain. *Journal of Neurophysiology, 2,* 494–499.

Fisher, C., Bognar, L., Turjman, F., & Lapras, C. (1995). Auditory evoked potentials in a patient with a unilateral lesion of the inferior colliculus and medial geniculate body. *Electroencephalography & Clinical Neurophysiology, 96,* 261–267.

Fowler, C. G. (2004). Electrophysiological evidence for binaural processing in auditory evoked potentials: The binaural interaction component. *Seminars in Hearing, 25,* 39–49.

Fox, L., & Dalebout, S. (2002). Use of the median method to enhance detection of the mismatch negativity in the responses of individual listeners. *Journal of the American Academy of Audiology, 13,* 83–92.

Geisler, C., Frishkopf, L., & Rosenblith, W. (1958). Extracranial responses to acoustic clicks in man. *Science, 128*, 1210–1211.

Gopal, K., & Pierel, K. (1999). Binaural interaction component in children at risk for central auditory processing disorders. *Scandinavian Audiology, 2*, 77–84.

Hall, J. (1985). The acoustic reflex in central auditory dysfunction. In M. Pinheiro & F. Musiek (Eds.), *Assessment of central auditory dysfunction: Foundations and clinical correlates* (pp. 103–130). Baltimore: Williams & Wilkins.

Jerger, J., & Musiek, F. (2000). Report of the Consensus Conference on the diagnosis of auditory processing disorders in school-aged children. *Journal of the American Academy of Audiology, 11*, 467–474.

Jerger, J., Thibodeau, L., Martin, J., Mehta, J., Tillman, G., Greenwald, R., Britt, L., Scott, J., & Overson, G. (2002). Behavioral and electrophysiologic evidence of auditory processing disorder: A twin study. *Journal of the American Academy of Audiology, 13*, 438–460.

Jerger J. F., & Hayes, D. (1980). Diagnostic applications of impedance audiometry: Middle ear disorder, sensori-neural disorder. In J. F. Jerger & J. L. Northern, (Eds.), *Clinical impedance audiometry*. Acton, MA: American Electromedics.

Jewett, D., & Williston, J. (1971). Auditory-evoked far fields averaged from the scalp of humans. *Brain, 94*, 681–696.

Jirsa, R. (1992). Clinical utility of the P3 AERP in children with auditory processing disorders. *Journal of Speech and Hearing Research, 35*, 903–912.

Jirsa, R. (2001). Maximum length sequence-auditory brainstem responses from children with auditory processing disorders. *Journal of the American Academy of Audiology, 12*, 155–164.

Jirsa, R., & Clontz, K. B. (1990). Long latency auditory event-related potentials from children with auditory processing disorders. *Ear & Hearing, 11*, 222–232.

Kemp, D. (1986). Otoacoustic emissions, travelling waves and cochlear mechanisms. *Hearing Research, 22*, 95–104.

Kemp, D., Ryan, S., & Bray, P. (1990). A guide to the effective use of otoacoustic emissions. *Ear & Hearing, 11*, 93–105.

Kilney, P., Paccioretti, D., & Wilson, A. F. (1987). Effects of cortical lesions on middle-latency auditory evoked responses (MLR). *Electroencephalography & Clinical Neurophysiology, 66*, 108–120.

Knight, R., Hillyard, S., Woods, D., & Neville, H. (1980). Effects of frontal and temporal-parietal lesions on the auditory evoked potential in man. *Electroencephalography & Clinical Neurophysiology, 50*, 112–124.

Kraus, N., & McGee, T. J. (1994). Mismatch negativity in the assessment of central auditory function. *American Journal of Audiology, 3*, 39–51.

Kraus, N., McGee, T., Carrell, T., King, C., Littman, T., & Nicol, T. (1994). Discrimination of speech-like contrasts in the auditory thalamus and cortex. *Journal of Acoustical Society of America, 96*, 2758–2767.

Kraus, N., McGee, T., Carrell, T. D., King, C., Tremblay, K., & Nicol, T. (1995). Central auditory system plasticity associated with speech discrimination training. *Journal of Cognitive Neuroscience, 7*, 25–32.

Kraus, N., Ozdamar, O., Hier, D., & Stein, L. (1982). Auditory middle latency response in patients with cortical lesions. *Electroencephalography & Clinical Neurophysiology, 5*, 247–287.

Kraus, N., Smith, D., Reed, N., Stein, L., & Cartee, C. (1985). Auditory middle latency responses in children: Effects of age and diagnostic category. *Electroencephalography & Clinical Neurophysiology, 62*, 343–351.

Laureys, S., Salmon, E., Goldman, S., & Majerus, S. (2003). Functional neuroimaging of auditory processing. *Acta Oto-Rhino-Laryngologica Belgica, 57*, 267–273.

McGee, T., Kraus, N., Comperatore, C., & Nicol, T. (1991). Subcortical and cortical components of the MLR generating system. *Brain Research, 544*, 211–220.

McPherson, D. (1996). *Late potentials of the auditory system*. San Diego: Singular Publishing.

Millen, S. J., Haughton, V. M., & Yetkin, Z. (1995). Functional magnetic resonance imaging of the central auditory pathway following speech and pure-tone stimuli. *Laryngoscope, 105*, 1305–1310.

Moller, A. R., Jannetta, P. J., & Moller, M. B. (1981). Neural generators of brainstem evoked potentials. Results from human intracranial recordings. *Annals of Otology, 90*, 591–596.

Musiek, F. E., Baran, J. A., & Pinheiro, M. L. (1992). P300 results in patients with lesions of the auditory areas of the cerebrum. *Journal of the American Academy of Audiology, 3*, 5–15.

Musiek, F. E., & Berge, B. E. (1998). How electrophysiologic tests of central auditory processing influence management. In F. Bess (Ed.), *Children with hearing impairment* (pp. 145–161). Nashville, TN: Vanderbilt-Bill Wilkerson Center Press.

Musiek, F. E., Gollegly, K., Kibbe, K., & Verkest, S. (1988). Current concepts on the use of ABR and auditory psychophysical tests in the evaluation of brainstem lesions. *American Journal of Otolology, 9*, 25–36.

Musiek, F. E., & Lee, W. (1995). Auditory brainstem response in patients with cochlear pathology. *Ear & Hearing, 16*, 631–636.

Osterhamel, P., Shallop, J., & Terkildsen, K. (1985). The effects of sleep on auditory brainstem response (ABR) and middle latency response (MLR). *Scandinavian Audiology, 14,* 47–50.

Ozdamar, O., & Kraus, N. (1983). Auditory middle latency responses in humans. *Audiology, 22,* 34–39.

Parthasarathy, T. K. (2000). Electrophysiologic assessment of CAPD. A review of basics. *The Hearing Journal, 53,* 52–60.

Parthasarathy, T. K. (2001). Aging and contralateral suppression effects on transient otoacoustic emissions. *Journal of the American Academy of Audiology, 12,* 80–85.

Picton, T., Woods, D., Baribeau-Braun, J., & Healy, T. (1977). Evoked potential audiometry. *J Otolaryngology, 6,* 90–119.

Purdy, S., Kelly, A., & Davies, M. (2002). Auditory brainstem response, middle latency response, and late cortical evoked potentials in children with learning disability. *Journal of the American Academy of Audiology, 13,* 367–382.

Rasmussen, G. L. (1946). The olivary peduncle and other fiber projections of the superior olivary complex. *Journal of Comparative Neurology, 84,* 141–220.

Ritter, W., Simson, R., Vaughan, H. G., & Macht, M. (1982). Manipulation of event-related potential manifestations of information processing stages. *Science, 218,* 909–911.

Robinett, M. (1992). Clinical observations with patients with transient evoked otoacoustic emissions with adults. *Audiology, 29,* 85–92.

Sams, M., Aulanko, R., Aaltonen, O., & Naatanen, R. (1990). Event-related potentials to infrequent changes in synthesized phonetic stimuli. *Journal of Cognitive Science, 2,* 344–357.

Sams, M., Hamalainen, M., Antervo, A., Kaukoranta., E., Reinikainen., K., & Hari, R. (1985). Cerebral neuromagnetic responses evoked by short auditory stimuli. *Electroencephaography & Clinical Neurophyiololgy, 61,* 254–266.

Scherg, M., & Von Cramon, D. (1986). Evoked dipole source potentials of the human auditory cortex. *Electroencephalography & Clinical Neurophysiology, 65,* 344–360.

Squires, K., & Hecox, K. (1983). Electrophysiological evaluation of higher level auditory processing. *Seminars in Hearing, 4,* 415–432.

Starr, A., & Achor, J. (1975). Auditory brainstem responses in neurological disease. *Archives of Neurology, 32,* 761–768.

Sutton, S., Braren, M., Zubin, J., & John, E. R. (1965). Evoked-potential correlates of stimulus uncertainty. *Science, 150,* 1187–1188.

Suzuki, T., Hirabayashi, M., & Kobayashi, K. (1983). Auditory middle responses in young children. *British Journal of Audiology, 17,* 5–9.

Tremblay, K., Kraus, N., Carrell, T. D., & McGee, T. (1997). Central auditory system plasticity: Generalization to novel stimuli following listening training. *Journal of the Acoustical Society of America, 102,* 3762–3773.

Walker, L. J., Carpenter, M., Down, C. R., Cranford, J. L., Stuart, A., & Pravica, D. (2001). Possible neuronal refractory or recovery artifacts associated with recording the mismatch negativity response. *Journal of American Academy of Audiology, 12,* 348–356.

Warr, W. B., & Guinan, J. J. (1978). Efferent innervation of the organ of Corti: Two different systems. *Brain Research, 173,* 152–155.

Wilson, R. H., & Margolis, R. H. (1991). Acoustic reflex measurements. In W. F. Rintelmann (Ed.), *Hearing assessment* (pp. 247–319). Austin, TX: Allyn & Bacon.

Woods, D., Clayworth, C., & Knight, R. (1985). Middle latency auditory evoked potentials following cortical and sub-cortical lesions. *Electroencephalography & Clinical Neurophyiology, 61,* 55.

Language-Based Assessment and Intervention of APD

Gail J. Richard
Eastern Illinois University

Vygotsky was among the first to challenge the professions of audiology and speech-language pathology to address the concept of processing auditory information. His book, *Thought and Language* (1962), introduced the term "process" by stating that the relationship between thought and words is not a "thing," but a "process"—a continual movement back and forth between thought and word, word and thought. Norma Rees fueled the fires of debate with her 1973 article, "Auditory Processing Factors in Language Disorders: The View from Procrustes' Bed." She raised questions regarding the parameters of "language" versus "auditory" processing. Ten years later, Duchan and Katz (1983) wrote an enlightening chapter that added the differential perspective—how the same client could be viewed as completely different when viewed through the lens of an audiologist versus speech-language pathologist.

The profession of audiology continues to struggle with a definitive diagnosis of auditory processing disorders. An increased awareness of neuropsychology has refocused researchers and practitioners on brain-based behavioral responses. All behavior is mediated in the brain, so professionals must evaluate behavioral responses in relation to the area of the brain involved in generating a response. Aberrant responses to auditory stimuli do not occur randomly; neurological structures are intimately involved in the resulting motor response. It is imperative that the professionals engaged in intervention understand the neurological correlates of presenting deficits. However, professionals have not reached agreement on definitive boundaries for the peripheral auditory system, central auditory system, and language system. Consequently, diagnostic labels are not consistent when introduced by audiologists following assessment procedures. The operational definition for auditory processing that one audiologist uses may differ significantly from the operational definition that another audiology colleague employs when evaluating clients.

The source of the definition variation is whether processing is an auditory phenomena (Katz, 1978; Keith, 1981; Tallal, Stark, Kallman, & Mellits, 1981) or a language-based phenomena (Gerber & Bryen, 1981; Kamhi, 1981, 1984; Rice, 1983; Rice & Kemper,

1984; Wiig & Semel, 1980). Most professionals now agree that it is both; acoustic and linguistic knowledge are necessary for accurate processing of an auditory signal.

The variation in definition of auditory processing disorders creates the final dilemma: What is the role of the audiologist versus speech-language pathologist in addressing auditory processing disorders? Audiologists are typically the professional involved in assessing and diagnosing auditory processing disorders. However, implementation of audiologist-generated recommendations generally falls on the speech-language pathologist. This becomes problematic with two autonomous professions. The person charged with remediation for the disorder did not complete the diagnostic assessment and may not agree with, or understand, how the audiologist arrived at his or her evaluation conclusion. Consequently, it is imperative that speech-language pathologists be able to functionally interpret audiologists' recommendations in regard to auditory processing disorders, as well as conduct assessment procedures to verify deficit areas before designing and implementing intervention goals.

RELATIONSHIP BETWEEN AUDITORY PROCESSING AND LANGUAGE ABILITIES

The debate among audiologists to reach a consensus definition of auditory processing disorders will not be resolved in the immediate future. Researchers and practitioners share differing views based on their theoretical perspective. Improved noninvasive medical technology is enabling professionals to examine the neurological structures intimately involved in auditory processing. While research continues to attempt differential diagnosis, speech-language pathologists must agree to some extent on a functional operational definition. Individuals seeking therapeutic services for auditory processing disorders are demanding assistance in overcoming and compensating for diagnosed deficits that contribute to academic and vocational problems.

In reality, it is difficult to separate neurological processing components. The ability to accurately perceive, transfer, and interpret an auditory stimulus is highly interactive and interdependent on multiple neurological structures. However, a basic conceptual model for understanding auditory processing is necessary if speech-language pathologists are going to provide effective intervention.

A. R. Luria (1970) proposed a functional organization of the brain that provides a hierarchical model for the brain and central nervous system. The Luria model, combined with information regarding the central auditory nervous system (CANS), provides a conceptual model that assists in understanding auditory processing within the perspective of remediation. Processing can be viewed on a continuum, beginning with emphasis on the integrity of the acoustic signal, and gradually transitioning into discrimination and interpretation of the signal. Figure 6.1 presents a graphic representation of the processing continuum.

First, an acoustic stimulus is received by an individual. This initial reception of the signal involves structures of the outer, middle, and inner ear. The signal is then transmitted through the central auditory nervous system, beginning with the eighth auditory nerve and working through the brain stem structures to eventually reach the upper cortex at Heschl's gyrus. Agreement and accuracy checks occur between hemispheres via the corpus callosum. The purest definition for central auditory processing is an intact transference of an acoustic signal from the peripheral auditory system to the upper cortex of the brain.

Second, the individual must discriminate features of the acoustic signal. The individual must recognize the auditory stimulus as meaningful and begin decoding

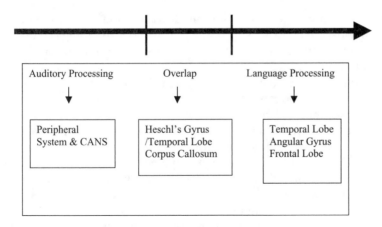

FIG. 6.1. Processing continuum.

its features within a phonetic linguistic code system. This aspect of discrimination involves both auditory and language processing aspects. The acoustic discrimination of one phoneme from another is partially based in the integrity of the hearing system, and partially based in the individual's linguistic knowledge of the sounds of a language. The ability to manipulate the signal involves discrimination of the acoustic units received, such as recognizing the last phoneme or sound in an acoustic signal.

Third, the acoustic signal must now be interpreted within language parameters. This requires an individual to know that a phonetic sequence of /k o t/ represents a clothing article that you wear when it is cold outside (i.e., coat). The pairing of meaning with the acoustic signal enters a language processing realm. If a person can receive the signal intact, reproduce it, and discriminate features within it (e.g., how many distinct sounds are heard), but cannot formulate an image of what the phonemic unit represents, then the deficit is in acquisition of the lexicon or vocabulary of a language, not a deficit in the ability to receive and discriminate characteristics of the acoustic stimulus. For example, an individual hearing a foreign language may be able to receive and even repeat what was heard (auditory processing) but cannot translate what the sounds mean (language processing).

The processing continuum as presented is simplistic in nature to emphasize the main features involved in processing auditory information. It is not intended to suggest that actual processing is as linear or discrete as this model. The graphic representation is intended to assist a professional charged with determining the type of difficulty or level of breakdown that an individual is experiencing, so that treatment can more accurately address the problem.

In reality, there are several models of processing that have been utilized in the fields of speech-language pathology and audiology. Once again, the auditory processing models delineate a discrete definition for a very complex, integrated task. The purpose is to help clarify the process conceptually, not neurologically define the reality of processing auditory information.

TOP-DOWN VS. BOTTOM-UP VS. COMBINATION APPROACHES

Massaro (1975) defined processing as "the ability to abstract meaning from an acoustic stimulus." There are a variety of approaches and models that exist in the literature regarding how the interpretation or attachment of meaning is accomplished. The importance of understanding the various models for processing information relates to the perspective used when assessing a client. Auditory processing is more focused on processing the acoustic parameters of an acoustic signal, while limiting the linguistic attachment of meaning.

Two classic approaches have been prevalent in the literature regarding how to address processing—top-down versus bottom-up. Numerous other theories can also be found, many of which combine features of these two primary approaches. Although none of the theories can definitively account for all aspects of processing auditory information, it is helpful to understand the fundamental principles in the varying approaches. In reality, auditory processing involves aspects of multiple theories and probably varies based on familiarity with the auditory stimulus being presented.

A bottom-up approach is most closely aligned with the audiology perspective. This approach advocates that an individual must become aware of the introduction of an acoustic stimulus in the environment. The stimulus is received in the peripheral auditory system as acoustic energy or formants. The acoustic formants combine to create phonemes or sounds. These sounds accumulate into words, which add up to phrases and eventually form a syntactic unit that represents a thought or idea. Emphasis is on the acoustic output. The acoustic signal is then translated using a linguistic code to attach meaning to the auditory signal.

Audiological assessment for auditory processing disorders generally follows a bottom-up model. The focus is on accuracy in receiving and transferring the acoustic signal as it moves from the peripheral auditory system through the central auditory system into the upper cortex. Assessment instruments emphasize recognition of various acoustic features of the signal, such as pitch, loudness, duration, and speed/timing.

A functional conceptual framework for bottom-up processing is to think of small parts being received to add up to the whole. Individual pieces must be accurately perceived to achieve an integration of the whole. An example to help illustrate is the process an individual goes through when learning to play the piano. Initial lessons introduce the individual piano keys and finger patterns. Those individual notes are added up to form tunes and melodies. The summative whole is a musical score, comprised of the small parts of varying tones/frequencies, durations, and intensities.

Top-down processing involves the opposite perspective. A summative whole or gestalt is perceived and then analyzed and broken down into component parts. The piano analogy would apply if reversed to the perspective of someone who learned to play music "by ear." The individual heard a song and reproduced it in total, without understanding the notes or musical aspects of composition. They might not know what notes they are playing or what the timing particulars are; they are focused on a functional whole product. The whole is then broken down into its smaller pieces.

Speech-language pathology is often based in a top-down approach. Functional communication is the goal or focus, so emphasis is on comprehension and taking in the acoustic stimulus as a whole unit. If the whole is meaningful and creates a thought or idea, then individual aspects can be analyzed, such as what words, sounds, gestures, or facial expressions were used to assist in relaying the message.

Examples of the two models exist in educational curriculum styles. A phonics approach to reading is bottom-up; a whole language approach is top-down. The cook who carefully follows a recipe is bottom-up, as opposed to the person who cooks by instinct with a pinch of this and dash of that to result in a delicious entrée. Figure 6.2 summarizes the top-down/bottom-up contrast.

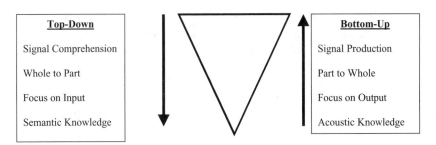

FIG. 6.2. Top-down versus bottom-up approach.

In reality, individuals use a combination of top-down and bottom-up models to deal with processing information. The approach will vary based on the individual's familiarity with the type of content. Familiar information tends to be dealt with in more of a top-down manner, getting the main idea and then focusing on particular details of importance. Unfamiliar information is more likely to be written down or focused on in more detail because the main idea of the message cannot be grasped quickly and the specifics become more important for accurate processing.

Other models have been proposed as theories for dealing with processing information, most of which address levels of linguistic processing rather than acoustic processing. For example, Wallach and Butler (1984) summarized aspects of the Multi-Store Model, which advocates a simplified transference of information for processing. The sensory information is received and, if pertinent, moved to short-term memory for initial processing. If considered relevant for the future, the information is then moved to long-term memory for storage and future retrieval. This model is illustrated in Fig. 6.3.

The Levels-of-Processing Model (Butler, 1984) was proposed by Craik and Lockart in 1972 in response to criticism regarding the simplicity of the Multi-Store Model. Research in the 1960s and 1970s began suggesting that the ability to recall information was dependent on the depth or level of meaning that was initially attached to the incoming stimulus. An individual could engage in shallow or deep interpretation of meaning on auditory information received. The variables influencing the processing depth were relevance of the material and amount of time spent with the information.

A combination model derived by Norman in 1979 (Butler, 1984) created a framework of cognitive processing using memory schemas to analyze auditory information. Schemas are personal experiences that an individual brings to the task of interpretation. If a schema exists for the information received, then the experience can facilitate improved processing of the stimulus. The memory–schema model attempted to replace the 'serial' models of processing with a model that was simultaneously driven by data and cognition.

The actual unit of processing has some bearing on the model or approach a professional prefers to use when attempting to justify assessment or remediation results. The actual unit has been proposed to be as small as an individual phoneme (Hirsh,

FIG. 6.3. Multi-store model of processing.

1966) or syllable (Abbs & Sussman, 1971; Niccum, Speaks, & Carney, 1976) to as large as major clause components of a sentence (Lieberman, Cooper, Shankweiler, & Studdert-Kennedy, 1967). The unit of processing and the approach that a professional embraces become important in later consideration of intervention techniques.

For example, Paula Tallal and her colleagues (1981) have concluded that many academic problems are the result of auditory perceptual impairments, primarily in temporal aspects of sound recognition. Collaborative work with Michael Merzenich (1997) has focused on modifying the rate of acoustic stimuli presentation to gradually strengthen neural pathways involved in sound recognition for reading and other core academic tasks. Computer-generated tasks provide exercises in signal detection, recognition, discrimination, memory, and sequencing. The Scientific Learning Corporation has founded several intervention programs, including *FastForWord* (1999), based on this principle.

The approach or model of intervention needs to match the assessment model for subsequent treatment to be effective. Discrimination of the level of auditory processing difficulty is critical for effective intervention. An audiologist will engage in administering a battery of tests to stress the auditory nervous system and reduce redundancy in an attempt to determine if an auditory processing deficit is present. Test results will be passed on to a speech-language pathologist, teacher, parent, or other professional to implement strategies to overcome and compensate for the auditory processing deficits. It is important that the diagnosing audiologist also share an explanation of the approach or philosophy that underlined assessment, so accurate intervention decisions can be made.

ASSESSMENT OF THE SPEECH-LANGUAGE PATHOLOGIST FOR AUDITORY PROCESSING DISORDERS

The speech-language pathologist's primary concern in auditory processing disorders is to provide appropriate and effective intervention. To determine appropriate treatment goals, the speech-language pathologist needs to engage in further assessment to differentiate the type of difficulty within the processing continuum that the individual is experiencing. The assessment procedures conducted by the speech-language pathologist can be informal or formal, but are a critical aspect of treatment. Intervention will be only as effective as the professional's detective work to determine the crux of the problem.

Utilizing the processing continuum outlined previously in this chapter (Fig. 6.1), the three assessment levels that should be pursued by the speech-language pathologist are the following:

- Signal reception
- Signal manipulation
- Signal interpretation

The first aspect of auditory processing that should be examined and substantiated by the speech-language pathologist is in regard to the acoustic integrity of the signal. The audiologic evaluation can examine acoustic parameters in more detail, such as discrimination of tone duration, pitch, or loudness. The speech-language pathologist's concern is if the individual is receiving an intact auditory signal. In other words, is the acoustic stimulus received accurately by the listener?

An audiologist will typically use dichotic or electrophysiological tests in the auditory processing battery to formally assess this aspect of the continuum, such as the *SCAN-C: Test for Auditory Processing Disorders In Children—Revised* (Keith, 1999). The SCAN is standardized on children and can assist the speech-language pathologist in determining if the individual is struggling to receive an intact acoustic signal. However, speech-language pathologists must remember that this is a screening instrument, not a diagnostic tool. Poor performance on the SCAN should result in a referral to an audiologist for more in-depth assessment.

Reception of the signal can be informally assessed very quickly and easily by the speech-language pathologist with a simple word repetition task. The speech-language pathologist can ask the child to repeat a word or phrase immediately after them. Nonsense words can be used if vocabulary development is a concern. Another easy method is to ask the student to point to items in the room that you name. If the student is successful in this task, the general acoustic signal is being received as grossly intact.

The second step in follow-up assessment for a speech-language pathologist is to evaluate functional discrimination of the acoustic signal. This involves tasks such as auditory closure, auditory segmentation, auditory blending, or phonemic discrimination. Careful evaluation of a child's ability to manipulate and analyze acoustic features of an auditory signal will help determine specific therapy goals. The area can be informally evaluated by presenting tasks that require the client to engage in auditory discrimination or phonemic manipulation of the signal.

An example of a standardized assessment tool to evaluate this aspect of the processing continuum is the *Phonological Awareness Test* (Robertson & Salter, 1997). The instrument includes multiple subtests that ask the individual to identify sound segments of presented stimuli, such as the first sound or last sound in a word or syllable. Other subtests request the individual to manipulate sounds, such as replace the first sound with another sound or reorder sounds within a word. This test is very helpful for determining if a child has acquired the phonemic awareness and discrimination skills to serve as a foundation for academic learning, especially reading and spelling.

The *Goldman-Fristoe-Woodcock Auditory Series* is another standardized instrument that evaluates skill areas within the overlap area on the processing continuum. Subtests include Auditory Discrimination, Auditory Selective Attention, Auditory Memory, and Sound–Symbol Association. Each subtest area evaluates one aspect of signal discrimination that is necessary or prerequisite for building an academic foundation for learning.

The third area of assessment for the speech-language pathologist should be in the area labeled as language processing on the continuum, or the ability to use the linguistic code to attach meaning to the acoustic signal. The speech-language pathologist must evaluate the child's ability to decode or attach meaning to the words received through an auditory modality. Deficits could be in the language realm of vocabulary acquisition, conceptual development, expressive word retrieval, or problem solving and reasoning.

Table 6.1 summarizes the three assessment aspects that speech-language pathologists should address when evaluating or treating individuals with auditory processing disorders. Example evaluation tasks are also included for each area.

One important principle that the speech-language pathologist must use to guide test selection in the language processing area of assessment is evaluation of discrete language skills. The assessment model used by audiologists is not based on evaluation of functional skills. The model promotes evaluation of discrete specific auditory skills that must then be integrated to perform functional auditory tasks. Assessment should

TABLE 6.1
SLP Assessment Concerns in Auditory Processing Disorder

Auditory Processing Differential Levels	Definition/Goal	Example Assessment Task	Example Assessment Instruments
Signal Reception	Receiving the signal—intact transmission	*Word Repetition *Tone Discrimination (high–low sequences) *Pattern Repetition (clapping patterns)	*SCAN-C
Signal Manipulation	Analyzing the signal—discrimination of acoustic segments	*Word segmentation *Rhyming *Sound Discrimination *Auditory Closure *Sound Blending *Sound–Symbol Correspondence	*Phonological Awareness Test (PAT) *Goldman-Fristoe-Woodcock Auditory Series *Lindamood Auditory Conceptualization Test (LAC)
Signal Interpretation	Understanding the signal—attaching meaning	*Identifying objects *Identifying concepts *Semantic Relationships (synonym, antonym, homonym) *Wh Questions *Compare/Contrast—Similarity/Difference	*Language Processing Test (LPT) *WORD Test *Comprehensive Assessment of Spoken Language (CASL) *Listening Test

not attempt to mirror real life; it should break down life skills into discrete components that are added together to function every day.

Speech-language pathologists and many of the standardized assessment instruments have a tendency to evaluate language within complex integrated tasks. When an individual performs poorly, the speech-language pathologist does not know which component is creating the problem and needs to be addressed in remediation. To provide treatment as a functional whole is not always an efficient manner in which to address language processing intervention.

For example, if a person wants to be a professional athlete, then lessons and practice will build specific discrete skills to gradually approach the whole. A basketball player must learn to stand and dribble the ball before learning to run and dribble the ball. He must learn to shoot a basket while standing still before he can run and shoot a basketball. It is not time-effective to teach within the context of the whole game; certain discrete motor skills must be developed first.

Language processing assessment should evaluate specific discrete language skills that are then integrated to perform functional language tasks. Vocabulary should be evaluated; basic concepts should be evaluated; syntactic/morphological rules should be evaluated. Independent language abilities must be assessed before analyzing language competence in connected functional contexts.

When an assessment task has multiple variables, poor performance does not lead to specific goals without further evaluation. For example, a child is given a language test that provides verbal directions for the child to follow. The examiner then instructs the child to "Put the red circle under the green square." If the child does not correctly comply, the speech-pathologist does not know which language variable contributed to the deficit performance. Could the child not discriminate color, shape, or spatial prepositions? Perhaps there is a memory deficit and the individual could not retain the direction to act on it. Although the subtest performance indicates a problem, the discrete language variable causing the problem has not been identified. Consequently, the direction for remediation has not been assisted by the assessment task.

Tests that work well to help the speech-language pathologist differentiate language processing areas of deficit have discrete, clearly identified subtest areas with language variables controlled. One example is the *Language Processing Test-Revised* (Richard & Hanner, 1995a). Subtest areas are arranged in a hierarchical order of language development. One language variable is assessed within each subtest. Complexity builds as the individual moves through the subtests to identify a level of language processing breakdown for intervention goals.

A higher-level language processing task that accomplishes assessment in the same manner is the *Comprehensive Assessment of Spoken Language (CASL)* (Carrow-Woolfolk, 1999). Subtests are arranged in areas of language competence (i.e., semantic, syntactic, pragmatic, supralinguistic) to assist the speech-language pathologist in writing goals.

Language processing assessment cannot be completely addressed in this chapter. The purpose of including it with the discussion of auditory processing disorders is to alert the speech-language pathologist to confusion among professionals as to when a deficit is not in the purview of auditory processing but, rather, in the area of linguistic interpretation or language processing. Some audiologists administer tests that are very language-based, and then diagnose an auditory processing deficit. Speech-language pathologists need to know how to interpret test results to determine the actual area of deficit so appropriate intervention can be addressed.

TEST INTERPRETATION BY THE SPEECH-LANGUAGE PATHOLOGIST

A practicing speech-language pathologist may receive a referral identifying a student as having an auditory processing disorder that includes recommendations for treatment. Due to the divergent opinions among practicing audiologists in defining auditory processing disorders, assessment procedures completed to result in diagnosis can vary widely. It is not unusual to have a diagnosis of an auditory processing disorder based on poor performance on the *Clinical Evaluation of Language Fundamentals-Fourth Edition (CELF)* (Semel, Wiig, & Secord, 2003), which is a language test.

Audiologic testing procedures for auditory processing disorders often require significant memory and language concept knowledge for the individual to accurately respond. For example, in a dichotic task, an audiologist may ask a child to repeat the *first* word heard in the *right* ear. This requires a child to know serial order number concepts as well as left and right—while retaining the words in memory to recall upon demand! A child with a significant language disorder or attention problem may fail an auditory processing assessment battery for the wrong reasons.

The speech-language pathologist should carefully evaluate the audiologist's report and try to assess the task demand for the instruments used. Variables that can significantly impact test results include the following:

- Attention
- Memory
- Word retrieval
- Language complexity

Children who have attention deficit disorders (ADD/ADHD) may appear to have an auditory processing disorder due to poor focus on academic tasks. When evaluated for auditory processing problems, it is not unusual for them to lose focus or interest in auditory stimuli being presented. It is important for the audiologist to factor in the ramifications of attention deficit disorder behaviors when evaluating children, as well as when interpreting results. Inconsistent results or performance that becomes worse as the session lengthens in time could be a function of waning attention rather than auditory processing deficits.

Some auditory processing tasks, particularly auditory synthesis and dichotic competing sentence tests, require that a child retain information to formulate a response. As the information load becomes larger, a child may begin making errors. The problem may lie not in auditory perception of the stimulus, but in the ability to retain information. If a child has a poor short-term memory, the audiologist or speech-language pathologist should try to determine whether the memory demand on certain tasks could have affected results.

Many children with language deficits also evidence word retrieval problems. Although most auditory processing tests minimize the retrieval component, it should be considered when interpreting results.

Another component that can influence results on some auditory processing tests is general language development. Children with significant delays in language acquisition may demonstrate poor performance on auditory processing tests because of poor concept knowledge, limited vocabulary, or difficulty understanding directions for a task. Unless the audiologist has a comfortable understanding of language demand within tasks, results could lead to the wrong impression and diagnosis. A speech-language pathologist charged with providing treatment for an auditory processing disorder should read the referral report carefully and be familiar with auditory processing tests. It is often advisable to speak with the referring audiologist to share language concerns or clarify any discrepancies in performance that could be attributed to documented language deficits.

Competent audiologists who have spent extensive time evaluating the central auditory system in children know how important it is to use a battery of tests for accurate diagnosis. An auditory processing disorder should not be diagnosed on the basis of poor performance on one subtest. A deficit in the CANS system should be consistently observed in multiple tests. False positive results can occur if an audiologist ignores normal results on multiple tests and diagnoses an auditory processing disorder on the basis of one subtest that was different or aberrant from the others. There are exceptions, such as some of the electrophysiological assessments. But, in general, the diagnostic conclusion that an auditory processing disorder is present should be based on impressions obtained from multiple assessment tasks that collectively substantiate a deficit central auditory nervous system.

MANAGEMENT OF AUDITORY PROCESSING DISORDERS BY THE SPEECH-LANGUAGE PATHOLOGIST

Once the speech-language pathologist has assimilated the audiologist's report and completed some formal or informal evaluation of signal reception, discrimination, and interpretation, intervention approaches and objectives can be determined. A differential analysis of the three broad areas on the auditory processing continuum can

TABLE 6.2
SLP Concerns in Treatment for Auditory Processing Disorders

Auditory Processing Differential Levels	Behavioral Objective/Goal	Example Intervention Tasks	Example Intervention Programs
Signal Reception	Receiving the signal—intact transmission	*FM System *Preferential Seating *Speech Reading *Tape Recording *Figure Ground	
Signal Manipulation	Analyzing the signal—discrimination of acoustic segments	*Auditory Closure *Sound Blending *Word Analysis (first, middle, last sound) *Grapheme–phoneme Correspondence	FastForWord Earobics Phonological Awareness LindamoodLiPS
Signal Interpretation	Understanding the signal—attaching meaning	*Concept Development *Word/Object Association *Answering wh Questions *Compare/Contrast Tasks	Language Processing Kit Concept Programs

result in more focused and effective treatment. Table 6.2 provides a summary of general treatment strategies for addressing auditory processing disorders.

If a child is experiencing difficulty in receiving an intact acoustic signal, then intervention should focus on enhancing or maximizing the signal while minimizing disruptions. Most of the treatment objectives to address problems for accurate reception of the signal will be compensatory strategies. Therapy in this case could include improving the signal-to-noise ratio by reducing extraneous background noise, recommending an FM system, or encouraging preferential seating. Direct intervention could work on speech reading, auditory localization, auditory figure ground, attention techniques for careful listening, supplementing auditory presentation with visual back-up, and tape-recording to allow repetition of a signal until heard accurately. Auditory memory to retain the signal could also be an aspect that needs to be addressed.

Signal manipulation deficits will be addressed through therapy that emphasizes phonemic analysis skills. Therapy could include direct instruction and practice drills on phoneme identification, grapheme–phoneme correspondence, sound blending phonemic synthesis, sound segmentation (e.g., first sound, last sound), rhyming, auditory closure, and auditory association.

Commercial programs have been developed in the past several years to address deficits in this area of auditory processing. The importance of literacy skills for effective learning has provided a focused emphasis on development of phonetic manipulation skills. *Earobics* (1996), *FastForWord* (1999), and *LiPS* (1999) are three of the most prominent programs in the media. Phonological awareness programs for classroom collaboration at the preschool and elementary grade levels also target acoustic signal manipulation skills.

Signal interpretation is when the individual requires skills at a linguistic level rather than primarily an auditory processing level. Tasks become very language-based with a focus on meaning, or the message contained within the acoustic stimulus, rather than the acoustic characteristics. Therapy goals for interpretation problems could include teaching vocabulary labels, concept terms, expressive language retrieval and organization, word meanings, and semantic relationships. A language processing focus emphasizes semantic aspects within treatment objectives.

If treatment is primarily in the semantic aspects of language, then it can be very misleading to label the deficit as an auditory processing disorder. The speech-language pathologist may need to help parents and other professionals understand differences in auditory processing expectations as the task moves along the continuum from neurological transference to linguistic interpretation. It may be helpful to use the illustration in Fig. 6.1 to differentiate an auditory processing deficit from a language processing deficit.

Treatment for auditory processing disorders should always include two primary types of goals, regardless of the level of breakdown on the processing continuum. The first type of goals should be compensatory in nature—addressing environmental aspects that should be controlled to enhance receipt of auditory stimuli. The second category of goals should be actual skill strategies that can be taught to improve the individual's ability to accurately process auditory information.

Examples of compensatory goals could include seating the child near the instructor in a classroom, tape recording lecture material, or using an FM system. The compensatory recommendations are not something accomplished with the student, but rather are modifications within the student's environment to make it more conducive for auditory processing.

Treatment for specific skills would include goals addressed directly with the individual to help him or her learn how to process auditory information more accurately. Examples are working on speech reading skills, drilling auditory closure, auditory discrimination, phonemic awareness, and participation in the *FastForWord* (1999) or *LiPS* (1999) program. The person with the auditory processing disorder would be developing specific skills to decrease effects of the deficit.

Auditory processing disorders never go completely away. A treatment plan should not try to fix the disorder or promise that the problem will be resolved. With a combination of compensatory modifications applied in the environment and specific skill strategies, the impact of the disorder should be diminished. The treatment outcome should focus on facilitating more productive processing of auditory information by the client in various functional environments.

SUMMARY

The speech-language pathologist serves an important role in auditory processing disorders. Whereas an audiologist assumes the responsibility for assessment and diagnosis, the speech-language pathologist is often responsible for interpreting and implementing recommendations. An additional challenge exists in the lack of agreement among audiologists in defining the disorder and its differential aspects.

As a result, the speech-language pathologist must engage in conducting additional informal or formal assessment to evaluate the specific nature of problems within the broad category of auditory processing. An operational definition to guide treatment decisions can be formulated using the various processing models that have been proposed over the years. A simplified, linear model identifies a continuum of processing that begins with acoustic signal reception, transitions to discrimination of the acoustic features, and eventually results in extrapolating meaning encoded within the acoustic stimulus.

Evaluation of abilities within these three aspects of auditory processing assists the speech-language pathologist in determining the nature of primary deficits, to then decide on treatment options. Intervention should include both compensatory and skill-based goals. Environmental modifications involve coordination with teachers and parents. Specific skills can be taught and practiced to facilitate the individual's improved competence in processing auditory information. The disorder does not disappear or completely resolve, but certainly the impact can be minimized. The functional outcome should be an individual who knows how to compensate to overcome the academic problems that can result from an auditory processing disorder.

REFERENCES

Abbs, J. H., & Sussman, H. M. (1971). Neurophysiological feature detectors and speech perception: A discussion of theoretical implications. *Journal of Speech and Hearing Research, 14,* 23–26.

Barrett, M., Huisingh, R., Bowers, L., LoGiudice, C., & Orman, J. (1992). *The listening test.* East Moline, IL: LinguiSystems.

Butler, K. (1984). Language processing: Halfway up the down staircase. In G. P. Wallach & K. G. Butler (Eds.), *Language learning disability in school-age children* (pp. 60–81). Baltimore: Williams & Wilkins.

Carrow-Woolfolk, E. (1999). *Comprehensive Assessment of Spoken Language.* Circle Pines, MN: American Guidance Service.

Duchan, J. F., & Katz, J. (1983). Language and auditory processing: Top down plus bottom up. In E. Z. Lasky & J. Katz (Eds.), *Central auditory processing disorders: Problems of speech, language, and learning* (pp. 31–45). Baltimore, MD: University Park Press.

Earobics. (1996). Evanston, IL: Cognitive Concepts.

FastForWord. (1999). Berkeley, CA: Scientific Learning Corporation.

Gaddes, W. H. (1980). *Learning disabilities and brain function—A neuropsychological approach.* New York: Springer-Verlag.

Gerber, A., & Bryen, D. N. (1981). *Language and learning disabilities.* Baltimore: University Park Press.

Goldman, R., Fristoe, M., & Woodcock, R. (1974). *Goldman-Fristoe-Woodcock Auditory Series.* Circle Pines, MN: American Guidance Service.

Hirsh, I. J. (1966). Audition in relation to perception of speech. In E. C. Carterette (Ed.), *Speech, language and communication. (Vol. III), Brain function.* Berkeley, CA: University of California Press.

Huisingh, R., Barrett, M., Bowers, L., LoGiudice, C., & Orman, J. (1990). *The WORD Test-Revised.* East Moline, IL: LinguiSystems.

Kamhi, A. (1981). Nonlinguistic symbolic and conceptual abilities of language-impaired and normally developing children. *Journal of Speech and Hearing Research, 24,* 446–453.

Kamhi, A. (1984). Problem solving in child language disorders: The clinician as clinical scientist. *Language, Speech & Hearing Services in Schools, 15,* 226–234.

Katz, J. (1978). Evaluation of central dysfunction. In J. Katz (Ed.), *Handbook of clinical audiology* (2nd ed., pp. 233–243). Baltimore: Williams & Wilkens.

Keith, R. (1981). *Central auditory and language disorders in children.* San Diego, CA: College-Hill Press.

Keith, R. (1999). *The SCAN-C: Test for Auditory Processing Disorders in Children-Revised.* San Antonio, TX: Psychological Corporation.

Lieberman, A. M., Cooper, F. S., Shankweiler, D. P., & Studdert-Kennedy, M. (1967). Perception of the speech code. *Psychological Review, 74,* 431–461.

Lindamood Phoneme Sequencing Program-LiPS. (1999). San Luis Obispo, CA: Lindamood-Bell Learning Center.

Lindamood, P., & Lindamood, C. (1971). *Lindamood Auditory Conceptualization Test (LAC).* San Antonio, TX: Psychological Corporation.

Luria, A. R. (1970). The functional organization of the brain. *Scientific American, 222,* 66–78.

Massaro, D. (1975). *Understanding language: An information-processing analysis of speech perception, reading, and psycholinguistics.* New York: Academic Press.

Niccum, N., Speaks, C., & Carney, E. (1976). Reversal in ear advantage with dichotic listening: Effects of alignment. *Journal of the Acoustical Society of America, 59,* Supplement 1, S–6.

Rees, N. S. (1973). Auditory processing factors in language disorders: The view from Procrustes' bed. *Journal of Speech and Hearing Disorders, 38*(3), 304–315.

Rice, M. L. (1983). Contemporary accounts of the cognition/language relationship: Implications for speech-language clinicians. *Journal of Speech and Hearing Disorders, 48,* 347–359.

Rice, M. L., & Kemper, S. (1984). *Child language and cognition.* Baltimore: University Park Press.

Richard, G. J. (2001). *The source for processing disorders.* East Moline, IL: LinguiSystems.

Richard, G. J. (2004). Redefining auditory processing disorder: A speech-language pathologist's perspective. *ASHA Leader, 9, 7,* 21.

Richard, G. J., & Hanner, M. A. (1995a). *The Language Processing Test-Revised.* East Moline, IL: LinguiSystems.

Richard, G. J., & Hanner, M. A. (1995b). *The language processing kit.* East Moline, IL: LinguiSystems.

Robertson, C., & Salter, W. (1977). *The Phonological Awareness Test.* East Moline, IL: LinguiSystems.

Semel, E., Wiig, E., & Secord, W. (2003). *Clinical Evaluation of Language Fundamentals* (4th ed.). San Antonio, TX: Psychological Corporation.

Tallal, P., & Merzenich, M. (1997). *FastForWord training for children with language-learning problems—National field trial results.* Presentation at ASHA Convention, Boston, MA.

Tallal, P., Stark, R., Kallman, C., & Mellits, D. (1981). A reexamination of some nonverbal perceptual abilities of language-impaired and normal children as a function of age and sensory modality. *Journal of Speech and Hearing Research, 24,* 351–357.

Wallach, G., & Butler, K. (1984). *Language learning disabilities in school-age children.* Baltimore, MD: Williams & Wilkins.

Wiig, E., & Semel, E. (1980). *Language assessment and intervention for the learning disabled.* Columbus, OH: Merrill.

Vygotsky, L. S. (1962). *Thought and language.* Cambridge, MA: MIT Press.

Linking Literacy Assessments to Diagnostic Instructional Strategies for Children With an APD

Stephanie L. McAndrews
Southern Illinois University Edwardsville

An auditory processing disorder (APD) is a physical hearing impairment that affects the development of the integrated processes of language (listening and speaking) and literacy (reading and writing) (Masters, Stecker, & Katz, 1998; American Speech-Language-Hearing Association, 1996). If problems are encountered in recognizing the sound system of language, then additional problems are likely to be encountered when the child is asked to begin to match "speech sounds" to their alphabetic representations, a skill that serves as the foundation for the development of subsequent reading and writing skills. This, in turn, can lead to comprehension problems and poor academic performance (Schminky & Baran, 1999; American Speech-Language-Hearing Association, 1996).

Reading and writing are reciprocal literacy processes in which the development of one process impacts the other. The reading process involves the integration of grapho-phonic, syntactic, and semantic cues in order to comprehend text (Goodman, 1996). Grapho-phonics is used when readers make connections between the grapheme (letter) and the phoneme (sound) in order to identify a word. Readers use syntax when they utilize their knowledge of sentence structure and grammar to aid in the identification of words. Semantics is used when readers think about the meaning of the text integrated with their prior knowledge.

The process of writing also involves grapho-phonics, syntax, and semantics in order to communicate ideas. In an alphabetic language such as English, children begin to learn to write by identifying the written symbols (graphemes) that represent speech sounds (phonemes) in words. They learn to use the rules of sentence structure and grammar (syntax) along with appropriate punctuation and capitalization for the specific genre. Writers organize and develop their ideas in a coherent manner in order for the audience to gain meaning from their writing (semantics). Research shows that there is a strong correlation between children having an auditory processing disorder and having reading and writing difficulties (Masters et al., 1998), and therefore it

TABLE 7.1
Literacy Processes and Related Processing Problems

Literacy Processes:	Phonological Awareness/Word Identification	Comprehension	Spelling	Writing Composition	Organization/ Executive Functioning
Definition:	To recognize and manipulate sounds in words/to use grapho-phonics, syntax, and semantics to identify words	To understand what is read	To use phonics and rules of spelling to write words	To write complete, coherent sentences or essays for a purpose	To organize and carry out tasks
Examples of Difficulties:	Rhyming, identifying sounds of letters, sounding out words	Retelling, answering questions, and making connections	Spelling in and out of context	Writing coherently with standard sentence structure, grammar, and punctuation	Organizing and accomplishing assignments
Related Processing Problems:	Phonemic decoding, Memory	Phonemic decoding, Memory, Integration	Phonemic decoding, Memory, Integration	Memory, Integration, Organization	Integration, Organization

is necessary to not only provide speech and language instruction, but also provide instruction to enhance their literacy development as well. Baraybar (2004) associated auditory processing problems such as phonemic decoding, memory, integration, and organization with specific literacy processes. Table 7.1, adaptedcite from Baraybar (2004), illustrates the connection between the literacy processes and related processing problems.

Children with auditory processing disorders are often referred to the Cougar Literacy Clinic, at Southern Illinois University Edwardsville, where specific literacy assessments are administered and then individual diagnostic instruction is planned and implemented. The literacy clinic focuses on all aspects of the literacy process: word identification, comprehension, spelling, and writing composition. This chapter emphasizes assessments and instructional strategies for each of these processes as they are also areas of deficit often identified in children with an auditory processing disorder. Table 7.2 lists all of the assessments that are described in this chapter and identifies which literacy process it is assessing.

The 11 assessments used in the Cougar Literacy Clinic were developed or adapted by the author, unless otherwise referenced. Each assessment is briefly described and then the actual record sheet for documenting children's responses can be found in the related appendix.

1. Literacy Interview Assessment (Appendix 1)

This 10-question interview adapted from Goodman, Watson and Burke (1987) is used to determine the child's perceived reading and writing strategies, strengths, and needs. The reading responses may be oriented toward phonics, grammar, meaning, or a combination. The writing responses may focus on content, spelling, or handwriting.

TABLE 7.2
Assessments and the Related Literacy Processes

Literacy Processes Assessments	Phonemic Awareness and Letter/Sound Identification	Word Identification	Comprehension	Spelling	Writing Composition
Literacy Interview		X	X	X	X
Concepts About Print	X	X			
Letter and Sound Identification	X				
Auditory Discrimination	X				
Phonemic Segmentation	X				
Word Identification	X	X			
Text Reading		X	X		
Oral Reading Strategies		X	X		
Writing Words	X			X	
Sentence Dictation	X			X	
Writing Composition	X			X	X

2. Concepts About Print Assessment (Appendix 2)

This 24-question assessment, adapted from Clay (1993), provides information about print concepts, such as directionality, one-to-one matching of words to print, and concepts of letters, words, and punctuation, in the context of following along in a book.

3. Letter and Sound Identification Assessment (Appendix 3)

This assessment provides information about the child's ability to identify the names and sounds of 26 capital and the 28 lowercase letters, adapted from Clay (1993). The letters a and g are presented with two different fonts. Each letter is presented one at a time and the child is asked the name, sound, and a representative word for each. The child is also prompted for both the short and long sounds of vowels and the hard and soft c and g sounds. The incorrect responses are analyzed for visual or auditory similarities.

4. Auditory Discrimination Assessment (Appendix 4)

The auditory discrimination assessment, based on the concept of the Wepman Auditory Discrimination Test (1958), is designed to determine the ability of children to recognize the fine differences between English phonemes. Each test consists of orally presenting 20 word-pairs that differ by the vowel phonemes or are the same.

5. Phonemic Segmentation Assessment (Appendix 5)

The *Yopp-Singer Test of Phoneme Segmentation* (Yopp, 1995) is used to identify the child's phonic knowledge by the rime patterns recognized in words. Segmenting words into their single letter sounds and synthesizing the sounds to form words are strategies used when decoding unfamiliar words. The phonetic elements that the child is unable to correctly segment are analyzed and correlated with those in other assessments.

6. Word Identification Assessment (Appendix 6)

There are two assessments for word identification: high-frequency word lists and graded word lists. The high-frequency word lists are selected from Fry's Instant Words and organized by grade level, pre-primer through Grade 12 (Fry, Kress, & Fountoukididis, 1993). These assessments are used to establish the child's basic sight vocabulary. The graded word lists come from the Qualitative Reading Inventory-3 (Leslie & Caldwell, 2001). These lists contain 20 words that are also found in the graded text passages. Three scores are calculated for each grade level word list: an automatic recognition score, an identified score (for words that were self-corrected or correctly decoded), and a total score.

This word identification information is used during instruction to help the child identify new words such as connecting known phonemes and words to identify unknown words. The text reading assessment begins at the child's highest instructional level (70% or above) on the grade level word lists.

7. Text Reading Assessment (Analysis Appendices 7–8)

The text reading assessment is used to gain information about the child's word identification in context and comprehension. Two informal reading inventories are used in the literacy clinic for pre- and post-assessment data: the *Developmental Reading Assessment* (DRA; Beavers, 2001) for emergent readers through Grade 2 and the *Qualitative Reading Inventory-3* (QRI-3; Leslie & Caldwell, 2001) for Grades 3 through high school. The key difference is that the DRA has multiple reading levels per grade that correlate to guided reading books, whereas the QRI has a more in-depth analysis and includes more expository passages.

The reading inventories identify the oral, silent, and/or listening levels of children using both expository and narrative grade leveled passages. To analyze children's oral reading behaviors, running records—a technique developed by Clay (1993)—are taken during oral reading and the patterns of miscues are analyzed. Appendix 7 shows the Oral Miscue Worksheet for analyzing the miscues. Miscues include substitutions of real words or decoded sounds, insertions, and omissions. The type of cue used for each substitution is also identified as grapho-phonic (initial, medial, and final), syntactic, or semantic. Self-corrections are subtracted from the total miscues, and repetitions are documented but do not count against word accuracy. Both a word accuracy score—the percentage of words read correctly—and a text meaning score, which includes those miscues that retained meaning of the text, are calculated. The meaning score is beneficial because there is a significant difference between a reader who substitutes decoded sounds or words that alter the meaning and a reader who deletes insignificant words or substitutes words that still make sense. Comprehension of each passage is also assessed through prior knowledge questions, then retelling and comprehension questions after oral reading, silent reading, or listening to each passage. The data are then documented on the Text Reading Summary Sheet (Appendix 8). The child's instructional level for book selection is based on the oral reading level criteria developed by Betts (1946). The minimum levels for word accuracy are: Independent 95%, Instructional 90%, Frustration 89% or below. The comprehension levels are based on Leslie and Caldwell's (2001) criteria: Independent 90%, Instructional 70%, Frustration 50% or below.

An analysis of word identification assessments can provide a window into the child's reading processing in order to plan instruction that can enhance the child's literacy development. These assessments are analyzed in five areas: What does the child perceive about his or her reading processing? What are the similarities or differences between the types of miscues a child makes in isolation versus in context? What problem-solving strategies does the child employ? What words and phonetic elements does the child know or indicate difficulties with? Finally, how does the child's word identification impact comprehension?

8. Oral Reading Strategy Assessments (Appendices 9 and 10)

Three assessments, developed by McAndrews (2002), provide an analysis of the child's use of oral reading strategies. The teacher assessment (Appendix 9) is a tally sheet of the number of times the child uses each strategy during a passage reading and then the additional prompts the teacher provides the reader when figuring out unknown words. The peer assessment provides children an opportunity to listen for the strategies other children use while they read and place a stamp each time one is used. This helps children focus on learning strategies rather than calling out words, which inhibits readers from problem solving on their own. The final oral reading assessment (Appendix 10) is the self-assessment, which enhances metacognition of problem-solving strategies. Children audiotape their reading, replay the tape, and mark all the strategies they used. They identify those that were effective and those that may help. An added benefit of this assessment is that the children often self-correct after hearing their reading and improve their comprehension of the text.

9. Writing Words Assessment (Appendix 11)

The purpose of the writing words assessment is to identify high-frequency words the child can correctly spell and known phoneme–grapheme relationships. This assessment as well as the writing dictation are also used to look at letter formation, especially at the kindergarten and first-grade levels. Children are asked to write words from the high-frequency word lists, based on Fry's Instant Words (Fry, Kress, & Foun-toukididis, 1993). The pre-primer through second grade words are listed in Appendix 9. For emergent writers, initially ask them to write their first and last names and any other words they know, then begin prompting them from the high-frequency word list. These tests can be scored in two ways: by using a developmental rubric (Table 7.3) or the traditional scoring of one point for each correctly spelled word. Using the developmental rubric, assign points for each word and then determine the child's overall developmental level for each grade level. This rubric provides a more accurate view of a child's spelling development than simply looking at correct or incorrect spellings.

10. Sentence Dictation Assessment (Appendix 12)

The dictation assessment is used to identify known writing vocabulary, the children's ability to divide words they hear into their sounds (phonemic segmentation),

TABLE 7.3
Developmental Spelling Scoring Rubric

Pre-phonetic	Semi-phonetic	Phonetic	Transitional	Conventional
Letters and/or shapes are written, but do not represent the sounds.	Some sound-symbol relationships	At least half of the sounds are represented graphically.	All sounds are represented graphically.	The word is spelled correctly.
0 point	1 point	2 points	3 points	4 points

write the letter or letters that represent them, and the children's ability to use a word analogy for known words to help them spell new words. These sentences were created based on incorporating as many phonograms as possible in the fewest words in the context of a story. The complete sentences are dictated to the child and then each word is repeated one at a time for him or her to write. There are two dictation sentences: one for Grades K–2 and the other for Grades 3 and up. The dictation sentences are scored by assigning one point for each correct phoneme–grapheme correlation. To analyze the sentence dictation, the clinician identifies the correct and incorrect phonetic elements or patterns of spelling in order to plan instruction. Punctuation and capitalization as well as handwriting are evaluated.

11. Writing Composition Assessment (Appendix 13)

Children are given a prompt to write either a narrative, expository, or persuasive writing sample. The writing is then analyzed using a plus, check, or minus scale plus comments for each of the following writing elements: ideas/details, organization, sentence fluency, word choice, grammar, punctuation, capitalization, and spelling. The evaluation is based on grade level or individual expectations.

12. Individual Phonics Summary Sheet (Appendix 14)

When all the assessments are completed, this phonics summary sheet is used to document missed phonetic elements from all the reading and writing assessments. It is important to note, however, that these phonic elements should be taught in the context of reading and writing, not in isolation.

DIAGNOSTIC INSTRUCTION AND STRATEGIES

According to Walker (2004), diagnostic teaching is "the process of using assessment and instruction at the same time to identify the instructional modification that enables problem readers (and writers) to become independent learners" (p. 5). After analyzing the results of the informal literacy assessments, the clinician identifies specific instructional objectives, materials, and strategies based on the child's strengths and needs. Instruction is then planned at the leading edge of the child's zone of proximal development, "the distance between the actual developmental level as determined by independent problem solving and the level of potential development as determined through problem solving under adult guidance or in collaboration with more capable peers" (Vygotsky, 1978, p. 86). The reading materials and strategies are selected based on the child's instructional level, so that with some scaffolding the child will be successful.

This chapter identifies strategies appropriate to develop each of the literacy processes: phonemic awareness/phonics, word identification, comprehension strategies, and writing strategies. The instructional strategies have been developed, selected, and adapted from a variety of sources. Reading recovery strategies are described by Clay (1993), Lyons, Pinnell, and DeFord (1993), and Pinnell and Fountas (1998). Six sources containing a compilation of instructional techniques and strategies are Walker (2004), Vaca et al. (2003), Allington and Cunningham (2002), Thomkins (2002), Tierney (2000), and Cunningham, Hall, and Sigmon (1999). Additional strategies were developed by the author and used with children in both classroom and clinical settings. Several of these strategies have been found to be beneficial for children with not only auditory processing disorders (Kelly, 1995), but other reading disabilities as well.

PHONEMIC AWARENESS AND LETTER/SOUND IDENTIFICATION

Phonemic awareness is the awareness of the sounds (phonemes) that make up spoken words, whereas phonics is the correlation between these sounds and the letters that represent them. These understandings are essential for learning to read an alphabetic language. The following activities support children's understanding of phonemic awareness and the correlation between letters and sounds:

Auditory Discrimination: Ask children to identify the initial, final, and then medial phonemes within words they hear in conversations or in books, for example, listen for initial /s/ or then later identify the initial sound in sat, sit, sip, and sad . . . or for long /e/ in me, see, and bee.

Blending Phonemes: Ask the child to orally blend phonemes into words, for example, /s/-/ă/-/t/ makes what word? This helps children eventually decode or sound out words.

Phoneme Segmentation: Ask child to orally break up words into component sounds, for example, goat = /g/-/ō/-/t/. This helps children eventually write words. One effective strategy is called Pushing Pennies. The child pronounces a word slowly and pushes one penny in each box on a card as he or she says each sound. Eventually, when they learn phonics, children can write the letters that represent each sound.

The correlation between the letters and sounds is phonics. When introducing each letter, model its corresponding sound and have children produce the sound themselves. At first, teach and work with only a few letter–sound correspondences that have high utility in many words (e.g., /m/ in man, mad, him, and ham). Postpone teaching less frequently occurring letters and consonant digraphs until the child has a firm understanding of how left-to-right spellings represent first-to-last sounds (alphabetic understanding). The following strategies came from the author's experience as well as adapting those presented by Thomkins (2002):

Environmental Print: Collect food labels, toy traffic signs, newspaper advertisements, and other environmental print for children to sort and use in identifying letters and words.

Letter Containers: Collect coffee cans or shoeboxes, one for each letter of the alphabet. Write upper and lowercase letters on the outside and the teacher can place several familiar objects that represent the letter in each container. The teachers use these containers to introduce the letters, and the children use them at a center for sorting and matching activities.

Show and Tell Bag: At home have children place items and pictures in a bag that represent a given letter or sound. They can share these items, or they can give clues as to what is in the bag for the others to guess.

Alphabet Books: Read aloud alphabet books to build vocabulary and teach children the names of words that represent each letter. Then, children reread the books and consult them to think of key words when making their own books about a letter.

Letter and Word Search: While reading books have children find particular letters or words beginning with that letter. You could make circle-shaped letter frames from tag board, plastic bracelets, or shape pipe cleaners or Wikki-Stix (Wax covered sticks) for children to highlight particular letters on charts or in big books.

Key Word Alphabet Charts: Use alphabet charts with a picture and word of a familiar object for each letter. They must be familiar with the object or they will not remember the key words. Recite the alphabet by pointing to each letter and saying "A-/ă/- apple, etc.

Letter Books and Posters: Children can make letter books or posters with pictures of objects beginning with a particular letter on each page. They can add letter stamps or stickers.

Magnetic Letters/Letter Tiles: Given a variety of letters, children pick all examples of a letter or match upper and lowercase letter forms. They also arrange the letters in alphabetical order and then use the letters to spell their names or other familiar words.

Letter Stamps: Children use letter stamps and ink pads to stamp letters on paper or in booklets. They also use letter-shaped sponges to paint letters and letter-shaped cookie cutters to make cookies or to cut out Play-Doh letters.

Making Letters: Children practice making letters while saying the sound that it represents using pipe cleaners, Play-Doh, writing in shaving cream, writing on sidewalks, in the air, and on white boards.

Letter and sound identification is one element of concepts about print. As seen in the Concepts About Print Assessment (Appendix 2), children need to be taught concepts such as directionality (reading left to right and the return sweep), one–one matching, the difference between letters and words, letter and word identification, and the purpose for punctuation marks. The teacher models these concepts about print to the class by using a pointer and asking questions while reading big books or by pointing and asking questions while reading with an individual.

WORD IDENTIFICATION STRATEGIES

The terms *word identification and word recognition,* although similar, differ slightly in their definitions. The *Literacy Dictionary* (Harris & Hodges, 1995) defines both word recognition and word identification as "the process of determining the pronunciation and some degree of meaning of an unknown word" (p. 282). However, word recognition is further defined as the "quick and easy identification of the form, pronunciation, and the appropriate meaning of a word previously met in print or writing" (p. 283). For words that are in a reader's meaning vocabulary, unlocking the pronunciation leads to the word's meaning. During assessment, word recognition is determined by those words the child is able to read automatically, while word identification is demonstrated by the processes children use in their attempts to read or self-correct an unknown word. Word identification processes include context clues, phonic analysis, and configuration clues. One technique that integrates all three of these processes is the Oral Strategy Assessments for Teachers or Self (McAndrews, 2002; Appendices 9 and 10) for instruction as well as assessment. To determine when to prompt for specific strategies, see the Oral Reading Strategy Prompts (Appendix 15). In order to differentiate the three processes used in word identification, the following definitions were paraphrased from the *Literacy Dictionary* (Harris & Hodges, 1995) and Pikulski (1997):

Phonic analysis is the identification of words by their sounds, which involves the association of speech sounds with letters and the blending of these sounds into syllables and words. Structural and analogy clues support phonic analysis. Structural analysis includes the identification of roots, affixes, compounds, hyphenated forms, inflected and derived endings, contractions, and, in some cases, syllabication. Readers also employ analogy clues by using the words they know to help them recognize words that are unfamiliar. Children can learn to manipulate the onsets (consonants before the vowel) and rimes (the vowel and consonants following it within a syllable).

For example, a child who is able to read *cat*, can change the onset to "s" when reading the new word *sat*. Being able to associate sounds with a cluster of letters, such as the rime "at," leads to more rapid, efficient word identification.

Context clues for word identification involve using information from the surrounding words, phrases, and sentences, such as semantic or syntactic clues, or using picture clues. The semantic or meaning clues help the reader by associating words with the topic of the text or sentences. For example, when reading a story about dogs, the expectation is that the text may also contain words such as bark, woof, and wagging. The syntactic clues help the reader to predict what part of speech the unknown word is based on the word order. The picture clues or illustrations can often help with the identification of a word if there is strong picture support for the unknown word. Context clues are helpful, but they need to be cross-checked with phonic cues.

Configuration clues involve using the shape or outline of the word to aid in word identification, especially the pattern the letters make above and below the main body of the word and the length of the word. In addition, noticing typography such as bold, capitalized, or italicized words draws attention to words that may be important.

PHONIC ANALYSIS STRATEGIES

Books With Specific Letter–Sound Patterns: Give children meaningful and predictable stories containing several examples of words that reflect the letter–sound pattern that is being taught. Encourage children to find those words. However, some books written for the purpose of teaching specific phonic elements are difficult to read because the child can only use the phonic strategy, without much context or meaning, such as "Nan can fan Dan."

Model Decoding Words: After children have mastered a few letter–sound correspondences, teach them to decode words or sound them out. Begin with small, familiar words. The teacher models sounding out the letters, left to right directionality, blending the sounds together, searching for the word in memory, and saying the word.

Known to Unknown: The teacher writes or demonstrates to the child the relationship between phonic elements in known words and those in unknown words in the text. Select one or two elements at a time to focus on.

Make-and-break Words: From text using magnetic letters or tiles, including onsets and rimes. Make the vowels in a different color than the consonants, so that the child knows that every word has a vowel. Initially select words that have one letter per sound. Scramble the letters needed to make the word and have the child reconstruct it. Then, have the child find and read the word in the story. The child can also make a familiar word and then make new words with the letters by changing the onset or the rime.

Missing Vowel Cards: Make index cards with each of the vowels (a, e, i, o, u) and then make cards with pictures of a variety of short vowel consonant–vowel–consonant (cvc) words (cat, pen, pig, fox, cup). Write the word under the picture but make a line where the vowel should be. Have the child sort the picture cards under the correct vowel.

Missing Vowel Mix and Match: Make tiles or cards with the vowels on them. Write consonant–vowel–consonant words with a box for the vowel. Have the children put different vowels in each box to make multiple words. Example word frames include: h_t, s_t, h_m, b_t, d_g, m_p, t_p, f_n, c_b.

Sorting by Sounds: Find a story that contains numerous examples of a single phonogram or phonograms with multiple sounds: c (/k/,/s/); g (/g/,/j/); ch (/ch/, /k/,/sh/); -ea (ē, ĕ, ā,); -ed (/ēd/, /d/, /t/). Make word cards to be sorted under the correct sound card. Have children create new word cards as they find them in print. Instead of teaching many phonic rules, teach the child to try alternate sounds, starting with the most common sound.

Word Family or Phoneme Books: Make books with one word per page that contain the same phonemic elements.

H Brothers Poster: Using pictures of four brothers, tell this story: This brother plays with trains and says /ch/. This brother blows his whistle and says /wh/. This brother doesn't want to play and sticks out his tongue and says /th/. This last brother says mom is coming, /sh/. Children refer to the poster for reading or writing consonant digraphs.

Vowel Farm Bulletin Board: As a resource, label farm pictures with key words and underline the vowel, for example, "oa" in goat.

Flap Books: Make silent –e flap books (mad → made), contraction books (cannot → can't), or word family books (eat → meat, heat, etc.).

"Words I know" and "Words I am learning" Envelopes or Boxes: Make two labeled envelopes or boxes. Put in word cards created from word wall words, sentence cut-ups, or other sight words the child is learning. As the child learns the words, they are moved from the "words I am learning" to the "words I know" envelope. Limit the "words I am learning" to no more than 5–7 words.

Personal Dictionaries: Introduce a few high-frequency words as they are encountered in text. As words are introduced, they can be written under the correct initial letter in a personal word chart or dictionary for ongoing reference. Children can draw picture clues if needed.

Dictionary or Glossary: This resource is generally best for looking up word meanings rather than pronunciation, unless children are at the fluent reading level, approximately Grade 4 and above, when they can understand the dictionary pronunciation key.

STRATEGIES FOR PHONIC ANALYSIS DURING READING

- Say the first three sounds and predict what makes sense.
- Write what the child said above what is written in the text. Have child compare them.
- Write down or say a known word with the same phonic element(s) as the unknown word to help the child make connections.
- Say "try a different sound" or suggest a specific sound.
- Ask, Does the word you said look like the word in the text?

STRATEGIES FOR STRUCTURAL ANALYSIS

Identify and learn meanings of prefixes and suffixes from text. Add different suffixes to words (play, plays, played, playing) with magnetic letters or word cards.

Make contraction flap books (open: cannot, closed: can't). During reading, break words in parts (prefixes, roots, suffixes, compounds) by covering each affix.

STRATEGIES FOR CONTEXT CLUES

Language Experience Approach (R. Van Allen in Tierney and Readence, 2000): The teacher takes dictation from a child about a personal experience. The teacher reads back the story so that the child can make ,any desired changes. Then, have the child read it to you, while pointing one to one. The child can use the context of the story to help read unknown words. Point out high-frequency words that are also in other stories they are reading.

   Predictable language approach: Read the child books that have predictable or patterned language. Have children read or chime in during the predictable or patterned part.

   Break up sentences: Model and demonstrate how to break short sentences into individual words. For example, use the sentence "Frogs eat bugs," and demonstrate with chips, cards, or other manipulatives how the sentence is made up of three words and how the order of the words matters.

   Sequencing sentences: Using manipulatives such as word cards, have the child put the cards in order to make sentences.

   Cut-up sentences (Clay, 1993; Lyons, Pinnell, & DeFord, 1993): Cut up sentences from a song, poem, or book. Have children select a sentence that they like or the teacher selects a sentence that the child had difficulty reading. Write the sentence on a thin strip of tag board. Cut between each word or word part, and cut off the punctuation. Write the sentence on an envelope. Have the child read the sentence, turn over the envelope, and reconstruct the sentence. To make it more challenging, the teacher can cut up individual words by onset/rime, by syllable, or by phonemes, depending on what the child needs to work on. This can then be sent home for homework.

   Cloze Procedure (Taylor, 1953) or Guess the Covered Word (Cunningham; Hall, & Sigmon, 1999): During reading, the child predicts the unknown word or part of the word that is deleted or covered with correction tape or Post-it.

   Read on and go back and read again: When reading, the teacher prompts the child to read on to collect clues or go back and read again. Ask, Does it make sense? Does it sound right? This is to encourage the child to be self- reflective during reading.

STRATEGIES FOR PICTURE CLUES

Select books with strong picture support.

   Before reading, ask the child to look at the pictures, discuss the pictures, and predict what the story will be about.

   While reading, say: Look at the picture and think about the story to figure out that word.

   Some books have rebus pictures above the word or in place of the word to help the beginning reader.

STRATEGIES FOR CONFIGURATION CLUES (USED FOR READING AND WRITING WORDS)

Configuration Boxes (Cunningham, Hall, & Sigmon, 1999): Draw the shape or outline around the words to indicate the pattern the letters make above the line (b, d, f, h, k, l, t), below the line (g, j, p, q, y), and between the lines for the rest of the letters. Make configuration boxes around newly introduced words to assist memory.

Oral Reading Strategies: While many children skip unknown words or wait until someone tells them the word, these are not the most effective strategies for problem solving. Initially a list of oral reading strategy prompts developed by McAndrews (2002) was selected that help readers when they come to unknown words after providing some wait time: Look at the pictures and think about the story; Say the beginning three sounds; Read on to collect clues then go back; Go back and read again; Break words into parts; Try different sounds; Think: Does it make sense, does it look right, does it make sense; Self-correct; and Summarize what you have read. These strategies are not sequential; the selected prompts given should be those that most efficiently result in self-correction. See Appendix 15 for when a teacher may chose a given prompt. These strategies can also be made into a bookmark and poster to remind children to use them while reading.

GUIDED READING

Word identification and comprehension are greatly enhanced when teachers use guided reading (Fountas & Pinnell, 1996). In guided reading, the teacher first selects books that are at the child's instructional level (at or above 90% accuracy in word recognition). The teacher guides the learning by reading aloud and discussing the book as the children follow along. Print concepts and using multiple reading strategies are emphasized along the way. The child then retells the story focusing on the beginning, middle, and end. Now the child rereads the text while the teacher prompts for problem solving of unknown words. The teacher can provide extension activities related to the text. The child then takes the book home and rereads it to enhance fluency.

COMPREHENSION STRATEGIES

According to Pearson and Fielding (1991), reading comprehension strategies are designed to: activate children's prior knowledge, guide children's reading of a text, foster active and engaged reading, reinforce concepts from text reading, encourage careful critical thinking when reading, and pursue inquiry on different topics. When comprehending both narrative and expository texts, it is important to emphasize all levels of Bloom's Taxonomy (Bloom, 1956): knowledge, understanding, application, analysis, synthesis, and evaluation. A compilation of effective strategies for before, during, and after reading can be found in numerous resources such as Walker (2004), Vacca et al. (2003), Thomkins (2002), and Tierney and Readence (2000). In addition, McAndrews (2004) provides information on comprehending nonfiction texts. While each of these strategies is beneficial, it is important to note that children need models of how to employ them and many opportunities to practice them in a group, in pairs, and individually. The reading comprehension strategies described are organized by the following types: background knowledge, concepts and vocabulary, questioning strategies, and summarization.

BACKGROUND KNOWLEDGE STRATEGIES

Developing background knowledge is directly related to schema theory, which states that comprehension depends on integrating new knowledge with a network of prior knowledge. In schema theory, reading is seen as an active process of constructing meaning by connecting old knowledge with new information encountered in text (Anderson, 2004). Activate prior knowledge through discussions about what children already know about a topic. Have discussions about direct and indirect experiences you planned for the children such as experiments, field trips, videotapes, computer programs, demonstrations, and guest speakers. An effective way of building background knowledge is by reading a variety of texts to and with the children. The following are suggestions for building background knowledge:

Book Introduction: Give children a hook or a purpose for reading the book. Read the title, author, and illustrator. Do a picture walk that includes looking at the pictures and predicting what the story may be about. Discuss important vocabulary words. For phonetically irregular words, have children predict what the initial letters would be and locate it in the text. Help the children make connections between what they already know and the story; think about the author, topic, events, structure, or visually similar words.

Predictions: Ask the child to predict what the text will be about before and during reading based on cover, introduction, and/or the beginning sentences.

Pre-Reading Plan (PReP) (Langer & Nicolich, 1981): First, engage children in group discussion around key concepts and then analyze the nature of the children's responses.

Prediction Maps (Walker, 2004): A conceptual flowchart to visually map the comprehension process of prediction and revision.

Anticipation Guide (Vaca et al., 2003): A handout prepared for the children in advance including key concepts and vocabulary words.

K-W-L and K-W-L Plus for Expository Text (Walker, 2004): Make three columns on a chart and elicit children's responses to complete each column: What you Know, What you Want to know, and What you Learned. The plus is creating a map or web of what was learned and then summarize the text.

Guided or Visual Imagery (Walker, 2004): The teacher uses sensory images related to the storyline to increase active comprehension and activate background knowledge about situations and characters or key concepts in expository text. For introducing the text, *My Side of the Mountain* by Jean Craighead George, the teacher for example might begin by saying: Close your eyes; picture yourself in the mountains; what can you hear; what can you see? You are all alone. How are you going to eat? Where are you going to sleep? Etc.

CONCEPT AND VOCABULARY STRATEGIES

When introducing new vocabulary words, provide children with visual, auditory, and kinesthetic methods of learning them. Specifically point out individual word parts such as affixes and roots. Have children read the word in context, practice pronouncing it, and then provide their own definition and example.

Semantic Mapping (Johnson & Pearson, 1984) or **List–Group–Label** (Taba, 1967) in Tierney and Readence (2000): Children dictate a list of words related to a given topic. The children then group the terms and give each group a label.

Word Sort (Walker, 2004): The child or teacher identifies key words, writes them on index cards, and then organizes them by relationship to each other.

Label Diagrams: Add vocabulary labels to drawings such as the skeletal system of the human body, the water cycle, or the life cycle of a butterfly.

TABLE 7.4
Semantic Feature Analysis

	Lives in Water	Breathes Air	Lays Eggs	Has Fur
Whales	+	+	−	−
Seals	+ sometimes	+	−	+
Sharks	+	−	+	−
Fish	+	−	+	−
Bears	−	+	−	+

Schematic Word Map (Tierney & Readence, 2000): Identify key concepts, using lines to show how words are hierarchically related. Develop the target concept, for example, reptiles. The supraordinate concepts would be cold-blooded, vertebrate, and animal. A coordinate concept would be amphibians, while subordinate concepts would be alligators, snakes, and lizards. Define the concept, present the concept, finish constructing the hierarchy, guide children to relevant and irrelevant attributes, and complete the map with additional examples and nonexamples.

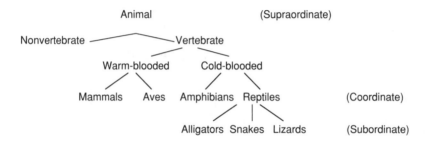

Semantic Feature Analysis Matrix (Johnson & Pearson, 1984 in Walker, 2004): Identify items to be classified, such as different kinds of animals. Identify attributes that make them similar and different. Classify each animal by the attribute, by putting a + or − in each box indicating the presence of each feature. Adaptation: Use the schematic word map to classify the animals. Table 7.4 provides an example of the semantic feature analysis grid.

Venn Diagram: Comparing and contrasting concepts. Draw three interlocking circles. Label each with the concepts such as whales, sharks, and seals. In each circle write attributes related only to that animal, such as sharks hatch from eggs. In the intersections write attributes that the two have in common, such as having live birth is attributed to both whales and seals. In the center write what all three have in common, such as they all swim in the water.

Contextual Processing (Walker, 2004): The teacher selects paragraphs from text where the meaning of new vocabulary is apparent from the surrounding context and writes it on the overhead or computer. After the children read the paragraph, the teacher asks, What does the paragraph tell you about the word ____? After the children reply, she probes and asks, "Why did you think that?" The teacher asks the children to write down what they think the word means. Then, the children think of other words with similar meanings.

Identifying Affixes and Latin Roots: The child or teacher writes prefixes, suffixes, and root words on separate index cards. Help child to make, pronounce, and define the parts of the words. For example, add the prefixes re- or pre- or suffixes -ing, -er, -ed to root words. In the child's personal dictionary, make a page for common definitions of affixes. Identify words with affixes in the text. Practice covering up parts of words in text to read unknown multisyllabic words.

4 block Vocabulary or Vocabulary Grid: For individual words, divide paper into four quadrants. Put the word in a circle in the center. In the rectangles, write the definition, the sentence where it was found, a new sentence demonstrating under-standing of the word, and draw a picture of it. For multiple words, fold the paper in five columns and put headings on each column such as: vocabulary word; definition; word that makes you think of it; sentence you can use it in; and an antonym, synonym, or example of it.

Vocabulary Self-Collection Strategy: While reading children write down words they cannot pronounce, understand, or are particularly interesting along with the page number where they can be found. The class or group discusses the words in the context of the story until its meaning is understood.

Figurative Language: Identify and discuss the meaning of figurative language as it is used in text.

Act out, visualize, or draw vocabulary words.

Personal Dictionaries: After learning new vocabulary words, the children can record them in their personal dictionaries or class vocabulary charts.

Cloze Procedure (Taylor, 1953; also in Walker, 2004): A tool for measuring read-ability and comprehension of a passage. In the cloze technique, words are omitted or covered in the text and the child needs to supply the missing words. The modified cloze technique uses semantic and syntactic clues to determine the covered vocabulary word. Grapho-phonic cues can be provided such as the beginning letter or letters.

QUESTIONING STRATEGIES

Question–Answer Relationships (Raphael, 1982; also in Walker, 2004): This is used to identify the type of response necessary to answer a question such as: right there, think and search, author and you, and on my own. Adaptation: Children can use highlighting tape to identify the answers to right there questions.

SQ3R (Walker, 2004): This procedure for studying content area texts includes five steps: Survey, Question, Read, Recite, and Review the text.

Question Generation Strategy (Walker, 2004): After reading, the children write and answer questions about important information in their reading. These ques-tions/answers are then compared to those the teacher wrote.

Self-Directed Questioning (Walker, 2004): Children write questions before and during reading and then answer them after reading.

ReQuest Procedure: Reciprocal Questioning (Manzo, 1968 in Tierney & Readence, 2000 and Walker, 2004): Children and teachers take turns asking and answering each other's questions about the text.

Questioning the Author (QtA) (Beck & McKeowan, 1997 in Tierney & Readence, 2000): The teacher identifies major understandings that the children are to construct and potential problems children may face while reading. The teacher then segments the text into meaningful parts. The teacher writes a series of initiating, follow-up, and narrative queries such as: What is the author trying to say here? Does the author explain it clearly? How does this connect to what the author has already told us? Does the author tell us why? Given what the author already told us about the character, what do you think will happen? How does the author let you know something has changed?

The teacher then strategically guides the children's contributions and discussions to help the children construct an understanding of the ideas in the text.

SUMMARY STRATEGIES

Retelling of Narrative Texts: While there are multiple strategies for retelling narratives both orally and in written form, they generally contain the following elements: Who (Characters), When (When did the story take place?), Where (Where did the story take place?), What (What events occurred? and What problem occurred?), Why? (Why was there a problem?), and How (How was the problem solved?). Children may provide an unaided retell or they may be allowed to look back in the text.

 Story Map (Walker, 2004): As a class or individually, write each element on the story map that contains vertical boxes for each element with sequential plot episodes.

 Herringbone Technique (Walker, 2004): In a fishbone diagram, write who, when, where, what, why, and how in each section. Across the backbone, write a main idea sentence using elements from the other sections.

 Beach Ball with Comprehension Questions: Toss beach ball with story element questions written on it. The children answer the question that a specified part of their hand touches.

 Chinese Folded Fortune Tellers with Comprehension Questions: Write story element questions on each of the flaps; children take turns asking and answering questions based on the story elements.

 Use or make puppets, pictures, or felt cut-outs to retell or sequence the events.

 Retelling of Nonfiction: Children need to be taught to retell the different text structures of expository texts, such as: cause–effect, comparison–contrast, sequence, description, problem–solution, question–answer, and generalizations or examples. Graphic organizers can be useful for organizing this information.

 Retelling with Word Sort: The child can write down important words from each chapter, then do a word sort that organizes the words by their relationship to each other.

 ERT: Everyone reads to ... (Cunningham, Hall, & Sigmon, 1999). Children read silently to a specific page, paragraph, section, or until they find the answer to a question. Then, they discuss what was read.

 Say Something (Walker, 2004): Children take turns saying something at intervals during the reading of the story. The children provide a personal response to the text.

 R.A.P.: Children **R**ead the paragraph, **A**sk questions, and **P**ut in their own words.

 GIST Procedure: Generating **I**nteractions between **S**chemata and **T**ext (Cunningham, 1982). The purpose is to improve children's abilities to comprehend the gist of the paragraphs. The steps include: (a) Select a paragraph, (b) The child reads the first sentence, (c) The child generates summaries, (d) The child then reads the first two sentences, (e) and Generates summary for sentences one and two, (f) Continue with the procedure for the remainder of the paragraph, and finally (g) Move from sentence approach to the paragraph approach.

 Triple Read Outline (Walker, 2004): Used for expository texts. Teacher states that the purpose for the first reading is to identify the main idea of each paragraph and she models it by writing it in the margin of a photocopy of the text. During the second reading, the purpose is to identify the supporting details. The third reading is to organize the information into an outline. The teacher then writes a summary of the passage using the main idea as the topic sentence and puts the details to support it.

She points out the irrelevant information that she left out. The children then follow the same procedure on their own using a new passage and compare their outline with what the teacher wrote.

SPELLING WORD STRATEGIES

While spelling is important in order to accurately convey a written message, it is only one aspect of the writing process. Spelling ability is dependent on the writer having a strong foundation of the sound–symbol correlations as well as being a reader, so that he or she is familiar with how words look. Children should be taught to spell high-frequency words in the context of reading and writing sentences and use inventive spelling using their spelling knowledge for unknown words. Children's writing will be stifled if they are limited to only writing words they can spell. Spelling skills are not necessarily sequential, so do not wait until a child has mastered one spelling pattern before moving on.

Introducing Words: Introduce high-frequency phonetically regular words first followed by phonetically irregular words. Teach children to spell words by sounding them out and writing the corresponding letters one by one. Model the sounding and spelling process for children as they spell. Begin with short words children can sound out, because these words follow regular spelling conventions, for example, "at," "can," and "go," instead of "see," "was," or "have."

Pushing Pennies (Clay, 1993): A strategy introduced during phonemic awareness when children pushed up pennies into a box for every sound they hear; they now write the letter(s) that represent each sound.

Magnetic Letters: Show the child how to make new words by changing the onset (the initial consonant(s) or the rime (the vowel and the following consonants in a syllable).

Sound Boxes (adapted from Elkonin, 1975): Make one box for every phoneme. If more than one letter represents that phoneme, divide that box with dotted lines between each letter. For example, the word *night* would have three boxes—n, igh, t—igh would be in the center box divided by dotted lines. For a silent –e at the end of a word, draw a line, since a box would indicate it has a sound. Have the child predict, then write the letters in each box.

Configuration Boxes (Cunningham, Hall & Sigmon 1999): Draw the shape of the word to indicate the letters that are above, below, and between the lines. Tell the children the word and have them write it in the configuration box.

Read, Cover, and Write Words (McAndrews, 2004): Select 3–4 high-frequency words the child had difficulties with during reading and/or writing. Fold paper in four columns. In the first column, the teacher writes 3–5 new words to learn. The child reads the first word, covers it up and then writes it in the second column, and opens it up and checks the spelling. This process is repeated for columns three and four. It is then repeated for each new word. This writing strategy allows the child to internalize the spelling rather than simply copying the letters.

Chanting Words: Have the children chant the letters or sounds for each word. Actions or arm movements can be added as each word is spelled. For example: Arms can be raised to the "attic" for tall letters that go above the line (b, d, f, h, k, l, and t); arms can be out straight for "main floor" letters that remain within the lines (a, c, e, i, m, etc.); arms can go down to the "basement" for letters below the line (g, j, p, q, and y).

Spelling Patterns: Introduce words with similar spelling patterns or rimes together. Using magnetic letters, children can make new words.

Word Wall Words (Allington & Cunningham, 2002): Introduce high-frequency words a few at a time. Place the words on the word wall underneath the initial letter. Have children refer to the word wall when they find words in books or want to write words that are on the wall. Often, these letters are written using an outline of the letter configurations as a clue.

Personal Dictionary: Have children create a spelling dictionary with words they can read and are learning to write. There should be one page for every letter of the alphabet. As the children desire to write new frequently used words, help them to add it to their dictionary.

Content Vocabulary Charts: The teacher can write important vocabulary for a topic or unit study on a poster for children to refer to while writing. Pictures could be added for recognition.

WRITING COMPOSITION STRATEGIES

While there are many strategies for writing depending on the genre or purpose, most importantly children need to reread what they write to be sure that it accurately and clearly conveys the message they want to communicate. To improve in their writing development, children need to write on a daily basis and for different purposes. They should also be given models to read of the type of writing that is expected.

While not all student writing needs to be published, those pieces that are, important need to go through the writing process. Direct instruction of the writing process includes: pre-writing activities, a first draft, revising for content, editing for mechanics, sharing draft, subsequent drafts, publishing, and sharing writing. To help children revise and edit their writing, they should be taught to use a writer's checklist such as the one based on the writing composition assessment. The ideas should be accurate and include sufficient details. The writing should be well-organized and flow from one part to another. The writing should include descriptive and topic-specific vocabulary. The sentences should be edited for grammar, punctuation, capitalization, and spelling. Teach children to refer to resources such as the word walls, vocabulary posters, a personal dictionary, or any reading materials for spelling words. For any additional words that they are unsure of the correct spelling, they should write it phonetically and circle it. Children should write on a daily basis for a variety of purposes such as letters, poems, invitations, advertisements, classified ads, reports, presentations, plays, personal journals, and subject-related journals. The following are a few writing strategies to improve writing composition:

Alternate Endings and Rewrites: Childs can write different endings or rewrite a story changing one or more of the story elements.

Sentence Combining (Walker, 2004): Using children's examples of short related sentences, the teacher shows how to delete repeated words or phrases and combine sentences with a variety of conjunctions and prepositions. Then children can edit their own writing by combining sentences.

Sentence Expanding: Model this process by writing a noun and a verb. Ask the child to add additional words to make an interesting sentence. Add parts of speech such as articles, adjectives, adverbs, conjunctions, prepositions, and pronouns. Now have children edit their own writing by expanding their sentences.

SUMMARY

The key to effective instruction is to first identify each child's specific literacy strengths and needs based on an analysis of informal reading and writing assessments administered. The assessments described were specifically designed to gather information about the children's reading and writing processing both in and out of context. The teacher is then able to plan instruction and select appropriate reading materials. The goal is for the teacher to scaffold the child's instruction in order to develop a self-extending system whereby the child can problem solve independently in order to comprehend text and effectively communicate ideas in writing. During the lessons, teachers assesses the child's learning and the impact of their teaching in order to monitor the child's progress and plan the next lesson. In order to evaluate the child's literacy growth over time, the teacher selects and readministers the appropriate assessments. A new educational plan can then be developed to further the child's literacy development.

In the clinic, two general types of readers with auditory processing disorders were found. These children had been receiving language therapy, and now were receiving individualized literacy tutoring. One child received significant training in developing language and she had a very high listening comprehension level, yet her phonics was very weak. Her instruction focused more on word identification strategies and writing words. Another child received a significant amount of phonics training, and yet was unable to comprehend what he read. His instruction focused more on comprehension strategies and composition writing.

The assessments and strategies described in this chapter have been effective in enhancing the literacy development of the children who attend the Cougar Literacy Clinic at Southern Illinois University Edwardsville. These children have been diagnosed with an auditory processing disorder, a language disorder, or a reading disability. In addition, practicing and pre-service teachers, who have used these assessments and strategies, have reported positive results in the reading and writing development of children with special needs as well as those in regular education.

REFERENCES

Allington, R. L., & Cunningham, P. M. (2002). *School that work: Where all children read and write*. Boston: Allyn & Bacon.

American Speech-Language-Hearing Association. (1996). Central auditory processing: Current status of research and implications for clinical practice. *American Journal of Audiology, 5*(2), 41–54.

Anderson, R. C. (2004). Role of the reader's schema in comprehension, learning and memory. In R. Ruddell, & N., Unrau (Eds.), *Theoretical models and processes of reading* (5th ed.). Newark, DE: International Reading Association.

Baraybar, R. (2004). Reading disorders, academics, and auditory processing. *Help for Kid's Speech*. Scottish Rite Foundation of Florida. Retrieved at http://www.helpforkidspeech.org/articles.

Beavers, J. (2001). *Developmental reading assessment*. Parsippany, NJ: Celebration Press.

Betts, E. A. (1946). *Foundations of reading instruction*. New York: American Book.

Bloom, B. S. (1956). *Taxonomy of educational objectives: Cognitive domain*. New York: McKay.

Clay, M. M. (1993). *An observational survey of early literacy achievement*. Portsmouth, NH: Heinemann.

Cunningham, J. W. (1982). Generating interactions between schemata and text. In J. A. Niles & L. A. Harris (Eds.), *New inquiries in reading research and instruction* (pp. 42–47). Thirty-first Yearbook of the National Reading Conference. Washington D.C.: National Reading Conference.

Cunningham, P., Hall, D., & Sigmon, C. (1999). *The teacher's guide to the four blocks: A multimethod, multilevel framework for grades 1–3*. Greensboro, NC: Carson-Dellosa.

Elkonin, D. B. (1975). USSR. In J. Downing (Ed.), *Comparative reading: Cross-national studies of behavior and processes in reading and writing*. New York: Macmillan.

Fountas, I. C., & Pinnell, G. S. (1996). *Guided reading: Good first teaching for all children.* Portsmouth, NH: Heinemann.

Fry, E., Kress, J., & Fountoukididis, D. (1993). *The reading teacher's book of lists* (3rd ed.). Englewood Cliffs, NJ: Prentice-Hall.

Goodman, K. (1996). *Ken Goodman on reading: A common-sense look at the nature of language and the science of reading.* Portsmouth, NH: Heinemann.

Goodman, Y. M., Watson, D., & Burke, C. L. (1987). *Reading miscue inventory.* New York: Owens.

Harris, T. L., & Hodges, R. E. (1995). *The literacy dictionary: The vocabulary of reading and writing.* Newark, DE: International Reading Association.

Kelly, D. A. (1995). *Central auditory processing disorders: Strategies for use with children and adolescents.* San Antonio, TX: Communication Skill Builders.

Langer, J. A., & Nicolich, M. (1981). Prior knowledge and its effect on comprehension. *Journal of Reading Behavior, 13,* 375–378. In R. J. Tierney, & J. E. Readence (Eds., 2000). *Reading Strategies and Practices: A Compendium.* (5th ed.). Boston: Allyn & Bacon.

Leslie, L., & Caldwell, J. (2001). *Qualitative reading inventory—3* (3rd ed.). New York: Longman.

Lyons, C. A., Pinnell, G. S., & DeFord, D. E. (1993). *Partners in learning: Teachers and children in reading recovery.* New York: Teachers College Press.

Masters, M. G., Stecker, N. A., & Katz, J. (1998). *Central auditory processing disorders: Mostly management.* Boston: Allyn & Bacon.

McAndrews, S. L. (2002). Enhancing reading strategies through teacher, peer, and self-assessment. *Illinois Reading Council Journal, 30*(3), 32–41.

McAndrews, S. L. (2004). Linking literacy to life: Teaching concepts through informational texts. *Missouri Reader, 28*(2), 55–64.

Pearson, P. D., & Fielding, L. G. (1991). Comprehension instruction. In R. Barr, M. Kamil, P. Mosenthal, & P. D. Pearson (Eds.), *Handbook of reading research: Vol. II.* New York: Longman.

Pikulski, J. J. (1997). *Teaching word identification skills and strategies: A balanced approach.* Houghton Mifflin. Retrieved from http://www.eduplace.com/rdg/res/teach on November 30, 2003.

Pinnell, G. S., & Fountas, I. C. (1998). *Word matters: Teaching phonics and spelling in the reading/writing classroom.* Portsmouth, NH: Heinemann.

Raphael, T. E. (1982). QARs, Question-answering strategies for children. *Reading Teacher, 36,* 186–190.

Schminky, M. M., & Baran, J. A. (1999). Central auditory processing disorders—An overview of assessment and management practices. *Deaf–Blind Perspectives,* Fall 1999. Teaching Research Division of Western Oregon University.

Taylor, W. L. (1953). Cloze procedure: A new tool for measuring readability. *Journalism Quarterly, 30,* 415–433.

Thomkins, G. E. (2002). *Language arts content and teaching strategies* (5th ed.). Upper Saddle River, NJ: Pearson Education.

Tierney, R. J., & Readence, J. E. (2000). *Reading Strategies and Practices: A Compendium* (5th ed.). Boston, MA: Allyn & Bacon.

Vacca, J. L., Vacca, R. T., Gove, M. K., Burkey, L. C., Lenhart, L. A., & McKeon, C. A. (2003). *Reading and learning to read* (5th ed.). Boston: Pearson Education.

Vygotsky, L. S. (1978). *Mind in society: The development of higher psychological processes* (M. Cole, V. John-Steiner, S. Scribner, & E. Souberman, Eds.). Cambridge, MA: Harvard University Press.

Walker, B. J. (2004). *Diagnostic teaching of reading: Techniques for instruction and assessment* (5th ed.). Upper Saddle River, NJ: Prentice-Hall.

Wepman, J. (1958). *Auditory discrimination test.* Chicago: Language Research Associates.

Yopp, H. K. (1995, September). A test for assessing phonemic awareness in young children. *Reading Teacher, 49*(1), 20–29.

APPENDIX 1

Literacy Interview

Child's Name: _____   Date: _____

Directions: "I am going to ask you some questions about what you do when you read and write. I am going to write down everything you say."

Reading Questions:

1. When you are reading and you come to a word you do not know, what do you do?
   Do you do anything else?
2. When you are reading and you do not understand something, what do you do?
   Do you do anything else?
3. How would you help someone who is having trouble reading?
4. What do you think you do well at during reading? Why?
5. What would you like to change about your reading? Why?

Writing Questions:

1. When you are writing and you come to a difficult part, what do you do?
   Do you do anything else?
2. If you were asked to write a story, what would you do first?
   Next?
   Then what?
   Last?
3. How would you help someone who is having trouble writing?
4. What do you think you do well at during writing? Why?
5. What would you like to change about your writing? Why?

APPENDIX 2

Concepts About Print (Modified Clay's Assessment)

Child's Name: _____ Date: _____

Title of Book: _____ Author: _____

Select a picture book with a picture and two–three lines of print on each page. For questions, 1–7 ask the questions then read the page. For questions 8–24, read each page, then ask the questions. Write all child's responses and √ if correct. Fill in the blanks on questions 15–17.

What you do	What you say	Response
Hold book with spine to child.	1. Where is the front of the book?	
Read title of book.	2. What do you think this book is going to be about? I'll read this story and you can help me. Read until you get to a page with pictures and print.	
Turn to first page with picture and print.	3. Where do I begin reading? Read page.	
Turn to the next page that has at least two lines. Ask questions 4–7, then read the page.	4. Show me where to start. 5. Which way do I go? 6. Where do I go next? 7. Point to it while I read it.	
Next page, ask questions then read.	8. Point to the first word on the page. 9. Point to the last word on the page. 10. Show me the bottom of the picture.	
Read along until you come to a period, question mark, comma & quotations, then stop, point, and ask questions.	11. What's this for (.)? 12. What's this for (?)? 13. What's this for (,)? 14. What are these for (" ")?	
Find two letters that have both a capital and lowercase on that page. Point to the capital letter and ask...	15. Can you find a little letter like this? (point to capital ____) 16. Can you find a big or capital letter like this? (point to lowercase ____)	
Find a page with two words that start with the same letter. Select one.	17. Can you find the word _____?	
Read page. Hand child two index cards and show them how to close them like a curtain.	18. I want you to close the cards like this until all you can see is one letter. 19. Now show me two letters. 20. Show me just one word. 21. Now show me two words. 22. Show me the first letter of a word. 23. Show me the last letter of a word. 24. Show me a capital letter.	
	Total Correct	/24

APPENDIX 3

Letter and Sound Identification Record Sheet

Child's Name: _____   Date: _____

	Letter	Sound	Word		Letter	Sound	Word
A				a			
F				f			
K				k			
P				p			
W				w			
Z				z			
B				b			
H				h			
O				o			
J				j			
U				u			
				a			
C				c			
Y				y			
L				l			
Q				q			
M				m			
D				d			
N				n			
S				s			
X				x			
I				i			
E				e			
G				g			
R				r			
V				v			
T				t			
				g			
Total	/26	/26		Total	/28	/26	

Recording: correct response: √ incorrect response: record what child says
Total Capital Letter Names: /26   Total Lowercase Letter Names: /28
Total Letter Sounds: /26
Visual Similarities: Auditory Similarities:
Unknown Letters: Unknown Sounds:
Comments:

APPENDIX 4

Auditory Discrimination Tests for Short & Long Vowels and Vowel Diphthongs, and –r and –l Controlled Vowels

Child's Name: _____

Date: _____ Grade: _____

Examiner's Name: _____

Directions: Sitting shoulder to shoulder facing opposite directions, the examiner says toward the child's ear: "I am going to say two words. I want you to tell me if they are the same or different."

Put a plus (+) if correct and a minus (−) if incorrect.

Short & Long Vowels		Different	Same	Vowel Diphthongs −r and −l Controlled Vowels		Different	Same
1. hat	hot			1. hall	hail		
2. him	him			2. pool	pole		
3. pat	pet			3. few	few		
4. pen	pin			4. her	here		
5. get	get			5. hook	hawk		
6. lad	led			6. foot	foot		
7. pit	pet			7. fear	fair		
8. not	nut			8. mood	mud		
9. mud	mad			9. care	care		
10. hut	hit			10. stir	steer		
11. me	me			11. grow	grew		
12. we	way			12. shook	shook		
13. not	note			13. town	tune		
14. mad	made			14. talk	took		
15. time	team			15. shoot	shut		
16. tone	tune			16. cloud	clawed		
17. heat	heat			17. our	or		
18. high	hay			18. fund	found		
19. hope	heap			19. pull	Paul		
20. cope	cape			20. for	fur		
Total Correct		/20=	%	Total Correct		/20=	%

Observational Notes and Summary:

APPENDIX 5

Yopp-Singer Test of Phoneme Segmentation Assessment

Child's Name: _____   Date: _____

Directions: Today we're going to play a word game. I'm going to say a word and I want you to break the word apart. You are going to tell me each sound in the word in order. For example, if I say "old," you should say "/ō/, /l/, /d/."

Practice Items: ride, go, man

Test Items: Circle those items that the child correctly segments; incorrect responses are recorded on the blank line.

1. dog	_____	12. lay	_____
2. keep	_____	13. race	_____
3. fine	_____	14. zoo	_____
4. no	_____	15. three	_____
5. she	_____	16. job	_____
6. wave	_____	17. in	_____
7. grew	_____	18. ice	_____
8. that	_____	19. at	_____
9. red	_____	20. top	_____
10. me	_____	21. by	_____
11. sat	_____	22. do	_____

Yopp, Hallie Kay. (1995, September). A test for assessing phonemic awareness in young children. *The Reading Teacher, 49*(1), 20–29.

APPENDIX 6

High-Frequency Reading Word Lists

Child's Name: _____ Date: _____

Write all child responses and √ if correct. For reading be sure to mark vowels for all decoding or attempts at words and put slashes between decoded parts of words. If at or above 14 correct or 70%, go to next list. If at or below 13 correct or 65%, go to previous list.

Pre-Primer Reading Words: ____ / 20 words = ____ %

a	to	in	is	he
I	at	have	go	see
cat	can	like	the	mom
on	dog	dad	and	we

Primer Reading Words: ____ / 20 words = ____ %

by	what	are	from	his
then	with	my	this	all
you	from	she	do	make
was	her	how	for	that

Grade 1 Reading Words: ____ / 20 words = ____ %

other	about	many	each	when
why	which	there	play	down
little	they	new	out	one
some	good	said	going	of

Grade 2 Reading Words: ____ / 20 words = ____ %

very	before	right	goes	always
around	works	great	their	don't
where	use	would	who	your
wanted	first	please	early	long

Grade 3 Reading Words: ____ / 20 words = ____ %

favorite	really	family	because	people
friend	again	another	everyone	sometimes
thought	walked	called	writing	carried
doesn't	early	once	we're	believe

Grade 4 Reading Words: ____ / 20 words = ____ %

been	difference	they're	beautiful	piece
pretty	knew	sign	brought	finally
trouble	learned	usually	excited	whether
half	weight	whole	through	tomorrow

APPENDIX 7

Oral Miscue Worksheet

Oral Miscue Worksheet

Name:						Teacher:				
Title:					Word Count:			Text Level:		

Student Response/Text	Type of Miscue					Type of Cues Used			Meaning Retained
	Substitution	Decoded	Omission	Insertion	Self-correct	Graphophonic Initial = I Medial = M Final = F	Syntactic	Semantic	√ = yes
1									
2									
3									
4									
5									
6									
7									
8									
9									
10									
11									
12									
13									
14									
15									
16									
17									
18									
19									
20									
21									
22									
23									
24									
25									
26									
27									
28									
29									
30									
Totals:									

APPENDIX 8

Text Reading Summary Sheet

Name:		Teacher:		Date:		
Title:			Word Count:		Level:	
Type of Score	Calculation				fraction	percentage
Word Accuracy Score	Words Correct = Word Count – Uncorrected Miscues / Word Count					
Text Meaning Score	Words Correct including meaning retain miscues / Word Count					
Self-Correction (S-C) Score	Self-Corrections / Miscues					
Type of Miscues	Omissions/ Miscues					
	Insertions/ Miscues					
	Substitutions of real words/ Miscues					
	Decoded Sounds/ Miscues					
Grapho-Phonic Cue Score	Number of Grapho-phonic Cues Used / Number of Miscues					
Syntactic Cue Score	Number of Syntactic Cues Used / Number of Miscues					
Semantic Cue Score	Number of Semantic Cues Used / Number of Miscues					

Accuracy Functioning Levels	Actual Score in %	Functioning Level
Oral Reading Accuracy		
Oral Reading Meaning		
Self Correction Score		
Comprehension		
Prior Knowledge Questions	__/__ __%	Familiar or Unfamiliar
Retelling Narrative Expository Setting Main Idea Goal Details Events Main Idea Resolution Details	Score: +√ –	Functioning Level

Comprehension Questions
   Explicit
   Implicit
   Total
	Fraction and %	Functioning Level

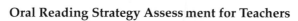

APPENDIX 9

Oral Reading Strategy Assessment for Teachers

Reader: _____   Date: _____

Title of Literature: _____ _____

Strategies: Put a tally mark each time a strategy is used by the student.

Teacher Prompts: Put a tally mark for each prompt given.

___ Wait time.

___ Look at the pictures and think about the story.

___ Say the beginning three sounds.

___ Read on to collect clues.

___ Go back and read again.

___ Break words into parts.

___ Try different sounds.

___ Miscues have similar meanings.

___ Miscues are visually similar.

___ Miscues have similar syntax.

___ Self-correct.

___ Summarize.

Observations:

___ Look at the pictures and think about the story.

___ Say the beginning three sounds.

___ Read on to collect clues.

___ Go back and read again.

___ Break words into parts.

___ Try different sounds.

___ Does that make sense?

___ Does that look right?

___ Does that sound right?

___ Where is the tricky part?

___ Are you right?

___ How do you know?

___ What else can you do?

___ Try that again?

___ Summarize.

APPENDIX 10

Oral Reading Strategy Assessment for Self

Name: _____ ___   Date: _____

Title of Literature _____   _____

After reading or listening to a tape recording of your reading, put a stamp each time you use a strategy.

1. Look at the pictures and think about the story.

2. Say the beginning 3 sounds. **B L O** blocks

3. Read on to collect clues.

4. Go back and read again.

5. Break words into parts.   paint + er = painter

6. Try different sounds.   cane

7. Think:
Does it make sense?

Does it sound right?

Does it look right?

8. Self-correct.

9. Summarize.

Strategy number that worked well ___ , Strategy number that might help ___

Comments:

APPENDIX 11

High-Frequency Writing Word Lists

Child's Name: _____   Date: _____

Dictate the following words and have the student write them on a separate sheet of lined paper. Write all incorrect student responses above each word or √ if correct in each box. Be sure to indicate reversals and capital letters. If at or above 14 correct or 70%, go to next list. If at or below 13 correct or 65%, go to previous list. You will obtain a percentage score as well as a developmental spelling level.

Pre-Primer Writing Words: Developmental Level: _____   ___/ ___words
asked = ___%

Ask, "Can you write your first name and last name?" _____

a	to	in	is	he
I	at	have	go	see
cat	can	like	the	mom
on	dog	dad	and	we

Ask, "Do you know how to write any other words?" _____
_____

Primer Writing Words: Developmental Level: _____   ___/20 words= ___ %

by	what	are	for	his
then	with	my	this	all
you	from	she	do	made
was	her	how	saw	that

Grade 1 Writing Words: Developmental Level: _____   ___/20 words= ___ %

of	about	many	each	when
why	which	there	play	down
little	they	new	out	one
some	good	said	going	other

APPENDIX 12

Sentence Dictation

Child's Name: _____   Date: _____

Directions: "I am going to read you a story and then I am going to go back and read one word at a time. I want you to write down each word, I say. If you do not know how to write a word, say the word to yourself and write down the letters for the sounds you hear." If the word is correct, put a check above the word. If the word is misspelled, write student's response above the word. Count one point per correct phoneme–grapheme correlation. Use the individual phonics summary sheet for analysis.

Sentence Dictation A: ___50 graphemes

Th e f ar m er s aw the b l a ck a n d wh i te t oy b oa t ou t o n the w a t er.
It f l oa t ed u n d er the sh i n y s t ee l b r i dge t o a s m a ll b ea ch.

Sentence Dictation B: ___154 graphemes

T o d ay I s aw a l i tt le g ir l w a l k i ng in th e c oo l w a t er a l o ng the br ee z y b ea ch in Fl or i d a. Sh e a s k ed, "Ch r is, d o y ou kn ow wh ere m y tw o bl ue t oy s ai l b oa t s ar e?" I s ai d, "I th i nk th ey f l oa t ed u n d er th a t n ew br i dge a n d the h u ge w a v es m igh t h a v e br ough t th e m u p o n the j a gg ed sh or e o v er th ere. Wh y d o n 't y ou p u t on y our sh oe s b e c au s e y ou c ou l d g et h ur t cl i mb i ng?" We f ou nd o n ly a s m a ll p ie c e of o n e boat i n th e s oi l. I e x c l ai m ed, "L e t 's h ea d b a ck, it 's g e tt i ng qu i te d ar k! N ow d o n 't w or r y, we 'll s t ar t l oo k i ng a g ai n ear l y t o m or r ow."

APPENDIX 13

Writing Composition Assessment

Child:_____ Date: _____

Title: _____ Genre: _____

Instructions: For each trait, circle the rating that best fits the writing. Underline any descriptive words that seem appropriate. Then weight each trait to equal a total of 50 points.

	Excellent	Satisfactory	Needs Work	Student/ Teacher Score
Content:				
Ideas/Details 10 points	Interesting. Well focused. Accurate. Specific details and description. Shows insight, originality, and careful thought. No irrelevant details.	Clear, but has limited details. Not very specific. Varied quality; some ideas important while others are not. Parts lack personal feeling or knowledge.	Seems to lack purpose or focus. Limited or unclear information. Doesn't seem meaningful or real. Lacks personal feeling or knowledge.	
Organization 10 points	Inviting introduction. The order makes sense and easy to follow. Ideas are connected with smooth transitions. Details fit. Strong conclusion adds impact.	The reader can follow what is being said but lacks focus and impact. The introduction and/or conclusion can be found but seem weak or forced. Some details seem confusing.	No identifiable introduction and/or conclusion. Details strung together without logical order. No transition. Gaps in information.	
Sentence Fluency 5 points	Complete. Clear meaning. Varied. Easy to read. Flowing, interesting word patterns. Natural dialogue. Paragraphs as needed.	Some sentences seem awkward. Most follow a single pattern. Fragments appear to be mistakes. Dialogue seems forced.	Difficult to understand. Choppy. Simplistic word patterns. Unnatural. Disjointed. Monotonous.	
Word Choice 5 points	Interesting. Precise and natural. Words are specific and accurate. Strong images and verbs. Description of multiple senses.	Words are ordinary, but convey message. Meaning comes through, but lacks precision. Some language seems over done.	Limited, vague, or abstract words. Repetitious, monotonous words and worn-out expressions. Few images. Weak verbs.	
Content Total:				
Conventions:				
Grammar 5 points	Correct grammar and word forms.	A few grammatical errors.	Several grammatical errors making it hard to read.	
Punctuation 5 points	Correct punctuation.	Ending punctuation correct, with minor other punctuation errors.	Several punctuation errors making it hard to read.	
Capitalization 5 points	Correct capitalization.	Correct capitalization at beginning of sentences, with minor mistakes on proper nouns.	Several capitalization errors.	
Spelling 5 points	Correct spelling.	Spelling correct on common words and decodable on others.	Spelling makes the writing hard to read.	
Conventions Total:				
Total Score:				

APPENDIX 14

Individual Phonics Summary

Child's Name: _____   Date: _____

Highlight in yellow for missed elements while reading. Highlight in blue for missed elements while writing. Highlight in green for missed elements in both reading and writing. Circle element once the child is able to read and write it correctly.

Consonants	Vowels
Initial Consonants b c d f g h j k l m n p qu r s t v w y z x /z/	Long Vowels a,e,i,o,u, y (/ē/, /ī/)
Final Consonants b d f g k l m n p t x z s /z/ v (followed by e)	Short Vowels a, e, i, o, u, y (/ĭ/) also a in "father" and o in "to"
Initial Blends br cr dr fr gr pr tr thr bl cl fl gl pl sl sc scr sk sm sn sp spl st str squ tw	Vowels with Silent -e a_e, e_e, i_e, o_e, u_e
Final Blends -ct -ld -mp -np -nk -nt -rb –rk –rl –rm -sk –sp	Vowel Digraphs ai, ea, ee, ei, eigh, ey, ie, igh, oa, oo, oe, ou /ŭ/, ow /ō/
Consonant Digraphs th(voiced,voiceless), wh, ch (/ch/,/k/,/sh/), ph, -ng, ck, dge, sh, ti, ci (/sh/) si (/sh/ or /zh/)	Diphthongs oi, oy, ou in ouch, ow in cow Irregular ough /ō/, /oo/, /ŭf/, /ŏf/, /aw/, /ŏw/
Hard and Soft C /c/ /s/	Vocalic –r /er/: er, ir, ur, wor, ear
Hard and Soft G /g/ /j/	-r, -l, and -w controlled vowels /ar/ /or/; /al/ in all, /aw/ in saw, /ew/ in new
Silent Consonants gh, kn, wr, pn, rh, b in lamb, l in could	Past tense –ed /ed/ /d/ /t/
Double consonants following short vowels Double consonants when adding suffixes	Spelling: change y to i when adding suffix.

Comments including patterns of known or unknown phonemes:

APPENDIX 15

Oral Reading Strategy Prompts

Strategy Prompt	When teacher would provide prompt
Wait Time	Be sure to provide wait time before any prompting. Allow the child the opportunity to read to the end of the sentence before prompting.
Look at the pictures and think about the story	Use if the picture, diagram, or the previous content can be used to figure out the unknown words.
Say the beginning three sounds (three was selected because it is more effective than predicting based only on the initial sound, and often more efficient than sounding out the entire word)	Use if child pauses for an extended time or guess based only on the initial sound.
Read on to collect clues	Use if the context of the rest of the sentence would help. Then prompt them to go back.
Go back and read again	Use if the beginning of the sentence or the previous sentence will help.
Break words into parts	Use if they know parts of the word or for multisyllabic words.
Try different sounds	Use when the child is mispronouncing phonemes. If necessary the correct sound can be provided.
Does that make sense?	Use when the child keeps reading after a miscue that doesn't make sense.
Does that look right?	Use when the miscue does not look like the correct word.
Does that sound right?	Use when the miscue is the wrong part of speech.
Where is the tricky part?	Use to help the child monitor when the child keeps reading well after the miscue.
Try that again	Use to indicate there are one or more miscues and child needs to problem solve.
Are you right? How do you know?	Highest Metacognitive Level: Use initially for self-evaluation of reading when child is correct,. Then use for both correct and incorrect reading.
What else can you do?	Use when child was unsuccessful with the first strategy.
Summarize what you read	Use to check comprehension of reading.

8

Interpretation of APD Test Results

Teri James Bellis
The University of South Dakota

Interpretation of APD test results may be undertaken for a variety of purposes. There-fore, the goal of the testing first must be taken into account. If the goal of testing is to determine presence versus absence of disorder, that is, to diagnose APD, then the eval-uation results should meet a specified diagnostic criterion. Furthermore, only those tests that have been shown to exhibit good sensitivity and specificity for disorders of the central auditory nervous system (CANS), as discussed in chapter 4, should be uti-lized for diagnostic purposes. Finally, it should always be kept in mind that, because APD is fundamentally an auditory-based deficit, audiologists are the professionals who diagnose APD (ASHA, 2004a, 2005a,b).

Test results should also be interpreted with an eye toward *differential* diagnosis. This requires input from a variety of modalities and disciplines to ensure that the auditory deficits noted on central auditory testing are not reflective of a higher-order, more global cognitive, multimodality, or related disorder. Central auditory test results should never be interpreted in a vacuum, as there exist many other disorders that will affect processing across modalities and result in abnormal findings on tests of APD. Instead, data regarding functioning across modalities should be viewed together.

A final goal of interpretation of APD test results is to determine the nature of the individual child's disorder so that a deficit-specific intervention and management pro-gram may be developed. Analysis of the child's performance on central auditory tests can provide information related to specific auditory processes and behaviors affected, as well as possible site-of-dysfunction within the CANS. When taken together with ad-ditional functional information, an overall picture of the child's patterns of strengths and weaknesses may be obtained. According to the American Speech-Language-Hearing Association's preferred Practices statement, speech-language pathologists (SLPs) collaborate in the overall assessment of children suspected of APD, as well as providing intervention in those cases in which speech, language, or related dys-function is present (ASHA, 2004b). Specifically, the SLP is uniquely qualified to delin-eate the cognitive-communication and/or language-related difficulties that may be associated with APD in a given individual. Similarly, information gleaned from psychologists, educators, physicians, and related professionals will provide important means of determining the real-world impact of APD and of developing individualized, ecologically valid treatment plans.

This chapter discusses the interpretation of APD test results for diagnostic and differential diagnostic purposes, as well as for the determination of the nature of the deficit so that development of individualized, deficit-specific, and ecologically valid intervention plans can be better guided.

DIAGNOSTIC CRITERIA FOR APD

As previously stated, the audiologist is the professional who diagnoses APD, and he or she does so using behavioral and physiologic tests of central auditory function that have been shown to be sensitive to dysfunction in the CANS. In its purest form, the purpose of diagnosis is simply to determine whether a disorder is present—a task that seems, on the face of it, easily accomplished merely by noting whether a given child's performance is "normal" or "abnormal." However, there is some controversy regarding the specific criteria for abnormality that should be adopted when interpreting results of central auditory diagnostic testing.

Some approaches to APD diagnosis recommend an absolute or norm-based interpretation construct. In other words, a child's performance on specific tests of central auditory function is compared to normative values and a discrete cut-off, usually expressed in terms of standard deviations (SD) below the mean, is selected for the determination of abnormality. However, this approach to APD diagnosis is problematic for several reasons. The use of norms for test interpretation is predicated on several assumptions, including that adequate normative groups have been sampled and that the data are normally distributed. Although general guidelines for age-specific normative values have been published for some of the more commonly used tests of central auditory function (see Bellis, 2003), most of these tests have not undergone standardization on a large group of normal control subjects. Even if adequate standardization has been completed and the data have been found to be normally distributed, one must recognize the implications of the choice of a specific cut-off value in which a difference of just 1 or 2% on a given test might classify a child as abnormal versus normal. For example, in the normal distribution, 16% of normals fall below 1 SD from the mean, and 2% fall below 2 SD. As such, no matter what cut-off is chosen, there is always some element of risk of making an error in which a normal child will be classified as abnormal (false alarm) or vice versa (miss). The more lax the criterion for abnormality is (e.g., 1.5 SD versus 2 SD), the greater is the likelihood that a false alarm error will be made. Therefore, it seems appropriate to question whether the use of comparisons against normative data alone represents the best approach to central auditory test interpretation and diagnosis (e.g., Bellis, 2002b, 2003; Jerger & Musiek, 2002).

Instead, it may be more useful to use the child as his or her own control by employing both intra- and inter-test analysis procedures for determination of abnormality. For example, in cases of symmetrical hearing sensitivity, the presence of clear ear differences that are greater than would be expected for age argues for a central, rather than peripheral, site of dysfunction. It also suggests that observed performance deficits are less likely to be due to attention, motivation, and related issues, as these confounds tend to affect performance in general, regardless of ear. Similarly, the presence of hemispheric differences (or electrode effects) on physiologic tests in which bilaterally symmetrical electrophysiologic activity would be expected would support a diagnosis of APD. Scatter across measures in which performance on one or more tests or under specific acoustic conditions is poor whereas performance on others is good also would suggest the presence of specific auditory deficit(s). As a general rule, global factors involving attention, motivation, and other higher-level functional issues typically will affect performance across measures, with no clear pattern of performance emerging from intra- and inter-test analysis. In addition, many physiologic measures of neural representation of auditory stimuli in the CANS often are normal in cases of higher-level, global deficits or confounds as well.

Another issue related to determination of abnormal versus normal performance is the number of tests that should be affected before a child's performance can be classified as "abnormal." According to ASHA (2005b), a diagnosis of APD should be enabled only when failure (often defined as > 2 SD below the mean) occurs on at least two tests of central auditory function. In addition, the audiologist should monitor for inconsistencies in performance across tests (e.g., left-ear deficit on one task accompanied by a right-ear deficit on another task) that might signal the presence of a nonauditory confound rather than an APD. Finally, for failure on one test to be considered sufficient support for an APD diagnosis, performance should exceed 3 SD below the mean and should be accompanied by significant functional difficulties. In these cases, it is always prudent to re-administer same test as well as another test that measures the same or similar process to confirm the finding (ASHA, 2005b).

As will be discussed later in this chapter, this author advocates an approach to diagnosis in which both norm-based and inter-/intra-test performance on behavioral and physiologic tests of central auditory function is analyzed for interpretation purposes. Results are examined for patterns that are consistent with dysfunction in specific auditory process(es) and/or neuroanatomical regions, and are related to multidisciplinary and multimodal measures for purposes of differential diagnosis.

DIFFERENTIAL DIAGNOSIS OF APD

One aspect critical to diagnosis of any disorder is the concomitant ruling out of other disorders. The term *differential diagnosis* refers to the differentiation among two or more disorders that have similar symptoms associated with them. There are many disorders that can mimic APD in some of their behavioral characteristics and that can lead to poor performance on behavioral tests of central auditory function, including but not limited to attention deficit hyperactivity disorder (ADHD), language processing disorders, autism, and mental retardation. To avoid misdiagnosis of these disorders as APD, attention must be paid to methods of differentially diagnosing APD.

The way in which APD is differentiated from other disorders will be determined by the manner in which APD is defined. Most definitions of APD emphasize the modality-specific nature of the disorder; that is, APD is a deficit that is specific to the processing of auditory information (e.g., Jerger & Musiek, 2000). These definitions have led some to assert that, for a diagnosis of APD to be enabled, one must demonstrate the presence of a disorder in the auditory system and nowhere else. Thus, demonstration of test validity and differential diagnosis of APD would require that poor performance on tests of central auditory function not be accompanied by or correlate with poor performance on similar tests in other modalities (Cacace & McFarland, 2002). This expectation of complete modality specificity of APD, combined with the lack of evidence in support of the existence of completely modality-specific auditory disorders, has led some to question the very existence of APD as a viable diagnostic entity (e.g., Cacace & McFarland, 1998; McFarland & Cacace, 1995).

However, current research regarding information processing in the brain suggests that there are few, if any, completely modality-specific neuroanatomical areas. Instead, complex, interactive networks influence the processing of basic sensory input (e.g., Calvert et al., 1997). For example, processing of basic, lower-level acoustic cues involving temporal and spectral aspects of the auditory signal is influenced greatly by higher-order factors such as linguistic experience and familiarity with the speech sounds of the language (e.g., Goldstone, 1994; Groenen, 1997; Salasoo & Pisoni, 1995). Neurophysiologic substrates of even the most fundamental auditory processing include nonprimary, subcortical regions that are multimodal in nature (e.g., Kraus et al.. 1994). Even the primary auditory cortex is not immune to multimodality influence, as it has been shown that visual input can alter the auditory cortical responses to sound (e.g., Mottonen, Schurmann, & Sams, 2004; Sams et al., 1991). Because of the complex interaction among primary and nonprimary systems and pathways throughout the CANS, it is not surprising that individuals with auditory temporal processing deficits may also exhibit discrete temporal processing deficits in other modalities (e.g., Tallal, Miller, & Fitch, 1993), or that aging adults who exhibit a significant decline in auditory interhemispheric abilities would also exhibit poor performance on visual–motor interhemispheric tasks reliant on the same or adjacent neurophysiologic regions (e.g., Bellis & Wilber, 2001). These and other findings cast doubts on the ecological validity of any definition of APD that assumes pure modality specificity of all auditory processing deficits as such definitions, quite simply, do not reflect the way auditory processing occurs in the real world. However, at present, most diagnostic frameworks for APD do not provide for examination of performance in other modalities. Thus, the potential comorbidity of disruptions in other sensory modalities is typically never addressed.

Therefore, this author advocates for a definition of APD that acknowledges both the heterogeneity of APDs and the potential for concomitant disorders in other modalities while, at the same time, emphasizing the auditory-specific nature of the APD itself. The focus in differential diagnosis shifts to disentangling the auditory-specific component from those that may exist at higher processing levels or in other modalities, rather than being solely on demonstrating the modality specificity of the disorder (Bellis, 2003; Jerger & Musiek, 2000).

This requires that APD not be evaluated or diagnosed in a vacuum. Instead, to differentially diagnose APD, information from other modalities and higher-level processing areas must be taken into account during the diagnostic process, and performance on analogous tasks in other sensory modalities should be examined (Ross & Bellis, 2005). At the same time, tests of central auditory function used to demonstrate the presence and nature of the auditory deficit(s) must employ appropriate psychophysical methods and control for higher-level linguistic, memory, attention, and related confounds, as discussed in chapter 4. Thus, because complete assessment of multimodality function is not within the Scope of practice of any one discipline or profession, differential diagnosis of APD from other, similar disorders requires multidisciplinary input.

It is this author's view that, for a diagnosis of APD to be enabled, it must be shown that (a) an auditory deficit exists in one or more specific auditory processes that *cannot reasonably be attributed to* higher-order, more global cognitive (e.g., memory, attention), language, or related confounds; (b) intra- and inter-test performance *patterns* exist that are consistent with well-established neurophysiologic tenets regarding dysfunction in specific brain regions; and (c) the observed deficits are accompanied by functional, real-world listening or related difficulties and complaints (Bellis 2002a,b, 2003; Bellis & Ferre, 1999). By using this multifaceted diagnostic construct, the audiologist is able both to identify the presence and nature of an APD as well as to determine the relative contribution of other, nonauditory factors to a child's test performance. Finally, this diagnostic construct sets the stage for the development of individualized, deficit-specific, ecologically valid intervention plans that will address the specific child's areas of difficulty.

DETERMINING THE NATURE OF THE AUDITORY DEFICIT(S)

Although the primary goal of diagnosis is to demonstrate the presence of a disorder, it is important that the nature of the disorder be examined so that deficit-specific intervention can occur. It should be emphasized that APD is a heterogeneous disorder and may impact functioning in a variety of ways. As discussed in chapter 4, auditory processing may be decomposed into several measurable auditory behaviors, each of which are presumed to underlie more complex, real-world listening and related behaviors. Therefore, the first step in determining the nature of the APD that is present in a given child is to identify the specific auditory processes that are impacted adversely. Although physiologic tests of central auditory function are instrumental in providing objective evidence of the presence of dysfunction in the CANS in some cases of APD, this author has found that only behavioral audiologic tests for APD provide the type and breadth of qualitative information necessary to shed light on the functional nature of the auditory deficit. Thus, this section will focus on process-based interpretation of behavioral tests of central auditory function.

Binaural Separation and Binaural Integration Deficits

Binaural Separation is the ability to attend to one ear while ignoring competing stimuli presented to the other ear, whereas Binaural Integration is the ability to attend to auditory information presented to both ears simultaneously. Both of these abilities are important for hearing and understanding speech in noisy environments. For example, the child with deficits in these areas may exhibit difficulty hearing the teacher when a fellow student is rattling papers or whispering nearby. Similarly, the ability to listen to two speakers at once, which is sometimes required during group discussions, may be impacted adversely by dysfunction in these behaviors. Performance deficits on dichotic speech tests that require report of one ear (Binaural Separation, e.g., Competing Sentences Test) and/or both ears (Binaural Integration, e.g., Dichotic Digits) are characteristic of this type of auditory disorder.

Monaural Separation/Auditory Closure Deficits

The hallmark of an Auditory Closure deficit is the inability to "fill in" the missing pieces of a message when portions of the input are distorted, obscured by noise, or otherwise degraded. Therefore, as with the previous auditory behaviors discussed, this behavior is important for speech understanding in backgrounds of noise or in other communicative situations in which the auditory signal is less than clear. Children with a deficit in this area will typically exhibit poor performance on tests of monaural low-redundancy speech (e.g., low-pass filtered speech, time-compressed speech) and speech-in-noise tests. However, as emphasized in chapter 4, it is important to recognize that poor performance on tests of speech-in-noise may be seen in a variety of auditory and nonauditory disorders; therefore, a finding of speech-in-noise difficulty should not, in and of itself, be considered diagnostic for APD.

Auditory Patterning/Temporal Ordering Deficits

Auditory pattern recognition and ordering is a complex skill requiring discrimination among auditory signals as well as the ability to sequence the signals over time. This skill is fundamental to speech understanding, which requires both discrimination and ordering of phonemes and words for comprehension of linguistic *content* as well as recognition of acoustic contours that underlie prosody, or the rhythm, stress, and intonational cues that express communicative *intent*. Tests such as Frequency Patterns and/or Duration Patterns tap the process of Auditory Patterning/Temporal Ordering.

Auditory Discrimination Deficits

For speech to be understood, the spectro-temporal acoustic components of the auditory signal must first be discriminated and recognized. Poor performance on tests of speech and nonspeech discrimination, including frequency, intensity, and duration difference limens, phoneme discrimination tasks, and similar measures, provide evidence for a deficit in Auditory Discrimination. Children with Auditory Discrimination deficits may confuse similar-sounding phonemes and words, or they may have difficulty distinguishing nonspeech, prosodic elements of the speech signal, leading to frequent misunderstandings. In addition, Auditory Discrimination is a fundamental element of most of the other auditory behaviors discussed in this section; therefore, children with Auditory Discrimination deficits may exhibit poor performance on other behavioral audiologic tests of central auditory function.

Binaural Interaction (Sound Localization and Lateralization) Deficits

Sound Localization and Lateralization, along with other binaural interaction abilities, are two skills that appear to be important fundamentals for understanding speech in noise, as the source of the auditory signal first must be located. Children with deficits in these areas may exhibit abnormal Masking Level Differences (MLDs) as well as poor performance on tasks requiring acute localization. It should be remembered that there is a paucity of good commercially available binaural interaction tests today; therefore, this ability often is regrettably overlooked in central auditory assessment.

Temporal Processing Deficits

In chapter 4, it was emphasized that temporal processing underlies virtually every auditory behavior and all APDs likely have some form of temporal processing deficit at their core. Timing is critical in the auditory system, whether it be relative timing of information arrival to the two hemispheres or ability to resolve acoustic signals that occur rapidly in time. Therefore, deficits in discrete temporal processing areas such as temporal integration, gap detection or auditory fusion, and related abilities may be associated with speech and nonspeech discrimination difficulties, binaural separation and integration problems, temporal patterning deficits, and binaural interaction dysfunction. More research is needed to delineate the relationship between specific types of temporal processing deficits and functional sequelae as well as to develop user-friendly, commercially available tests of temporal processing.

ANALYZING PATTERNS IN CENTRAL AUDITORY TESTS RESULTS

Once the deficit(s) are identified, it is important to examine the overall test findings for intra- and inter-test patterns that are consistent with what is known about effects of dysfunction in various brain regions on behavioral tests of central auditory function. Although most children with APD do not exhibit organic lesions in the CANS per se, pattern analysis of test findings can be a useful guide to test battery interpretation for several reasons. First, the presence of a clear pattern across performance areas assists in increasing confidence in the test findings themselves. It also helps to rule out the possibility of attention, motivation, cognitive, or other higher-order, more global confound in that these types of deficits typically do not yield specific patterns consistent with CANS dysfunction. Instead, attention and related confounds tend to result in one of four possible findings: (a) normal performance on all tests, (b) abnormal performance on all tests, (c) abnormal performance on some tests with no clear pattern consistent with CANS dysfunction emerging, or (d) inconsistent performance across and within tests.

Each of the processing areas discussed above is relatively more reliant on different mechanisms, levels, and loci within the CANS. Thus, the child who exhibits difficulty in all of these processing areas would, therefore, be exhibiting deficits in virtually all brain regions at all levels of processing. This finding would argue strongly for a more global disorder—or perhaps even poor motivation—rather than an APD. On the other hand, the child who exhibits a pattern of deficits that is consistent with those seen in confirmed cases of CANS dysfunction is more likely to be exhibiting a true APD. Therefore, it behooves the clinician to be familiar with the types of patterns that, based on well-established neuroscience research, occur with dysfunction in specific brain regions. Audiologists should be cautioned, however, that most children with APD do not exhibit frank lesions of the CANS pathways; therefore, these patterns are to be used as guides only. In addition, isolated processing deficits can and do occur in many cases of APD, which result in significant difficulty on one test or in one processing area, accompanied by functional difficulties in real-world communicative situations reliant on that specific process or behavior. For a more comprehensive discussion of neurophysiologic mechanisms underlying various auditory processes, readers are referred to Bellis (2003).

Left-Hemisphere Dysfunction

The left hemisphere of the brain is considered to be language-dominant in the majority of both right- and left-handed individuals. As such, this area of the brain is instrumental in fine-grained auditory discrimination, especially speech–sound discrimination, temporal processing, and auditory closure. The pattern on behavioral tests of central auditory function that is typically associated with left-hemisphere, primary auditory cortex dysfunction is that of poor performance on tests of monaural low-redundancy speech (auditory closure) and bilateral or right-ear deficit on dichotic speech tasks. In some cases, poor performance may also be noted on Frequency and Duration Patterns testing in the linguistic labeling condition only, as this ability is influenced by left-hemisphere integrity. In addition, fine-grained temporal processing often is disrupted, resulting in elevated gap detection thresholds as well as speech–sound discrimination difficulties. Localization of sound sources in the right auditory field also may be compromised. Typically, left-hemisphere dysfunction that occurs in association cortex areas, such as those seen in cases of receptive (or Wernicke's) aphasia, will lead to right-ear or bilateral deficit on dichotic speech tasks and bilateral deficits on Frequency or Duration Patterns testing in the linguistic labeling report condition. Performance on tests of auditory closure and fine-grained temporal processing often is normal in these cases.

Right-Hemisphere Dysfunction

The primary auditory functions of the right (or non-language-dominant) hemisphere relate to part-to-whole synthesis, sequencing of auditory events, and perception of the melodic aspects of speech that make up speech prosody. The pattern that is typically seen on behavioral tests of central auditory function in cases of right-hemisphere dysfunction is that of left-ear deficit on dichotic speech tasks accompanied by poor performance on Frequency and/or Duration Patterns in both the linguistic labeling and humming conditions. Nonspeech–sound discrimination abilities also may be poor. Typically, performance is normal on tests of monaural low-redundancy speech, speech–sound discrimination, and fine-grained temporal processing.

Interhemispheric Dysfunction

The interhemispheric pathways, most notably the corpus callosum, have been implicated in a wide variety of auditory and nonauditory abilities, including the linking of emotional, prosodic aspects of communication with linguistic content (Klouda et al., 1988); speech perception in noise and other aspects of binaural hearing (Hoptman & Davidson, 1994; Springer & Gazzaniga, 1975); bimanual coordination abilities (Jeeves et al., 1988; Sauerwein et al., 1981); and visuospatial and visuoperceptual skills (Trevarthen & Sperry, 1973). In fact, integrity of interhemispheric pathways is critical for virtually any activity that requires the two hemispheres of the brain to work together.

The classic pattern found on behavioral tests of central auditory function that is characteristic of interhemispheric (corpus callosum) dysfunction is that of left-ear deficit on dichotic speech tasks combined with poor performance on Frequency and/or Duration Patterns in the linguistic labeling condition *only*. Typically, performance on tests of monaural low-redundancy speech, temporal patterning in the nonverbal report condition, and binaural interaction is not affected. Localization abilities may also be disrupted in cases of interhemispheric dysfunction, as communication between the cerebral hemispheres is important for the development of the concept of auditory space and direction.

Brainstem Dysfunction

Brainstem dysfunction typically results in ipsilateral ear deficits in performance, elevated MLDs, and, in some cases, poor performance on other tests of binaural interaction (e.g., Binaural Fusion). Localization and lateralization may be disrupted, and unilateral findings may be seen on tests in which bilateral symmetry typically is expected (e.g., monaural low-redundancy speech tests, speech-in-noise tests, temporal processing tests). As a general rule, this author recommends that auditory brainstem response (ABR) testing be conducted in all cases of suspected brainstem dysfunction, and medical follow-up for possible space-occupying lesion or other condition requiring medical or surgical intervention be conducted immediately. Behavioral test findings consistent with left-hemisphere, right-hemisphere, interhemispheric, and brainstem auditory dysfunction are summarized in Table 8.1.

Determining the nature of the auditory deficits will provide guidance as to specific auditory training activities that may be indicated for a particular child with APD, and pattern analysis of the findings will assist in enhancing confidence in the test results as well as differential diagnosis endeavors. However, in order to fully understand the myriad ramifications of the auditory deficit(s) and to develop a comprehensive management and intervention program, it is necessary to go one step further by examining the relationship between the auditory deficits identified and the child's functional complaints and difficulties in everyday communicative and learning situations.

TABLE 8.1
Effects of Neurophysiologic Site of Dysfunction on Central Auditory Test Performance

Site of Dysfunction	Central Auditory Test Findings
Left Hemisphere, Primary Auditory Cortex	Bilateral or right-ear deficit on dichotic speech tasks Bilateral or right-ear deficit on tests of monaural separation/auditory closure *Possible* deficit on auditory patterning/ temporal ordering tests in linguistic labeling report condition Fine-grained temporal processing deficits (e.g., gap detection) Poor speech–sound discrimination
Left Hemisphere, Association Cortex	Bilateral or right-ear deficit on dichotic speech tasks Possible deficit on auditory patterning/ temporal ordering tests in linguistic labeling report condition
Right Hemisphere	Left-ear deficit on dichotic speech tasks Deficit on auditory patterning/temporal ordering tests in BOTH labeling and humming conditions Poor nonspeech discrimination
Interhemispheric Dysfunction	Left-ear deficit on dichotic speech tasks Deficit on auditory patterning/temporal ordering tests in linguistic labeling condition ONLY Possible deficit on localization tasks and speech-in-noise tests
Brainstem Dysfunction	Possible ipsilateral ear deficits on most/all tests Elevated Masking Level Differences (MLD) Deficit on binaural interaction tests Poor localization/lateralization and speech-in-noise abilities

RELATING AUDITORY FINDINGS TO FUNCTIONAL SEQUELE

Our current conceptualization of APD asserts that these auditory disorders can lead to or be associated with a variety of learning, language, and communication difficulties. However, because of the heterogeneity of APDs and the unique higher-order abilities and capacities that each individual child possesses, it is often difficult to demonstrate a precise one-to-one correlation between discrete auditory deficits and higher-order learning and related function. Put quite simply, different auditory deficits may impact different children in different ways. This may be one reason why some researchers have failed to find a significant predictive relationship between discrete measures of auditory processing and higher-order abilities such as reading and spelling (e.g., Watson & Kidd, 2002).

Several models have been proposed that link central auditory test findings to learning, language, and communication sequelae. One such theoretical model is the Bellis/Ferre Model of APD (Bellis, 1996, 2002a, 2002b, 2003; Bellis & Ferre, 1999). In this model, subtypes of APD are delineated in which neurophysiologically tenable patterns of auditory deficits are related to concomitant functional difficulties. The model is based on a vast body of literature in the general and cognitive neurosciences, auditory neuroscience, and neuropsychology that supports the existence of patterns of performance deficits consistent with dysfunction in various brain regions. It should be emphasized that the Bellis/Ferre Model, like all models of APD, is theoretical in nature and has yet to be empirically validated. Furthermore, this model is not intended to provide a lock-stepped, cookie-cutter approach to APD diagnostics, nor is it intended to suggest that all children will fit cleanly into one of the APD subtypes proposed. Instead, the model is offered as a guidance tool to assist clinicians in examining information from central auditory and multidisciplinary evaluations for performance patterns that are consistent with well-established neuroscience tenets. The model emphasizes the development of functional deficit profiles for use in both diagnostic and deficit-specific intervention endeavors.

The Bellis/Ferre Model consists of three primary subtypes of APD, corresponding to patterns consistent with left-hemisphere, right-hemisphere, and interhemispheric dysfunction. Each of the three primary subtypes yields a different pattern of performance on central auditory testing as well as different functional learning, language, and communication sequelae. Two additional, secondary subtypes have also been proposed; however, these secondary subtypes likely reflect higher-order language and attention-based deficits and, thus, probably would not accurately be considered subtypes of APD. Nevertheless, because both of the secondary subtypes are associated with auditory complaints, auditory-based intervention often is indicated, and they are included in the model for that purpose alone.

Again, it should be emphasized that the three primary profiles suggested by the Bellis/Ferre Model are not the only manners in which APD can manifest itself. Isolated deficits that impact performance on just one diagnostic test or in just one auditory area also can exist, and brainstem dysfunction is not, at present, considered in the model. These profiles can occur singularly or in combination; however, one profile is typically primary and the combinations usually arise from anatomically adjacent brain areas. If a child or adult exhibits deficits in all auditory processes assessed, or a combination of all three profiles, one should consider the possibility of a more global, higher-order cognitive, memory, attention, or related disorder rather than APD being the primary contributing factor to his or her difficulties. The three primary subtypes of the Bellis/Ferre Model are Auditory Decoding Deficit, Prosodic Deficit, and Integration Deficit.

Auditory Decoding Deficit

Auditory Decoding Deficit is perhaps the "purest" and most auditory-modality-specific of the three primary APD subtypes included in the Bellis/Ferre Model. Characterized by primary deficits in Monaural Separation/Auditory Closure and speech–sound discrimination abilities, children with Auditory Decoding Deficit often appear as though they have hearing loss even when peripheral hearing sensitivity is normal, especially in noisy or reverberant listening environments or when speech is distorted or degraded, as when listening to heavily accented speakers. Secondary sequelae associated with Auditory Decoding Deficit include reading and spelling difficulties; however, these difficulties are usually confined to phonological decoding (or word attack) skills and it is theorized that reading and spelling difficulties are reflections of poor phonological (speech–sound) representation at the cortical level. Therefore, Auditory Decoding Deficit likely interferes with the "sound" portion of the sound–symbol association needed for reading and spelling. Children with Auditory Decoding Deficit may also exhibit poor vocabulary and other language-based concerns. They may complain of auditory fatigue, especially in challenging listening environments, and they usually benefit significantly from the addition of visual or multimodality cues and from methods of enhancing the signal-to-noise ratio via assistive listening devices or other means. Other characteristics of Auditory Decoding Deficit include Verbal poorer than Performance IQ on cognitive testing, better performance in nonlanguage-based classes (e.g., math calculation), difficulty learning a foreign language, good sight word reading skills, and preserved visual–spatial processing. Phonological deficits may be present, and idiosyncratic speech errors typically involve substitutions and/or omissions of speech sounds (usually consonants) that are very similar acoustically.

Diagnostically, Auditory Decoding Deficit yields a pattern of poor performance on monaural tests of degraded speech and binaural or right-ear deficits on dichotic speech tests. Speech–sound discrimination abilities are typically deficient, especially for phonemes that involve rapidly changing spectrotemporal acoustic features (e.g., stop consonants). Fine-grained temporal processing (e.g., gap detection, auditory fusion) may be disrupted as well. Electrophysiologically, individuals with Auditory Decoding Deficit may exhibit reduced cortical response amplitudes over left-hemisphere recording sites, especially in response to speech stimuli. Overall, the pattern of findings on central auditory and multidisciplinary assessment tools argues for a left-hemisphere, primary auditory cortex site of dysfunction in Auditory Decoding Deficit.

Prosodic Deficit

Also referred to as right-hemisphere APD, Prosodic Deficit is characterized by difficulty processing the prosodic elements of speech that allow a listener to gauge communicative intent. Children with Prosodic Deficit often exhibit problems understanding what is *meant* in relation to what is *said*. Put another way, Prosodic Deficit interferes with perception of the *intent* rather than the *content* of the message, leading to difficulties comprehending subtle communication forms such as sarcasm and humor. Typically, hearing in noise and other binaural abilities are good in cases of Prosodic Deficit because auditory closure and discrimination abilities, performance with degraded acoustic signals, and related skills are preserved.

Secondary sequelae often associated with Prosodic Deficit may include poor pragmatics or social communication skills, and poor music or singing skills. Speaking and reading voices may be somewhat monotonic or lack appropriate affect and intonation. Children with Prosodic Deficit frequently exhibit reading and spelling difficulties confined to right-hemisphere-based, Gestalt patterning, sight-word abilities; however, phonological decoding (word attack) skills are typically intact. Thus, Prosodic Deficit likely interferes with the *symbol* portion of sound–symbol association. Other right-hemisphere-related sequelae may be present as well, including difficulties with sequencing information, topic maintenance, mathematics calculation, and visual–spatial tasks. Performance (or nonverbal) IQ is often lower than verbal IQ. It should be emphasized that these cross-modality difficulties are not attributed to the auditory deficit per se, but rather are thought to coexist with right-hemisphere-based auditory findings because of shared neuroanatomical regions. Therefore, Prosodic Deficit may be more accurately conceptualized as the auditory manifestation of right-hemisphere involvement, rather than as a purely isolated auditory-specific deficit unaccompanied by difficulties in other modalities. The auditory findings in Prosodic Deficit represent merely one aspect of the greater constellation of difficulties that characterize right-hemisphere dysfunction.

On diagnostic tests of central auditory function, children with Prosodic Deficit usually exhibit a pattern of poor performance on duration and/or frequency patterns testing in *both* the humming and labeling report conditions, suggesting difficulty with auditory pattern perception and sequencing combined with a left-ear deficit on dichotic speech tests. Frequency, duration, and intensity difference limens also may be elevated, and localization of sounds in the contralateral (i.e., left) auditory field may be impacted. On physiologic measures, Prosodic Deficit may yield smaller auditory cortical responses recorded over the right hemisphere. Typically, performance on tests of monaural low-redundancy speech, fine-grained temporal processing, speech–sound discrimination, and similar measures more reliant on left-hemisphere integrity is within normal limits.

Integration Deficit

Integration Deficit is conceptualized as the auditory manifestation of inefficient communication between the two cerebral hemispheres, most likely related to corpus callosum dysfunction. Children with Integration Deficit may have difficulty with any task that requires interhemispheric cooperation. Thus, the functional impact of this deficit is quite heterogeneous. From an auditory perspective, children with Integration Deficit tend to exhibit difficulties in binaural skills such as tracking moving sound sources, understanding speech in noise, and linking the linguistic (speech–sound and related) content with communicative (prosodic) intent for purposes of understanding the whole message, especially when forms such as sarcasm are used in which the tone of voice may not match the actual linguistic content of the message. Reading and spelling difficulties may exist in which children have difficulty linking the orthographic symbol on the page with its corresponding speech sound (i.e., the *association* portion of sound–symbol association). Performance and verbal IQ scores may be equal; however, scatter may be seen across subtests with poorer performance in those tasks that are more interhemispheric in nature. Subtle deficits may exist in bimanual coordination skills and other abilities requiring interhemispheric integration; however, the auditory deficits are typically primary. Finally, children with Integration Deficit may actually perform more poorly when visual or multimodality cues are added in an attempt to augment auditorily presented information.

As discussed previously, the classic pattern of central auditory test findings characteristic of corpus callosum dysfunction is that of left-ear deficit on dichotic speech tasks, combined with poor performance on tests of temporal patterning *in the linguistic labeling condition only* (performance in the humming condition is not affected). Typically, performance on discrete temporal resolution (e.g., gap detection) and auditory discrimination tasks, along with auditory closure tasks involving monaural low-redundancy speech, is within normal limits as well; however, speech-in-noise often is affected adversely, as is the case with most APDs. Physiologically, children with Integration Deficit may exhibit atypical hemispheric asymmetry in auditory cortical event-related potentials involving speech stimuli or dichotically presented stimuli; however, standard evoked potential findings are usually normal. The central auditory test findings and functional sequelae of Auditory Decoding Deficit, Prosodic Deficit, and Integration Deficit are summarized in Table 8.2.

It was mentioned previously that the Bellis/Ferre Model also includes two secondary subtypes. The first secondary subtype, Associative Deficit, yields a pattern of deficit on central auditory tests that is suggestive of left-hemisphere involvement (i.e., right-ear or bilateral deficit on dichotic speech tasks). However, other measures of discrete auditory processing, including auditory closure, temporal processing, auditory discrimination, and related tasks, are typically normal, suggesting intact primary auditory cortex function. It is possible that the dichotic listening findings are due to auditory association cortex involvement and, indeed, a similar pattern is often seen in aphasic adults following left-hemisphere stroke in association cortex (or Wernicke's area). As such, Associative Deficit may be more accurately conceptualized as a language disorder and this deficit's functional manifestations typically consist of symptoms that are associated with receptive language deficit.

Output-Organization Deficit, the other secondary subtype, is characterized by difficulty organizing responses to auditory information or instructions, especially complex auditory input. Children with Output-Organization Deficit typically exhibit difficulty on any central auditory task that requires report of more than two critical elements, regardless of task. In addition, Output-Organization Deficit often includes significant difficulty hearing in noise, which may require specific auditory-based management and intervention recommendations. Because no true performance pattern consistent with a specific neurophysiologic region of dysfunction occurs with Output-Organization Deficit, it is most likely that this deficit reflects more of an attention-related or executive function disorder. Indeed, Campbell (2003) demonstrated that children diagnosed with ADHD often exhibit performance findings consistent with Output-Organization Deficit, casting doubt on the appropriateness of its inclusion in a model of APD. However, abnormal contralateral acoustic reflexes and contralateral otoacoustic emission suppression have also been reported in selected cases of Output-Organization Deficit, suggesting that there may be an auditory efferent component to this disorder in some instances. More research is needed to explore this issue more fully.

SUMMARY

In this chapter, several methods of interpreting central auditory test results have been discussed. Audiologists have available to them a number of avenues for identifying the presence of an auditory deficit, including norm-based interpretation and analysis of inter- and intra-test and cross-disciplinary performance for purposes of examining

TABLE 8.2

Summary of the Primary Subtypes Included in the Bellis/Ferre Model of APD

Subtype	Presumed Site of Dysfunction	Auditory and Associated Symptoms
Auditory Decoding Deficit	Primary auditory cortex (left hemisphere)	Difficulties in speech–sound discrimination, speech-in-noise, reading and spelling (word attack skills), foreign language learning, phonological awareness. May complain of auditory fatigue in challenging listening environments. Verbal poorer than performance IQ. Preserved sight-word reading skills, visual–spatial processing, and nonlanguage-based abilities (e.g., math calculation). Benefit from addition of visual or multimodality cues.
Prosodic Deficit	Right hemisphere	Difficulties in comprehension of prosodic elements of speech, reading and spelling (sight word skills), pragmatics. Speaking or reading voice may be monotonic. Associated right-hemisphere symptoms include math calculation and visuo-spatial difficulties, difficulties with topic maintenance, poor sequencing abilities. Performance IQ may be poorer than Verbal IQ.
Integration Deficit	Corpus callosum	Difficulties in any task requiring interhemispheric cooperation, including linking linguistic and prosodic elements of speech, understanding speech in noise, and reading/spelling (association of written symbol with corresponding speech sound). Performance IQ and verbal IQ equal, with deficits in task-specific areas. Bimanual coordination and other interhemispheric difficulties may be present, but auditory deficits are primary. Addition of visual or multimodality cues may confuse rather than clarify.

data for neurophysiologically tenable patterns of performance. Identification of the specific auditory process(es) that are deficient is important for developing deficit-specific treatment plans, as is relating auditory deficit(s) to functional language, learning, and communication symptoms and complaints. Finally, subtyping models like the Bellis/Ferre Model of APD may be useful guides in linking central auditory test findings to both the underlying neurophysiology and the functional sequelae. For a more in-depth treatment of the topics discussed in this chapter and the science underlying process-based and site-of-dysfunction interpretation of APD test results, as well as subtyping methods, readers are referred to Bellis (2002a, 2003).

ACKNOWLEDGMENTS

The author would like to thank Jody Ross and Desirae Steffen Vobr for their invaluable assistance in the preparation of chapters 4 and 8.

REFERENCES

American Speech-Language-Hearing Association. (2004a). Scope of practice in audiology. *ASHA*. Suppl. no. 24.

American Speech-Language-Hearing Association. (2004b). Preferred practice patterns for the profession of speech-language pathology. Available: http://www.asha.org/members/deskref-journals/deskref/default.

American Speech-Language-Hearing Association. (2005a). (Central) auditory processing disorders— The role of the audiologist [Position Statement]. Available: http://www.asha.org/members/deskref-journals/deskref/default.

American Speech-Language-Hearing Association. (2005b). (Central) auditory processing disorders [Technical Report]. Available: http://www.asha.org/members/deskref-journals/deskref/default.

Bellis, T. J. (1996). *Assessment and management of central auditory processing disorders in the educational setting: From science to practice*. San Diego: Singular Publishing Group.

Bellis, T. J. (2002a). *When the brain can't hear: Unraveling the mystery of auditory processing disorder*. New York: Pocket Books.

Bellis, T. J. (2002b). Considerations in diagnosing auditory processing disorders in children. *American Speech-Language-Hearing Association Special Interest Division 9 (Hearing and Hearing Disorders in Children)*, 12, 3–9.

Bellis, T. J. (2003). *Assessment and management of central auditory processing disorders in the educational setting: From science to practice* (2nd ed.). Clifton Park, NY: Thomson Learning.

Bellis, T. J., & Ferre, J. M. (1999). Multidimensional approach to the differential diagnosis of central auditory processing disorders in children. *Journal of the American Academy of Audiology*, 10, 319–328.

Bellis, T. J., & Wilber, L. A. (2001). Effects of aging and gender on interhemispheric function. *Journal of Speech, Language, and Hearing Research*, 44, 246–263.

Cacace, A. T., & McFarland, D. J. (1998). Central auditory processing disorder in school-aged children: A critical review. *Journal of Speech, Language, and Hearing Research*, 41, 355–373.

Cacace, A. T., & McFarland, D. J. (2002). Factor analysis in CAPD and the "unimodal" test battery: Do we have a model that will satisfy? *American Journal of Audiology*, 11, 7–9.

Calvert, G. A., Bullmore, E. T., Brammer, M. J., Campbell, R., Williams, S. C. R., McGuire, P. K., Woodruff, P. W. R., Iverson, S. D., & David, A. S. (1997). Activation of auditory cortex during silent lipreading. *Science*, 276, 593–596.

Campbell, N. G. (2003). *The central auditory processing and continuous performance of children with Attention Deficit Hyperactivity Disorder (ADHD) in the medicated and non-medicated state*. Unpublished doctoral dissertation, University of South Africa, Pretoria.

Goldstone, R. L. (1994). Influences of categorization on perceptual discrimination. *Journal of Experimental Psychology*, 123, 178–200.

Groenen, P. (1997). *Central auditory processing disorders: A psycholinguistic approach*. Nijmegen, Netherlands: University Hospital of Nijmegen.

Hoptman, M. J., & Davidson, R. J. (1994). How and why do the two cerebral hemispheres interact? *Psychological Bulletin, 116*, 195–219.

Jeeves, M. A., Silver, P. H., & Milne, A. B. (1988). Role of the corpus callosum in the development of a bimanual motor skill. *Developmental Neuropsychology, 4*, 305–323.

Jerger, J., & Musiek, F. (2000). Report of the consensus conference on the diagnosis of auditory processing disorders in school-aged children. *Journal of the American Academy of Audiology, 11*, 467–474.

Jerger, J., & Musiek, F. (2002). On the diagnosis of auditory processing disorder. *Audiology Today, 14*, 19–21.

Klouda, G. V., Robin, D. A., Graff-Radford, N. R., & Cooper, W. E. (1988). The role of callosal connections in speech prosody. *Brain and Language, 35*, 154–171.

Kraus, N., MGee, T. J., Littman, T., Nicol, T., & King, C. (1994). Nonprimary auditory thalamic representation of acoustic change. *Journal of Neurophysiology, 72*, 1270–1277.

McFarland, D. J., & Cacace, A. T. (1995). Modality specificity as a criterion for diagnosis central auditory processing disorders. *American Journal of Audiology, 4*, 36–48.

Mottonen, R., Schurmann, M., & Sams, M. (2004). Time course of multisensory interactions during audiovisual speech perception in humans: A magnetoencephalographic study. *Neuroscience Letters, 363*, 112–115.

Ross, J. B. M., & Bellis, T. J. (2005, April). Development of visual analogs to central auditory tests. Poster presented at American Academy of Audiology annual convention, Washington, D.C.

Salasoo, A., & Pisoni, D. B. (1995). Interaction of knowledge sources in spoken word identification. *Journal of Memory and Language, 24*, 210–231.

Sams, M., Aulanko, R., Hamalainen, M., Hari, R., Lounasmaa, O. V., Lu, S. T., & Simola, J. (1991). Seeing speech: Visual information from lip movements modifies activity in the human auditory cortex. *Neuroscience Letters, 127*, 141–145.

Sauerwein, H. C., Lassonde, M. C., Cardu, B., & Geoffrey, G. (1981). Interhemispheric integration of sensory and motor functions in agenesis of the corpus callosum. *Neuropsychologia, 19*, 445–454.

Springer, S., & Gazzaniga, M. (1975). Dichotic testing of partial and complete split-brain patients. *Neuropsychologia, 13*, 341–346.

Tallal, P., Miller, S., & Fitch, R. H. (1993). Neurobiological basis of speech: A case for the preeminence of temporal processing. *Annals of the New York Academy of Science, 682*, 27–47.

Trevarthen, C., & Sperry, R. W. (1973). Perceptual unity of the ambient visual field in human commissurotomy patients. *Brain, 96*, 547–570.

Watson, C. S., & Kidd, G. R. (2002). On the lack of association between basic auditory abilities, speech processing, and other cognitive skills. *Seminars in Hearing, 23*, 83–93.

Management Strategies for APD

Jeanane M. Ferre
Audiology Private Practice, Oak Park, IL

You can't treat effectively that which has not been diagnosed specifically.

This statement is true in many disciplines including speech-language pathology and audiology. Presented with a diagnosis of "language disorder," the speech-language pathologist would first ask, "What kind of language disorder?" before starting a treatment program. Similarly, given a diagnosis of "hearing loss," the audiologist must know the type and degree of loss in order to provide meaningful recommendations for management. Audiologists seek to specify the nature of more broadly labelled disorders in order to use resources for intervention wisely and efficiently, and to affect positive change for the clients served. Recommendations that may be appropriate for one type of language disorder or one type of hearing loss may be wholly inappropriate for another type of similarly labelled disorder. Thus, the assessment process is used to define as clearly as possible the nature of the disorder in order to develop effective management strategies.

This premise MUST also apply when discussing management for an "auditory processing disorder" (APD). Appropriate management of APD *begins* with differential diagnosis. A review of the literature makes it clear that the term "auditory processing disorder" refers to deficiency in one or more of a complex set of skills subserved by the central nervous system rather than to one singular disorder. While the precision of this definition may continue to be debated, it is a usable framework within which to operate. Documents published by the American Speech-Language-Hearing Association (ASHA, 1996), the American Academy of Audiology (Jerger & Musiek, 2000), and others (Bellis, 2003) indicate that the central auditory processes include the following skills: binaural interaction skills—the ability of the two ears to work together, dichotic listening skills—the ability of the two hemispheres to work together, temporal processing skills—the ability to use timing aspects of the target, and speech–sound discrimination skills—the ability to encode acoustic features of the target.

The assessment/diagnostic process for auditory processing disorder is designed to distinguish an auditory processing disorder from other neurocognitive disorders that may have similar behavioral manifestations; to describe the specific perceptual nature of the auditory processing disorder itself; and to identify the impact that the disorder is likely to have on a listener's educational success, communication skills, and psychosocial well-being.

The goals of the management plan are to minimize the adverse effects of the disorder on the client's day-to-day life and to improve deficient skills. Because auditory processing disorders can have varied manifestations, case management should, like the assessment process, be multidisciplinary in nature. Results from a comprehensive evaluation of auditory function should be included when discussing the overall academic, communicative, and psychosocial needs of the listener. Presence of an auditory processing disorder can exacerbate and be exacerbated by other sensory and/or neurocognitive dysfunction. As a member of the assessment/management team, the audiologist offers insight regarding possible impact of a specific auditory processing disorder as it relates to other life skills. The audiologist works with other team members to develop specific, meaningful, and realistic intervention strategies designed to improve auditory and related skills as well as to minimize the day-to-day impact of the disorder on the listener's academic success, communication abilities, and/or well-being.

In-depth discussions of the diagnostic/assessment process relative to APD are given elsewhere in this text. In addition, several models are available that allow the audiologist to describe the specific functional nature of the auditory processing disorder (Bellis & Ferre, 1999; Katz, 1992; Medwetsky, 2002). While the relative merits of each of these models can be debated, it is clear that without a sound diagnostic framework by which to specify the nature of the auditory processing disorder, management will be, at best, little more than a "laundry list" of generic accommodations, compensations, and available treatment options. As Myklebust (1954) eloquently pointed out, "unless a differential diagnosis is made, [children's] potentialities are lost" because different types of problems will result in different language–learning–listening needs. When considering the day-to-day needs of the clients we serve, audiologists must consider the "different types of problems" that contribute to those needs. Similarly, as more and more remediation programs appear on the market, all promising to improve an array of processing and related skills, it is obvious that specifying the nature of the auditory processing disorder is critically important to choosing appropriate remediation.

THE MANAGEMENT TRIPOD

Regardless of the specific type of APD that has been diagnosed, management of an auditory processing disorder must include modification of the environment, use of compensatory strategies, and direct remediation. Figure 9.1 illustrates how, like a tripod, effective management of an auditory processing disorder requires all three of these components. Environmental modifications are designed to alter the quality and/or structure of signal, thereby improving the listener's access to the information. Compensatory strategies allow the listener to "work around the deficit" and access different means/methods for processing. By modifying the environment and encouraging the listener to use compensatory strategies, the adverse effects of the APD on day-to-day skills are minimized greatly. Direct remediation allows the opportunity to improve auditory and related skills identified as deficient and to teach new skills and compensatory strategies.

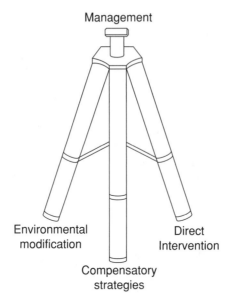

FIG. 9.1. APD Management Tripod.

This chapter describes common environmental modifications, compensatory strategies, and treatment options for use with clients diagnosed with auditory processing disorder. Case examples are used to illustrate the application of these strategies and programs for listeners with specific auditory processing disorder.

ENVIRONMENTAL MODIFICATIONS

Universal among recommendations for environmental modifications are those that involve direct signal enhancement including noise abatement, enhanced signal quality via assistive listening technology, changes in the speaker's oral presentation, and classroom seating options.

NOISE ABATEMENT

In general, a listener's ability to function in background noise depends upon (a) the type of noise present, (b) the loudness of the noise relative to the target, and (c) task demands (Crandall & Smaldino, 2002). It is generally agreed that any listener will benefit from reduction of extraneous noise in the listening environment. Recommended classroom signal-to-noise ratios should exceed +15dB with reverberation time of less than 0.4 seconds (ASHA, 1995). Classroom noise abatement can be accomplished by carpeting rooms; using curtains, drapes, and/or acoustic ceiling tiles; placement of baffles within the listening space; eliminating open classrooms; or damping highly reflective surfaces. Placing bookcases perpendicular to each other or creating a 6–8-inch space between side-by-side bookcases can create baffles and minimize noise. Cork bulletin boards and/or covering hard surfaces with fabric can dampen reflective surfaces and increase the amount of sound-absorbing material in the environment. Felt pads on the bottoms of chair and table legs minimize furniture-to-floor noise. For a detailed discussion of classroom acoustics, the reader is referred to Rosenberg (2002) and/or Crandall and Smaldino (1996, 2002).

For some students, noise abatement can be accomplished through the use of noise-reducing earplugs to attenuate background noise. However, extreme caution must be exercised in these cases as earplugs are designed to decrease all signal levels reaching the ear, thereby creating a temporary conductive hearing loss for the wearer. Noise-reducing earplugs should be considered for use only while studying, to reduce background noise in the home or at school. They should not be used on an ongoing basis throughout a student's academic day. Finally, for some listeners, "noise" abatement is accomplished not by reducing extraneous noise but by masking it with another signal. Some listeners benefit from the introduction of background music or other steady-state signals while studying as a way to mask random, aperiodic environmental noises that may disrupt concentration, similar to the use of tinnitus maskers or "sleep machines" by other listeners.

Signal Enhancement VIA Assistive Technology

Direct signal enhancement can be achieved through the use of assistive listening devices (ALDs) in which the signal-to-noise ratio reaching the child's ear is improved. In the personal FM system arrangement, the teacher wears a microphone and the child wears earphones or earbuds. Unlike traditional amplification where the speech signal and any ambient noise may both be amplified, the physical configuration of the personal ALD (FM system) has the effect of pulling the target signal away from the noise via very mild gain amplification, thereby pushing the noise further into the perceptual background. This results in a significantly more favorable signal-to-noise ratio and, in turn, improved speech reception. Soundfield FM systems likewise enhance the target signal for groups of students via standing, wall-mounted, or ceiling-mounted speakers. More recently, so-called personal soundfield systems are available. In this arrangement, the teacher wears a microphone and the signal is transmitted to a small desktop speaker used by the student. In this arrangement, not only does the student in need of signal enhancement benefit, but also students seated nearby. When used with proper diagnosis and monitoring, personal assistive listening devices can improve auditory attention, short-term memory, auditory discrimination, and perception (Shapiro & Mistal, 1985, 1986; Stach et al., 1987; Blake et al., 1991). For detailed discussions of assistive listening technology, the reader is referred to Rosenberg (2002) and Stein (1998).

Changes in Oral Message Presentation

Alterations in message presentation typically involve recommendations to speak more slowly or to repeat or rephrase information. Recent research by Bradlow (2003) indicated that slowing the overall speaking rate enhanced speech recognition for all listeners. By slowing the speaking rate, articulatory precision is enhanced. Altering the prosodic characteristics of the signal (i.e., changing the timing, pacing, and/or emphasis of portions of a message) can enhance the salience of key points. Repeating information with an accompanying related visual or tactile cue (e.g., pointing, gesturing) or breaking lengthy messages into smaller chunks would enhance reception for many clients with auditory processing disorder. However, for some listeners, simple repetition of the target does not improve understanding. These listeners require enhanced linguistic clarity rather than enhanced acoustic clarity. By offering this listener a more familiar and/or less ambiguous target, comprehension is improved. For example, the sometimes ambiguous instruction to "sit still" should be replaced with "Keep your hands (or feet, or head) still". To gauge the student's understanding, replace "Do you understand?" with "Tell me what you think I said". That is, ask the child to paraphrase instructions or statements rather than repeating them verbatim.

Classroom Seating Considerations

As indicated previously, perception of speech in a classroom is affected by presence of noise or reverberation and signal loudness. In general, signal loudness decreases as a function of increasing distance from the source, with distances of 3–6 feet considered optimal for audibility (Boothroyd, 2004). Thus, sitting nearer the sound source should improve signal audibility. The addition of visual (e.g., lipreading/speechreading) cues enhances the listening experience for most clients. In preferential classroom seating, an effort is made to maximize *both* the acoustic and visual aspects of the target. One way to achieve preferential seating is through the "Arc of the Arms" rule. Have the teacher stand at the location in the classroom most often used for instruction with arms outstretched at a 45-degree angle. Visually extend the lines formed by arms another 2–3 feet. By connecting the endpoints of these lines, an "arc of the arms" will be formed. Seat the student, facing the speaker, anywhere within the arc. This seating arrangement optimizes audibility of the signal as well as accessibility of visual (e.g., facial, lipreading) cues by placing the student at no more than a 45-degree angle from the speaker and at a distance not greater than 6 feet. Figure 9.2 illustrates the use of the "Arc of the Arms" rule for three different classroom seating types. For many

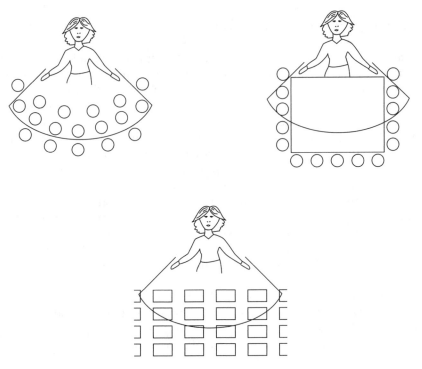

FIG. 9.2. Preferential seating using the "Arc of the Arms" rule for three classroom types—theater-style, conference, and traditional row seating.

listeners with an auditory processing disorder, seating near and facing the speaker allows the listener to "look and listen", minimizing the adverse effects of the disorder by enhancing the clarity of the target.

However, not all listeners with APD benefit from "looking AND listening" simultaneously. Some listeners are deficient in their ability to integrate auditory and visual information. Thus, the addition of visual cues may create further confusion. In these cases, the "look and listen" rule should be modified to "look *or* listen" (Bellis, 2003; Ferre, 1997). Additionally, at times, individuals may be asked to copy material from a board or screen while simultaneously listening to related information. In these situations, some listeners will need to "look *then* listen" (sequential processing) in order to minimize potential overload on their integration and/or organization skills (Bellis, 2003; Ferre, 2002b).

COMPENSATORY STRATEGIES

As noted above, preferential seating is used to increase access to the visual cues of the signal. While useful as a means to enhance the signal directly, addition of visual cues also can assist listeners with APD to *compensate* for their auditory deficiencies. Addition of visual cues may take the form of written copies of verbally presented material, notes written in margins, highlighted text, diagrams, or other visual aids that help the listener visualize the concept or make the message more explicit and familiar. Some listeners will require outlines or checklists to assist them; others will need explicit multisensory instruction that includes use of manipulatives. Other compensatory strategies include instructional modifications and changes in the curriculum or assessment process.

Instructional Modifications/Compensations

Preteaching or previewing material is designed to enhance familiarity with the target. For any listener, the more familiar one is with the target, the easier the processing becomes. Books on tape,[1] copies of teachers' notes/texts, Cliff's Notes™, seeing movies, and reading aloud to children can enhance their familiarity with the subject, task demands, main ideas, key elements, and/or vocabulary. In addition, allowing students to tape-record lectures, class discussions, or instructions for later playback can improve familiarity as well as allow students to verify information. For many students with APD, knowledge of the rules, structure, and task demands "up front" will minimize overload. However, it is important to note that for students with processing disorders, this knowledge is not acquired through mere exposure, but through explicit instruction and repeated practice and review across a variety of contexts/settings.

Many students with APD, regardless of specific type, report experiencing excessive auditory fatigue. Scheduling breaks in the listening day helps to minimize this reported auditory overload. For example, intersperse lecture classes with those that are more hands-on or less academic (e.g., physical education class scheduled between lessons in reading and grammar). Allow the student to have some "downtime" after school rather than scheduling homework or therapy immediately after school. Allowing frequent breaks while studying, extending project completion time, and/or reducing assignment size can lessen potential processing overload.

---

[1] A resource for obtaining books on tape is Recordings for the Blind and Dyslexic (RBD) 1-800-772-3248.

Extended time for test taking also may be needed. For some students with APD, timed tests underestimate true knowledge/skills. In general, tests with closed set questions (multiple choice or fill-in) are preferred rather than those with more open-ended questions. Some students may need to write answers in a test booklet rather than on a computer-scored answer sheet, especially for standardized testing. For other tests, it may be necessary to read the questions to the student to ensure understanding. Use of separate rooms for test taking and study/work carrels may be needed for some students with auditory processing disorder.

Changes in Curriculum or Assessment Procedures

When determining particular courses or curricular requirements, presence of an auditory processing disorder should be considered. For some students, consider a non-verbal alternative (e.g., ASL) for meeting foreign language requirements. Many states not only recognize American Sign Language (ASL) as a foreign language but also accept it for credit at the high school and collegiate levels (NICD, 2001). Other students may require a waiver or substitution (e.g., a culture course) for a foreign language requirement due to the nature of their auditory–language difficulties. Some processing deficits adversely effect the ability to intuit multisensory and/or unisensory patterns. In these cases, the foreign language chosen should minimize the demands on these skills. Consider a highly structured and well-ordered language (e.g., Hebrew or Latin) as a second language choice for these students. Finally, regardless of the second language, consider and minimize any potential adverse impact on expressive speech and language (verbal and written), recall, and/or planning skills (e.g., allow dictated responses on written exams, minimize oral language exams).

During the multidisciplinary assessment process, presence of possible auditory processing disorder should be considered when choosing test instruments. Because auditory processing can adversely effect language competence, results on standardized tests, especially IQ tests, may underestimate true potential. Use of non-language-biased or nonverbal instruments (e.g., Test of Nonverbal Intelligence or Leiter Performance Inventory) may provide a more reliable estimate of potential. The inclusion of both types of testing instruments may assist the team in clarifying the nature of a student's suspected difficulties.

DIRECT REMEDIATION

As noted previously, effective behavioral management of an auditory processing disorder is incomplete without the inclusion of direct remediation. The inclusion of remedial activities in any management plan is based on neural plasticity research. Neural plasticity refers to the brain's ability to organize and reorganize itself in response to internal and/or external changes. Hebb (1949) identified synaptic changes within the central nervous system in response to changes in stimulation and suggested that these changes were essential to learning. Skinner (1957) observed that behavior could be modified by systematic and/or adaptive training. Plasticity theory and behavior modification theory combine to form the basis for traditional speech–language, auditory, and other neurocognitive therapies. These same principles have been applied to (re)habilitate auditory processing skills. Therapy programs designed to improve specific auditory processes, to apply linguistic rules, and/or to integrate auditory and nonauditory stimuli have been developed and should be included in the management plan.

When choosing a specific therapy, the clinician should consider three key questions:

- Does treatment efficacy data exist to support the use of the therapy for a specific child or groups of children?
- Is the therapy founded on sound neuroscientific principles and/or observations?
- Is the therapy approach appropriate to the specific deficit area(s) identified through the assessment process?

Treatment efficacy continues to be of paramount importance in all aspects of the discipline. The consumer, whether a health plan, school district, client, or parent, deserves to have financial and human resources used effectively. Treatment outcome data can meet this need. To document treatment efficacy, one must establish that real change has occurred as the result of the treatment and not of some uncontrolled factor, or in the case of a child, maturation (Goldstein, 1990). In addition, one must demonstrate real change for a specifically defined population. Anecdotal reports, while having face validity, are not reliable indices of specific treatment efficacy. Treatment outcome data may be obtained using traditional treatment–no treatment paradigms (Alexander & Frost, 1982), or examination of pre- and post-therapy electrophysiologic and/or behavioral data for single clients (Kraus et al., 1993; Ferre, 1998; Seats, 1998) or groups of listeners (Tallal & Merzenich, 1997; Tremblay et al., 2001; Tremblay & Kraus, 2002). Because auditory performance does not operate in isolation, determination of efficacy may include evidence of improved performance on tests of central auditory function as well as documented change in related functional skills at home, work, or school (Chermak & Musiek, 1997). Finally, outcome data may include change for both objective (e.g., test scores) and subjective (e.g., self-assessment scales of disability) measures. Therapy programs that offer reliable documentation regarding efficacy will likely be given greater consideration when developing an intervention plan.

The lack of a strong record of efficacy should not, however, result in a program's out-of-hand dismissal for inclusion in the management plan. While many currently available treatment programs include some efficacy data, this area remains a pressing discipline-wide research need. In cases where conclusive efficacy research is lacking, one must consider the extent to which the program rests on sound neuroscientific principles. That is, if one cannot answer the question of "Does the program work?", consider the issue of "*Should* the program work?" When presented with a "new" treatment program, we must insist that it adhere to currently accepted neuropsychological, neurophysiological, and/or neuroscience principles. Therapy programs that cannot be shown to be founded on these basic principles should not be considered in the management plan for auditory processing disorder.

Because of the complexity of the central nervous system as well as the interactive and dynamic nature of the many skills it subserves, it can be safely said that there is no "silver bullet" among the various remediation programs currently available for use with listeners with auditory processing disorders. Clients with similar disorders may have vastly different day-to-day needs and similar needs may be the result of different types of disorders. If we accept that no one test can measure all areas in question, then we must not be misled to believe that any one treatment program can "fix" all areas in need. Just as the diagnostic process is differential in nature, we must also employ differential management when choosing a therapy program. A program that may be effective for one type of auditory processing disorder may be ineffective for another. Appropriate therapy programs for auditory processing disorder are those that are deficit-specific and target needs identified through the assessment process. In general, most therapies currently available to improve auditory processing and related skills fall into one of two types: "bottom-up" or "top-down".

Bottom-up processing refers to information processing that is data driven, in which the stimuli are the primary determinants of a higher-level representation (Chermak & Musiek, 1997). Early speech-processing theory argued that perception of speech depended on the encoding of an incoming acoustic signal as patterns of neural activity that varied in their spectral characteristics (Liberman et al., 1967). Thus, poor "processing" resulted from poor acoustic perception. Bottom-up therapies are based on the notion that the listener's ability to encode incoming signals is deficient but can be improved through adaptive stimulation. In contrast to data-driven processing theory is one suggesting that auditory processing problems are the result of deficient "top-down" information processing. In a top-down model, processing is concept driven, with higher-level constraints guiding the interpretation of input from lower levels (Chermak & Musiek, 1997). Top-down therapies do not seek to alter the listener's ability to perceive a target, but rather focus on improving the listener's ability to apply rules of language and cognition to the communication event. Depending on the specific deficit area(s) to be addressed, therapists may choose from among therapies that are considered bottom-up or those that have a top-down emphasis. For many listeners with auditory processing disorder, techniques of both types will be employed to varying degrees.

Bottom-Up Therapy

Bottom-up therapies typically involve specific auditory training activities that target the auditory deficits identified during diagnostic testing. Training may include, but is not limited to, activities that target auditory discrimination of speech and nonspeech targets, binaural processing, and temporal patterning skills. Training in related skills, such as interhemispheric transfer of information, auditory vigilance, speech-to-print skills, ability to recognize speech in noise, and lipreading skills, also may be useful additions to the therapy program for some listeners.

Discrimination Training. Early attempts at sensory-based adaptive auditory training include portions of the Central Auditory Abilities (CAA) Teaching Program (Flowers, 1983). In the CAA, the listener's ability to identify phonemes and effect auditory closure on the incoming signal was trained by presenting targets that had been electronically high-pass filtered to attenuate the power of the vowel portion and accentuate the presence of the consonant. Alexander and Frost (1982) described an experimental training program in which the stimuli were lengthened to improve their perceptibility. They noted that repetition of these time-altered targets improved perception more than simple repetition of unaltered (or naturally produced) targets.

Sloan's phoneme training program (1980, 1995) focused on the listener's ability to discriminate, identify, and recognize consonant sounds and to judge an incorrect perception. The program involves systematic presentation of minimally contrasted consonant pairs (e.g., m versus n) in which the salience of the target sound is enhanced by having the clinician prolong the production of the targets (e.g., the pair /p, b/ becomes "puhhh" and "buhhh") and/or increase vocal loudness. The program progresses in difficulty from discrimination of consonant sounds in isolation to those presented in a variety of VC, CV, or VCV contexts (e.g., pa versus da, pe versus de, and epa versus eda).

With advances in computer technology, programs have now become available that allow for very subtle enhancement and/or manipulation of the acoustic characteristics of the signal that cannot be accomplished via live voice. Recent commercially available computer-assisted training programs include Fast ForWord (Scientific Learning Corporation, 1997), Earobics (Cognitive Concepts, 1997, 1998), and SoundSmart (Sandford, 2001). These programs use computer-synthesized and/or digitized natural speech presented in an adaptive training paradigm to improve the listener's perception of the target. The Fast ForWord programs focus on improving temporal processing skills that are important for auditory discrimination. The listener plays a variety of games in which target sounds or words have been electronically elongated and minimally amplified to increase target salience. Tasks include discrimination, analysis, and identification of speech sounds as well as temporal ordering of stimuli. While appropriate for children with auditory discrimination difficulties, the Fast ForWord programs can only be used by a clinician certified by the Scientific Learning Corporation. The program is intensive in terms of both time and money, requires an Internet connection with client's progress uploaded to a central site, and does not allow the on-site clinician to judge progress or to manipulate any task parameters. The Earobics programs use digitized naturally produced, but also acoustically altered, speech. Like Fast ForWord, listeners play an array of games designed to train discrimination, auditory closure, attention/awareness, rhyming, and sequencing skills. Less costly than Fast ForWord, the Earobics programs do not require specialized training for use and allow the clinician to manipulate a variety of task parameters including level of difficulty, length of play, and stimulus presentation. Finally, SoundSmart is the newest addition to the computer-assisted training program market. This program also uses adaptive game play to enhance a listener's discrimination, attention, and memory skills. Although costly, SoundSmart does not require specific certification for use and allows the clinician flexibility in implementation.

Nonspeech discrimination training includes intensity training, frequency training, and duration training. The listener may be asked simply to determine whether two signals are the same or different. A more challenging task is to require the listener to indicate which of two targets is, for example, shorter or longer, faster or slower, higher or lower, or louder or softer while varying the increment of difference between signals from relatively large to just noticeable. A number of authors describe nonspeech discrimination training including Flowers (1983), Carrell et al. (1999), Chermak and Musiek (1997, 2002), and Bellis (2003). Nonspeech discrimination training appears particularly useful for listeners with temporal processing deficits, as well as those with poor vowel recognition skills (Bellis, 2003).

Binaural Processing Training

Training in binaural processing would be appropriate to improve binaural integration/separation skills (how the two cerebral hemispheres work together) or binaural interaction skills (how the two ears work together). To improve binaural integration, dichotic listening training is used in which the listener hears two (or more) different targets, presented simultaneously, to each ear and is asked to attend to the signal(s) in both ears. The relative intensity of the two signals is systematically varied as are the materials presented to each ear. For example, the listener may hear and be asked to repeat words or sentences presented to each ear. An alternative method to train binaural integration is to ask the child to listen to and report two targets emanating from different speakers (Chermak & Musiek, 2002). Although most children rarely need to listen to and report two different targets at once, binaural integration plays a role in listening comprehension as well as the ability to listen to and follow lengthy and/or complex directions and extract the meaning and/or intent of a message.

Binaural separation refers to the ability to listen to one target while ignoring another, a skill many students require. Again, a dichotic listening or soundfield paradigm may be used. However, in this training, the listener is asked to repeat the information to one ear (or from one speaker) only and ignore the other. For example, the client may be presented with single words spoken via live voice to one ear with a recorded story presented to the other ear and be asked to report only the words given. Another, more challenging, pairing consists of the presentation of two different stories, with the listener asked to retell only one. By increasing the intensity of the "competing signal" relative to the target or by presenting increasingly similar targets to each ear, binaural separation skills can be improved (Bellis, 2003).

Localization refers to the ability to determine the location of a sound source in space and relies on intact binaural interaction skills. Localization training can be accomplished in a variety of ways and has been described by a number of authors (Bellis, 2003; Chermak & Musiek, 1997; Kelly, 1995). A simple method for use with very young children is "get my keys". In this activity, the child stands with eyes closed and the clinician or parent simply shakes a set of keys at various locations near the child's head (e.g., above, below, and to the left) and asks the child to point to or try to take the keys. Another activity involves asking a child to point to the speaker from which the target sound emanates. Very recent research has examined performance in a virtual localization task, in which the listener wears a headset programmed to simulate sounds emanating from sources at varying angles and elevations from the head (Besing et al., 2003). For example, the listener may experience the sound as coming from directly behind, directly ahead, or high and to the right. While not in use at this time with listeners with auditory processing disorder, virtual localization appears promising as a therapy tool to improve localization and binaural interaction skills.

Temporal Patterning Training

Temporal ordering and patterning exercises are designed to improve the listener's ability to use timing aspects of the signal. Activities of this type include identifying the sweep direction for a short-duration toneburst (Chermak & Musiek, 1997), sequencing a string of words or environmental sounds (Protti et al., 1980; Kelly, 1995; Cognitive Concepts, 1997, 1998), recognizing two- or three-tone patterns (Scientific Learning Corporation, 1997), or imitating rhythmic (e.g., long–short–long) or tonal (e.g., high–low–high) patterns by humming or tapping the response. As skills improve, the task can be made more challenging by altering the interstimulus interval of the pattern or emphasizing parts of the pattern (Bellis, 2003). Phoneme sequencing and sound blending programs can enhance both speech–sound discrimination and patterning skills. Clinicians may choose to include diadokokinetic exercises in therapy for this purpose. Programs that include this type of patterning activity are the Phoneme Synthesis Program (Katz & Fletcher, 1982), Processing Power (Ferre, 1997), and the Lindamood-Bell Phoneme Sequencing (LiPS) program (Lindamood-Bell Learning Processes, 1998).

Training Related Skills

Many authors report activities to improve bottom-up-related skills, including auditory attention, vigilance, interhemispheric communication, speech recognition in noise, speech-to-print skills, and lipreading. Activities to improve attention and awareness are included in programs developed by Protti et al. (1980) and Kelly (1995). Related to auditory attention is auditory vigilance, the ability to sustain attention over time and respond to a change in the signal. The clinician may say a string of words, intermittently inserting a "target" word, and the listener is asked to respond each time the target word is said (e.g., the target word *boy* interspersed in a string of common monosyllabic words). The Earobics program (Cognitive Concepts, 1998) uses pseudoword phonemes and asks the listener to respond only when the target changes. By varying the degree to which the target differs from the common signal (e.g., from /ma/ embedded in a string of /ba/ to /ma/ embedded in a string of /muh/), vigilance tasks also train auditory discrimination skills.

Exercises to improve interhemispheric transfer of information involve those tasks for which cross-hemisphere communication is required. Activities such as musical instrument training, singing, and linguistic labelling of tactile stimuli (e.g., reach into this bag and describe what you are touching without looking at it) will stimulate the communication between the two hemispheres. However, these activities need not be wholly auditory or linguistic in nature. The key criteria are that the activity require a single or double transfer of information across the corpus callosum and include frequent repetitions (Bellis, 2003). Thus, sports, karate, video games that involve auditory–visual or bimanual coordination, activities that involve auditory–motor response (e.g., Simon Says), and activities that involve bipedal (e.g., dance) or bimanual coordination (e.g., tossing a ball from one hand to another) can improve communication across the corpus callosum for listeners exhibiting binaural integration and/or interhemispheric deficits.

Speech Recognition in Noise

Difficulty recognizing speech in noise is a common complaint among listeners with auditory disorder, including auditory processing disorder. Noise tolerance training can be useful in improving a number of processing skills, including speech–sound discrimination and binaural integration/separation. Ferre (1997) used an adaptation of Garstecki's (1981) auditory–visual training paradigm for hearing-impaired adults to develop a noise tolerance training program with quantifiable objectives for use with children with auditory processing disorders. In this program, the level of competing multispeaker babble, acoustic/linguistic redundancy of the target, and presence/absence of visual cues are systematically varied (one parameter at a time) in an adaptive paradigm to create increasingly difficult listening situations. Noise desensitization also is included in programs described by Masters (1998) and Kelly (1995).

Speech-to-Print Skills Training

In speech-to-print training, the listener is asked to "go beyond" speech sound discrimination and demonstrate the connection between the sound and its printed grapheme. For example, the student may be asked to point to the letter representing the sound they heard from a two-, three-, or four-alternative set. Another activity would be to ask the child to identify which of two (or more) printed words contains the target sound. Sloan's (1995) phonemic training program concludes with extensive speech-to-print training activities. Computer-assisted speech-to-print training can be found in the Earobics programs (Cognitive Concepts, 1997, 1998).

Lipreading/Speechreading Training

Although not an "auditory" training activity, the inclusion of lipreading exercises is an important component of the aural rehabilitation program of the listener with auditory processing disorder. As previously discussed, addition of visual (e.g., lipreading) cues enhances the listening experience for most clients. Using adaptive techniques similar to those described for other types of training, the listener's ability to use lipreading cues can be quantifiably improved. Ferre's (1997) Processing Power program contains lesson plans for lipreading to use with children as young as 6 years of age. The child is first asked to identify whether two targets, presented visually only (i.e., mouthed but not spoken aloud), are the same or different. This activity is followed by asking the child to describe how various sounds "look" when produced. Those sounds with similar visual characteristics are grouped together on a viseme chart for further discussion. Training activities involve asking the child to choose the target word (usually a compound word), and later, target sentence, from among a closed set of printed or pictorial representations. Work on lipreading also is included, either implicitly or explicitly, in many phoneme training programs (e.g., Sloan, 1995; Lindamood-Bell Learning Processes, 1998).

Top-Down Therapy

The reader may note that the latter three training programs described above move well beyond bottom-up encoding skills and also target more top-down concept driven abilities. In speech-in-noise, speech-to-print, and lipreading/speechreading training, adaptive exercises are interspersed with explicit instruction in metalinguistic and metacognitive rules and strategies. Metalinguistic strategies refer to the listener's ability to apply higher-order linguistic rules when confronted with adverse listening situations (Chermak, 1998). These include auditory closure (i.e., using context to fill in missing pieces), schema induction (i.e., using expectations and experience to fill in the message), use of discourse cohesion devices (e.g., learning to "key-in" to tag words and conjunctions), and prosody training (i.e., learning to use the rhythmic and melodic features of the signal to "get the message"). Metacognitive strategies refer to the listener's ability to think about and plan ways to enhance spoken language comprehension (Chermak, 1998). These strategies include attribution training (i.e., self-identification of the sources of listening difficulties), use of metamemory techniques (e.g., chunking, mnemonics), and self-advocacy (i.e., learning to modify one's own listening environment). Taken together, metalinguistic and metacognitive strategies enable the listener to be an active, rather than passive, participant in a communication event. This listener learns to use all available cues as well as his or her own knowledge and experience, altering behavior as needed, to improve processing and communication. Clinicians now have a wealth of sources from which to choose that describe in detail specific metacognitive and metalinguistic strategies and their use with individual and/or groups of listeners with auditory processing disorder. The reader is referred to chapters in this text by Richard and Kelly (chapters 6 and 12, respectively) as well as texts by Bellis (2003) and Chermak and Musiek (1997) for a more detailed discussion. Additional resources for training these strategies are given in Appendix A.

Two of the more "auditory" among the metalinguistic strategies are auditory closure training and prosody training. As noted above, key metacognitive strategies include metamemory skills and metacognitive attribution training, and self-advocacy/ assertiveness training. These metacognitive strategies are discussed briefly here.

Auditory Closure Training

Auditory closure involves predicting a missing target word or sound based on context. In so doing, the listener learns to listen to the whole message rather than trying to decode each word. Simplest among these is asking the listener to fill in a missing word in a sentence. Tasks usually begin with familiar material such as nursery rhymes (e.g., Mary had a little _) or predictable everyday sentences (e.g., After you eat, you should brush your _). As skills improve, and/or for older students and adults, use more linguistically challenging materials such as common expressions (e.g., Don't cry over spilt _) or sentences in which specific parts of speech have been omitted (e.g., omission of the object, The boy threw the tennis _ to the dog). More challenging auditory closure activities include asking the listener to predict targets with a missing syllable (e.g., el-e- _) or missing sound (e.g., tele _ one).

Prosody Training.   Prosody training is the top-down extension of temporal pattern training in which the listener learns to attach meaning to the prosodic or suprasegmental aspects of speech including melody, rhythm, timing, and emphasis. In prosody training the focus is on the intent of the message rather than the words themselves (i.e., the way you said something, not what you said). A common area for practice includes recognizing sarcasm. In addition, the client may need practice with heteronyms, words that change meaning based on syllabic stress (e.g., CONvict versus conVICT, obJECT versus OBject), or to recognize changes in sentence meaning based on changes in stress or intonation (e.g., Stop the car!, Stop! The car!, Stop the car?). This kind of sentence recognition will likely include a discussion of the ways in which prosodic cues are coded in print (e.g., commas, exclamation points, question marks), thereby enhancing speech-to-print skills. A fun introduction for children to metalinguistic strategies including use of prosody is the Grammar Rock video from the Schoolhouse Rock!® video series.

Metamemory Skills Training

Most listeners regularly apply metamemory language strategies when listening to verbally presented information. Listeners with auditory processing disorder often require specific instruction in the use of strategies such as reauditorization, verbal rehearsal, chunking, and use of mnemonics. Reauditorization is used to verify perception/reception of individual pieces of information. For example, when taking a phone message, we might repeat each letter of a person's name to ensure that we heard each sound correctly. In contrast, verbal rehearsal involves self-repetition of whole messages or chunks of messages in order to retain or store the information as well as to verify comprehension. For example, having stopped and asked for directions, the listener may repeat all or portions of the instructions a number of times to him/herself while driving (e.g., turn right at the next light and then left two blocks after that; right at the next light, left two blocks after that; right next light, then left two blocks). Verbal rehearsal is particularly important when the information is not available in writing.

Chunking information, important for rehearsing it, involves organizing or reorganizing lengthy messages into smaller, more manageable segments (e.g., grocery lists organized by product category, phone numbers, identification numbers) to improve retention of the information. Mnemonic elaboration refers to using acronyms or easy-to-remember rules or rhymes to organize information for storage and recall. For example, HOMES is the acronym to remember the names of the Great Lakes; *i* before *e*, except after *c* assists spelling. Care should be taken, however, to avoid mnemonics that are themselves so long or complex that the associated information is lost. For example, most readers of this text can easily recite the "silly sentence" associated with the order of the 12 cranial nerves. However, many of us may still have difficulty recalling the name of the specific nerve associated with each word of that lengthy mnemonic sentence.

Attribution and Self-Advocacy Skills Training

In attribution training, listeners learn to identify the sources of their listening difficulties that are under their control (e.g., I have trouble hearing if I'm not looking at the speaker). In self-advocacy or assertiveness training, the listener learns appropriate ways to modify those sources of difficulty that are under their control (e.g., I should look at the speaker to get the message). The extent to which a client can demonstrate use of attribution and self-advocacy, as well as other metacognitive skills, can be used as a subjective measure of the treatment program's efficacy. At a therapy visit, one young client of this author was found seated in the clinician's chair rather than his own. The client's chair was placed in front of and between the two loudspeakers from which background noise emanated, while the clinician's chair was located behind the speakers. When questioned about this seating change, he responded, "It's too noisy over there [his location]. I'm going to sit here today so I can hear better". In this case, the client had identified the source of his listening difficulty and, more importantly, acted on his own behalf to improve the situation.

The Games We Play

As the preceding discussions have indicated, therapy for listeners with auditory processing disorders relies on the use of challenging, yet engaging activities that tax both bottom-up perceptual skills and top-down conceptual abilities. Toward this end, the clinician will employ a variety of formal and informal games in the therapy session. For therapy to be truly effective, however, we must enlist clients and their families to repeat these activities and "play our games" at home. Yet, this home therapy need not be limited to scheduled times during the week when mom or dad sits down with a child to practice "listening games". Instead, we should encourage clients and their families to engage in, on a daily basis, simple games that complement formal therapy activities and stimulate development of targeted auditory processing and related skills to enhance carryover of newly acquired behaviors. Appendix B lists 30 common games and activities that can enhance auditory processing and related skills. In general, these games are free or inexpensive, require little or no specialized equipment, are easy to learn, and can be played by individuals or groups of children and/or adults.

CASE EXAMPLES IN DEFICIT-SPECIFIC MANAGEMENT OF APD

As indicated previously, the challenge for most clinicians is not what kinds of modifications, compensations, or therapies are available for use with listeners with auditory processing disorder but, rather, knowing when and with whom to use them. Bellis and Ferre (1999) delineated five specific auditory processing deficits based on key central auditory test findings and described typical behavioral manifestations associated with each deficit. The model includes three primary auditory processing deficits characterized by presumed underlying site of dysfunction. Two secondary deficit types are included that, while yielding unique patterns of results on central auditory tests, may be appropriately described as manifestations of more supramodal or cognitive–linguistic disorder. These auditory processing profiles are described briefly here.

Auditory decoding deficit is characterized by poor discrimination of fine acoustic differences in speech with behavioral characteristics similar to those observed among children with peripheral hearing loss. Auditory decoding deficit can create secondary difficulties in communication (e.g. vocabulary, syntax, semantics, and/or second language acquisition) and/or academic (e.g. reading, decoding, spelling, notetaking, and/or direction following) skills.

Integration deficit is likely due to inefficient interhemispheric communication and is characterized by deficiency in the ability to perform tasks that require intersensory and/or multisensory communication. The child does not synthesize information well, may complain that there is "too much" information, and has difficulty intuiting task demands, starting complex tasks, transitioning from task to task, or completing tasks in a timely fashion. Impact on communication is variable with more typical observation of academic effects in reading, spelling, writing, and other integrative tasks.

Prosodic deficit is characterized by deficiency in using prosodic features of a target, a predominantly right-hemisphere function. The child displays difficulty in auditory pattern recognition, important for perceiving running speech, but also may have difficulty recognizing and using other sensory patterns (e.g. visual, tactile). Adverse effects are observed in pragmatic language (e.g. reading facial expressions, body language, and gestures or recognizing or using sarcasm or heteronyms), rhythm perception, music, and nonverbal learning.

Auditory associative deficit, a secondary CAPD subtype, is characterized by significant auditory–language processing difficulties. Children with this deficit do not intuit the rules of language as well as their peers. While normal processors too often do not "think outside the box," these children rarely are "in the box"—the "box" being those rules of language, both explicit and implicit, that we use to "get the message" of an auditory–verbal target. They may exhibit specific language impairments in syntax, vocabulary, semantics, verbal and/or written expression, pragmatics, or social communication. More importantly, however, they exhibit functional communication deficits even in the absence of specific language impairment. A key behavioral characteristic is a finding of adequate academic performance in early elementary grades with increasing difficulty as linguistic demands increase in upper grades. This child may present with subaverage to subnormal intellectual potential when assessed using standard (language-biased) intelligence tests.

Another secondary subtype showing a unique pattern on CAP tests is output-organization deficit. This deficit is characterized by difficulty on tasks requiring efficient motor path transmission/motor planning and may actually be a behavioral manifestation of impaired efferent function or planning/executive function deficit. Behaviorally, the child may be disorganized, impulsive, and a poor planner/problem solver. Difficulties in expressive language, articulation, and syntactic skills may be observed as well as educational problems in direction following, note-taking, and remembering assignments. The following five cases represent these deficit types and summarize the management strategies described above that are appropriate for each.

PRIMARY APD SUBTYPES:

Daniel, age 10

Auditory processing profile: Auditory decoding deficit

Primary characteristics: difficulty on tasks of speech–sound discrimination, auditory closure and some aspects of temporal processing for each ear, may exhibit difficulty on tests of binaural integration/separation for one or both ears

Recommended modifications and compensations:

- preferential classroom seating
- noise abatement at school and at home
- direct signal enhancement via trial with an FM system
- signal repetition
- American Sign Language as his second language choice
- use of tape recorder in class
- adjusted class schedule to minimize auditory overload
- preteaching of new information, especially vocabulary
- multisensory educational environment with verbal material complemented in writing or graphically

Recommended direct remediation activities:

- discrimination training using speech and nonspeech targets
- noise tolerance training
- lipreading/speechreading skills
- auditory closure activities
- schema induction
- reauditorization
- attribution and self-advocacy training

The games he played:

- Earobics for children (both levels)
- telephone game
- rhyming games, including A Rhyme in Time
- Wheel of Fortune
- sound blending games
- vigilance games

- Hanna's last-sound game, problem-solving games
- Read My Lips

Rachel, age 12

Auditory processing profile: Integration deficit

Primary characteristics: poor interhemispheric integration characterized by difficulty on temporal patterning tasks requiring verbal mediation and left ear difficulty on dichotic listening tasks

Recommended modifications and compensations:

- allowed to look *or* listen
- repetition of information with associated visual cue, demonstration, or model
- always told task demands "up front," preteaching
- information presented sequentially rather than simultaneously
- untimed tests and extended time for projects/assignments
- on standardized tests, allowed to write answers in test booklet rather than on computer-scored answer sheet
- tape recorder or notetaker
- books on tape
- increased use of study guides, including Cliff's Notes™
- played classical music tapes while studying at home

Recommended direct remediation activities:

- interhemispheric transfer exercises
- dichotic listening exercises
- speech-in-noise training
- speech-to-print skills training
- verbal rehearsal
- schema induction
- atribution and self-advocacy skills training

The games she played:

- Name that tune
- Feely bag
- UpWords
- Rummikub
- Bopit
- Brain Warp
- Simon
- piano lessons
- gymnastics
- Twister

Ryan, age 8

Auditory processing profile: Prosodic deficit

Primary characteristics: difficulty analyzing/synthesizing acoustic patterns characterized by difficulty on temporal patterning tasks (for each ear) regardless of response type and left ear difficulty on dichotic listening tasks, may exhibit nonverbal
processing deficits

Recommended modifications and compensations:

- multisensory learning environment
- trial use of assistive listening device
- preferential classroom seating
- noise abatement at home and school
- repetition of information with emphasis on key portions, altered speaking rate
- placement with "animated" teacher
- preteaching
- notetaker, as needed
- untimed tests and extended time on assignments

Recommended direct remediation activities:

- temporal patterning training
- prosody training
- verbal rehearsal
- speech-language therapy for pragmatic and social language
- attribution and self-advocacy skills training
- lipreading/speechreading

The games he played:

- Simon
- Rummikub
- Twister
- watched sing-along tapes/videos including Schoolhouse Rock!
- rebus puzzles
- enrolled in a summer drama camp

SECONDARY APD PROFILES:

Marc, age 14

Auditory processing profile: Associative deficit

Primary characteristics: poor auditory–language association, exhibits bilateral difficulty on dichotic listening tasks

Recommended modifications and compensations:

- rephrasing and clarification
- avoidance of ambiguous language

- preteaching rules and vocabulary
- waiver of second language requirement
- assessed using both WISC-3 and TONI tests
- books on tape, study guides, and Cliff's Notes™

Recommended direct remediation activities:

- speech-to-print skills training
- dichotic listening training
- metalinguistic and metacognitive skills training
- speech-language therapy for receptive/expressive language skills

The games he played:

- Password
- Plexers
- Catch Phrase
- Taboo
- Quizzles (logic puzzles)
- Scattergories
- Clever Endeavour

Cameron, age 9

Auditory processing profile: Output-Organization deficit

Primary characteristics: difficulty organizing, acting upon, or responding to auditory information, difficulty on tasks with multiple or lengthy targets, ordering errors noted

Recommended modifications and compensations:

- trial use of assistive listening device
- notetaking service
- preteaching rules
- use of outlines and checklists
- closed-set tests
- allowed to give oral responses for written exams, used keyboarding and word processing for written assignments
- untimed tests
- on standardized tests, allowed to write answers in test booklet rather than on computer-scored answer sheet

Recommended direct remediation activities:

- reauditorization and verbal rehearsal
- metaliguistic and metacognitive strategies
- speech-in-noise training
- speech-language therapy for improved expressive language skills

The games he played:

- Catch Phrase
- alphabetizing games
- Bopit and Bopit Extreme

SUMMARY

Auditory processing disorders can adversely affect an array of skills including academic achievement, communicative success, and life skills. These deficits can coexist with other disorders and may exacerbate and be exacerbated by speech-language and/or neurocognitive dysfunction. The differential diagnosis of auditory processing disorder leads to differential management. In differential management, "general" recommendations are made deficit-specific, therapies are chosen that target specific skills, and this deficit specificity is infused into the listener's entire day. In so doing, a management plan is developed that not only uses personnel and financial resources effectively but also creates positive change in the lives of the clients served.

ACKNOWLEDGMENTS

The author gratefully acknowledges Alyce Faleni for artistic renderings.

A Rhyme in Time is a registered trademark of Poet and Didn't Know It.

Battleship and Twister are registered trademarks of Milton Bradley, Inc.

Boggle, Scattergories, Simon, Scrabble, Bopit, Bopit Extreme, Catch Phrase, Brain Warp, Taboo, and UpWords are registered trademarks of Hasbro, Inc.

Clever Endeavour is a registered trademark of Mind Games, Inc.

Cliff's Notes is a registered trademark of Hungry Minds, Inc.

Earobics is a registered trademark of Cognitive Concepts, Inc.

Fast ForWord is a registered trademark of Scientific Learning Corporation.

Mad Gab is a registered trademark of Patch Products.

Password is a registered trademark of Mark Goodson Productions, LLC.

Plexers is a registered trademark of Plexers, Inc.

Rags to Riches is a registered trademark of Super Duper Publications

Read My Lips and Rummikub are registered trademarks of Pressman Toy Corporation.

Schoolhouse Rock! is a registered trademark of Walt Disney Video.

SoundSmart is a registered trademark of BrainTrain.

Wheel of Fortune is a registered trademark of Merv Griffin Enterprises, LLC.

REFERENCES

Alexander, D. W., & Frost, B. P. (1982). Decelerated synthesized speech as a means of shaping speed of auditory processing of children with delayed language. *Perceptual & Motor Skills, 55*, 783–792.

American Speech-Language-Hearing Association. (1995). Guidelines for acoustics in educational environments. *ASHA, 37* (supplement 14). Rockville, Pike, MD: Author.

American Speech-Language-Hearing Association. (1996). Central auditory processing: Current status of research and implications for clinical practice. *American Journal of Audiology, 5*, 41–54.

Bellis, T. J. (2003). *Assessment and management of central auditory processing disorders in the educational setting: From science to practice* (2nd ed.). Clifton Park, NY: Thomson-Delmar Learning.

Bellis, T. J., & Ferre, J. M. (1999). Multidimensional approach to differential diagnosis of central auditory processing disorders in children. *Journal of the American Academy of Audiology, 10*, 319–328.

Besing, J., Koehnke, J., & Abouchacra, A. U. (2003). *SLIQ & SPLINT: Clinical tests of spatial localization in quiet and noise.* Paper presented at the annual meeting of the American Speech-Language-Hearing Association, Chicago, IL.

Blake, R., Field, B., Foster, C., Plott, F., & Wertz, P. (1991). Effect of FM auditory trainers on attending behaviors of learning disabled children. *Language Speech & Hearing Services in the Schools, 22*, 111–114.

Boothroyd, A. (2004). Room acoustics and speech perception. *Seminars in Hearing, 25*, 155–166.

Bradlow, A. R. (2003). *Sentence perception in noise by children with learning disabilities.* Paper presented at the annual meeting of the American Speech-Language-Hearing Association, Chicago, IL.

Carrell, T. D., Bradlow, A. R., Nicol, T. G., Koch, D. B., & Kraus, N. (1999). Interactive software for evaluating auditory discrimination. *Ear & Hearing, 20*, 175–176.

Chermak, G. D. (1998). Metacognitive approaches to managing central auditory processing disorders. In M. G. Masters, N. A. Stecker, & J. Katz, (Eds.), *Central auditory processing disorders: Mostly management* (pp. 49–61). Boston: Allyn & Bacon.

Chermak, G. D., & Musiek, F. E. (1997). *Central auditory processing disorders: New perspectives.* San Diego, CA: Singular Publishing Group.

Chermak, G. D., & Musiek, F. E. (2002). Auditory training principles and approaches for remediating and managing auditory processing disorders. *Seminars in Hearing, 23*, 297–308.

Cognitive Concepts, Inc. (1997). *Earobics$_R$ auditory development and phonics program* [Computer software]. Evanston, IL: Author.

Cognitive Concepts, Inc. (1998). *Earobics$_R$, step two auditory development and phonics program* [Computer software]. Evanston, IL: Author.

Crandall, C. C., & Smaldino, J. J. (1996). Soundfield amplification in the classroom: Applied and theoretical issues. In F. Bess, J. Gravel, & A. Tharpe, (Eds.), *Amplification for children with auditory deficits* (pp. 229–250). Nashville, TN: Bill Wilkerson Center Press.

Crandall, C. C., & Smaldino, J. J. (2002). Room acoustics and auditory rehabilitation technology. In J. Katz (Ed.), *Handbook of clinical audiology* (5th ed., pp. 607–630). Philadelphia: Lippincott Williams & Wilkins.

Ferre, J. M. (1997). *Processing power: A guide to CAPD assessment and management.* San Antonio, TX: The Psychological Corporation.

Ferre, J. M. (1998). The M3 model for treating CAPD. In M. G. Masters, N. A. Stecker, & J. Katz (Eds.), *Central auditory processing disorders: Mostly management* (pp. 103–115). Boston: Allyn & Bacon.

Ferre, J. M. (2002a). Behavioral therapeutic approaches for central auditory problems. In J. Katz (Ed.), *Handbook of clinical audiology* (5th ed., pp. 525–531). Philadelphia: Lippincott Williams & Wilkins.

Ferre, J. M. (2002b). Managing children's central auditory processing deficits in the real world: What teachers and parents want to know. *Seminars in Hearing, 23*, 319–326.

Flowers, A. (1983). *Auditory perception, speech, language, and learning.* Dearborn, MI: Perceptual Learning Systems.

Garstecki, D. (1981). Auditory-visual training paradigm for hearing impaired adults. *Journal of the Academy of Rehabilitative Audiology, 14*, 223–238.

Goldstein, H. (1990). Assessing clinical significance. In L. B. Olswang, C. K. Thompson, S. F. Warren, & N. J. Minghetti, N.J., (Eds.), *Treatment efficacy research in communication disorders* (pp. 91–98). Rockville Pile, MD: ASHA.

Hebb, D. O. (1949). *The organization of behavior.* New York: Wiley.

Jerger, J., & Musiek, F. (2000). Report on the consensus conference on the diagnosis of auditory processing disorders in school-age children. *Journal of the American Academy of Audiology, 11*, 467–474.

Katz, J. (1992). Classification of auditory disorders. In J. Katz, N. Stecker, & D. Henderson (Eds.), *Central auditory processing disorders: A transdisciplinary view* (pp. 81–91). St. Louis: Mosby Year Book.

Katz, J., & Fletcher, C. H. (1982). *Phonemic synthesis: Blending sounds into words.* Vancouver, WA: Precision Acoustics.

Kelly, D. A. (1995). *Central auditory processing disorders: Strategies for use with children and adolescents.* San Antonio, TX: The Psychological Corporation.

Kraus, N., McGee, T., Ferre, J. M., Hoeppner, J., Carrell, T., Sharma, A., & Nicol, T. (1993). Mismatch negativity in the neurophysiologic/behavioral evaluation of auditory processing deficits: A case study. *Ear & Hearing, 14*, 223–234.

Liberman, A. M., Cooper, F. S., Shankweiler, D., & Studdert-Kennedy, M. (1967). Perception of the speech code. *Psychological Review, 74*, 431–461.

Lindamood-Bell Learning Processes. (1998) *LiPS: Lindamood Phoneme Sequencing Program.* San Luis Obispo, CA: Author.

Masters, M. G. (1998). Speech and language management of central auditory processing disorders. In M. G. Masters, N. A. Stecker, & J. Katz (Eds.), *Central auditory processing disorders: Mostly management* (pp. 117–129). Boston: Allyn & Bacon.

Medwetsky, L. (2002). Central auditory processing testing: A battery approach. In J. Katz, (Ed.), *Handbook of clinical audiology* (5th ed., pp. 510–524). Philadelphia: Lippincott, Williams & Wilkins.

Myklebust, H. (1954). *Auditory disorders in children.* New York: Grune & Stratton.

NICD: National Information Center on Deafness. (2001). *States that recognize American Sign Language as a foreign language.* Washington, DC: Gallaudet University.

Protti, E., Young, M., & Bryne, P. (1980). The evaluation of a child with auditory perceptual deficiencies: An interdisciplinary approach. *Seminars in Speech, Language, and Hearing, 1*, 167–180.

Rosenberg, G. G. (2002). Classroom acoustics and personal FM technology in management of auditory processing disorder. *Seminars in Hearing, 23*, 309–318.

Sandford, J. (2001). *BrainTrain* [Computer software and manual]. Richmond, VA: SoundSmart™ Author.

Scientific Learning Corporation. (1997). *Fast ForWord training program for children. Procedure manual for professionals.* Berkeley, CA: Author.

Seats, T. (1998). *Treatment efficacy of temporal exercises in habilitating children with central auditory processing disorders.* Paper presented at annual meeting of the American Speech-Language-Hearing Association, San Antonio, TX.

Shapiro, A., & Mistal, G. (1985). ITE-aided auditory training for reading and spelling-disabled children: Clinical case studies. *Hearing Journal, 38*, 14–16.

Shapiro, A., & Mistal, G. (1986). ITE-aided auditory training for reading and spelling-disabled children: A longitudinal study of matched groups. *Hearing Journal, 39*, 14–16.

Skinner, B. F. (1957). *Verbal behavior.* New York: Appleton-Century-Crofts.

Sloan, C. (1980). Auditory processing disorders in children: Diagnosis and treatment. In P. J. Levinson & C. Sloan (Eds.), *Auditory processing and language: Clinical and research perspectives* (pp. 117–133). New York: Grune & Stratton.

Sloan, C. (1995). *Treating auditory processing difficulties in children.* San Diego, CA: Singular Publishing Group.

Stach, B., Loiselle, L., Jerger, J., Mintz, S., & Taylor, C. (1987). Clinical experience with personal FM assistive listening devices. *Hearing Journal, 40*, 24–30.

Stein, R. (1998). Application of FM technology to the management of central auditory processing disorders. In M. G. Masters, N. A. Stecker, & J. Katz (Eds.). *Central auditory processing disorders: Mostly management* (pp. 89–102). Boston: Allyn & Bacon.

Tallal, P., & Merzenich, M. (1997). *Fast ForWord training for children with language-learning problems: National field test results.* Paper presented at the annual meeting of the American Speech-Language-Hearing Association, Boston, MA.

Tremblay, K., & Kraus, N. (2002). Auditory training induces asymmetrical changes in cortical activity. *Journal of Speech, Language, Hearing Research, 45*, 564–572.

Tremblay, K., Kraus, N., McGee, T., Picton, C., & Otis, B. (2001). Central auditory plasticity: Changes in the N1-P2 complex after speech–sound training. *Ear & Hearing, 22*, 79–90.

APPENDIX A

Resources and Materials for Metalinguistic and Metacognitive Skills

Connections—activities for deductive thinking/reasoning, from Dandy Lion Publications, San Luis Obispo, CA.

Quizzles—logic problems, from Dale Seymour Publications, Palo Alto, CA.

Great Ideas for Teaching!—variety of activities to enhance auditory–language processing skills, from Great Ideas for Teaching, Inc., Wrightsville Beach, NC.

Puzzlemania, Which Way USA, Top Secret Adventures—variety of paper/pencil puzzles to enhance language learning and related processing skills, from Highlights for Children, Clifton, NJ.

Central Auditory Processing Kit, from LinguiSystems, Inc., Rock Island, IL.

Central Auditory Processing Disorder: Strategies for use with children and adolescents by D. Kelly, The Psychological Corporation, San Antonio, TX.

It's time to listen: Metacognitive activities for improving auditory processing in the classroom, by P. McAleer-Hamaguchi, Pro-Ed, Austin, TX.

Language Exercises for Auditory Processing (LEAP), by L. Mattes and P. Schuchardt, Academic Communication Associates, Oceanside, CA.

A metacognitive approach for treating auditory processing disorders, by P. McAleer-Hamaguchi, Pro-Ed, Austin, TX.

Processing Power: A Guide to CAPD Assessment and Management by J. M. Ferre, The Psychological Corporation, San Antonio, TX.

The Source for processing disorders, by G. Richard, LinguiSystems, Inc., Rock Island, IL.

Treating auditory processing difficulties in children, by C. Sloan, Singular Publishing Group, San Diego, CA.

APPENDIX B

Thirty great games/books to enhance auditory processing and related skills.

Game	Auditory processing or related skill(s)
A Rhyme in Time®	speech sound discrimination, auditory closure
Battleship®	active listening, visual patterning, integration
Blind Man's Bluff	localization, binaural interaction
Boggle®	pattern recognition, integration
Bopit®, Bopit Extreme®	integration, vigilance
Brain Warp®	vigilance, integration, problem solving
Card games (e.g., Rummy)	pattern recognition, sequencing
Catch Phrase®	integration, vocabulary development, output
Clever Endeavour®	metalinguistic strategies, critical listening
Feely Bag	interhemispheric communication
Hanna's last-sound game[2]	auditory discrimination
Mad Gab®	temporal patterning, metalinguistic skills
Marco Polo	localization, binaural interaction
Musical Chairs/Cake Walks	auditory vigilance
Name that tune	interhemispheric transfer of function
Password®	vocabulary building, metalinguistic skills
Plexers®	metalinguistic strategies
Rags to Riches®	metalinguistic skills (idioms)
Read My Lips®	lipreading/speechreading
Red Light–Green Light	auditory vigilance, active listening
Rummikub®	patterning, problem solving, integration
Scattergories®	vocabulary building, metalinguistic strategies
Scrabble®	integration, linguistic skills, visual patterning
Simon®	auditory–visual patterning
Simon Says	auditory vigilance, active listening
Taboo®	vocabulary building, metalinguistic strategies
Telephone game	attention, active listening, discrimination
Twister®	integration, critical listening
UpWords®	integration, visual patterning
Wheel of Fortune®	auditory closure

---

[2] Hanna's last-sound game: Each player says a word that starts with the last sound of the previous word (e.g., shoP—PaT—TiMe—MoTH—THuMb . . .).

ADHD: Diagnosis and Current Treatment Options to Improve Functional Outcomes

David Duesenberg
Mercy Health Research, St. John's Mercy Medical Center

Auditory processing disorders and attention deficit disorders share many signs, symptoms and behaviors. How to distinguish between the disorders, or how to identify if both disorders coexist, is integral to appropriate intervention. Through exploring the diagnosis and treatment of ADHD, this chapter provides an overview to better identify those traits which are consistent with ADHD and gives insight into approaches used to remediate ADHD.

The understanding and labeling of the pattern of maladaptive behavior associated with and now classified as ADHD, has been found in the medical literature for over a century. Terms such as "minimal brain damage," "minimal brain dysfunction," and "hyperkenetic reaction of childhood or adolescence" (American Psychiatric Association {APA}, 1968), have given way to a more empirically based disorder described in 1980 (APA, 1980) as attention deficit disorder (ADD). In 1994, ADD was renamed attention deficit hyperactivity disorder (APA, 1994). What has been learned since 1980 is that ADHD is a biologically based disorder affecting 3–7% of school-age children (APA, 1994), 60% of whom continue to manifest the disorder into adulthood (Schweitzer, 2001). The male to female ratio varies from 6:1 to 1:1 (Barkley, 1998a) depending on the study, age group being evaluated, and the diagnostic criteria utilized. ADHD affects all races and cultures worldwide (Goldman, Genel, & Bezman, 1998).

To encapsulate the diagnostic criteria together with results of accepted research, attention deficit hyperactivity disorder can be best understood as a chronic neuropsychiatric disorder characterized by developmentally inappropriate levels of inattention and/or hyperactivity/impulsivity. Onset of symptoms occurs prior to the age of 7 and leads to clinically significant impairment in two or more settings. Four important concepts need to be highlighted in these statements: first, onset before the age of 7; second, developmentally inappropriate levels of inattention and/or hyperactivity/impulsivity; third, significant impairment in two or more settings; finally, chronic neuropsychiatric disorder.

ETIOLOGY

The onset of symptoms prior to the age of 7 underscores the early manifestation of this disorder. Although the specific pathophysiology has yet to be delineated, early manifestation of symptoms reflect the mounting data consistent with the biological basis of ADHD. Through family (Faraone, Biederman, & Spencer, 2000), twin (Goodman, 1989; Hudziak et al., 1998), and adoption (Deutch, Matthysse, Swanson, & Farkas, 1990) studies, the estimated hereditability index for ADHD most frequently reported is approximately 0.75. This means that about 75% of the phenotypic variance can be attributed to genes. This leaves about 25% of the phenotypic variance due to environmental factors. Additional studies reveal that siblings of children with ADHD have a two to three times increased risk of having the disorder (Journal of the American Academy of Child and Adolescent Psychiatry {JAACAP} 1997). Similarly, first-degree family members of children with ADHD have a higher risk of this disorder than relatives of controls (Biederman et al., 1990; Cantwell, 1972; Morrison & Stewart, 1971). On the other hand, adoptive relatives of children with ADHD are less likely to have the disorder than biological relatives of these children (Alberts-Corush, Firestone & Goodman, 1986; Morrison & Stewart, 1973).

Other proposed biological etiologies of ADHD that have been studied or are currently under investigation include areas of brain size (Castellanos et al., 2002); metabolism (Zametkin et al., 1990); blood flow; fetal development; acquired brain damage through trauma, infections, lead, alcohol, smoking, or other toxins; and the impact of diet. While these variables may have some role in the overall expression of ADHD, from the evaluation of both the complex, intricate biological markers to the outward clinical manifestations, the most compelling data point to a genetic basis for this disorder. However, as in all psychiatric disorders, there is clearly an interplay between genetic expression and the environment that leads to full embodiment of the disorder.

DIAGNOSIS

The diagnostic criteria for attention deficit hyperactivity disorder (Table 10.1) specify that an individual must manifest six or more symptoms of inattention and/or six or more symptoms of hyperactivity and impulsivity. These symptoms must have persisted for at least 6 months and at a level considerably more frequent than most people of the same developmental stage. Symptoms must have presented prior to the age of 7. Impairment must be noted in two or more settings and there must be clear evidence of clinically significant impairment in school, academic, or occupational functioning. The symptoms do not occur exclusively during the course of a pervasive developmental disorder, schizophrenia, or psychotic disorder, and are not better accounted for by another mental disorder (mood disorder, anxiety disorder, dissociative disorder, personality disorder, etc.). There are four ADHD subtypes: the combined type, the predominantly inattentive type, predominantly hyperactive/impulsive type, and the not otherwise specified type. The combined type is the most frequent type, followed by the inattentive type. The predominantly hyperactive/impulsive type is quite rare. The ADHD not otherwise specified type is reserved for individuals who do not meet full criteria for ADHD. A common example of this is the diagnosis of an adult who cannot substantiate symptoms prior to the age of 7 years old. Given that one of the diagnostic criteria specifies that the person must have symptoms prior to the age of 7 years, all diagnostic criteria will not have been fulfilled.

TABLE 10.1
DSM-IV Diagnostic Criteria for Attention-Deficit/Hyperactivity Disorder

A.	Either (1) or (2)

(1) **Six (or more)** of the following symptoms of **inattention** have persisted for at least 6 months to a degree that is maladaptive and inconsistent with developmental level:
  (a) often fails to give close attention to details or makes careless mistakes in schoolwork, work, or other activities
  (b) often has difficulty sustaining attention in tasks or play activities
  (c) often does not seem to listen when spoken to directly
  (d) often does not follow through on instruction and fails to finish schoolwork, chores, or duties in the workplace (not due to oppositional behavior or failure to understand instructions)
  (e) often has difficulty organizing tasks and activities often avoids, dislikes, or is reluctant to engage in tasks that require sustained mental effort (such as schoolwork or homework)
  (g) often loses things necessary for tasks or activities (e.g., toys, school assignments, pencils, books, or tools)
  (h) is often easily distracted by extraneous stimuli
  (i) is often forgetful in daily activities

(2) **Six (or more)** of the following symptoms of hyperactivity-impulsivity have persisted for at least 6 months to a degree that is maladaptive and inconsistent with developmental level:

Hyperactivity
  (a) often fidgets with hands or feet or squirms in seat
  (b) often leaves seat in classroom or in other situations in which remaining seated is expected
  (c) often runs about or climbs excessively in situations in which it is inappropriate (in adolescents or adults may be limited to subjective feelings of restlessness)
  (d) often has difficulty playing or engaging in leisure activities quietly
  (e) is often "on the go" or often acts as if "driven by a motor"
  (f) often talks excessively

Impulsivity
  (a) often blurts out answers before questions have been completed
  (b) often has difficulty awaiting turn
  (c) often interrupts or intrudes on others (e.g., butts into conversations or games)

B.	Some hyperactive-impulsive or inattentive symptoms that caused impairment were present before age 7 years.
C.	Some impairment from the symptoms is present in two or more settings (eg, at school [or work] and at home).
D.	There must be clear evidence of clinically significant impairment in social, academic, or occupational functioning.
E.	The symptoms do not occur exclusively during the course of a Pervasive Developmental Disorder, Schizophrenia, or other Psychotic Disorder and are not better accounted for by another mental disorder (e.g., Mood Disorder, Anxiety Disorder, Dissociative Disorder, or Personality Disorder).

Reprinted with permission from the Diagnostic and Statistical Manual of Mental Disorders. Copyright 2000. American Psychiatric Association.

The Diagnostic Statistical Manual IV (DSM-IV) for ADHD and the International Classification of Diseases (ICD-10), (World Health Organization {WHO}, 1992) for hyperkenetic disorder—the European diagnostic counterpart for the DSM-IV ADHD classification—are fundamentally the same. It is important to note four keys to understanding these 18 symptoms. First, the expression of symptoms does not constitute the disorder to the exclusion of other diagnostic criteria. Second, the symptoms describe behavior consistent with the developmental stage of the child, but occur at a frequency and level of severity beyond what one would expect at that developmental stage. Third, symptoms vary considerably in severity and frequency of occurrence from one individual to another. Fourth, it is the persistence of the symptoms that leads to significant impairments. Application of these keys is important in order to maintain the integrity of the diagnosis. If the symptoms are considered in isolation from the other symptoms or other diagnostic criteria, these symptoms can be interpreted as not distinctly different from normal behavior. This error in evaluation lends itself to misinterpretation of the patient, missed diagnosis, and at the extreme, questions the validity of the disorder. Moreover, application of symptoms described for a child's developmental stage to that of an adolescent or an adult may lead one to erroneously believe that a person "grows out of the disorder." As will be discussed, symptom manifestation will change with maturation and changing developmental tasks. Finally, in addition to these diagnostic criteria, the clinician needs to take a complete history detailing the impairments and pervasiveness of the disorder. Despite great strides in understanding the neurobiological basis of this disorder, there is no quick laboratory test, neuroimaging study, computer evaluation, or other biologically based examination that can make the diagnosis. Only a skilled clinician performing a thorough evaluation is able to do so.

THE PRESENTATION

There are three main reasons why ADHD is considered a pediatric disorder. First, due to the biological basis of the disorder, children will be the first age group to manifest the disorder. Second, at no other time in a person's life will he or she be grouped with a large number of same-aged peers. Given that the diagnostic criteria specify "developmentally inappropriate level" of behaviors, the classroom becomes a medium of comparison and measure for behaviors that are considered to be "normal" versus "abnormal." Given that the teacher is the primary observer of this group of similarly aged individuals, it should come as no surprise that the teacher is the primary source of referrals for individuals who may have ADHD. Finally, historically people have been educated using the classic description of the individual who displays ADHD. This includes the DSM-IV diagnostic criteria, which describe symptoms in pediatric terms. Given this description and the prior training of professionals that this is a pediatric disorder, the medical community is in the process of "catching up" on what the latest research has revealed. Research clearly documents that this disorder continues into adolescence as well as adulthood (Barkley et al., 1990; Biederman et al., 1996).

The classic presentation of a child with ADHD is a child struggling with academic and social issues. As a result of difficulty in focusing, making careless mistakes in schoolwork, and receiving only "sound bites" of information, the child is unable to assimilate information required to perform to his or her potential. Similarly, the child will miss social cues, which consequently impedes social development and appropriate responses. Due to social immaturity, the child with ADHD often plays with children 2–3 years younger. The ability to make and maintain appropriate friendships is impaired. Combining these traits with impulsivity, making inappropriate statements, or displaying behavior that is restless, fidgety, or hyperactive, the ADHD child is routinely redirected by parents, teachers, and people of authority. The frequent, consistent redirections and disciplinary actions become internalized, leading to low self-esteem/self-concept (Hachtman, 2000b). For children who have personality characteristics that internalize these confrontations, depression and anxiety disorders become seeded. For those who interpret these confrontations as controlling and threatening, they will reciprocate with externalizing behaviors that are consistent with symptoms of oppositional defiant disorder and conduct disorder. The impulsive, hyperactive behavior may also lead to increased frequency of behavior that is noisy, intrusive, demanding, and noncompliant. Frustrated, the ADHD child may experience frequent and excessive temper tantrums (Rief, 1998).

Adolescents who present with ADHD continue to have difficulty. At this stage, the focus shifts from one of keeping a child in their seat to keeping a child in school. The symptoms of inattention lead to greater difficulty with homework, organization, impatience, and distractability (Greenhill, 1998). The adolescent with ADHD is three times more likely to have failed one or more grades or to have been suspended or expelled (Barkley, 1998a). Other developmental tasks associated with this stage include driving, sexuality, smoking, illicit drugs, and delinquent behavior. Adolescents with ADHD are more likely to be involved in automobile accidents and cited for traffic violations (Barkley et al., 1993). There is an increase rate of unplanned pregnancies as well as sexually transmitted diseases (Biederman et al., 1997). Smoking and illicit substance abuse are considerably higher (Barkley, 1998b). Also, the adolescent with ADHD is three times more likely to be involved with the judicial system (Barkley, 1998c).

Problems of childhood and adolescence are perpetuated into adulthood. Given the academic struggle in the formative years, adults with ADHD often complete less formal education. Without adequate education, they tend to have low job status and occupational underachievement (Manuzza et al., 1993). These individuals fail to plan ahead, are disorganized, have difficulty initiating and finishing tasks (Brown, 2000), misjudge time, and are fired more frequently (Biederman et al., 1993). They may also make impulsive decisions related to money, travel, jobs, and social plans (Conners & Jett, 1999). Divorce rates are twice as high in the adult with ADHD than in the general population (Brown, 2000). Adults with ADHD have greater rates of motor vehicle accidents, traffic violations, substance abuse, and suicide (Barkley et al., 1993; Faraone et al., 2000; Heiligenstein et al., 1999). Given the scope of this text, these behaviors may not be necessary to know in order to make the diagnosis of ADHD in adults. However, knowledge of these behaviors serves our understanding of the behavior of the parent of the child for whom care is being provided.

To sum up, as an individual with ADHD matures, four trends are seen. First, as a person ages, the level of hyperactivity tends to diminish while the symptoms of inattention persist (Biederman et al., 2000; Castellanos, 1997). Second, as the individual matures, the presenting complaint transitions from behaviors reflecting *symptoms* to complaints reflecting *impairments*. For example, in childhood the complaint is usually a specific behavior to be addressed, such as "he can't sit still and focus on his work." The adult's chief complaint tends to be broad and generalized statements such as "I can't get my work done" and "people complain that I don't listen." Third, the child is referred for care by another individual and is accompanied by the parent. On the other hand, the adult is the one who seeks his or her own care, perhaps on the prompting of another adult. Finally, adults have had more time to develop comorbidities. Therefore, the adult with ADHD may present with complaints focusing on symptoms associated with a comorbid disorder instead of symptoms related to ADHD.

ASSESSMENT

Assessing an individual suspected of having ADHD is a labor-intensive task. Information beneficial to a comprehensive assessment includes: a comprehensive clinical interview of the patient and parent; rating scales completed by parents, teachers, and clinicians; standardized test results; report cards; prior psychiatric and medical records including vision and hearing tests; a developmental history; family psychosocial and psychiatric history; and a physical exam. Combined, these assessments provide the foundation for making a well-informed clinical diagnosis.

COMORBIDITIES AND DIFFERENTIAL DIAGNOSIS

Complicating the evaluation of the ADHD child are issues pertaining to comorbidities and ulterior motives. In regards to comorbidities, upwards of 70% of children (MTA Cooperative Group, 1999) and 80% of adults (Brown, 2000) have one or more conditions occurring simultaneously with ADHD. The most frequent childhood comorbidities include behavior disorders (oppositional defiant and conduct disorder), mood disorders (unipolar and bipolar depression), anxiety disorders, and learning disorders (Barkley, 1998b; Pliszka, 1998). In adolescents and adults, the most frequent comorbidities include mood disorders, anxiety disorders, and substance abuse/dependence disorders (Biederman et al., 1994). Personality traits may also complicate the evaluation of the adolescent and adult. Oppositional defiant disorder, conduct disorder, and antisocial personality traits are higher in individuals with ADHD. Other disorders to be included in the differential diagnosis include central auditory processing disorder; encephalopathies including those associated with infection, trauma, or metabolic etiologies; and environmental conditions such as family adversity, abuse, neglect, stress, or inappropriate school placement. Also, individuals may be motivated by obtaining medications that can be performance-enhancing, a means by which to get "high," or to obtain medications used for dietary or weight-loss objectives.

Differentiating between ADHD and a comorbidity can be complicated. Knowing the patterns of various disorders is crucial in guiding the clinician through the evaluation. First, ADHD is pervasive, not episodic. While ADHD symptoms may become more pronounced during structured activities requiring cognitive effort, people who have anxiety, depression, mood, or other psychiatric disorders have discrete episodes of symptoms consistent with those comorbid disorders. Second, symptom onset for ADHD is evident before the age of 7. Rarely will other frequently associated comorbidities be manifested at such an early age unless clear environmental stressors (loss of significant person, injury, illness, attacks, etc.) precipitate such illnesses. Third, except for behavior disorders, comorbidities are frequently precipitated by environmental stressors. The continuous nature of ADHD symptoms reflects a quality of character of the individual that does not significantly change in response to external events. Fourth, mood disorders have neurovegetative symptoms (change in sleep schedule, eating habits, energy level, etc.) and changes in levels of interest in activities normally seen as enjoyable. Anxiety symptoms have symptoms of autonomichyperactivity (muscle tension, increased rate of breathing, shortness of breath, tachycardia, sweating, etc.) and thoughts of apprehension and fear. ADHD disorders have persistent and stable physiological parameters and maintain normal interest and response patterns. Fifth, ADHD patients do not have delusional or psychotic thoughts associated with pure ADHD symptomatology. Depression, bipolar disorders, anxiety disorders, and psychotic disorder patients can have changes in thought content. Sixth, the main "pearl" is that the majority of individuals have more than just ADHD occurring. Treat the most debilitating illness first. Once the severity of that illness is reduced, evaluate further to determine if there are underlying conditions. If underlying conditions exist, treat the underlying condition concomitantly. The masking of ADHD by a comorbid disorder becomes an important consideration especially when the individual's response to treatment is less than expected.

TREATMENT

It has been said that the best patient is the well-informed patient. The care of the person dealing with ADHD is an excellent example of this statement. Educating the individual and/or parent about ADHD begins the process of gaining control over a condition that is often interpreted as being out of control. For example, to acknowledge ADHD's biological basis prepares the way to introduce pharmacotherapy, addresses the guilt that is often misplaced on a parent for not implementing adequate parenting techniques, confronts misperceptions about the disorder, and stimulates hope for "recovery." In addition to education about the etiology of ADHD, the clinician should discuss psychotherapeutic interventions, pharmacological choices, and resources for education and support.

Psychotherapeutic interventions include classroom interventions, parent training, social skills therapy, and "coaching." Classroom interventions may include: establishing a clear, structured routine; communicating attainable expectations; reducing environmental distractions by placing the child in the front row or next to the teacher's desk; establishing a reward system for appropriate behavior; writing specific "to do" lists; developing visual and auditory aids; allowing extra time for exams; frequent communication between the teacher and parent; and providing resource classes. Resource classes allow for general skills training (organizational, self-study, and self-monitoring skills), remedial work (reading, writing, etc.), and individualized testing environments.

Resources for education and support include national and local organizations and some laws. Children and Adolescents with Attention Deficit Disorder (CHADD) and the national Attention Deficit Disorder Association (ADDA) are comprised of patients, families, and professionals who are steeped in and have firsthand experience with the disorder. These and other organizations provide education, medical, and legal support. Section 504 of the Rehabilitation Act of 1973 provides the basis for eligible individuals to attain special education services, classroom accommodations, and social work services.

PHARMACOTHERAPY

Pharmacotherapy is a cornerstone in the treatment of ADHD. First used by Bradley in the 1930s (Bradley, 1937), many medications have been developed and used for controlling symptoms associated with ADHD. The most recent guidelines published on the care of individuals with ADHD come from the American Academy of Child and Adolescent Psychiatry (AACAP) (Bernet, Dulcan, Greenhill, & Pliszka, 2004). These guidelines identify three medications that have been approved by the Food and Drug Administration (FDA) for the treatment of ADHD and hence are considered first-line therapies: amphetamine based medications, methylphenidate based preparations, and selective norepinephrine reuptake inhibitors (Table 10.2). The amphetamine and methylphenidate preparations are referred to as stimulants and the selective norepinephrine reuptake inhibitor is considered to be a nonstimulant medication.

TABLE 10.2
Medications Approved by the FDA for ADHD

Generic Class Brand Name	Dosage Form	Typical Starting Dose	FDA Max/Day	Off-Label Max/Day	Comments
Amphetamine Preparations					
Short-acting (4–5 hr)					
Adderall*	5, 7.5, 10, 12.5, 15, 20, 30 mg tab				• All-day stimulant coverage may decrease appetite for supper • Adderall XR cap may be opened and sprinkled on soft food.
Dexedrine*	5 mg tab				
DextroStat*	5, 10 mg tab				
Intermediate-acting (6–8 hr)					
Dexedrine Spansule	5, 10, 15 mg cap				
Long-acting (10–12 hr)					
Adderall XR	5, 10, 15, 20, 25, 30 mg cap				
Methylphenidate Preparations					
Short-acting (3–4 hr)					
Focalin	2.5, 5, 10 mg tab				• All-day stimulant coverage may decrease appetite for supper • Metadate CD and Ritalin LA caps may be opened and sprinkled on soft food
Methylin*	5, 10, 20 mg tab				
Ritalin*	5, 10, 20 mg tab				
Intermediate-acting (6–8 hr)					
Metadate ER	10, 20 mg tab				
Methylin ER	10, 20 mg tab				
Ritalin SR*	20 mg tab				
Metadate CD	10, 20, 30 mg cap	20 mg qam	60 mg	> 120 lb: 80 mg	
Ritalin LA	20, 30, 40 mg cap				
Long-acting (12 hr)					
Concerta	18, 27, 36, 54 mg cap	18 mg qam	54 mg	72-108 mg	• Swallow whole with liquids • Nonabsorbable tab shell may be see in stool
Selective Norepinephrine Reuptake Inhibitor					
Atomoxetine (24 hr)					
Strattera	10, 18, 25, 40, 60 mg cap	Children and adolescents < 155 lb: 0.5 mg/kg/d for 4d; then 1.2 mg/kg/d	L:esser of 1.4 mg/kg or 100 mg	Lesser of 1.8 mg/kg or 100mg	• Not a schedule II medication • Give qam or divided bid • Slower titration may reduce uncomfortable side effects • Do not open cap

Reprinted with permission of the author, T. Wikens, and IGC. Managing AD/HD Guideline Pocketcard Version 2.0.

Pemoline is also a stimulant medication, but given its association with life-threatening hepatic failure (Shevell & Schreiber, 1997) it is rarely used. Regardless of which medication is chosen to treat ADHD, a positive response, meaning a reduction in symptoms of impairment and improvement in functional outcome, does not validate the diagnosis of ADHD.

Results of many randomized controlled trials document that stimulant medications improve attention and reduce hyperactivity and impulsivity (American Academy of Pediatrics, 2001). This occurs as a result of the stimulant medication's effect on the neurotransmitters dopamine and norepinephrine. The primary effect of the stimulant medication is the release of dopamine from the neuron. To varying degrees, these medications may also inhibit dopamine and norepinephrine reuptake back into the neuron (Cyr & Brown, 1998). Although the exact biochemical mechanisms of these medications remain unknown, Solanto (1998) reported evidence that neurons from the locus ceruleus to the prefrontal cortex may account for improved working memory, executive function, and delaying responses. Executive function can be understood as one's ability to focus in on information, analyze it, and make a decision. Delaying responses reduces impulsivity. However, the dopamanergic activity on the striatum and nucleus accumbens may account for the effects on motor activity and reinforcement processes, respectively. The effect on motor activity can lead to tics. The effects on reinforcement processes can lead to habits of abusing the medication.

The nonstimulant—the specific norepinephrine reuptake inhibitor atomoxetine—also affects the catecholamine system. Atomoxetine's primary effect is on blocking the reuptake of norepinephrine by the presynaptic neuron. In the prefrontal cortex, this blockade of the norepinephrine reuptake receptor also leads to increased levels of dopamine (Bymaster et al., 2002; Stahl, 2003c). Given the increase levels of norepinephrine and dopamine between two neurons, the clinical responses seen with atomoxetine are similar to those with the stimulant medications (Kratochvil et al., 2002). These responses include improved attention and reduced hyperactivity and impulsivity (Michelson et al., 2002; Pliszka, 2003). However, atomoxetine has not been associated with abuse or adverse motor activities such as tics.

Adverse events associated with stimulant and nonstimulant medications overlap in the type of event, but the frequency and severity differ. The similarities and differences of these shared events are detailed in Michelson's work (Michelson, 2002).

Other differences between these two medication classes are important. As noted above, stimulant and nonstimulant medications differ in their potential for abuse (Fig. 10.1). Stimulant medications are classified by the FDA as Class II agents due to their potential for diversion and abuse. Atomoxetine is not classified given that no abuse potential has been seen. In a disorder in which chemical abuse and dependency is a frequent comorbidity, this issue may be of importance to the patient and the family. Other areas in which there may be differences include how these two classes of medications deal with growth velocity and exacerbation of tics. Considerable debate continues as to whether stimulant medications decrease overall height (Biederman, Faraone, & Monuteaux, et al., 2003; Safer, Alllen, & Barr, 1972; Spencer et al., 1998) and if Class II medications should be contraindicated in individuals with tics or Tourette disorder (Findling & Doggin, 1998; Lowe et al., 1982). Atomoxetine does not appear to have a negative effect on height or precipitate tics (Wernicke et al., 2002). As delineated in the American Academy of Child and Adolescent Psychiatry table of medications approved by the FDA for treatment of ADHD, several medications are considered "long-acting" or "extended release" (Bernet et al., 2004). Given the biological basis of ADHD and the functional impairments associated with the disorder that are

Comparative Adverse Events: >10% NRI vs Stimulant			
Event	**Atomoxetine (n=129) %**	**Methylphenidate (n=37) %**	**Placebo (n=124) %**
Headache	30.2	45.9*	28.2
Abdominal pain	31.0	29.7	21.8
Rhinitis	25.6	13.5*	32.3
Poor appetite	21.7*	32.4*	7.3
Pharyngitis	16.3	10.8	15.3
Vomiting	14.7	13.5	12.1
Cough increased	13.2	16.2	11.3
Nervousness	13.2	16.2	6.5
Somnolence	9.3	10.8	8.1
Nausea	10.1	16.2	10.5
Insomnia	7.0	27.0*,†	8.9
Diarrhea	6.2	16.2	6.5
Fever	6.2	18.9†	9.7
Dizziness	3.9	13.5†	4.0

*$P<0.05$ vs placebo; †$P<0.05$ vs Atomoxetine
Michelson, D.

FIG. 10.1. Stimulant and non-stimulant medication adverse events.

documented throughout waking hours, the pharmaceutical industry is striving to provide longer-acting medications. It is believed that by controlling symptoms longer, functional outcomes improve (Frankel et al., 1999). Wilens & Spencer (2000) maped the duration of the effect of the commonly used FDA-approved medications (Fig. 10.2).

ALTERNATIVE THERAPIES

Various alternative therapies have been proposed for the treatment of ADHD. These include medications that are FDA approved for other indications, vitamin/herbal remedies, dietary changes, and other interventions. Other medications that are used as "second-line" or "third-line" agents include bupropion, venlafaxine, tricyclic antidepressants, monoamine oxidase inhibitors, clonidine, guanfacine, and some atypical antipsychotics. While these medications may be helpful in decreasing the severity of symptoms, they do not have the efficacy of controlling the symptoms to the extent that the first-line agents have demonstrated (Conners et al., 1996; Connor, 1998; Wilens, 1999). Amino acid supplementation (Wood, Reimherr, & Wender, 1985) simple sugar restriction (Wolraich et al., 1994; Wolraich, Wilson, & White, 1995) and megavitamin supplementation (Haslam, Dalby, & Rademaker, 1984) have not been effective in the treatment of ADHD as demonstrated in controlled studies. Fatty acid supplementation, herbal remedies, biofeedback, and immune therapies lack controlled studies.

MTA STUDY

The National Institute of Mental Health and the United States Department of Education sponsored a multicenter, randomized, controlled trial to evaluate the efficacy of psychosocial intervention and pharmacotherapy in the treatment of ADHD. This

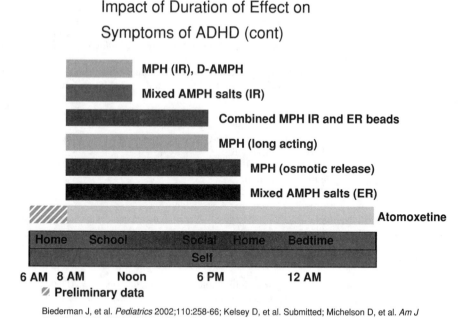

FIG. 10.2. Duration of action of medications used for treating ADHD.

study, entitled the Multimodal Treatment of Children with ADHD or the MTA study (MTA Cooperative Study Group, 1999), was comprised of four treatment arms. These arms include: medication management only, intensive behavior therapy only, medication management and behavioral therapy, and community-based care. The MTA study utilized the ADHD field's best method for medication and therapy with a rigorously controlled design and implementation. The overall results demonstrated that all treatments lead to improvements in core ADHD symptoms. The combined medication management and behavioral therapy did the best but was nearly equal to that of medication management alone at ameliorating the core symptoms of ADHD. This indicates that behavior therapy intervention did not significantly add to effectiveness of medication management alone. However, combination therapy did better for the management of the associated comorbid symptoms and behaviors. Given that the majority of individuals who have ADHD have co-occurring disorders, combination therapy is considered to be the best practice method (Jensen et al., 2001).

SUMMARY

ADHD is a genetically based neurobehavorial disorder that presents in childhood and continues to cause complications into adulthood. Those who suffer from the disorder have significant impairment in multiple aspects of their life. Adding to the complications of ADHD are the comorbidities that frequently accompany the disorder. Combined, these disorders further erode one's potential to have a rewarding and content life. Fortunately, various pharmacological agents are available to treat ADHD. These medications in combination with education and psychotherapeutic techniques can provide means by which to diminish the symptoms, regain control of one's life, and improve functional outcomes.

REFERENCES

Alberts-Corush, J., Firestone, E. P., & Goodman, J. T. (1986). Attention and impulsivity characteristics of the biological and adoptive parents of hyperactive and normal controlled children. *American Journal of Orthopsychiatry, 56,* 413–423.

American Academy of Pediatrics. (2001). Clinical practice guideline: Treatment of the school-aged child with attention-deficit/hyperactivity disorder, Subcommittee on Attention-Deficit/Hyperactivity Disorder, 108, 1033–1044.

American Psychiatric Association. (1968). *Diagnostic and statistica manual of mental disorders* (2nd ed.). Washington, D.C.: American Psychiatric Association.

American Psychiatric Association. (1980). *Diagnostic and statistica manual of mental disorders* (3rd ed.). Washington, D.C.: American Psychiatric Association.

American Psychiatric Association. (1994). *Diagnostic and statistica manual of mental disorders* (4th ed.). Washington, D.C.: American Psychiatric Association.

American Psychiatric Association. (2000). *Diagnostic and statistica manual of mental disorders* (4th ed., text revision). Washington, D.C.: American Psychiatric Association.

Barkley, R. A. (Ed.). (1998a). Attention-deficit hyperactivity disorder. *A handbook for diagnosis and treatment* (2nd ed.). New York: Guilford.

Barkley, R. A. (1998b). Comorbid disorders, social relations, and subtyping. In R. A. Barkley (Ed.), *Attention deficit hyperactivity disorder: A handbook for diagnosis and treatment* (2nd ed., pp. 139–163). New York: Guilford.

Barkley, R. A. (1998c). Developmental course, adult outcome, and clinic-referred ADHD adults. In R. A. Barkley (Ed.), *Attention deficit hyperactivity disorder: A handbook for diagnosis and treatment* (2nd ed., pp. 186–224) New York: Guilford.

Barkley, R. A., Fischer, M., Edelbrock, C. S., et al. (1990). The adolescent outcome of hyperactive children diagnosed by research criteria: I. An 8-year prospective follow-up study. *Journal of American Academy of Child and Adolescent Psychiatry, 29,* 546–557.

Barkley, R. A., Guevremont, D. C., Anastopoulos, A. D., et al. (1993). Driving-related risk and outcomes of attention deficit hyperactivity disorder in adolescents and young adults; 3-2, 5-year follow-up survey. *Pediatrics, 92,* 212–218.

Bernet, W., Dulcan, M. K., Greenhill, L. L., Pliszka, S. R. (2004). Managing attention deficit/hyperactivity disorder. Baltimore, MD. International Guidelines Center.

Biederman, J., Faraone, S., Lapey, K. (1994). Gender differences in a sample of adults with attention deficit hyperactivity disorder. *Psychiatry Research, 53,* 13.

Biederman J., Faraone, S., et al. (1997). Correspondence between DSM-III-R and DSM-IV attention deficit/hyperactivity disorder. *Journal of American of Child and Adolescent Psychiatry, 36,* 1682–1687.

Biederman J, Mick E., & Faraone S. (2000). Age-dependent decline of symptoms of attention deficit hyperactivity disorder: Impact of remission definition and symptom type. *American Journal of Psychiatry, 157,* 816–818.

Biederman, J., Faraone, S. V., Keenan, K., et al. (1990). Family–genetic and psychosocial risk factors in DSM-III attention deficit disorder. *Journal of American Academy of Child and Adolescent Psychiatry, 29,* 526–533.

Biederman, J., Faraone, S., Milberger, S., et al. (1996). A prospective four-year follow-up study of attention deficit hyperactivity and related disorders. *Archives of General Psychiatry, 53,* 437–446.

Biederman, J., Faraone, S. V., Monuteaux, M. C., et al. (2003). Growth deficits and attention deficit/hyperactivity disorder revisited: Impact of gender, development, and treatment. *Pediatrics, 111,* 1010–1016.

Biederman, J., Faraone, S. V., Spencer, T., et al. (1993). Patterns of psychiatric comorbidity, cognition, and psychosocial functioning in adults with attention deficit hyperactivity disorder. *American Journal of Psychiatry, 150,* 1792–1798.

Bradley, C. (1937). Behavior of children receiving benzedrine. *American Journal of Psychiatry, 94,* 577–585.

Brown, T. E. (2000). Attention deficit disorders and comorbidities in children, adolescents, and adults. Washington, D.C.: American Psychiatric Press.

Bymaster, S. P., Katner, J. S., Nelson, D. L., et al. (2002). Atomoxetine increases extra cellular levels of norepinephrine and dopamine in prefrontal cortex of rat: *A potential mechanism for efficacy in attention deficit/hyperactivity disorder. Neuropsychopharmacology, 27,* 699–711.

Cantwell, D. P. (1972). Psychiatric illness in the families of hyperactive children. *Archives of General Psychiatry, 27,* 414–417.

Castellanos, F. X. (1997). Toward a pathophysiology of attention-deficit/hyperactivity disorder. *Clinical Pediatrics, 36*, 381–393.

Castellanos, F. X., Lee, P. P., Sharp, W., et al. (2002). Developmental trajectories of brain volume abnormalities in children and adolescents with attention-deficit/hyperactivity disorder. *Journal of American Medical Association, 288*, 1740–1748.

Conners, C. K., Casat, C. D., Gualtieri C. T., et al. (1996). Bupropion hydrochloride in attention deficit disorder with hyperactivity. *Journal of American Academy of Child and Adolescent Psychiatry, 35*, 13–21.

Conners, C. K., & Jett, J. L. (1999). *Attention deficit hyperactivity disorder (in adults and children): The latest assessment and treatment strategies.* Kansas City, MO: Compact Clinicals.

Connor, D. F. (1998). Other medications in the treatment of children and adolescents ADHD. In R. A. Barkley (Ed.), *Attention-deficit hyperactivity disorder: A handbook for diagnosis and treatment.* (2nd ed., pp. 564–581). New York: Guilford

Cyr, M., & Brown, C. S. (1998). Current drug therapy recommendations for the treatment of attention deficit hyperactivity disorder. *Drugs, 56*, 215–223.

Deutch, C. K., Matthysse, S., Swanson, J. M., Farkas, L. G. (1990). Genetic latent structure analysis of dismorphology in attention deficit disorders. *Journal of the American Academy of Child and Adolescent Psychiatry, 29*, 189–194.

Faraone, S. V., Biederman, J., Spencer, T., et al. (2000). Attention-deficit/hyperactivity disorder in adults: An overview. *Biological Psychiatry, 48*, 9–20.

Findling, R. L., & Doggin, J. W. (1998). Psychopharmacology of ADHD: Children and adolescents. *Journal of Clinical Psychiatry, 59* (suppl-7), 42–49.

Frankel, F., Cantwell, D. P., Myatt, R., et al. (1999). Do stimulants Improve self esteem in children with ADHD and peer problems? *Journal of Child and Adolescent Psychopharmacology, 9*, 185–194.

Gittelman, R., Landa, B., Mattes, J., & Klein, D. (1998). Methylphenidate and growth in hyperactive children: A controlled withdrawal study. *Archives of General Psychiatry, 45*, 1127–1130.

Goldman, L. S., Genel, M., Bezman R. J., et al. (1998). Diagnosis and treatment of attention-deficit/hyperactivity disorder in children and adolescents. *Journal of American Medical Association, 279*, 1100–1107.

Goodman, R., & Stevenson, J. (1989). A twin study of hyperactivity-II. The etiological role of genes, family relationships, and perinatal adversity. *Journal of Child Psychological and Psychiatry, 30*, 691–709.

Greenhill, L. L. (1998). Diagnosing attention-deficit/hyperactivity disorder in children. *Journal of Clinical Psychiatry, 59* (suppl-7), 31–41.

Hachtman, L. (2000a). Assessment and diagnosis of attention-deficit/hyperactivity disorder. *Child and Adolescent Psychiatric Clinics of North America, 9*, 481–498.

Hachtman, L. (2000b). Subgroups of adult outcome of attention-deficit/hyperactivity disorder. In T. E. Brown (Ed.), *Attention-deficit disorders and comorbidities in children, adolescents, and adults.* (1st ed., pp. 437–452). Washington, D.C.: American Psychiatric Press.

Haslam, R. H. A., Dalby, J. T., & Rademaker, A. W. (1984). Effects of mega vitamin therapy on children with attention deficit disorder. *Pediatrics, 74*, 103–111.

Heiligstein, E., Guenther, G., Levy, A., et al. (1999). Psychological and academic functioning in college students with attention deficit hyperactivity disorder. *Journal of American College Health, 47*, 181–185.

Hudziak, J. J., Heath, A. C., Madden, P. F., et al. (1998). Latent class and factor analysis of DSM-I.V., ADHD: A twin study of female adolescents. *Journal of American Academy of Child and Adolescent Psychiatry, 37*, 848–857.

Jensen, P. S., Hinshaw, S. P., Swanson, J. M., et al. (2001). Findings from the NIMH multimodal study of ADHD (MTA): Implications and applications for primary care providers. *Journal of Developmental Behavior of Pediatrics, 22*, 60–73.

Kratochvil, C. J., Heilistein, J. H., Dittmann, R., et al. (2002). Atomoxetine and Methylphenidate Treatment in Children with ADHD: A prospective randomized, open-label trial. *Journal of American Academy of Child and Adolescent Psychiatry, 41*, 776.

Lowe, T. L., Cohen, D. J., Detlor, J., et al. (1982). Stimulant medications precipitate Tourette's syndrome. *Journal of American Medical Association, 247*, 1729–1731.

Mannuzza, S., Klein, R. G., Bessler, A., et al. (1993). Adult outcome of hyperactive boys. Educational Achievement, occupational rank, and psychiatric status. *Archives of General Psychiatry, 50*, 565–576.

Michaelson, D., Eli Lilly and Company, Data on file.

Michelson, D., Allen, A. J., Busner, J., et al. (2002). Once daily atomoxetine treatment for children and adolescents with attention deficit hyperactivity disorder: A randomized placebo-controlled study. *American Journal of Psychiatry, 159*, 1896–1901.

Morrison, J. R., & Stewart, M. A. (1971). A family study of the hyperactive child syndrome. *Biological psychiatry, 3*, 189–195.

Morrison, J. R., & Stewart, M. A. (1973). The psychiatric status of the legal families of adopted hyperactive children. *Archives of General Psychiatry, 28*, 888–891.

The MTA Cooperative Group. (1999). A 14-month randomized clinical trial of treatment strategies for attention-deficit/hyperactive disorder. The MTA Cooperative Group. Multimodal treatment study of children with ADHD. *Archives of General Psychiatry, 56*, 1073–1086.

Pliszka, S. R. (1998). Comorbidity of attention-deficit/hyperactivity disorder with psychiatric disorder: An overview. *Journal of Clinical Psychiatry, 59* (suppl-7), 50–58.

Pliszka, S. R. (2003). Non-stimulant treatment of attention-deficit/hyperactivity disorder. *CNS Spectrum, 8*, 253–258.

(1997). Practice parameters of the assessment and treatment of attention-deficit/hyperactivity disorder. *Journal of American Academy of Child and Adolescent Psychiatry, 36*, (suppl-10), 85S–121S.

Rief, S. F. (1997). *The ADD/ADHD checklist*. San Francisco, CA: Jossey-Bass Inc.

Safer, D., Allen, R., & Barr, E. (1972). Depression of growth in hyperactive children on stimulant drugs. *New England Journal of Medicine, 287*, 217–220.

Schweitzer, J. B. (2001). Attention-deficit/hyperactivity disorder. *Medical Clinics of North America, 85*(3), 757–777.

Shevell, M., & Schreiber, R. (1997). Pemoline-associated hepatic failure: Critical analysis of the literature. *Pediatric Neurology, 16*, 14–16.

Solanto, M. V. (1998). Neuropsychopharmacological mechanism of stimulant drug action in attention-deficit/hyperactivity disorder: A review and integration. *Behavior Brain Research, 94*, 127–152.

Stahl, S. M. (2003a). Neurotransmission of cognition, part 1. Dopamine is a hitchhiker in frontal cortex: Norepinephrine transporters regulate dopamine. *Journal of Clinical Psychiatry, 64*, 4–5.

Stahl, S. M. (2003b). Neurotranmission of cognition, part 2. Selective NRIs are smart drugs: Exploiting regionally selective actions on both dopamine and norepinephrine to enhance cognition. *Journal of Clinical Psychiatry, 64*, 110–111.

Stahl, S. M. (2003c). Neurotransmission of cognition, part 3. Mechanism of action of selective NRIs: Both dopamine and norepinephrine increase in prefrontal cortex. *Journal of Clinical Psychiatry, 64*, 230–231.

Wernicke, J. F., Kratochvil, C. J., Milton, D., et al. (2002). Long-term safety of atomoxetine in children and adolescents with attention-deficit/hyperactivity disorder {Coaster Presentation}. American Psychiatric Association Annual Meeting, Philadelphia, PA: May 18–23, 2002. *Advanced Studies of Medicine, 2*, 929–930.

Wilens, T. E. (1999). *Straight talk about psychiatric medications for kids*. New York: Guilford.

Wilens, T. E., & Spencer, T. J. (2000). The stimulant revisited. *Child and Adolescent Psychiatric Clinics of North America, 9*, 573–603.

Wolraich, M. L., Lindgren, S. D., Stumbo, P. J., et al. (1994). Effects of diets high in sucrose or aspartame on the behavior and cognition performance of children. *New England Journal of Medicine, 330*, 301–307.

Wolraich, M. L., Wilson, D. B., & White, J. W. (1995). The effect of sugar on behavior or cognition in children. A meta-analysis. *Journal of American Medical Association, 274*, 16–21.

Wood, D. R., Reimherr, F. W., & Wender, P. H. (1985). Amino acid precursors for the treatment of attention deficit disorder, residual type. *Psychopharmacological Bulletin, 21*, 146–149.

World Health Organization. (1992). *International statistical classification of diseases and related health problems* (10th rev.). Geneva, Switzerland.

Zametkin, A. J., Nordahl, T. E., Gross, M., et al. (1990). Cerebral glucose metabolism in adults with hyper-activity of childhood onset. *New England Journal of Medicine, 323*, 1361–1366.

APPENDIX A

Resources for Education and Support

American Academy of Child and Adolescent Psychiatry (AACAP) http://www.aacap.org

American Academy of Pediatrics (AAP) http://www.aap.org

American Medical Association (AMA) http://www.ama.assn.org

Children and Adults with Attention Deficit/Hyperactivity Disorder (CHADD) http://www.CHADO.org

National Association of the Mentally Ill (NAMI) http://www.nami.org

National Attention Deficit Disorder Association (ADDA) http://www.add.org

National Institute of Mental Health (NIMH) http://www.NIMH.nig.gov

Individual Educational Planning and Resources for APD

Cheryl Deconde Johnson
Colorado Department of Education

Auditory processing disorders (APD) can pose an enigma for parents and professionals when navigating the various options for services in the school setting. Support services range from basic management strategies in the general education classroom to services through special education. In order to understand this process, this chapter discusses the assessment to eligibility process as well as the mechanisms through which services can be provided, including the Individual Educational Program (IEP), as required under the Individuals with Disabilities Education Act (IDEA) and Section 504 of the Rehabilitation Act of 1973. However, before discussing the special education process, some fundamental premises regarding auditory processing (AP), AP assessment, and services for APD require clarification.

VARIANCE IN AUDITORY PROCESSING ABILITIES

As with many conditions, auditory processing exists along a continuum from mild auditory processing *problems* to severe auditory processing *disorders*. Further affecting how students perform is their ability to compensate for the problem. Factors such as intellectual ability, health conditions, and self-esteem contribute to why some do it well while others do not. The teacher's ability to accommodate the student is yet another factor. Again, some teachers differentiate instruction and manage accommodations better than others. Another complication in APD is the lack of a well-defined audiologic assessment process. Variability in the number and type of tests administered and the criteria used to identify abnormal performance yields questions regarding the efficacy of the diagnosis of auditory processing disorders. These issues have led to inconsistencies in the diagnosis among audiologists, speech-language pathologists, psychologists, and others involved in AP assessment, which in turn leads to confusion among parents and other professionals that are involved with the student. This lack of definition, combined with inexperience with special education practices, often results in intervention decisions that challenge the educational system. Therefore, it is essential that both school and nonschool professionals understand how all children with auditory processing issues can be supported in this system.

SCHOOLWIDE SUPPORT MODEL

Recent discussions in special education have focused on the concept of "response to intervention" (RTI) for at-risk students (Fuchs, Mock, Morgan, & Young, 2003), especially those with learning problems. The rationale behind RTI is to promote more partnering of school professionals in implementing interventions and providing differentiated instruction to support all students and to provide an alternative to the IQ discrepancy model for identification of learning disabilities. When applied to students with auditory processing and/or language-learning problems, this premise hypothesizes that by providing more universal supports to all students to promote access skills, reading instruction, and literacy development, the number of students needing special education services should be reduced to those who have true reading and/or language disorders. Through progress monitoring, students who are resistant to the general education language and reading interventions and who, therefore, require targeted or intensive/individualized supports through accommodations or modifications such as those provided through special education, are identified.

The RTI concept has been acknowledged through the IDEA reauthorization discussions and is expected to be reflected in the reauthorization regulations. There are also potential funding implications as the number of students requiring special education could be reduced, ostensibly resulting in more funding for those who require special education services. However, there are a number of questions associated with this model and little data to date. Questions that need to be answered include:

- What kind of information is needed to clarify the student's problems?
- Who should be involved in determining the universal interventions?
- How many interventions need to be tried before a student is determined to be "resistant" to intervention and, therefore, eligible for special education?
- How long should each intervention be applied?
- How should student progress be monitored?
- When should the student be elevated to the targeted intervention level?

The schoolwide support model shown in Fig. 11.1 is based on that fact that 80–90% of all students' learning is supported at the universal level, 5–10% at the targeted level, and 1–5% at the intensive/individualized level. Nationally, special education representation occurs at the rate of approximately 10% of all students. When applied to students with auditory processing difficulties, this model demonstrates how students on the continuum from auditory processing or learning problems to those with auditory processing disorders can be supported and served in schools. The right side of the model provides examples of specific services that would be considered at each of these levels. The outside triangle of this model represents the linkages between the home, the school, and the student's community. Services, for example, accommodations and

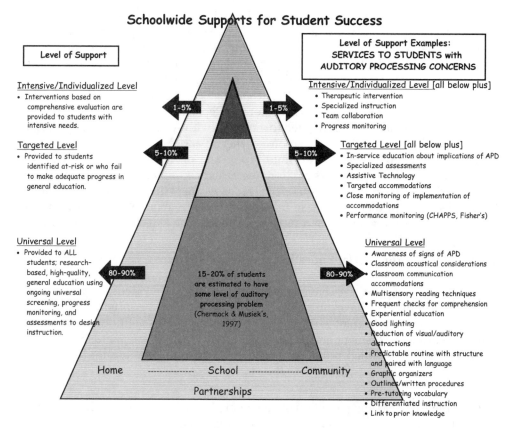

FIG. 11.1. Schoolwide interventions for auditory processing disorders.
Note: Schoolwide support model adapted for auditory processing disorders by Cheryl Deconde Johnson, Colorado Department of Education, Exceptional Student Services Unit (2004).

modifications for students with auditory processing problems, will be discussed in more depth later in this chapter.

THE IEP PROCESS

Step 1. Identification of Concern

When concern arises in the school regarding a student's processing abilities, the audiologist, speech-language pathologist (SLP), school psychologist, or other school specialist should discuss the concern with the teacher and the building special education team. Parents may also initiate a concern either based on their own observations or in conjunction with professionals who may have conducted testing in centers outside of the school setting. A screening questionnaire, such as the *Children's Auditory Processing Performance Scale* (CHAPPS; Smoski, 1990) or the *Fisher's Auditory Problems Checklist* (Fisher, 1985), may be used to (further) focus the teacher's or parent's concerns. Regardless of the source, home perspectives should always be considered in any discussion of the student.

The interventions that have been used to assist the student within the general education classroom and the data that describe the student's response to those interventions must be documented prior to a formal referral for special education. For a student with AP difficulties, these supports include those that would be available to all students as listed under universal supports in Fig. 11.1. Management strategies, such as those in the Appendix 1 handout, *Guidelines for Classroom Management of Children with Auditory Processing Disorders* (Colorado Department of Education, 1997), that have been traditionally recommended for students with AP problems are appropriate accommodations to assist the classroom teacher in addressing potential processing concerns. For many students with mild processing problems, the implementation of accommodations that address environmental and communication issues may provide sufficient support to alleviate a referral for assessment through special education. School districts call this first step in initiating a concern about a student by various names but it is usually known as a prereferral conference or a child study meeting.

Step 2. Referral for Special Education and Related Services

Once intervention strategies have been implemented and evidence exists that the student is continuing to have difficulties, a formal referral for special education may be initiated. At this time, parent permission is required as well as notification of parents' rights regarding assessment and services. These procedural safeguards include the following rights from the United States Code of Federal Regulations for IDEA (Final Regulations, 1999):

- Examine records and parent involvement in placement decisions [34CFR300.501]
- Independent educational evaluation [34CFR300.502]
- Participation in meetings [34CFR300.503]
- Prior written notice to initiate a meeting or change the identification, evaluation of educational placement or provision of FAPE, content of notice, and notice in understandable language [34CFR300.503]
- Procedural safeguard notice [34CFR300.504]
- Parental consent [34CFR300.505]
- Mediation [34CFR300.506]
- Impartial due process hearing [34CFR300.507]

Multidisciplinary Assessment Requirements. Assessment is necessary to accurately identify auditory strengths and weaknesses and to relate them to communication and learning. Assessment must include auditory, language, speech, cognitive, and academic measures as well as consideration of social and health issues. Depending on the concerns, assessments may be formal (standardized) or informal (curriculum-based). For cognition, intelligence tests, such as the Wechsler Intelligence Scale for Children (WISC), have traditionally been used to assess cognitive functioning to identify students with learning disabilities by applying the discrepancy model, for example, a discrepancy between verbal and performance subtests of the IQ test. The finding of a significant discrepancy generally indicates that the student has at least average ability but that processing problems may be impacting the student's ability to perform commensurate with that ability. As less emphasis is placed on the discrepancy model, it is expected that the use of intelligence testing will diminish and the identification process for learning disabilities will become more functional based on the RTI model. Regardless of the types of assessment used to acquire the information, a complete profile of a student's abilities is necessary to consider a diagnosis of APD.

This multidisciplinary approach to AP requires nonschool-based providers, as well as those who are employed by schools, to create a structure by which the audiologist, speech-language pathologist, special education teacher, psychologist, classroom teacher, parent, and any other relevant parties (such as nurse, social worker, and counselor) are included in the assessment process. While public schools already have these teams in place and are required to consider current functioning in all areas, most nonschool-based professionals do not. Collaboration is therefore necessary between schools and other private or public sector facilities or individuals to complete a multidisciplinary assessment.

Role of the Audiologist in AP Assessment. There are a number of ways for the audiologist to be involved in AP assessment.

- **As a consultant:** Considering the continuum of AP problems to disorders, it is appropriate for the SLP to conduct screening measures that can identify AP problems. If sufficient auditory processing information is available to develop an appropriate intervention plan or if the assessment clearly points to a language disorder as the basis for the problem, the audiologist may only be involved with review and interpretation of the existing data and circumstances.
- **As a screener:** The audiologist, based on the resources and experience of the multidisciplinary team, may screen for AP problems as part of the multidisciplinary team process.
- **As a diagnostician:** The audiologist conducts a range of audiological assessments that provide performance data at a variety of AP levels (dichotic, low redundancy monaural speech, temporal processing, binaural interaction, speech-in-noise) based on the referring concerns and that lead to a diagnosis that may include APD. The assessments performed are determined by recommended professional practices (ASHA, 1996). This diagnostic assessment is important when further clarity is needed for eligibility and for the development of an appropriate intervention plan.
- **No involvement:** It is also possible that the audiologist will not be involved in AP assessment. However, *if a diagnosis* of APD is to be considered, the audiologist must be included in the assessment process.

Considerations Prior to Assessment. Before a child is assessed, each of the following areas should be considered. As a result, it may be determined that an AP assessment is not appropriate or that the assessment will need to be modified or confined to specific instruments.

- **Age**—screening is generally not appropriate until a child is 4 or 5; assessment until 7 or 8 years; age criteria recommended with each screening or assessment instrument should be followed; age criteria is important as it reflects the developmental component of the central auditory pathways and resulting developmental abilities of the child.
- **Peripheral hearing**—the hearing status of the student must be determined prior to any screening or assessment and usually AP assessment is not conducted when

hearing loss is present unless there are legitimate concerns that AP problems may coexist with the hearing loss. If any hearing sensitivity loss is present, the AP screening or assessment must be administered by an audiologist in a sound booth where appropriate APD tests that are resistant to peripheral hearing loss can be administered.

- **Cognitive ability**—performance on AP tasks is affected by cognitive ability; therefore any student assessed should have cognitive ability within a normal range. However, both auditory and visual processing problems can coexist that may mask a student's actual ability. When these concerns present, the psychological assessment is crucial to sorting out the processing issues.
- **Primary language/language competence**—children with poor language skills generally have more difficulty on AP tasks, particularly those which require more sophisticated language processing. Results must be interpreted carefully and extra caution is recommended with bilingual students. When possible, assessments should be given in the child's native language. Special education eligibility may not be considered if the student has not had sufficient opportunity to learn English.
- **Speech abilities**—when children exhibit excessive phonology errors, it may be necessary to utilize measures that are based on picture-pointing responses rather than repetition so that response interpretation errors can be eliminated.
- **Motivation and emotional status**—significant test variability can occur based on these factors; when either is suspected, repeat assessment may be necessary to determine the reliability of the test responses.
- **Attention and/or distractibility**—ditto above; test accommodations may be necessary to assure that the student is attending for each test item; any test modifications should be noted on the protocol and must be taken into consideration in the test interpretation.

Screening or Diagnostic Assessment? The goals of assessment are twofold: first, to determine eligibility for special education and related services and, second, to develop a specific intervention plan for each student. Assessment tools range from screening to diagnostic depending on the presenting concerns, history, and interventions attempted. It may not be necessary to conduct a diagnostic assessment in each area to reach either of these goals. Disciplines should collaborate in assessment planning to ensure that all areas of suspected difficulty are considered and the degree to which each assessment occurs. A speech-language pathologist, for example, in the course of the language evaluation may decide to add screening tests to explore AP areas. Based on the assessment findings, the SLP or multidisciplinary team may decide that they have sufficient information to determine eligibility and to develop an appropriate intervention plan without proceeding with a full diagnostic AP evaluation. Or, in the course of the speech-language evaluation, the SLP may determine that it is necessary to bring the audiologist into the assessment process to evaluate the auditory domain so that they can sort out language versus auditory-based problems. If a diagnosis of an auditory processing disorder is to be determined, the audiologist must conduct an appropriate audiologic assessment. School teams, including the school audiologist, benefit from working together to develop a reasonable assessment approach.

Once appropriate assessment has been completed, questions must be answered to determine if a child is eligible to receive special education or other services. As part of this discussion, it is often helpful to lay out all of the assessment results in

Name: ____SM_____   Birthdate: _____ CA: __7-9__ Date: _3/03_

Auditory Acuity: _X_ Normal   __See audiogram   Auditory Evoked Potentials: _____

	Below Average			Average			Above Average		
Standard Deviation	-3	-2		-1		+1	+2		+3
Standard Score	1 2 3	4 5 6		7 8 9	10 11	12 13	14 15 16	17 18	19
	55	70		85	100	115	130		145
Percentile Rank	1 2	5 9		16 25 37	50 63	75 84	91 95 98	99	
AUDITORY:									
SCAN: FW				■					
AFG		■							
CW			■						
Composite									
CS: Binaural	30%								
RE	30%								
LE		40%							
Spondee Bin Fusion	35%								
Dichotic Digits(single)		■							
Auditory Fusion Test-R	CNT								
Pitch Pattern	CNT								
Duration Pattern	CNT								
ACPT (63errors/≥32sig)									
vigilance	1%								
LANGUAGE:									
PPVT-III		■							
TOLD-P:2 SLQ				■					
LIQ				■					
SpQ				■					
SeQ				■					
SyQ				■					
PhQ					■				
COGNITIVE:									
WISC-III									
Verbal IQ					■				
Performance IQ							■		
SOCIAL/EMOTIONAL:									
No concerns					■				
EDUCATIONAL: WJ3									
Broad Reading		■							
Broad Math				■					
Broad Written Lang	■								
Total Achievement		■							

OBSERVATIONS/COMMENTS:

Both parents deaf, no significant birth or health history, no concerns for 14yo and 4yo siblings; acts like a kid with hearing loss

Strengths: Enjoys playing with friends, likes to build things

Weaknesses: Delayed expressive language, attention problems, easily distracted

FIG. 11.2. Central Auditory Processing Assessment Profile. (Colorado Department of Education (1997), Auditory processing disorders: A team approach to screening, assessment and intervention practices. Appendix F, p. 30.)

a profile such as the one in Fig. 11.2. In addition to the test results that show the student's strengths and concern areas, the visual representation helps ensure that all areas have been evaluated and that sufficient information is available to respond to eligibility determination. For the student represented in this case, the profile shows significant AP issues confounded by attention deficits, vocabulary delays but average language function, average to above average cognitive ability with significantly higher nonverbal skills, and academic deficits in reading and language. No emotional or social concerns were identified.

Eligibility for Special Education. For a student being considered for special education services as a result of auditory processing issues, questions include:

- Based on the multidisciplinary assessment, is there evidence of an AP problem or disorder?

- Does the severity of the problem or disorder cause an adverse effect on learning and qualify this student for special education and/or related services?

- What are the characteristics or profile of the AP problem/disorder?
- What are the possible services that might be considered for the child, for example, speech-language, audiology, academic support or instruction, counseling, health?

Because there is not a federal category of disability for auditory processing, part of eligibility also includes identifying the type of disability under which the student qualifies. In most states, the disability areas are either speech-language disability or learning disability. Members of the multidisciplinary team should be familiar with the criteria under each category in order to make the most appropriate determination. Parents should also be aware of these categories so that they understand how AP applies within them. These IDEA 2004 federal definitions are:

A. **Specific learning disability [34CFR300.8(10)]**

  (i) **General.** The term means a disorder in one or more of the basic psychological processes involved in understanding or in using language, spoken or written, that may manifest itself in an imperfect ability to listen, think, speak, read, write, spell, or to do mathematical calculations, including conditions such as perceptual disabilities, brain injury, minimal brain dysfunction, dyslexia, and developmental aphasia.

  (ii) **Disorders not included.** The term does not include learning problems that are primarily the result of visual, hearing, or motor disabilities, of mental retardation, of emotional disturbance, or environmental, cultural, or economic disadvantage.

B. **Speech or language impairment [34CFR300.8(11)]** means a communication disorder, such as stuttering, impaired articulation, a language impairment, or a voice impairment, that adversely affects a child's educational performance.

Once eligibility is determined, development of an intervention plan, the Individual Education Program (IEP), occurs for the student. Figure 11.3 captures the components of this eligibility process.

504: Supports to Students Who Are Not Eligible for Special Education. If the student is not found to be eligible for special education services under IDEA, accommodations under 504 (Section 504 of the Rehabilitation Act of 1973) may be considered. Section 504 prohibits discrimination against persons with a disability in any program that receives federal funds. The Act defines a person with a disability as anyone who:

Has a mental or physical impairment that substantially limits one or more major life activities (major life activities include activities such as caring for one's self, performing manual tasks, walking, seeing, hearing, speaking, breathing, learning, and working).

Similar to IDEA, schools have responsibility to identify, evaluate, and, if the child is determined to be eligible, to afford access to appropriate educational services. Parents who disagree with the determination made by the school have a right to a hearing with an impartial hearing officer. The Family Educational Rights and Privacy Act (FERPA) also specifies rights related to educational records. Under FERPA, the parent or guardian has the right to:

- Inspect and review the child's educational records;
- Make copies of these records;
- Receive a list of all individuals having access to those records;

Eligibility Process at a Glance[1]

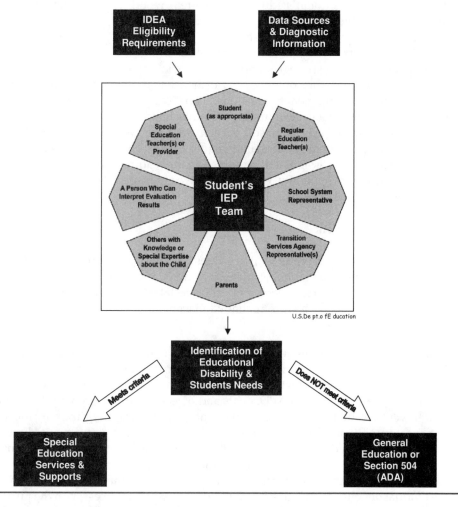

*Graphic from "A Guide to the Individualized Education Program" developed by the U.S. Department of Education, with the assistance of the National Information Center for Children and Youth with Disabilities (NICHCY). www.nichcy.org/resources.

FIG. 11.3. Assessment process.
Note: [1]Colorado Department of Education Exceptional Student Services, www.cde.state.co.us

- Ask for an explanation of any item in the records;
- Ask for an amendment to any report on the grounds that it is inaccurate, misleading, or violates the child's rights;
- A hearing on the issue if the school refuses to make the amendment.

As part of the referral process, the school should identify the reason for referral, the accommodations and interventions that have been attempted, and whether the child has been referred, evaluated, and/or received services from special education. Evaluation procedures (types of tests, qualifications of evaluator, test interpretation) should follow the same guidelines as for students being evaluated for special education. Eligibility for 504 is established in a meeting that determines the condition and its impact on the student's education, the areas where accommodations will be necessary to assist the student, and then a detailed list of the accommodations and services that will be provided. Plans should be reviewed periodically but there are no specific requirements specifying review timelines.

Accommodations are strategies applied to provide access to the education program. They do not alter the content or performance expectations. Accommodations include classroom management suggestions, acoustical requirements, and use of communication strategies. Modifications, on the other hand, alter the content or course requirements so that a student can still participate in the general education program but with fewer or different performance requirements. These include reducing the quantity or length of an assignment or adjusting the reading level of class materials. A modified curriculum generally requires services under special education. A sample 504 Plan is located in Appendix 2.

Step 3. IEP Development

The IEP team must complete several activities to develop the student's IEP. These include determining goals and objectives, accommodations and modifications, participation in state and district assessments, the special education and related services that will be provided, and the recommended placement.

1. *Goals and Objectives.*
   IEP goals and objectives are based on needs that are identified as a result of the assessment process and reflect the specific interventions that are recommended. Goals and objectives must also reflect state and district standards and benchmarks. For students with APD, goals and objectives are focused on therapeutic interventions that include two components: cognitive strategy training for compensatory skill development and self-management of the problem and direct intervention for auditory/listening skill development. This model of intervention is often referred to as a top-down (cognitive compensatory strategies)/bottom-up (skill development) approach. Both areas are determined by the specific individual deficits identified through the AP assessment process with the purpose of improving skills in deficit areas and for learning compensatory strategies. Profiles of various AP problems (Bellis & Ferre, 1996; Bellis, 2003; Katz, 1992) can further guide appropriate interventions based on certain types of processing difficulties.

   In addition to being standards-driven, IEP goals should be written using "SMART" terminology. SMART goals are Specific, Measurable, Attainable, Research-based, and Time-phased. Each goal/objective on the IEP should be tested against these parameters. Some examples of "SMART" goals are shown on the sample IEP in Fig. 11.4. Each IEP goal development process should include indicators of progress toward meeting the goals (short-term objectives), how the indicators are evaluated, the schedule for achievement of the objective, and progress toward the objective.

2. *Accommodations and Modifications.*
   In addition to goals, accommodations are also determined that allow the student to access and participate in the general education program, including district and state assessments.

Specific

Annual Goal to be measure by achievement of benchmarks #1: (goals should reflect standards/key components/access skills)

Annual Goal: Mary will demonstrate comprehension of a short passage (about 200 words) that is read to her in a classroom with typical background noise present using effective auditory processing strategies to receive and understand the meaning of what was spoken with 100% accuracy as measured by the following objectives:

Attainable

Measurable

Research-based
(see objectives)

Time-phased

Objective: Beginning date: 09/10/2003; Target completion date: 09/10/2004

1. When listening to single words presented in background noise at the same loudness level as the noise, Mary will repeat the words.

Baseline: Can repeat words with a low degree of background noise with 70% accuracy but only 50% accuracy when the noise level is equal to the presentation level. Criteria/Evaluation: Correct repetition in 23/25 attempts using dolch words lists.

Objective: Beginning date: 09/10/2003; Target completion date: 09/10/2004

2. When listening to a short paragraph of 3 critical elements presented in background noise at the same loudness level as the noise, Mary will describe the elements.

Baseline: Can identify the 2/3 critical elements 66% of the time with an equal degree of background noise.
Criteria/Evaluation: Identify 3/3 critical elements 90% of the time using teacher/curriculum-based materials.

Objective: Beginning date: 09/10/2003; Target completion date: 09/10/2004

4. When listening to a passage containing 5 critical elements, presented in background noise at the same loudness level as the noise, Mary will describe each element in the proper order of occurrence.

Baseline: Can identify 2/5 critical elements 66% of the time but gets flustered when the passage length increases.
Criteria/Evaluation: Identify 5/5 critical elements 90% of the time using teacher/curriculum-based materials.

FIG. 11.4. Sample IEP SMART goals/objectives.

Classroom Management. All students with APD require an optimum listening environment as well as one that incorporates bisensory (auditory and visual) presentation of materials. Classroom management includes environmental accommodations to help the student access information as well as purposeful strategies to enhance teacher–student communication interactions. Students should be taught self-advocacy skills to manage their own communication environment as early as possible. Examples of classroom management strategies are described in Table 11.1 and are also included in the *Auditory Processing Disorders IEP Checklist for Accommodations and Modifications* (Appendix 3).

Instructional Accommodations and Modifications. Purposeful adaptations made by the teacher to improve the child's opportunity to learn are considered under the umbrella of instructional accommodations and modifications. As discussed under 504, accommodations are changes made in the learning process in order to provide students access to information and an equal opportunity to demonstrate knowledge and skills without altering learning standards. Examples include use of a notetaker, visual supplements, study guides, pre-teaching, peer partners, adjusted pace of instruction, repetition of ideas, and reduced language level. Modifications are changes made in the instructional level, content, or performance criteria. Examples include reducing the difficulty of the material, shortening assignments, providing alternative assignments, and utilizing an alternative grading system. The Auditory Processing Disorders IEP Checklist located in Appendix 3 is again useful for identifying appropriate individual adaptations for students. The IEP team must also identify the accommodations and modifications that the student requires for participation in state and district assessments or the state's alternative assessment if appropriate.

3. *Assistive Technology: Assistive Listening Devices (ALDs)*.
   Assistive technology is defined in IDEA Part B & C (34CFR300.5-6; 34CFR303.12):

> "Assistive technology device" means any item, piece of equipment, or product system, whether acquired commercially off the shelf, modified, or customized, that is used to increase, maintain, or improve the functional capabilities of children with disabilities.
>   "Assistive technology service" means any service that directly assists a child with a disability in the selection, acquisition, or use of an assistive technology device. The term includes
> a. The evaluation of the needs of a child with a disability, including a functional evaluation of the child in the child's customary environment;
> b. Purchasing, leasing, or otherwise providing for the acquisition of assistive technology devices by children with disabilities;
> c. Selecting, designing, fitting, customizing, adapting, applying, retaining, repairing, or replacing assistive technology devices;
> d. Coordinating and using other therapies, interventions, or services with assistive technology devices, such as those associated with existing education and rehabilitation plans and programs;
> e. Training or technical assistance for a child with a disability or, if appropriate, that child's family; and
> f. Training or technical assistance for professionals (including individuals providing education or rehabilitation services), employers, or other individuals who provide services to, employ, or are otherwise substantially involved in the major life functions of children with disabilities.

Improvement in the audibility of the sound source (e.g., the speaker's voice, audio equipment) with FM, induction, or infrared systems can provide significant

TABLE 11.1
Classroom Management Strategies[a]

Classroom environment considerations to assure an appropriate acoustic learning environment:

Physical design considerations relative to noise and reverberation:	• Classroom placement within the building—away from high-noise areas such as cafeterias, gym, music-room)
	• Window placement—away from busy streets, playground areas
	• Ventilation/heating systems—noise levels should not exceed 35dB
	• Walls—should be permanent walls with nonmovable partitions
	• Room shape—avoid long disproportionately shaped or circular rooms
Adaptations to improve the classroom:	• carpet
	• rubber tips on chair legs or desk if carpet not available
	• drapes for windows/walls
	• cork board for bulletin boards
	• bookshelves as room dividers for quiet classroom area
	• cushions for chairs
	• position mobile bulletin boards at angle (not parallel) to walls to reduce reverberation
	• creative landscaping to reduce outside noise (trees, burms)
	• louvered shutters for outside window covers
	• close door to hallway noise
	• suspended acoustic tile
	• adequate lighting and reduction of reflective surfaces

Teacher–student communication considerations to promote student access to information:

STRATEGY	BENEFIT
Special seating near teacher or speaker with full face-to-face view.	• provides louder, less reverberent signal • provides advantage of visual instruction aids • provides access to visual spoken language • helps maintain attention and interest in task
Train students to "look and listen."	• student will usually comprehend better if watching person who is speaking
Check student's comprehension of verbal information.	• determines student's level of understanding of information • identifies information that needs to be restated • verifies when student is ready to move into new material
Earmuffs should be available and utilized when appropriate to reduce auditory distractions; quiet study areas that are free from visual distractions should also be available.	• helps to minimize problems with auditory and visual distractions, improving concentration and productivity
Monitor student for fatigue and length of attending time, providing breaks when necessary.	• permits student to have "downtime" and then redirection of attention
S = state the topic to be discussed P = pace your conversation at a moderate speed with occasional pauses to permit comprehension E = enunciate clearly, without exaggerated lip movements E = enthusiastically communicate, using body language and natural gestures CH = check comprehension before changing topics	• mnemonic device highlighting basic strategies for dealing with attending, memory, and receptive language deficits

[a] Colorado Department of Education (1997), Auditory processing disorders: A team approach to screening, assessment and intervention practices. Appendix H, pp. 32–33.

benefit to *certain* students with AP problems or disorders. These ALD systems enhance the signal by bringing the source directly to the ear with behind-the-ear receivers, earbuds, or headphones or through speakers placed on the student's desk or strategically in the room. In order to ensure proper candidacy, selection, and use of ALDs, the audiologist must be involved in the fitting of any system. Prior to including the ALD in the IEP, a 30–60-day trial is advised to demonstrate and appropriately document the effectiveness of the device. The trial should include a pre–post listening evaluation (e.g., CHAPPS, Fisher's Auditory Problems Checklist, or an evaluation like the FM Listening Evaluation protocol in Appendix 4) and should be of sufficient time to allow the student to demonstrate benefit as well as sustained use of the system. Once it is determined that the ALD is appropriate, it should be described under assistive technology on the IEP. Rather than specifying the brand and name of the device, a description of the characteristics of the device should be made. The purpose for this general description is to provide flexibility so that the IEP team does not have to reconvene to revise the type of ALD should the student's listening requirements be altered with classroom changes or when a student moves to another school or school district.

```
    DO SAY on the IEP: ``an amplification system
       that achieves a minimum of a +10 dB SNR"

DO NOT SAY: ``Phonak MicroEar," ``Soundfield classroom
               system," or personal FM"
```

Whenever assistive technology is provided, a determination of the accompanying assistive technology services (e.g., evaluation, fitting, monitoring, training) must also be made. If the service is part of accommodations, it should be included with accommodations; if use of assistive technology requires specific training, the training should be included under the IEP goals/objectives.

4. *Determination of Special Education and Related Services.*
The IEP team determines the services that the student will receive including:
- The type of service provider
- Projected beginning and ending dates of the services
- The hours of services that will be provided by each provider in the general education classroom and outside the general education classroom or by consultation.

The IEP team must also determine if the child will be eligible for extended school-year services, require special transportation, assistive technology, or require any special plan to accommodate behavior or other special characteristics identified in the state's special education regulations.

5. *Recommended Placement in the Least Restrictive Environment.*
The final determination is the location where the student will receive his or her services. For most students with APD, this placement will be in the student's neighborhood school. However, some students may attend a program at another school if the IEP team recommends that placement as the one that is most appropriate (and therefore least restrictive) for the student. In addition to the place

of services, the IEP team must determine the amount of time the student will spend outside and within the general education classroom. These time options are determined by the federal IDEA reporting requirements:

- Less than 21 percent outside the general education classroom
- 21 to 60 percent outside the general education classroom
- More than 60 percent of the time outside the general education classroom

Although generally not relevant to students with APD, other placement options include the home, hospital, community, and separate private or public facilities.

TRIENNIAL EVALUATIONS AND REASSESSMENT

97 IDEA requires that the IEP for each student be reviewed at least annually, with more in-depth evaluations every 3 years. It is recommended that students with APD have their AP assessments repeated at these 3-year intervals to monitor developmental or other potential performance changes. Lack of progress, a decrease in educational performance, or a significant change in behavior of a student should trigger more frequent consideration for assessment. Additional assessment may also be necessary to further define the processing abilities of a student so that interventions can be better matched to the student's processing profile.

INFORMATION AND RESOURCES

The parent partnership for home–school support and collaboration is essential to maximizing services for any student, including those with AP problems or disorders. Training is especially important in an area like AP where the problem is not well defined and understood. The *Frequently Asked Questions* (FAQ) handout in Appendix 5 can be a helpful tool for parents as well as professionals in defining some of the issues about auditory processing. Other resources include websites and textbooks. Professionals should screen these materials to try to assure that they represent a multi-disciplinary focus and promote evidenced-based practices. The National Information Center for Children and Youth with Disabilities (NICHCY) is a particularly useful website that is funded by the U.S. Department of Education. Good publications about IEPs include *A Student's Guide to the IEP, Questions Often Asked by Parents about Special Education Services*, and, for more in-depth information, *Questions and Answers about IDEA*. Some of these publications are also available in Spanish. The NICHCY Web site is: www.nichcy.org/resources.

SUMMARY

The IEP process includes consideration of universal interventions as well as 504 accommodations. As additional definition comes forth in the AP field, we will have more tools and resources available to better inform our school colleagues and parents and especially to guide the intervention practices with students with AP problems. In the meantime, it is imperative that we address these learning problems using the resources that are available to us.

REFERENCES

American Speech-Language-Hearing Association. (1996). Central auditory processing: Current status of research and implications for clinical practice. *American Journal of Audiology, 5*(2), 41–45.

Bellis, T. (2003). *Assessment and management of central auditory processing disorders in the educational setting: From science to practice* (2nd ed.). Clifton Park, NY: Thomson-Delmar Learning.

Bellis, T., & Ferre, J. (1996). Assessment and management of CAPD in children. *Educational Audiology Association Monograph, 4* , 23–27.

Chermack, G., & Musiek, F. (1997). Conceptual and historical foundations. *Central auditory processing disorders: New perspectives.* San Diego, CA: Singular Publishing Group.

Colorado Department of Education, Special Education Services Unit. (1997). Auditory processing disorders: A team approach to screening, assessment and intervention practices. Self.

Colorado Department of Education. (2001). *Section 504/ADA guidelines for educators and administrators.* Self.

Fisher, L. I. (1985). Learning disabilities and auditory processing. In R. J. Van Hattam (Ed.), Administration of speech language service in schools: A manual (pp. 231–290). San Diego, CA: College-Hill Press.

Fuchs, D., Mock, D., Morgan, P., & Young, C. (2003). Responsiveness-to-intervention: Definitions, evidence, and implications for the learning disabilities construct. *Learning Disabilities Research & Practice, 18*(3), 157–171.

Katz, J. (1992). Classification of auditory processing disorders. In J. Katz, N. Stecker, & D. Henderson (Eds.), *Central auditory processing: A transdisciplinary review* (pp. 81–91). St. Louis: Mosby Year Book.

Smoski, W. (1990). Use of the CHAPPS in a children's audiology clinic. *Ear and Hearing, 11*(5 Suppl.), 53S–56S.

APPENDIX 1

Guidelines for Classroom Management
of Children with Auditory Processing Deficits[1]

Children with auditory processing deficits typically demonstrate one or more of the following problems:

- Poor auditory attending skills
- Deficits in foreground/background discrimination
- Limitations in auditory memory and retrieval
- Delays in receptive auditory language development

These guidelines are based on strategies designed to minimize the impact of such problems upon academic achievement.

1. **Classroom Placement.** Determine the available options for classroom placement. Consider such critical factors as: the acoustics of the classroom relative to noise level and reverberation, the amount of structure within the classroom, and teacher's communication style. In general, a self-contained structured situation is more effective for children with auditory deficits than an open, unstructured teaching environment.

2. **Look and Listen.** Children with even mild auditory problems function much better in the classroom if they can both look and listen. Therefore, preferential seating is a major consideration in managing such children.

3. **Classroom Seating.** Children with auditory deficits should be assigned seats away from hall or street noise and not more than 10 feet from the teacher. Such seating allows the child to better utilize hearing and visual cues. Flexibility in seating better enables the child to attend and actively participate in class activities.

   In some cases, central auditory testing by the audiologist will reveal a significant difference in processing skills between the child's two ears. In such an instance, preferential classroom seating so the child can favor the better ear is recommended.

   Some audiologists also will recommend plugging the poorer ear with a custom earplug or earmuff as a means for improving the child's auditory function. At present there is no research to either support or refute this practice.

4. **Gain Attention.** Always gain the child's attention before giving directions or initiating class instruction. Calling the child by name or giving a gentle touch will serve to alert the child and to focus attention upon the classroom activity.

5. **Check Comprehension.** Ask children with auditory deficits questions related to the subject under discussion to make certain that they are following and understanding the discussion.

6. **Rephrase and Restate.** Encourage children with auditory processing problems to indicate that they do not understand what has been said. Rephrase the question

---

[1] Adapted with permission from Noel D, Matkin, Ph.D. Director, Children's Hearing Clinic, University of Arizona; Colorado Department of Education (1997), Auditory processing disorders: A team approach to screening, assessment and intervention practices. Appendix D-1, pp. 11–13.

or statement since certain words contain sounds or blends that are not easily discriminated. Also, most children with auditory problems have some delay in language development and may not be familiar with key words. By substituting those words and simplifying the grammar, the intended meaning may be more readily conveyed.

7. **Use Brief Instructions.** Keep instructions relatively short; otherwise, the child with limited auditory memory will be lost.

8. **Pre-tutor.** Read ahead on a subject to be discussed in class so that the child is familiar with new vocabulary and concepts, and thus can more easily follow and participate in classroom discussion. Such pre-tutoring is an important activity that the parents can undertake.

9. **List Key Vocabulary.** Before discussing new material, list key vocabulary on the blackboard. Then try to build the discussion around this key vocabulary.

10. **Visual Aids.** Visual aids help children with limited auditory skills by capitalizing upon strengths in visual processing and thus providing the auditory/visual association often necessary for learning new concepts and language.

11. **Individual Help.** The child with auditory deficits needs individual attention. Whenever possible, provide individual help in order to fill gaps in language and understanding stemming from the child's auditory problems. Attempt to develop specific auditory skills such as closure or memory span through direct training.

12. **Quiet Study Areas.** Provide an individual study area relatively free from auditory and visual distractions. Such an area helps minimize the child's problem in foreground/background discrimination.

13. **Involve Resource Personnel.** Inform resource personnel of planned vocabulary and language topics to be covered in the classroom so that pre-tutoring can supplement classroom activities during the individual therapy.

14. **Write instructions.** Children with auditory problems may not follow verbal instructions accurately. Help them by writing assignments on the board so they can copy them in a notebook. Also, use a "buddy system" by giving a classmate the responsibility for making certain the child is aware of the assignments made during the day.

15. **Encourage Participation.** Encourage participation in expressive language activities such as reading, conversation, storytelling, and creative dramatics. Reading is especially important, since information and knowledge gained through reading help compensate for what may be missed because of auditory deficits. Again, parents can assist the child through the participation in local library reading programs and carry over activities in the home.

16. **Monitor Efforts.** Remember that children with impaired auditory function become fatigued more readily than other children. Subsequently, they do not attend because of the continuous strain resulting from efforts to keep up and to compete in classroom activities. Therefore, provide short intensive periods of instruction with breaks during which the child can move around.

17. **Inform Parents.** Provide parents with consistent input so that they understand the child's successes and difficulties, as well as the need for individual tutoring at home.

18. **Evaluate Progress.** Don't assume a program is working. Instead, evaluate the child's progress on a systematic schedule. It is far better to modify a program than to wait until a child has encountered yet another failure.

S-P-E-E-CH. The following mnemonic device entitled "SPEECH" has been found helpful by teachers and parents over the past few years when communicating with hearing-impaired children. More recently teachers working with children having auditory deficits have reported the same mnemonic to be helpful in classroom management. An analysis of "SPEECH" highlights basic strategies for dealing with attending, memory and receptive language deficits, while capitalizing upon strengths in visual processing.

S	=	State the topic to be discussed
P	=	Pace your conversation at a moderate speed with occasional pauses to permit comprehension
E	=	Enunciate clearly, without exaggerated lip movements
E	=	Enthusiastically communicate, using body language and natural gestures
CH	=	Check comprehension before changing topics.

(Adapted from R. Peddicord, Ph.D.)

APPENDIX 2

Sample 504 Plan[1]

SECTION 504/ADA GUIDELINES FOR EDUCATORS

SECTION 504
Child Accommodation Plan

Child:_____   Date:_____
School:_____   DOB:_____
Review Date:_____   Case manager:_____

1. The child has a physical or mental impairment which substantially limits one or
      more of the major life activities: [ ] YES   [ ] NO

      [ ] caring for one's self   [ ] hearing
      [ ] performing manual tasks   [ ] speaking
      [ ] walking   [ ] working
      [ ] seeing   [ ] learning
      [ ] breathing

2. The disability impacts the child's education.   [ ] YES   [ ] NO

3. Is the child disabled under Section 504?   [ ] YES   [ ] NO

4. Briefly document the basis for determining the disability:
      _____
      _____
      _____

5. Describe areas of need and action to be taken:
      _____
      _____

6. Accommodation Plan
      Area of Difficulty:_____
      Accommodations:_____
      _____
      _____
      Evaluation:_____
      _____

      Area of Difficulty:_____
      Accommodations:_____
      _____
      _____
      Evaluation:_____
      _____

I give permission for my child to receive the above mentioned services.

      Parent   Date

---

[1] Colorado Department of Education (2001). Section 504/ADA Guidelines for Educators, p. 103.

APPENDIX 3

Auditory Processing Disorders Checklist:
Accommodations and Modifications[1]

STUDENT_____ DATE_____ COMPLETED BY_____

The following adaptations are appropriate and necessary for this student (check all that apply). Accommodations are in regular print; *modifications are italicized.*

ENVIRONMENT
____Quiet-acoustically appropriate classroom
____Reduce/minimize distractions:
    Visual_____   Spatial_____
    Auditory_____   Movement____
____Alter physical room arrangemen
____Special seating: classroom(s)_____
    Lunchroom_____   Bus_____
    Auditorium_____   Gym_____

PACING
____Decrease rate of speaking & delivery of instructions; use pauses before & after important points
____Extend time requirements for processing, responding, and task completion
____Allow breaks
____Send school texts, materials home for preview/review

PRESENTATION OF MATERIAL
____Obtain student's attention prior to delivery of information
____Monitor student for fatigue/length of attending time; provide breaks if necessary
____Provide teacher notes
____Use NCR paper for peer to provide notes
____Use functional application of academic skills
____Present demonstrations (model)
____Utilize manipulatives
____Emphasize critical information
____Pre-teach vocabulary
____Make/use vocabulary files
____Share activities
____Use visual sequences
____Use outlines, overheads, graphic highlighting, organizers
____*Reduce language level or reading level of assignments*
____*Vary content (amount to be learned & conceptual level)*

MATERIALS
____Use highlighted texts/study guides
____Use supplementary materials
____Provide note taking assistance: carbonless or Xerox copy of notes of regular students
____Type teacher material
____*Vary type of materials*

ASSIGNMENTS
____Give directions in small, distinct steps
____Use written back-up for oral directions
____Use pictorial directions
____Give extra cues or prompts
____*Vary amount to be practiced*
____*Reduce paper-pencil tasks*
____*Adapt worksheets, packets*
____*Utilize compensatory procedures by providing alternate assignment/strategy when demands of class conflict with student capabilities*
____*Vary grading system (homework, class discussions, special projects); avoid penalizing for spelling errors or penmanship*

SELF-MANAGEMENT/FOLLOW THROUGH
____Use visual daily schedule and calendars
____Train students to "look and listen"
____Check often for understanding/review
____Request parent reinforcement
____Have student repeat directions
____Teach study skills
____Use study sheets to organize material
____Design/write/use long-term assignment timelines
____Review and practice in real situations
____Plan for generalizations
____Organize long-term assignments
____*Vary type of response (copying, recognition, recall with cues, recall)*

TESTING ADAPTATIONS
____Taped (high quality headphones necessary)
____Pictures
____Read test to student
____Paraphrase instructions and test items
____Preview language of test questions
____Test administration by resource person
____Extend time frame
____*Vary amount to be tested*
____*Vary grading system*
____*Vary response expectations—provide guides with cues*

SOCIAL INTERACTION SUPPORT
____Peer partners
____Cooperative learning groups
____Home-school communication notebook

---

[1] Colorado Department of Education (1997), Auditory processing disorders: A team approach to screening, assessment and intervention practices. Appendix H, p. 34.

APPENDIX 4

FM Listening Evaluation[1]

Name:_____ **Date of Birth:**_____

Completed by:_____ **Date:**_____

___parent   ___audiologist   ___teacher   other-specify_____

Length of FM usage:_____   FM brand/model:_____

___FM used daily   Number of hours per day used _____

___FM used occasionally   Number of hours per week used _____

Please rate the following skills based on the child's behavior or performance on typical days.
Indicate if performance was obtained   ☐ with FM or   ☐ without FM (baseline).
To score, subtract any NA (not applicable) items from the total, then determine percent for total
performance and for each situation.

	SELDOM		SOMETIMES		USUALLY	
1. Student responds to his/her name when spoken to:						
a. In a quiet room, within 3 feet	1	2	3	4	5	NA
b. In a quiet room, at 10 feet	1	2	3	4	5	NA
c. In a noisy room, within 3 feet	1	2	3	4	5	NA
d. In a noisy room, at 10 feet	1	2	3	4	5	NA
e. Without visual cues	1	2	3	4	5	NA
f. From another room	1	2	3	4	5	NA
g. Outside/in the community	1	2	3	4	5	NA
2. Student attends to person speaking:						
a. In a quiet room, within 3 feet	1	2	3	4	5	NA
b. In a quiet room, at 10 feet	1	2	3	4	5	NA
c. In a noisy room, within 3 feet	1	2	3	4	5	NA
d. In a noisy room, at 10 feet	1	2	3	4	5	NA
e. Without visual cues	1	2	3	4	5	NA
f. From another room	1	2	3	4	5	NA
g. Outside/in the community	1	2	3	4	5	NA
3. Student distinguishes between words that sound alike (e.g., bay for day, sink for think, or sun for fun):						
a. In a quiet room, within 3 feet	1	2	3	4	5	NA
b. In a quiet room, at 10 feet	1	2	3	4	5	NA
c. In a noisy room, within 3 feet	1	2	3	4	5	NA
d. In a noisy room, at 10 feet	1	2	3	4	5	NA
e. Without visual cues	1	2	3	4	5	NA
f. From another room	1	2	3	4	5	NA
g. Outside/in the community	1	2	3	4	5	NA

---

[1] © Cheryl DeConde Johnson, 2004

	SELDOM		SOMETIMES		USUALLY	
4. Student responds accurately to spoken directions and/or questions:						
a. In a quiet room, within 3 feet	1	2	3	4	5	NA
b. In a quiet room, at 10 feet	1	2	3	4	5	NA
c. In a noisy room, within 3 feet	1	2	3	4	5	NA
d. In a noisy room, at 10 feet	1	2	3	4	5	NA
e. Without visual cues	1	2	3	4	5	NA
f. From another room	1	2	3	4	5	NA
g. Outside/in the community	1	2	3	4	5	NA
5. Student comprehends oral instruction & concepts:						
a. In a quiet room, within 3 feet	1	2	3	4	5	NA
b. In a quiet room, at 10 feet	1	2	3	4	5	NA
c. In a noisy room, within 3 feet	1	2	3	4	5	NA
d. In a noisy room, at 10 feet	1	2	3	4	5	NA
e. Without visual cues	1	2	3	4	5	NA
f. From another room	1	2	3	4	5	NA
g. Outside/in the community	1	2	3	4	5	NA

TOTAL SCORE: _____/(175)   = ☐ %   ____with FM   ____without FM

Situational Analysis: Quiet (a,b) _____/(50) = ☐ %   **Noise (c,d,g)** ____/(75) = ☐ %

Auditory only (e) _____/(25)   = ☐ %   **Distance (b,d,f)** ____/(75) = ☐ %

Information on FM Use:

FM system is easy to operate:	1	2	3	4	5	NA
FM system has remained in good working order:	1	2	3	4	5	NA
FM system is comfortable to use:	1	2	3	4	5	NA
Student tries to turn FM system off:	1	2	3	4	5	NA
Feedback (whistling noise) is present with HA/FM:	1	2	3	4	5	NA
Student refuses to use FM:	1	2	3	4	5	NA

Indicate types of activities the FM is used for?

____listening/language/speech therapy   ____story-time/reading   ____all academic classes
____PE/Art/Music   ____recess   ____lunch   ____extra-curricular activities other
(describe)_____

For which of the above activities do you think the FM was most beneficial?

What do you think is the greatest benefit(s) of the FM system?

What do you think is the greatest challenge(s) with the FM system?

APPENDIX 5

FAQs: Auditory Processing Disorders[1]

Hearing is a complex process which involves sensitivity to sound (e.g., one's ability to detect that sound is present), as well as interpretation of sound, resulting in meaningful recognition and comprehension of information. Many individuals who have normal hearing sensitivity have difficulty with the latter causing problems understanding conversations in noisy environments, sustaining or dividing attention, learning new vocabulary words, following complex directions, and learning foreign languages. This type of auditory problem is referred to as a central auditory processing disorder (CAPD). These problems can affect a student's ability to develop language skills, succeed academically, and communicate effectively. In recognition of the complexity of issues involved in CAPD assessment, the Colorado Department of Education has published guidelines, *Central Auditory Processing Disorders: A Team Approach to Screening, Assessment and Intervention Practices* (CDE, Special Education Services Unit, 1997).

What is CAPD?

The following definition, developed through a Consensus Conference on CAPD sponsored by the American Speech-Language-Hearing Association, reflects the complexity of the many functions involved in the processing of auditory information.

Central auditory processes are the auditory system mechanisms and processes responsible for the following behavioral phenomena:
- Sound localization and lateralization
- Auditory discrimination
- Temporal aspects of audition including temporal resolution, temporal masking, temporal integration, and temporal ordering
- Auditory performance with competing acoustic signals
- Auditory performance with degraded signals

These mechanisms and processes apply to nonverbal as well as verbal signals and may affect many areas of function, including speech and language. (ASHA, 1996, p. 41)

How is CAPD differentiated from learning disabilities, language disorders, ADD, and ADHD?

All of these disorders share common characteristics and are often inter-related. Hence, there is significant co-morbidity within this group of problems. The etiologies may be developmentally or neurologically-based. CAPD is differentiated from these other disorders when the deficit is primarily in the interpretation of auditory information. However, it is often also accompanied by attention, memory, and language/learning problems, making the identification of CAPD complex.

How is CAPD assessed and who makes the CAPD diagnosis?

The assessment of CAPD requires a multidisciplinary approach involving audiologists, speech language pathologists, psychologists, classroom and special education

---

[1] Cheryl D. Johnson, Ed.D. and Kathleen Fahey, Ph.D., Colorado Department of Education, Exceptional Student Services Unit, 2000.

teachers, and school nurses. A physician or psychiatrist may be involved when attention deficit disorder is suspected or other significant health or neurological conditions exist. The diagnosis of CAPD should be determined by the multidisciplinary team.

Assessment tools range from screening to diagnostic depending on the presenting concerns, history, and interventions attempted. Disciplines should collaborate in assessment planning to insure that all areas of suspected difficulty are considered. School teams will benefit from working together to develop a reasonable assessment approach. Factors which may preclude assessment include age, cognitive ability, peripheral hearing status, and primary language used by the student. The Colorado CAPD Guidelines offer a referral and evaluation process as well as suggested assessment tools.

What are the educational implications of CAPD and how is it treated?
CAP disorders may be manifested in a variety of ways depending on the student and the nature of the problem. While students with CAPD share many common characteristics, specific profile differences result in different educational outcomes for each student. Academic, social, and vocational issues need to be considered when determining interventions. Interventions should include classroom management (e.g., acoustical environment, communication strategies), appropriate accommodations and modifications, treatment which includes specific auditory-based training and metacognitive learning strategies, as well as consideration of assistive listening devices.

How can assessment data be used to make treatment decisions?
The goal of the multidisciplinary assessment is to determine a specific intervention plan for each student. Students with CAPD are often categorized in 3–4 primary profile types. These profiles should assist the team in the identification of specific intervention goals and activities for each of the four intervention areas.

How do children with CAPD qualify for Special Education?
CAPD is not a category within the special education disability definitions. Therefore, students who exhibit CAPD must qualify with either a speech-language disability or a perceptual/communicative disability. If the problems are not significant enough to meet the eligibility criteria of these categories, students may be eligible for support under Section 504. Please refer to the Colorado Department of Education Rules for the Administration of the Exceptional Children's Act (ECEA) and the CDE 504 Handbook for complete special education definitions and 504 regulations.

For more information about CAPD see your school audiologist or speech language pathologist.
This document can be downloaded from the Colorado Department of Education website: www.cde.state.co.us.

Reference:
American Speech-Language-Hearing Association (1996). Central auditory processing: Current status of research and implications for clinical practice. *American Journal of Audiology*, 5(2), 41–45.

Suggestions for Parents, Teachers, Speech-Language Pathologists, and Students: Enhancing Functional Outcomes in Children with APD

Dorothy A. Kelly
St. Joseph's College

Before considering suggestions to strengthen outcomes for parents, teachers, speech-language pathologists, and students with auditory processing disorder (APD), it is helpful to describe the impact of this complex challenge on the child's life. Fundamentally, the child with APD is a *child* who *happens* to have *auditory processing disorder*.

This child most likely has a family, siblings, and friends. The child's life is similar to that of other children. The difference is that the child with APD *processes* auditory stimuli through a diffuser. The child hears, but does not always comprehend. The child tries to *listen*, but the pathway from the ear to the brain seems short-circuited (Boone, 1987).

Everyday experiences for this child may be frustrating, isolating, and confusing. Because school performance is often erratic or weak, the child may feel stupid. Predictably, self-esteem and social/behavioral problems are common (Keller, 1998). In fact, according to Keith (2000), low self-esteem may be the *inevitable* result of failures in several contexts (e.g., social, academic, and linguistic). The child may appear withdrawn, sullen or shy, while even more complex issues underlie these behaviors (Bellis, 1996).

The information that follows is sensitive to the well-being of the *whole* child (i.e., the *student*). It includes suggestions to make home and school easier places to navigate. Some suggestions are pragmatic (e.g., tips for recalling information or reducing background noise); others address the student's attitude, perspective, and self-image. This combination is practical for obvious reasons. To disregard the child's feelings and emotions would be impractical. The *child* is not the *disorder*. It is a child who goes to school and becomes a student.

The present perspective is eclectic, drawing from a variety of theoretical bases. Important discussions of auditory processing approaches and diagnostic categories (e.g., Musiek, Gollegly, & Ross, 1985; Ferre, 1992; Katz, Stecker, & Masters, 1994; Bellis, 1996) are best served elsewhere.

This chapter is divided into five sections:

    I. Suggestions for Parents;
    II. Suggestions for Teachers (and Other Professionals);
    III. Suggestions for Speech-Language Pathologists;
    IV. Suggestions for Students—and, because *the process* extends well beyond discharge from therapy—
    V. Suggestions for Transition and Carryover.

Sections I through IV are each divided into two categories: Basics and Specifics. Information provided in the former category is fundamental in nature, while that found in the latter category is more detailed and descriptive.

SUGGESTIONS FOR PARENTS

Basics: Fundamentally, parents need *information* (Bellis, 1996). To understand auditory processing disorder in the home, parents should recognize possible symptoms. A child with APD may demonstrate:

- difficulty recalling names, dates, times, numbers, words, and so on;
- difficulty following simple, complex, or deferred directions;
- problems processing in noisy or distracting settings;
- better performance in small groups;
- disorganization/messiness;
- need for statements or questions to be repeated;
- inappropriate responses to questions and in conversations;
- slow response to questions;
- confusion with words, sounds, and so on;
- poor self-esteem;
- poor social skills/few friends (Kelly, 1995);
- easily distracted by ambient sounds;
- diffculty attending to relevant auditory stimuli;
- inability to complete meaning from material presented orally (Gillet, 1993);
- has difficulties with receptive and expressive language;
- has reading, Spelling and other academic difficulties;
- has behavior problems (Keller, 1988);
- says "Huh?" and "What" repeatedly;
- forgets what is said within a few minutes;
- learns poorly through the auditory channel;
- lacks motivation to learn;
- daydreams (attention drifts); (Fisher, 1976).

Successful social interactions require facile language skills. Interactions often involve rapid verbal exchanges between two or more children. The child with APD may not interpret and follow quickly produced speech (e.g., conversations). This child may also display logic problems (Bellis, 1996). The appropriate selection, structuring, and sequencing of verbal exchanges are difficult. Social interactions become intrinsically challenging for this child.

Predictably, the child often finds social interactions with age-peers intimidating. Willeford (1985) maintained that many children with APD seek friendships with younger children due to social failures with age-peers. Some children, described by parents as *loners*, seem to find *all* social interactions troubling.

Problems for children with APD are not limited to social interactions. Failure in school is understandable (Bellis, 1996). The majority of learning activities involve speaking and listening (Palmer, 1997). Teachers must be heard and understood before information can be assimilated. Fundamentally, the child with APD has difficulty attending to information through the auditory channel (Fisher, 1976). The student may demonstrate problems with auditory comprehension, auditory discrimination, auditory memory, auditory figure–ground (i.e., the ability to screen out background noises), and auditory attention, among others. Listening and learning may become frustrating and exhausting experiences.

Reading tasks often become particularly troublesome (Gillet, 1993). Sound–symbol associations and auditory–visual connections (e.g., heard and seen phonetic sounds and symbols), among other skills, are often weak. This child may confuse sounds or words, making spelling tests, following directions, and dictation difficult (Kelly, 1995).

Many children with auditory processing difficulties also experience an increased incidence of otitis media (Keller, 1998), resulting in frequent absences from school. This child may have to play *academic catch-up* with a limited set of tools.

Specifics: The greatest gift a parent can give a child with auditory processing disorder is *acceptance*. Home should be a safe zone, a refuge from the stresses and demands of the outside world (i.e., school and social settings). Parents should not expect the same level of listening effort at home as in school. The child will soon *burn out* under such circumstances.

Social, emotional, and behavioral challenges may be intrinsic to APD (Keller, 1998). Parents are asked to *Blame the disorder, not the student*, when challenging behaviors arise (Bellis, 2002a). Suggestions to ease processing and behavioral challenges may be tailored to individual needs within the home setting. For example, family members may discuss what works and what does not work within their unique home environment. They may analyze communication challenges that occur at particular times of the day, in certain rooms, or with particular communication partners. Family members may discuss types/levels of information (e.g., complicated/deferred directions, conversations, telephone messages, or detailed explanations) that seem difficult (Bellis, 2002a). In general, everyone benefits when speakers agree to be specific and succinct and when conversation partners allow extra processing time when needed. The child's *wheels are turning*, but perhaps at a slower rate (Bellis, 2002a).

Other suggestions for parents include: talk with and listen to your child daily, gain his or her attention visually and auditorily before starting a conversation, use picture cards or key words to help sequence routine tasks, insist on completion of ability-level activities, and be objective/realistic/patient. If a task is too difficult, parents should move on to one that is easier. Then they should return to the original task, modifying it so that the student can be successful (Florida Department of Education, 2001).

Perhaps most importantly, parents should be *easy on themselves*. Parents did not create their child's auditory processing problems. It is *human* to feel impatient, weary, and overwhelmed at times. Help is available from several sources including the pediatrician, speech-language pathologist, teacher, or psychologist (Colorado Department of Education, 1997).

SUGGESTIONS FOR TEACHERS

Basics: Teachers should understand the impact of APD on academic and classroom performance. They also need classroom management strategies (Bellis, 1996). Important team members, teachers are in the best position to identify academic progress and observe social skills (among other behaviors).

It is helpful for teachers to recognize symptoms of APD in order to modify teaching techniques and identify learning strategies that result in better academic performance. Symptoms may include:

- poor reading, writing, spelling, and academic skills;
- difficulties with attention;
- difficulties with learning a foreign language;
- behavioral, psychological, or social problems;
- difficulties in taking notes (Baran, 1998b);
- poor phonics and sound discrimination;
- poor receptive/expressive language abilities;
- poor auditory memory (span and sequence) skills;
- slow/delayed response to verbal stimuli;
- difficulty learning through the auditory channel;
- low frustration tolerance/poor self-control;
- poor social/peer relations (Keller, 1998);
- difficulty with simple, complex, immediate, or deferred directions;
- difficulty with dictated materials;
- better performance in one-to-one settings;
- difficulty with verbal math problems;
- difficulty with categorizations and associations;
- difficulty interpreting abstract materials (Kelly, 1995);
- deficient fine or gross motor skills;
- may be withdrawn or Sullen;
- inability to effectively participate in class discussions;
- verbal IQ scores often lower than performance scores;
- requires considerable structure/organization in the classroom;
- poor singing and music skills;
- skill scatter across subtests, with weaknesses in auditory-dependent areas (Bellis, 1996);
- difficulty listening in noisy environments;
- inconsistent response to speech;
- difficulty in identifying sound source/direction;
- difficulty following complex directions (Keith, 1995); and others.

Hood and Berlin (1996) identified other characteristics including poor auditory integration, poor auditory closure (e.g., recognizing that_ase_all is *baseball*), weak auditory localization (noting sound sources), weak auditory figure–ground skills (i.e., the ability to screen out background noises), and inadequate auditory sequencing skills, among others. Keith (2000) added that children with auditory processing disorder may demonstrate inconsistent responses to auditory stimuli and unexplainable fear of loud noises.

Owens, Metz, and (2003) Haas summarized symptoms simply: The child eventually diagnosed with auditory processing disorder often initially presents with an apparent inability to *listen in a classroom environment*. This inability is often related to the acoustics in a typical classroom. Rarely does a teacher present information in a completely quiet classroom at optimal distance from all listeners. The result is often degraded speech (analogous to listening to a poorly tuned radio). The student with APD may experience *more* difficulty in perception than the typical listener (Roseberry-McKibbon & Hegde, 2000). The impact on classroom performance is clear.

The child with auditory processing disorder often presents a confusing and inconsistent profile to the classroom teacher. For example, the student may have strong auditory memory skills (e.g., auditory memory for sentences), yet appear unable to complete directions (i.e, executive difficulties). The student may follow directions in quiet settings, but be unable to complete similar directions in the classroom (i.e., a noisy setting). Many children perform well academically until third grade, when concepts and tasks become more abstract.

Test results may also confuse the teacher. For example, the student's profile may include adequate or better nonverbal intelligence (perhaps indicating fundamental cognitive potentials). Yet academic performance may be weak, leading parents and teachers to mistakenly assume the child is simply *not trying hard enough*.

When pressed for reasons for poor academic performance, such students are also confused. They do not know why they cannot follow directions or remember homework assignments. The child does not know why he or she can prepare for spelling tests at home the night before and *know* all the words, yet fail the following day. The result of such confusion is a cycle of decline (psychologically and academically), as the student experiences pressure to perform better. It is easier to *give up* than to continue trying.

Teachers should recognize that although the accurate and timely diagnosis of APD is challenging enough, it is often comorbid with learning disability (Martin, 1997) or attention deficit disorder (Keller, 1998), among other complications. All symptoms are mistakenly associated with the more apparent disorder.

Difficulties with auditory processing may even appear in preschool-age students. *At-risk* behaviors include a greater likelihood of *ignoring* a speaker when engaged in activity, unusual reaction/sensitivity to sounds or noise, difficulty with sound localization, confusion with similar-sounding words, and difficulties with complex directions produced in single sentences (Paton, copyright 1996–2003. http://www.ldonline.org/ld_indepth/process_deficit/capd_paton.html). According to Masters (1998), other at-risk behaviors include word-finding difficulties, cluttering, and poor recall of rote memory rhymes (e.g., nursery rhymes and the alphabet song). Other at-risk behaviors include difficulty using and understanding why questions poor awareness of conversation rules and ineffective short-term memory (Richard, 2001).

Programs that identify *at-risk* preschoolers and provide appropriate stimulation, may reduce symptoms that impact on literacy and language. Specifically, Musiek and Chermak (1994) recommended that programs target auditory skills development (e.g., sequencing games, listening to stories and responding to questions, and auditory discrimination activities). Bellis (1996) noted that although comprehensive assessment is not possible in preschool-age children, intervention is needed as soon as APD is suspected.

Specifics: When teachers have a clear understanding of the diverse symptoms associated with auditory processing disorder in the classroom (and their impact on language and academics), strategies often become apparent. Difficulties specific to individual students may be identified through observation, assessment, and consultation with the speech-language pathologist.

Difficulties in following directions (simple/complex or immediate/deferred) are particularly common in the classroom. The process may be complicated by factors such as emotional status, memory/attention/language deficits, and background noise, among others. Directions embedded in other information are often confusing and particularly troublesome for the student with APD. It is helpful to break up complicated or complex directions into shorter, simpler units. The student may be asked to restate the direction as he or she understands it. Teachers should be specific, brief, and clear. Speech should be expressive, slightly louder and slower than usual. Eye contact is usually helpful (Kelly, 1995).

The student with APD may require additional processing time. Under such circumstances, the repetition of information stops the processing process and often adds an emotional overlay. Students are often quick to pick up impatience or irritation.

The student with APD often experiences other academic challenges in the classroom. Materials and curriculum modifications are often helpful. They may include: simplify vocabulary in written directions; complete spelling activities in resource or therapy room; use *hands-on* activities when possible; reduce the number (and complexity) of verbal math problems; build awareness of word families, root bases, and rhyming words; use a combination of logical phonics and sight vocabulary to facilitate decoding and encoding; and identify points of irregularity in irregularly spelled words (Lindamood & Lindamood, 1979), among others.

Teaching techniques and styles may also be modified. They may include: encourage speechreading or communication reading (i.e., ask the student to watch the speaker's face, gestures, and body language); teach mnemonic devices; repeat and rephrase when needed; reduce distractions; allow peer or adult tutors; allow cooperative learning experiences; maintain structure and routines; preview, state, and review information; gain the student's attention before speaking; write homework assignments on the blackboard; allow use of tape recorders; write directions out; emphasize nonverbal (gestures and facial expressions) and paraverbal (intonation and rate/rhythm) cues; monitor the student's fatigue and comprehension; and encourage participation in class activities (Baran, 1998a).

Frequent checks for comprehension may eliminate misunderstanding of auditory information. The teacher may also preteach vocabulary and new information (Bellis, 2002b). This strategy involves providing key concepts and vocabulary in writing before the topic is introduced, so that the student is more comfortable with the information presented.

In addition, the teacher may provide salient cues, such as, *This is important* or *These are the main points* (Florida Department of Education, 2001). Perhaps the teacher may adopt a language production style used by caregivers of young children (i.e., *motherese*). This technique involves slow, sing-song, simplified speech accompanied by slightly exaggerated facial expressions and gestures (Masters, 1998). This style should be modified to suit the age and processing needs of the student.

Another modification involves the teacher's speaking rate. A decrease in speech rate from 150 words per minute (average) to 110 words per minute can increase comprehension for children with auditory processing difficulties (Peck, LaPointe, Abbott, & Mercer, 1978).

Teachers (and parents) have found the SPEECH mnemonic helpful when working with hearing-impaired children. It has been successfully used with students with auditory processing difficulties as well, to capitalize on visual strengths while minimizing attention, memory, and language weaknesses.

S . . . . State the topic to be discussed.

P . . . Pace conversation at a moderate speed (with occasional pauses to facilitate comprehension).

E . . . . Enunciate clearly.

E . . . Enthusiastically communicate, using body language and natural gestures.

CH . . . Check comprehension before changing topics (adapted from R. Peddicord Colorado Department of Education).

The classroom listening environment may be modified in several ways to suit individual needs. Suggestions include: reduce reverberation and ambient noise; provide a quiet work space; allow frequency-modulated (FM) systems and other technology (e.g., desktop soundfield systems); when appropriate, encourage small group or one-to-one interactions; use visual aids when possible; avoid open classrooms; use cork board for bulletin boards; and use suspended acoustic tile for ceilings and use cushions on chairs, among others. Some children may benefit from wearing earmuffs (very selectively) to reduce auditory distractions. Preferential seating should be flexible to accommodate student listening and visual needs. Students should be able to see and hear the teacher without interference. It can be a mistake to place the student too close to the teacher. A slightly greater distance usually allows broader speechreading or communication reading (i.e., gestures and body language, not just lip movements).

Lighting in the room can affect speechreading skills. Fluorescent lighting can be harsh and produce glare. Also, speakers should not stand in front of windows (talking when they are backlit). Writing on the chalkboard (with the teacher's back to the student) or looking down at notes can also negatively affect speechreading performance (Bellis, 2002b).

Academic expectations may be adjusted to suit student needs. Modifications include:

- untimed tests;
- alternative test formats;
- test administration in alternative settings (e.g., therapy or resource room);
- reduced course loads;
- video-recording or audio-recording of lectures;
- provision of outlines, lecture notes, or preview materials;
- waiving or modifying academic requirements (e.g., foreign language);
- scheduling of classes and therapy sessions to accommodate fatigue issues (Baran, 1998b);
- use of Palm Pilots or personal device assistants (PDAs);
- vary type of materials presented;

- vary amount of material to be tested;
- vary grading system;
- use pictorial directions; and
- preview the language used in test directions (Colorado Department of Education, 1997).
- use of assistive listening devices (ALDs)
- use of peer notetaker
- allow preferential or roving seating (Ciocci, 2002)

Fatigue and burnout (in both teachers and students) can be prevented by identifying and addressing listening, language, and environmental issues in the classroom. Teachers who work cooperatively and proactively with students with APD (in team-like fashion) may realize unexpected positive outcomes.

SUGGESTIONS FOR SPEECH-LANGUAGE PATHOLOGISTS

Basics: Speech-language pathologists (SLPs) assess the effects of auditory processing disorder on language and language-dependent behaviors. They also provide direct intervention (remediative activities) for deficient auditory skill areas; address weak language and academic skills; teach compensatory strategies; often serve as team coordinators; and provide important information to parents, teachers, and others. SLPs often implement appropriate management strategies (e.g., environmental modifications, such as carpeted flooring and use of wall hangings to reduce reverberation).

In general, management programs are categorized into two approaches. The SLP focuses on language, academic, and compensatory auditory skills. The challenge to the clinician is to identify the student's individual profile of auditory processing assets and deficits, relate it to academic and social functions, and tailor an intervention program that optimizes potentials and minimizes challenges. While there are well-received, commercially produced programs (e.g., Fast ForWord, Brain Gym, and Earobics) designed to improve auditory processing skills, the SLP should know that no single program is suited to all children. Cognitive therapy that focuses on language improvement, auditory training, and organizational skills may also prove helpful (Northern & Downs, 2002).

The audiologist focuses on enhancing the acoustic environment by improving the signal-to-noise ratio. Recommendations may include the use of assistive listening devices (e.g., personal auditory trainers and soundfield systems). Audiologists and speech-language pathologists should work closely together to monitor the function and use of all technology.

Detailed discussion of intervention and management options is best served elsewhere. This section will offer suggestions applicable to *many* students with auditory processing disorders. The insightful clinician uses suggestions selectively with individual students.

Suggestions are divided into three subcategories: *Suggestions for School*, *Suggestions for Other Settings*, and *Clinical Suggestions*. The first two subcategories represent suggestions that may be taught to improve social and academic functioning; the latter includes practical ideas to facilitate the clinical process.

Specifics:

Suggestions for School

As noted earlier, following directions can be particularly troublesome for the student with APD and is worthy of additional attention. Difficulties may be due to:

- deficits in auditory memory (i.e., the student cannot recall the information),
- deficits in language (i.e., the student cannot understand the direction),
- deficits in execution (i.e., the student cannot carry out any direction, cannot transition from one part of a direction to the next, or cannot carry out a direction that is too general or too complicated),
- deficits in attention (i.e., the student cannot maintain attention long enough to absorb the direction; this student may simply be drained from processing information throughout the school day),
- difficulties with time (i.e., the student can carry out the direction now, but not later or the student cannot process the direction quickly),
- difficulties with auditory figure–ground skills (i.e., the student cannot process the direction in noise),
- difficulties with sensory integration (i.e., the student may not be able to carry out a direction that involves an integrated response, such as writing and listening as in a spelling test; the student may not be able to carry out a direction that involves an integrated production, such as when the teacher speaks and writes on the board simultaneously),
- difficulties in reverberant environments (i.e., the student cannot process the direction due to the *echo effect* or sounds bouncing off flat, hard surfaces at a slight time delay),
- or any combination of the above . . . or other reasons.

When the student's particular difficulties are identified, suggestions often become apparent. For example, if the student demonstrates a sensory integration deficit, the clinician (or teacher) may provide the direction in parts (e.g., first state that a direction will follow; then state the direction; then provide a visual cue such as pointing, highlighting, and so on; then repeat if needed). If the student has difficulty following directions in noisy (and even less noisy) environments, the clinician (or teacher) may modify the listening environment by reducing classroom chatter, closing hallway doors, carpeting floors, or shutting windows. If reverberant environments (classrooms) present challenges, then wall hangings, drapes, and area rugs may help.

When the student's problem in following directions involves a poor auditory memory, the speech-language pathologist may encourage the student to repeat the direction aloud. This technique must be modified under certain circumstances. For example, the repetition of information at conversation-level volume may be disruptive in the classroom. The student may need to repeat the information in a low voice (or in his or her head). Verbatim repetition of information (including directions) may be less efficient than the repetition of key words or phrases (Masters, 1998). Critical elements of a direction (fewer words) may be recalled more easily. Sometimes, it is helpful for students to visualize themselves carrying out the direction.

The SLP addresses other language, academic, and processing needs as well. A brief summary of representative suggestions follows:

- subvocalization: A cueing device to recall information by repetition in a low voice (Kelly, 1995).
- reauditorization: A higher-order cueing device to recall information by repetition in one's mind (Kelly, 1995).
- syllabication skills: To improve spelling, reading, decoding, and writing skills by *hearing* the parts/segments of words.
- auditory chunking/auditory clustering: To organize material into fewer bits of information; to group information into logical units, such as categories (Masters, 1998); to recall unrelated sequences such as phone numbers/to recall by meaning or association (Sloan, 1998).
- other recall cues: Deferred recall of information may improve with the use of visual cues such as stickers (on notebooks or wrist) or strings (around wrist or fingers).
- note-taking skills: A skill taught in steps (e.g., writing to simple dictation with a time delay, identifying/highlighting key words, phrase writing, summarizing in one's own words, and so on). The note-taker must be able to identify key details and rephrase information. Such skills must be *taught*. For example, the student may be asked to recognize important points in a text as it is read aloud, then fill in the blanks on a prepared sheet (Masters, 1998).
- organization: All forms of organization including the use of routines, lists, calendars, homework pads, and chore lists increase predictability and decrease processing challenges.
- responsibility: The student is ultimately responsible to manage his or her listening environment. For example, he or she must ask for clarification when needed, employ recall strategies, and prepare for spelling tests, as directed (perhaps using a tape recorder and lists).
- context cues for auditory logic: The student should note surroundings and time (e.g., classroom after lunch) as cues to apply listening logic (e.g., *She must be talking about the spelling test because we always have a test on Fridays after lunch*).

The speech-language pathologist may teach the student strategies to facilitate higher-order comprehension:

- Use grammatical context cues (e.g., structure patterns in sentences and phrases).
- Form visual images in mind to aid recall.
- Catalog new information into already existing information or categories.
- Notice speaker's delivery style, voice characteristics, and so on.
- Identify the intent of a message (as opposed to literal content).
- Identify the main ideas of a message, ignoring less critical information.
- Identify redundant messages.
- Identify ambiguous and unclear information (Kelly, 1995).

Butler (1983) suggested *alternative means* to derive meaning from auditory (verbal) information. These techniques allow the student to hear and process auditory information with a new set of *tools*. Strategies include teaching mnemonic strategies, analysis of new ideas, paragraphing, and the use of key words to think systematically.

Suggestions for Other Settings

Listening skills are critical to many aspects of *social* competence. Many students with auditory processing disorder experience unsatisfying interpersonal relationships, in part due to poor listening skills (Kelly, 1995; Bellis, 2002a). The student with APD who develops stronger listening skills may be more likely to initiate and engage in social conversations.

Pease (1981) devised the LISTEN mnemonic for *clients* (not specific to children with APD) who need a retrievable framework to improve listening skills in social settings. After the client learns the mnemonic, Parente' and Hermann (2003) suggested the clinician videotape a short conversation. Afterwards, the client is asked to identify which components of the LISTEN mnemonic were followed and which were not. A modification of the LISTEN mnemonic is particularly suited to students with auditory processing difficulties:

L: *Look* at the person with whom you are speaking (eye contact aids in speech-reading);

I: *Interest* yourself in the conversation (pay attention and listen generously/politely);

S: *Speak* less than half the time (it allows more time to process and comprehend);

T: *Try* not to interrupt or change the subject (reduces the likelihood of missing information and aids in comprehension);

E: *Evaluate* what is said (do not simply hear information; listen, assess, and consider carefully; use auditory logic—*Does this makes sense*?).

N: *Notice* body language and facial expressions (much of communication is produced in nonverbal form; what is missed in words may often be found in gestures, facial expressions, and body language).

The speech-language pathologist may further add to the LISTEN mnemonic by teaching other listening techniques. For example, teach the student to identify timing (e.g., rate and rhythm) and language-based acoustic cues (e.g., intonation and accent) to enhance comprehension. *How* something is said is as important as *what* is said.

Clinical Suggestions

Suggestions to improve clinical/therapy outcomes are many. Detailed discussion is not practical here. A brief summary of *clinical tips* follows: The student with auditory processing disorder requires a more flexible, evolving, collaborative, and innovative approach to assessment and therapy design. In general, it is not productive to *compare* the student with APD to more typically functioning students (except for purposes of perspective or documentation). Even comparisons to other students with APD are often misguided (due to the degree of diversity within the population).

Insightful assessment of APD results in an understanding of how individual auditory processing skill deficits interrelate (e.g., how poor auditory attention impacts auditory memory functions in a noisy classroom), among other findings. Treatment planning reflects an understanding of how the student's individual skill profile affects academic and language functions (e.g., how auditory discrimination deficits may affect spelling or decoding performance). The clinician should ask, What is my rationale for implementing this goal with this student at this time?

The identification of an appropriate therapy setting is highly individualized. For example, at particular points in the *process* of intervention, *push-ins* (supposedly less disruptive to schedules and more naturalistic) may not be more productive than *pull-outs*. Some students cannot function well with a clinician in close proximity (providing a second set of information to process, often in a noisy, distracting classroom). In some cases, this challenging setting and dynamic is best suited to the end of a therapy program.

Decisions about *time* from various perspectives are important as well. *More* therapy time is not necessarily better than *less* therapy time. Targeted, time-efficient therapy is often more productive and less disruptive to the student's schedule. It is often difficult for the student with language processing and academic difficulties to "catch-up" upon return to class.

In addition, identification of how the student's profile evolves *over time* is important. Last year's problems are not necessarily consistent with this year's problems. Progress and maturation (among other factors) may influence skill levels. Ask, *Is this student better able to function within the classroom today as compared to last year? How may he or she function next year? How can we get there?*

Perhaps the most important clinical tip has little to do with assessment or management. It has everything to do with the nature of the clinician–student interaction. The quality of the rapport between the SLP and student may significantly affect clinical and academic outcomes. It may affect the student's self-esteem, motivation, effort, and progress. Psychology and speech-language pathology are intricately intertwined. Again, it is a *child* who *happens* to have an auditory processing disorder.

SUGGESTIONS FOR STUDENTS

Basics: Students need to become aware of their particular auditory processing challenges, be able to identify difficult listening circumstances (and do what is needed to alleviate them), and apply strategies acquired in therapy on a regular basis. The student must become responsible for *keeping up his or her end of the bargain*. For example, when the student fails a spelling test, it may be because he or she has *chosen* not to prepare for it adequately (e.g., by using a tape recorder and subvocalization strategies). The student must understand the cause–effect relationship between choices made and consequences.

The student must be realistic. Therapy may not remediate all auditory processing challenges. However, it may provide coping strategies that make listening easier. Perhaps the most fundamental suggestion for students is to realize that *who* they are is not reflected by a diagnostic label, grades, or how they compare to siblings or peers. Intelligence, skill, talent, and worth are describable by many parameters. Performance in school, although important, is not the only indicator. Comparison to or competition with others is never productive. However, competition with oneself (*Can I do better in math this year than last year? How can I do this?*) is often motivating.

Specifics: Before identifying specific strategies for school and home, broader notions about the student him or herself are helpful. The better-prepared student is knowledgeable about his or her own auditory processing strengths and challenges. When the full range of auditory processing skills is examined, the student with APD often demonstrates areas of strength, perhaps previously unidentified. (Too often, teachers, parents, and the student notice the weaker areas and ignore or minimize the stronger areas). These strengths can become the foundations upon which an intervention program is planned. The student who believes he or she has *tools* to work with is often motivated to improve outcomes (e.g., better grades and less confusion at home). This student becomes vested in the *process*.

Psychological/academic burnout is far too common in students with auditory processing disorder. They have already *given up*. This unfortunate *outcome* may be the result of inadequate or delayed identification/assessment, poor program planning, or ineffective communication within the intervention team, among other reasons. Burnout can occur as early as in the lower grades. What happened to the student who happily got on the bus, anxious to go to school in kindergarten?

Suggestions for School

School is a dynamic and challenging environment that requires *active listening*. Bellis (2002a) offered suggestions for active (conscious) listening.

- Sit/stand up straight. This position facilitates alertness and participation.
- Lean the upper body toward the speaker (suggests undivided attention).
- Keep eyes on the speaker. This behavior results in greater concentration and facilitates speechreading. Much of *face-to-face* communication is nonverbal (e.g., gestures) or paraverbal (e.g., intonation or prosody) in nature.
- Eliminate or reduce unnecessary movements. Do not watch television, read, or play video games while listening. Energy should be directed toward listening.
- Do not allow the mind to drift. Force it back to the listening task at hand.

Additional suggestions include:

- Do it now, not later. You are less likely to forget tasks.
- Study aloud. Read notes aloud, while listening to your voice.
- Proofread written materials aloud. Listen to your own voice cues (e.g., *I paused here. My voice went up here*). They can help identify run-on sentences, punctuation markers, and so on.
- Spell and decode difficult words aloud. Hear word parts and syllabication cues.
- Get organized. Wear a watch, work in an uncluttered work space, follow routines, and so on (Kelly, 1995).
- Notice that women's voices are different than men's voices. Men's voices are often a little louder, fuller, and lower in pitch. Sometimes they appear less expressive than women's voices (with fewer intonation cues). Women tend to support their speech with more gestures and facial expressions (Kelly, 1998).
- Get the *whole picture*. Everyone has strengths, as well as challenges. APD is not related to intelligence.

Sloan (1998) identified integral components to active listening:

.... know the purpose of the listening task. *Why am I listening? What am I asked to learn or do?*

.... associate new ideas with known information. *What do I know about this already?*

.... question the sense of the information. *Does this make sense to me?*

.... use context cues to predict. *What may happen next? What is the next step?*

.... get the main point. *What is the main point? What is most important to know?*

Auditory memory is fundamental to active listening skills. Chermak and Musiek (1992) offered suggestions to improve auditory memory. They include chunking, mnemonics, imagery (see yourself carrying out the task), and drawing pictures to cue recall. The student may also view the listening task as an event; that is, the more memorable the event, the easier it is to remember. For example, a 10th birthday party may be recalled, but not lunch 2 days ago. The speaker's voice (intonation cues), body language, and facial expressions as well context (location and surroundings) may be noted. Such observations add to the richness of the experience.

Active listening can be stressful and fatiguing. The hearing-impaired student who speechreads all day often arrives home exhausted. The student with APD may share a similar burden. This student should take brief breaks (from listening) when needed. Other *active* strategies are not restricted to the listening process. They include speaking up (e.g., ask questions when understanding is incomplete, request a change in seating if noise is distracting, and so on) and generally taking responsibility for personal progress (Baran, 1998b). This self-reliance will serve the student well beyond the classroom years.

TRANSITION AND CARRYOVER

Students with auditory processing disorder experience numerous transitions. Some take place as the student progresses from one level of therapy to the next. Others involve educational placement (e.g., the student may move from a self-contained setting to a mainstreamed classroom). Academic transitions occur as the student moves from grade school to middle school, then to high school and graduation.

Transitions may also involve the student's use of strategies. Because processing difficulties may be temporary or lingering in nature, some strategies may be appropriate for a limited period of time, while others must be maintained indefinitely. The need for strategies may decrease with gains in development, health status, or therapy.

Transitions also involve locations. Skills acquired in the therapy room are not assured in other environments, especially in highly distracting settings. Therapy may begin in the therapy room, but does not end there. The clinician may introduce the student to more challenging and naturalistic environments (e.g., therapy room to classroom, to cafeteria, to playground, and so on) as therapy progresses.

A significant transition takes place upon discharge from therapy. A positive and realistic attitude is critical to successful transition from therapy to independence. The student who must maintain strategies indefinitely may view this as an unfair *burden*. However, parents and clinicians can help the student place this *burden* into perspective. It may be compared to that of the student who must wear glasses. The student can complain about the need for uncomfortable or unattractive glasses and *choose* to not wear them. That student has *chosen* not to *see* the world clearly (Kelly, 1995). Similarly, the student with auditory processing challenges must also choose to *hear* the world more clearly.

Transition from therapy to independence may also involve a decreasing dependence on assistive listening technology. It is unfortunate when a student who has become dependent on FM technology graduates into real life without adequate preparation. FM technology, however portable, does not always easily function in typical daily activities and environments.

A transition plan for students about to graduate may include career counseling. Students may not fully understand how processing difficulties may affect job performance. Without information, the student may experience failure and a loss of self-esteem. Counseling facilitates appropriate career and education choices (Baran, 1998b).

A *transition period* upon discharge from therapy is often helpful. During this time (perhaps months or even a year), the SLP may monitor the student's status using brief observations, assessments, and conversations with parents and others. Carryover of skills gained in therapy is always a concern. Before discharge, the SLP should sensitize the student to current status and possible changes over time. If the student needs a brief *recharge* (i.e., perhaps a few sessions of therapy), the Individual Education Plan may provide accommodations for this necessity (Kelly, 1995). This flexibility reduces costs to a school district over time. By providing needed *pit stops*, extended services may be unnecessary later.

Communication between all team members should continue as long as needed (before and after discharge). Successful transition experiences are the result of extended and insightful planning by *all* team members.

SUMMARY

Students with auditory processing disorders present a significant challenge to family members, teachers, and clinicians. This diverse group of students experience a wide range of processing difficulties that are influenced by task, linguistic context, and listening environment, among other variables. Because of the heterogeneous nature of auditory processing disorders, educators and clinicians may find predicting academic and clinical outcomes daunting.

Strategies and suggestions for functional outcomes were offered in this chapter. All such recommendations reflect a fundamental concept: The most *functional* outcome is independent *functioning* (to whatever extent possible). Strategies and suggestions are designed toward that end. Team members may view many strategies *relationally* in terms of both short-and longer-term outcomes; that is, more immediate strategies are helpful in achieving longer-term goals.

Other fundamental concepts may be summarized as follows:

1. Comprehensive and timely diagnosis is critical to the development of appropriate strategies for home and school settings. The psychological impact of incomplete or late diagnosis for the student should not be underestimated.
2. Management and intervention must involve a team effort in which all members (including the student) participate. All members communicate and share responsibilities.
3. Management and intervention plans must remain flexible, evolving as needed over time. Symptoms and behaviors of APD are affected by maturation, intervention, and the use of technology, among other influences.
4. The student with auditory processing challenges is a *child* who attends school, socializes with friends, and lives at home with family. Strategies for functional

outcomes must involve all settings. Plans for transitions (e.g., from grade school to junior high school; graduation to work or college) should become part of a comprehensive plan.

5. The aware and realistic student with APD is often more academically and socially successful. This student *understands* personal challenges, learns to self-advocate, and uses strengths to balance weaker skills.

REFERENCES

Auditory processing disorders: A team approach to screening, assessment and intervention practices (1997). Colorado Department of Education. Denver, Colorado. Retrieved August 8, 2004 from http://search.netscape.com/ns/boomframe.jsp?query=%22centr.

Auditory processing disorders—Technical assistance paper/ #10967/FY2001-9 (August, 2001). Bureau of Instructional Support: Florida Department of Education.

Baran, J. A. (1998a). *Classroom strategies. Central auditory processing disorders in students, Part 2: Management.* Short course presented at the American Speech-Language-Hearing Association's annual conference, San Antonio, TX.

Baran, J. A. (1998b). Management of adolescents and adults with central auditory processing disorders. In M. G. Masters, N. A. Stecker, & J. Katz (Eds.), *Central auditory processing disorders: Mostly management* (pp. 195–214). Needham Heights, MA: Allyn & Bacon.

Bellis, T. J. (1996). *Assessment and management of central auditory processing disorders in the educational setting: From science to practice.* San Diego: Singular.

Bellis, T. J. (2002a). *When the brain can't hear.* New York: Pocket Books.

Bellis, T. J. (2002b). *Basic principles of APD management—All the world's a stage: Environmental modifications at school.* Learning Disabilities Online. Retrieved November 19, 2003 from http://www.ldonline.org/ld_indepth/process_deficit/apd_management_school.html.

Boone, D. R. (1987). *Human communication and its disorders.* Englewood Cliffs: NJ: Prentice-Hall.

Butler, K. G. (1983). Language processing: Selective attention and mnemonic strategies. In E. Lasky & J. Katz (Eds.), *Central auditory processing disorders: Problems of speech, language and learning* (pp. 297–315). Baltimore: University Park Press.

Chermak, G. D., & Musiek, F. E. (1992). Managing central auditory processing disorders in students and youth. *American Journal of Audiology, 1*(3), 61–65.

Chermak, G. D., & Musiek, F. E. (1997). *Central auditory processing disorders: New perspectives.* Albany, NY: Singular Thomson Learning.

Ciocci, S. R. (2002). Auditory Processing Disorders: An Overview ERIC EC Digest E634. The Council for Exceptional Children Arlington, VA.

Colorado Department of Education. (1997). Auditory Processing Disorders: A team approach to screening assessment and intervention practice. Task Force on APDs. Denver, CO.

Ferre, J. (November, 1992). *CAT files: Improving the clinical utility of central auditory function tests.* Paper presented at the American Speech-Language-Hearing Association's Annual Convention, San Antonio, TX.

Fisher, L. I. (1976). *Fisher's auditory problem checklist.* Cedar Rapids, IA: Grant Woods Area Educational Agency.

Florida Department of Education. (August, 2001). *Auditory processing disorders—Technical assistance paper/#10967.*

Gillet, P. (1993). *Auditory processes* (rev. ed). Novato, CA: Academic Therapy Publications.

Hood, L. J., & Berlin, C. I. (1996). Central auditory function and disorders. In J. Northern (Ed.), *Hearing disorders* (3rd ed., pp. 227–243). Needham Heights, MA: Allyn & Bacon.

Katz, J., Stecker, N., & Masters, M. G. (March, 1994). *Central auditory processing: A coherent approach.* Paper presented at the ASHA Task Force on Central Auditory Processing Consensus Development Conference, Albuquerque, NM.

Keith, R. W. (1995). Tests of central auditory processing. In R. J. Roeser & M. P. Downs (Eds.), *Auditory disorders in school children* (pp. 101–116). New York: Thieme Medical Publishers.

Keith, R. W. (2000). *SCAN-C: Test of auditory processing abilities in children* (rev. ed.). San Antonio, TX: The Psychological Corporation.

Keller, W. D. (1998). The relationship between attention deficit hyperactivity disorder, central auditory processing disorders and specific learning disorders. In M.G. Masters, N. A. Stecker, & J. Katz (Eds.), *Central auditory processing disorder: Mostly management* (pp. 33–47). Boston: Allyn & Bacon.

Kelly, D. A. (1995). *Central auditory processing disorder: Strategies for use with children and adolescents*. San Antonio: Communication Skill Builders.

Kelly, D. A. (1998). *A winner's workbook: Reproducible activities for students with attention deficit disorder*. San Antonio, TX: Communication Skill Builders.

Lindamood, C. H., & Lindamood, P. C. (1979). *The LAC test: Lindamood auditory conceptualization test—Revised edition*. Austin: PRO-ED.

Martin, F. N. (1997). *Introduction to audiology* (6th ed.) Needham Heights, MA: Allyn & Bacon.

Masters, M. G. (1998). Speech and language management of central auditory processing disorders. In M. G. Masters, N. A. Stecker, & J. Katz (Eds.), *Central auditory processing disorder: Mostly management* (pp. 117–129). Boston: Allyn & Bacon.

Musiek, F., & Chermak, G. (1994). Three commonly asked questions about central auditory processing disorder. *American Journal of Audiology, 3*(3), 23–27.

Musiek, F., Gollegly, K., & Ross, M. (1985). Profiles of types of auditory processing disorders in students with learning disabilities. *Journal of Students with Communication Disorders, 9*, 43.

Northern, J. L., & Downs, M. P. (2002). *Hearing in children* (5th ed.). Philadelphia: Lippincott Williams & Wilkins.

Owens, R. E., Metz, D. E., & Haas, A. (2003). *Introduction to communication disorders: A lifespan perspective* (2nd ed.). Needham Heights, MA: Allyn & Bacon.

Palmer, C. V. (1997). Hearing and listening in a typical classroom. *Language, Speech, and Hearing Services in Schools, 28*(3), 213–217.

Parente', R., & Hermann, D. (2003). *Retraining cognition: Techniques and applications* (2nd. ed.). Austin: PRO-ED.

Paton, J. W. (1996–2003). *Central auditory processing disorders: CAPDs*. Retrieved November 21, 2003 from http://www.ldonline.org/ld_indepth/process_deficit/capd_paton.html)

Peck, D. J., LaPointe, L. L., Abbott, T. B., & Mercer, C. D. (1978). *The effects of presentation rates on the comprehension of learning-disabled children*. Paper presented at the annual convention of the American Speech and Hearing Association, San Francisco.

Pease, A. (1981). *Signals*. Toronto: Bantam.

Richard, G. J. (2001). *The source for processing disorders*. E. Moline, IL: Lingui Systems.

Roseberry-McKibbin, C., & Hegde, M. N. (2000). *An advanced review of speech-language pathology*. Austin, TX: Pro-Ed.

Sloan, C. (1998). *Central auditory processing disorders in students, Part 2: Management*. ASHA Short Course, American Speech-Language-Hearing Association Annual Conference, San Antonio, TX.

Willeford, J. A. (1985). *Assessment of central auditory disorders in children*. In M. J. Pinheiro & F. Musiek (Eds.), *Assessment of central auditory dysfunction: Foundations and clinical correlates* (pp. 239–255). Baltimore: Williams & Wilkins.

Current Controversies in CAPD: From Procrustes' Bed to Pandora's Box

Dennis J. McFarland
Wadsworth Laboratories

Anthony T. Cacace
The Neurosciences Institute and Advanced Imaging Center, Albany Medical College

For over three decades, the concept of central auditory processing disorder (CAPD) has been a lightning rod for controversy. Controversial issues have been explored from a variety of perspectives ranging from whether or not this disorder actually exists to what might be the best evaluation instruments and potential treatments (e.g., Rees, 1973, 1981; Cacace & McFarland, 1995, 1998; Watson, 1994; Jerger, 1998). In this chapter, we discuss controversial issues from a psychometric perspective. We consider the rationale for evaluating auditory specific perceptual deficits in school-aged children and focus on the reliability and validity of available tests. Treatment is probably the least studied area and one worthy of critical examination. Ethical concerns naturally follow, particularly when treatments are advocated based on limited data, unsubstantiated models, or theories that have questionable support or validity. Even the terms used to characterize this disorder are not agreed upon and/or are under flux (CAPD vs. APD). Therefore, our overall intent is to examine areas of concern, attempt to clarify pertinent issues, encourage debate, and take the optimistic position that this information will lead to a better understanding of contentious domains.

As we have indicated in chapter 3, antecedents to testing children began with studies in adults with lesions to the central nervous system (CNS). At the time of these early lesion-based studies (circa 1950–1970s), imaging technology was crude in comparison to today's standards. Lesions (primarily tumors and cerebrovascular abnormalities) were often very large, not well circumscribed, and probably not always limited to auditory areas or processes (e.g., Jerger et al., 1969; Lynn & Gilroy, 1977). Although criticizing this area through retrospection is a convenient mechanism for discussion, there are elements in this literature that are positive, relevant to present-day concerns, and worth mentioning. For example, in a detailed case report of bilateral temporal lobe lesions due to recurrent occlusion of the left and right middle cerebral arteries, Jerger and colleagues showed that temporal lobe lesions impaired speech intelligibility, intensity discrimination, temporal order for pitch, and absolute and relative localization abilities. Of particular interest to current-day concerns was their use of multimodality testing, at least for one of their tasks. For example, to evaluate whether impaired performance on the relative spatial localization task was modality-specific and not representative of a more generalized deficit in the judgment of angles, an analogous visual perceptual task was performed. Because performance on the visual perceptual task was found to be normal, Jerger and colleagues concluded that diminished performance observed on the relative localization task was indeed a modality-specific effect. Thus, what distinguished Jerger and colleagues from other early pioneers in this area was the strategic use of multimodal testing to clarify the modality specificity of test performance. What is not clear, however, is why there was a departure from the multimodality framework of testing, particularly as the initial application of this novel methodology was successful.

It is frequently stated that lesions of the auditory CNS are unaffected by simple monaural tasks, invoking the redundancy (crossed and uncrossed nature) of ascending auditory pathways to support this view. This conceptualization has provided a rationale to increase complexity of testing paradigms and reduce redundancy of the stimulus as a means to challenge the processing resources of the auditory system and uncover the effects of lesions. Consequently, this has led to the development of so-called sensitized tests (i.e., use of filtered speech, competing messages, time compression, dichotic presentation in various forms, etc.). While the need for sensitized tests is often espoused by workers in the field, experiments in animals over 50 years ago based on ablation of auditory cortex, suggested that discrimination thresholds to simple stimuli can be sensitive to lesion effects in this neuroanatomical area (e.g., Evarts, 1952). Questions concerning precisely what underlying processes were being measured when stimuli were sensitized have never adequately been addressed.

An issue of utmost importance is the development of an explicit definition of CAPD including what criteria should be applied for differential diagnosis between this and other common disorders of childhood. Indeed, researchers such as Friel-Patti (1999) have similar concerns: "If we are to do more than diagnose symptoms, it is essential that clinical criteria for CAPD be well-specified. Furthermore, this collection of behavioral, electrophysiologic, and even neurological correlates must be definitively linked to auditory perception, so that other cognitive, language or attention-based disorders can be distinguished. That is, we must demonstrate that this is fundamentally an *auditory* processing problem and not a language impairment or a disorder of general information processing. Ultimately, the diagnostic criteria must also reflect an impairment in some underlying mechanism(s) that has functional consequence" (p. 346). Thus, rather than having speech pathologists, audiologists, psychologists, and other professionals approach CAPD from different perspectives, like the blind man and the elephant parable, a unified definition, as proposed below, is a necessary and important precondition to differential diagnosis in order to avoid confusion and misunderstanding.

MODALITY SPECIFICITY

We have argued elsewhere that modality specificity should be a criterion for identifying disorders of auditory perception (McFarland & Cacace, 1995). This approach provides an objective means of distinguishing auditory perceptual abilities from more general skills that are involved in the processing of information from multiple sensory modalities. In this context, we have advocated multimodal testing as a way to clarify issues and to delineate CAPD from other common communication disorders of childhood (Cacace & McFarland, 1998). However, several authors have raised objections to this approach. Keith (1999) asserted that the construct of CAPD proposed by Cacace and McFarland (1998) is exclusive because it includes only nonlinguistic factors, and "limits the approach to assessment and remediation that a professional would take." Bellis and Ferre (1999) contended that our "unitary view of CAPD as a deficit in the processing of acoustic–phonetic features of speech is unrealistically narrow." As we noted in chapter 3, the points of view expressed by Keith and Bellis and Ferre either misrepresent or are contrary to our position. We have discussed in detail both modality-specific language disorders, such as pure-word deafness (McFarland & Cacace, 1995) and modality-specific disorders such as auditory agnosia, that are not language-specific (McFarland & Cacace, 1995). We emphasize that the concept of modality specificity as a criterion for identifying auditory perceptual processes does not exclude linguistic or nonlinguistic processes. Indeed, adopting modality specificity as a criterion for diagnosis of CAPD allows for constructs such as auditory attention deficit. However, merely conceptualizing such entities does not make them useful. It is also necessary to establish their validity.

USE OF APD VERSUS CAPD

A recent conference suggested that use of the term CAPD be replaced with the term APD (Jerger & Musiek, 2000). The change in terminology was suggested to maintain an operational definition, to avoid imputation of anatomic locus, and to emphasize interactions between peripheral and central sites. Probably, the main impetus for this change in terminology stems from greater emphasis placed on cases of "auditory neuropathy," a primary disorder of the auditory nerve where peripheral dysfunction can lead to poor performance on tests of central processing. Nevertheless, as we discuss below, an operational definition of auditory processing disorders may not be appropriate. Furthermore, knowledge of the neuroanatomical basis of any disorder of the central nervous system would ultimately be beneficial. In any case, this modification in terminology does not change basic issues with regard to psychometric concerns, which center on two key concepts: *reliability* and *validity* of this diagnosis.

PROBLEMS WITH PREVIOUS DEFINITIONS

The ASHA consensus statement (ASHA, 1996) asserted that CAPD may stem from some more general dysfunction such as attention deficit. Likewise, Chermak (2002) stated that "APD is not a label for a unitary disease, but rather a description of functional deficits," and furthermore "auditory processes involve the deployment of nondedicated, global mechanisms of attention and memory in service of acoustic signal processing" (p. 733). This view associates the presence of CAPD with failure on specific tests and is not concerned with underlying mechanisms (Cacace & McFarland, 1998; Friel-Patti, 1999). Moreover, this view follows from a definition of CAPD in terms of specific behaviors (i.e., performance on tests of sound localization and lateralization, auditory discrimination, auditory pattern recognition, etc.) rather than auditory perceptual processes. While it is possible to define CAPD in a one-to-one manner with performance on tests that involve only auditory stimuli, this "operational approach" has not proved useful in other fields and it has not withstood the test of time. For example, in the early days of intelligence testing, intelligence was operationally defined in terms of whatever the intelligence test measured (Boring, 1923). This approach was subsequently abandoned when the circular nature of this definition was recognized and researchers became aware of the inherent difficulties of applying it to the variety of tests that had been developed (Tyler, 1965). When similarly applied to CAPD, the extreme form of an operational view would have a specific type of auditory processing deficit associated with each specific test.

Defining a disorder in terms of whatever the tests measure does not provide a definition that can be usefully generalized to practical situations. For example, if the intent is to understand auditory-based learning problems of a student, it is not particularly helpful to characterize these difficulties as involving deficits in the perception of pitch patterns or dichotic digits. Rather, it is useful to describe auditory processing by more general constructs such as auditory pattern perception and auditory stream segregation. These are constructs that are more widely applicable but, at the same time, are not associated with test performance in a one-to-one manner. Thus, dichotic listening should be viewed as one of many tests that involve auditory stream segregation as well as other factors such as attention and memory. If a child has problems with auditory stream segregation, then a consistent pattern of performance would be expected across tests involving this construct. At the same time, similar tests in the visual modality should not show impairments. In this way, the hypothesis that a child has a deficit in "auditory" stream segregation would be supported. Presumably, this deficit would also be manifested in a noisy classroom listening environment.

TEST RELIABILITY

The concept of reliability refers, among other things, to the extent to which test results are repeatable at different points in time. If reliability is low, then it is unlikely that the results of an initial test will be repeated a second time. Moreover, if reliability is low, then it is also unlikely that two tests measuring the same construct will obtain the same results. Diagnosing CAPD is typically based on results of a battery of tests. Contemporary discussions of CAPD test batteries generally do not deal with the issue of reliability (e.g., Medwetsky, 2002) either in the context of individual tests or in terms of the profile of test results obtained. The issue of test profile reliability is not unique to the audiological literature—debates on this topic exist in the psychology and neuropsychology literature as well (e.g., Livingston et al., 2003). With respect to the audiological literature, the general lack of discussion of reliability may be due in part to the fact that many tests of auditory processing do not have good documentation with respect to this metric (Cacace & McFarland, 1995). The SCAN test, however, is an exception; documentation provided in manuals accompanying this test includes information concerning test–retest correlations obtained in the standardization sample. In addition, Amos and Humes (1998) have reported results of an independent study of SCAN test reliability.

The SCAN test (SCAN-A for adolescents and adults; SCAN-C for children) is a battery of auditory processing tests that is widely used (Emanuel, 2002). The SCAN-A consists of four subtests: Filtered Words, Auditory Figure–Ground, Competing Words, and Competing Sentences. Test–retest reliability for the total test score was reported to be 0.69 (Merz, 1998). A question that naturally arises is whether or not this value represents an acceptable level of stability for repeated measures. More specifically, what is an acceptable value for test–retest reliability? For example, the Test of Basic Auditory Capabilities (TBAC), which includes three subtests that include simple to complex discriminations, has been reported to yield test–retest correlations for the majority of tests in the range of 0.8 (Christopherson & Humes, 1992). Although the age ranges are not entirely equivalent with respect to the present discussion, test–retest reliability is substantially higher than the SCAN-A but similar to forms of testing such as the Wechsler Adult Intelligence Scale (WAIS) used in neuropsychological testing (The Psychological Corporation, 1997).

To consider this important question, we examined this issue by simulating test performance using a simple statistical model in order to gain insight as to what might be an acceptable level of reliability. In this model, test scores were a function of a true trait value and random error. Simulation of test–retest data involved generating pairs of scores with the same trait value and different error values. Reliability is then a function of the relative magnitude of the trait value and error. Scores were computed based on Equations 1 and 2 below:

$$Y_1 = X + E_1 \tag{1}$$

$$Y_2 = X + E_2 \tag{2}$$

where Y_1 and Y_2 represent separate test score results, X represents the single underlying trait, and E_1 and E_2 represent the two independent sources-of-error. For each observation, X was determined by a single draw from a random numbers generator having a Gaussian distribution, each E was determined from a separate draw for each Y test score value, and each point consisted of 100,000 simulated observations.

We first considered agreement between a single test score (Y_1) and the true trait value (X) given different reliabilities (correlation between Y_1 and X). Figure 13.1 shows concordance between the frequency of trait values (X) below 1 standard deviation (SD) and test values (Y_1) below 1 SD. A false alarm is scored when the test value is below 1 SD but the trait value is not. Likewise, a miss is scored when the trait value is below 1 SD and the test value is not. When both values are below 1 SD, a correct detection is scored. The percentages of each of these categories are presented for four different reliabilities.

As can be seen in Fig. 13.1, percent correct detection is below that or either false alarms or misses when the reliability is 0.60. For a reliability of 0.70, each of these

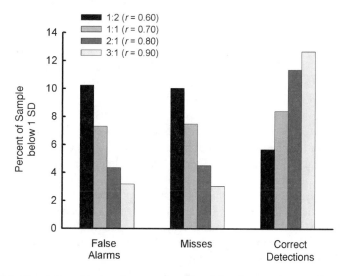

FIG. 13.1. Simulation of test performance based on false alarms, misses, and correct detections, where $n = 100,000$. The percentages of each of the three categories is presented for four different reliabilities ($r = 0.60; r = 0.70; r = 0.80; r = 0.90$). The simulation shows that it is only when reliabilities approximate 0.80 that correct detections exceed error rates.

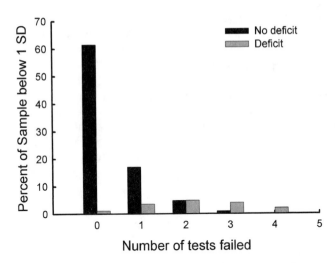

FIG. 13.2. Simulation of a battery of four tests, where all tests measure the same trait and the reliability is 0.70.

categories is approximately equal. It is only when reliabilities reach 0.80 that correct detections are greater than error rates. This same pattern of results is obtained if a more stringent criterion of 2 SDs is used, the main difference being that the overall percentages are lower but the ratios are the same. These results show that a practice of considering 0.80 to be a threshold for acceptable reliability makes considerable practical sense. Below this level, error rates exceed detection rates.

The statistical model for test–retest reliability is the same as the statistical model for two tests that measure the same trait. The correlation between two tests measuring the same trait depends on both the amount of shared variance and the error that is unique to each test. In either case, this represents the correlation between Y_1 and Y_2 from Equations 1 and 2. The results of a simulation of a test battery where each of four tests measures the same trait and has a reliability of 0.70 is shown in Fig. 13.2. Here, the percent of the sample falling below 1 SD on 1, 2, 3, or all 4 tests is presented separately for cases where the true trait value is below 1 SD (deficit group) or above 1 SD (no-deficit group). As can be seen in Fig. 13.2, the number of cases failing at least one test is greater in the no-deficit group than in the deficit group. For two tests, the rate is about equal. It is only for the cases that fail 3 or 4 tests that the rate of correct detections exceeds the false alarm rate.

Figure 13.3 shows a comparison of results for a single test with a reliability of 0.70 and the average of four tests with reliabilities of 0.70. As can be seen in Fig. 13.3, error rates are considerably better when the four test results are averaged.

Consideration of these simulation results illustrates several points. When reliability is low, the frequency of diagnostic errors will be high. Use of multiple tests with low reliabilities will produce even larger rates of misclassification, if failure on a small number of tests is considered diagnostic. Averaging the results of several tests that measure the same trait improves reliability (i.e., use of the composite score on the SCAN test, as suggested by Amos and Humes, 1998). A similar alternative would be to apply the cross-check principle (Jerger & Hayes, 1976), which requires agreement between tests measuring the same construct. Finally, when we apply these considerations to the composite test–retest correlation of 0.69 reported for SCAN-A

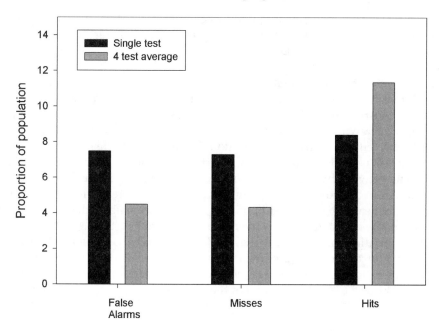

FIG. 13.3. Comparison of results for a single test and four tests using the same reliability coefficient, $r = 0.70$. Better error rates are observed when four tests are averaged.

(Merz, 1998), we can see that the expected consistency of test scores with this instrument is rather low.

Error in measurement is due to specific psychological processes operating on various time scales (Schmidt & Hunter, 1999). Understanding sources-of-error in measurement is an important part of understanding the phenomena under study. In the case of vigilance, a component of attention thought to be assessed on continuous performance tests (CPTs), there are moment-to-moment variations, day-to-day variations, and variations between subjects. Variation over time represents *state effects* and contributes to error. Variation between subjects represents *trait effects* and is the topic of interest. In addition, there are test-specific sources-of-error. For example, if our intent is to measure individual differences in attention, then test effects due to language ability represent a source-of-error. Averaging scores over several tests of the same construct reduces test-specific error. If the construct of interest is a perceptual ability, using parallel tests in multiple sensory modalities allows for the size of variations in nonperceptual factors to be estimated.

The reliability of tests can also be improved by modifications in test design. For example, studies indicate that many dichotic listening tests have poor reliability (Bradshaw, Burden, & Nettleton, 1986). Use of a target detection task rather than the usual recall procedure dramatically improves test–retest reliability (Voyer, 2003). Use of a detection task also minimizes factors related to response selection by minimizing factors related to response production so the validity of dichotic listening as a perceptual measure would be strengthened. Reliability is an important issue and an appeal has been made that more attention should be directed to this issue in the CAPD literature (Cacace & McFarland, 1995).

ISSUES OF VALIDITY

Tests of auditory processing are frequently evaluated by the sensitivity and specificity of test performance (e.g., Delb et al., 2002; Oyler et al., 1998), terms often associated with signal detection theory (SDT). However, applying SDT to CAPD requires a "gold standard" (i.e., a valid reference point needed to delineate different diagnostic categories). A gold standard is generally lacking in this area of investigation. Rather, studies typically evaluate sensitivity and specificity against some vague categorization such as "suspected CAPD." Swets (1988) has discussed problems in applying SDT when it is not known with certainty whether or not a case is positive or negative with respect to a specific diagnostic classification. In this context, the generic term "diagnostic systems" is used for the ability of a particular device or instrument to detect or discriminate between two alternatives categories, such as distinguishing signal from noise, truth from lies, tumor from no tumor, and so on. Whereas it is argued that SDT is germane to measuring diagnostic accuracy, it is also recognized that problems arise when the quality of test data "is not everything it should be" (Swets, 1988). Therefore, several qualifications are offered so that SDT can be applied optimally. These include consideration of the following criteria: (a) adequacy of truth, (b) independence of truth determination and system operation, (c) independence of test sample and truth determination, and (d) representation of the sample.

Adequacy of Truth

In evaluating for CAPD, the tester should know for certain whether or not tests accurately classify individuals with respect to the trait in question. Inaccurate classification will depress measures of accuracy. In this context and as noted above, the need for a gold standard is emphasized. In medical imaging, for example, surgery or autopsy becomes the gold standard, such that determining the presence or absence of an abnormality (i.e., cancerous tumor) is validated by a tissue sample and confirmed by appropriate histopathological examination.

Independence of Truth Determination and System Operation

Truth should be determined without regard to the system's operation. If this condition is not met, then truth will be inappropriate for scoring the system and its measured accuracy will be inflated. This can be considered analogous to comparing the inclusive framework used to assess for CAPD versus the more clear-cut concept of modality specificity. For example, if the accuracy of measurement is scored against a determination of truth set forth by an inclusive (ASHA, 1996) or potentially erroneous classification scheme, then accuracy of a diagnostic system may be viewed more generously than in fact it actually is.

Independence of Test Sample and Truth Determination

Procedures to establish the truth should not affect the selection of cases.

Representation of the Sample

The sample of test items should fairly reflect the population of cases to which the diagnostic system is usually applied. The various types of events should occur in the sample in the same proportion as they do in practice.

In addition, it is probable that auditory processing abilities lie along a continuum, rather than being simply disordered or not. For these reasons, the concept of validity is more appropriate for evaluation of the CAPD construct.

Test Validity

Validity refers to the extent to which a test measures what it is intended to measure. As such, the concept of modality specificity is one aspect of CAPD validity. However, this is not the only concern. One of the most influential discussions of validity has been put forth by Campbell and Fisk (1959). They discussed convergent and discriminant validation as two important aspects of test development. They argued that a test score reflects both the trait in question and method-specific effects. As a result, several methods must be employed that converge in the measurement of the same trait. In addition, they argued that discriminant validity must be shown before introducing a construct into science. That is, the construct should add something unique to our ability to predict performance. We examine each of these concepts separately and discuss how they apply to CAPD testing.

Convergence of several measures using different methods is necessary in order to ensure that test scores do not simply reflect some unique property of the measuring instrument. For example, the most popular account of SDT is that it involves both a sensory process and a decision process (e.g., Green & Sweets, 1966). In this context, both the input stimulus and the subject's responses are known. In contrast, the sensory and decision processes are theoretical constructs. For example, if we assess the sensory abilities of a subject in a simple two-choice experiment, the score reflects both the trait-of-interest and a method effect due to response bias. We could also assess subjects' detection ability with a three-alternative forced-choice paradigm. Whereas this method controls for response bias, it also requires that a greater reliance be placed on the subjects' memory, and hence introduces a different method effect. If the deficit occurs with one of these methods but not the other, then it is reasonable to conclude that some method-specific ability is involved, rather than the ability to detect the stimulus. If a given subject truly has a deficit in detecting a stimulus, then this should be apparent when testing is performed with both methods. This example would represent convergent validity, the concept that alternative measures of the same construct produce similar results.

Discriminant validity refers to the requirement that a new construct should be shown to measure a trait that is distinct from existing constructs. For example, a variety of sensory discrimination tasks have been shown to correlate with IQ (Deary et al., 2004). Some of the highest correlations with IQ are obtained with discrimination tasks that use rapidly presented stimuli to measure a construct called "inspection time" (e.g., Deary & Stough, 1996; Olsson et al., 1998; Bates, 2004). A number of investigators in the field of intelligence testing feel that inspection time is related to speed of information processing, which is conceptualized as a fundamental component of intelligence and one that is independent of the sensory modality (Bates & Eysenck, 1993). Cacace et al. (2000) have discussed this topic in the context of interpreting performance on temporal processing tasks as applied to remediation-resistant reading-impaired children. This topic was pertinent in distinguishing hypotheses relevant to the rapid processing of stimuli in multiple sensory modalities as our results showed that performance on multimodal temporal processing tasks was neither modality-specific nor temporal-specific. Thus, the principal of establishing discriminant validity would require that it be shown that the construct of auditory temporal processing involves something in addition to supramodal constructs such as speed of information processing and IQ.

The conceptualization that test scores reflect method-specific effects as well as the trait-of-interest and the fact that it is necessary to demonstrate discriminant validity, provide the rational for Campbell and Fisk's (1959) multitrait–multimethod approach. This approach involves the simultaneous assessment of multiple traits with multiple methods. The multitrait–multimethod approach allows for evaluation of convergent validity and discriminant validity by examining the pattern of intercorrelations of test scores. One methodology for this evaluation is the use of structural equation modeling (SEM; Eid et al., 2003), although other approaches are possible.

We now consider two studies that have evaluated multiple tests of auditory processing. One of these studies (Schow et al., 2000) examined intercorrelations between several tests of auditory processing. The second study (Hulslander et al., 2004) examined intercorrelations between tests of auditory and visual sensory processing, phonological awareness, IQ, and reading. We will examine these reports from the standpoint of what they can tell us about the convergent and discriminant validity of tests of auditory processing.

Schow et al. (2000) applied SEM to test scores from children given the SCAN and the Multiple Auditory Processing Assessment (MAPA) battery. The MAPA consists of the selective auditory attention test (SAAT), dichotic digits, competing sentences, and pitch patterns. In their model, left and right ear scores were entered separately for SAAT, dichotic digits, and pitch patterns. They included four factors in their model. Two of these factors consisted of loadings on tests involving only left and right ear scores (dichotic digits and pitch patterns). This provides a means of evaluating method-specific effects that relate to left versus right ear testing. However, there are other method-specific effects with the use of dichotic digits. For example, in addition to the construct of binaural integration that this test is supposed to reflect, dichotic digits also involves retention of numbers in immediate memory, a task similar to the digit span test included on IQ batteries such as the WAIS (Burton et al., 2002) and divided attention. An appropriate evaluation of convergent validity would also include tests of binaural integration that use methods other than dichotic digits. At best, the results of Schow et al. (2000) suggest that binaural integration, as measured by dichotic digits, is distinct from their other constructs, such as binaural separation, that were measured by two other dichotic tests (competing words and competing sentences). However, McFarland and Cacace (2002) reanalyzed the data of Schow et al. (2000) and showed that a structural equation model that included a single general auditory factor and several method-specific factors could easily account for their data as well. Thus, it is not at all clear that the battery of tests used by Schow and colleagues measures more than one auditory construct. Because the study by Schow et al. (2000) did not include any measures outside of the MAPA test battery, it cannot be concluded that these tests measure anything distinct from global constructs such as IQ. Furthermore, there is no information concerning how these tests might predict important outcome measures such as classroom performance and academic achievement.

Hulslander et al. (2004) examined the relationship between auditory amplitude modulation detection, frequency modulation detection, visual motion, visual form detection, several measures of phonological awareness, IQ, ADHD ratings, and reading ability. Multiple regression was used to evaluate whether effects were independent. Auditory amplitude and frequency modulation detection as well as visual motion detection were significantly related to reading ability, independent of ADHD ratings. However, these sensory processing measures did not account for a significant amount of variation in reading ability independent of IQ. In contrast, measures of phonological processing made significant independent contributions to the prediction of reading ability. Thus, this study does not provide support for the discriminant validity of auditory frequency and amplitude modulation detection as predictors of reading.

Carrol (1993) has undertaken an extensive analysis of correlational studies of human abilities. In this book, an entire chapter is devoted to tests of auditory abilities. Carrol concluded that there is evidence for distinct auditory abilities. However, the tests analyzed by Carrol differ from those generally included in CAPD batteries. Although some evidence for discriminant validity of the construct of auditory abilities exists within the psychometric literature, validation of CAPD test batteries has generally not included information on other pertinent domains (e.g. correlations with IQ, classroom grades, reading ability, standardized achievement test scores) that would allow for evaluation of discriminant validity.

An exception is the study by Watson et al. (2003)[1] that involved a cross-discipline epidemiological longitudinal multivariate design using experts in the fields of audiology, psychoacoustics, clinical and cognitive psychology, and optometry. Four hundred seventy students entering first grade in the Benton Indiana School District were evaluated over a 3-year period. The battery of 36 tests encompassing sensory (auditory and visual), linguistic, and cognitive skills were administered. These were used to predict success in reading, math, and overall academic achievement. Factor analysis reduced 60 variables into four factors: reading-related skills, visual cognition, verbal cognition, and speech processing. Based on a multivariate causal model of academic failure, four factors adequately described these data. The factor related to reading accounted for the majority of variance, followed by visual cognition, verbal cognition, and speech processing. Interestingly, most measures on which clusters of children showed deficits were standardized tests of the ability to understand speech under difficult listening conditions (SCAN). However, the analysis showed that the abilities tested were unrelated to reading achievement as measured by teacher-assigned grades and accounted for very little variance. The authors indicated that these data provide *no* support for therapies or remedial training programs that address reading disorders through auditory training methods (e.g., Tallal et al., 1996).

As we have indicated above, the psychometric approach deals with issues of convergent and discriminant validity by examining the pattern of intercorrelations between test scores. An alternative way of dealing with these same issues is to demonstrate modality specificity of effects using similar tests in multiple sensory modalities. For example, if auditory and visual test performance can be dissociated, then distinct abilities can be inferred and discriminant validity would be demonstrated. In the neuropsychological literature, for example, the *double* disassociation represents the coup d'état in experimental design, because of its value in demonstrating both the sensitivity of the task and the specificity of function that is examined. An example of the double disassociation has been provided in the context of demonstrating

---

[1] The study by Watson and colleagues (2003) is one of the most comprehensive reports to date dealing with sensory, cognitive, and linguistic variables that predict school performance. The brief description reported here does not do justice to the thought and design of this cross-disciplinary work. Therefore, interested readers are encouraged to evaluate this work in its entirety.

modality specificity for tests of short-term recognition memory using forced-choice psychophysical methods in an individual with a temporal lobe lesion (Cacace et al., 1992). In Fig. 5 of Cacace and colleagues (1992), we showed that recognition memory is normal for a visual color pattern task but abnormal for a matched auditory pitch pattern task. Therefore, by using comparable tasks in multiple modalities, dissociation of function can be observed and the modality specificity of a recognition deficit can be determined.

If visual and auditory tests are similar in all respects and differ only in terms of sensory modality, then method-specific effects are controlled. Psychometrically matched auditory and visual tests provide a simpler means of addressing these issues, as it is not entirely clear how general cognitive abilities should be measured. While IQ is a popular measure, test batteries purported to measure this construct (e.g., the WAIS) can have a complex structure (Burton et al., 2002). Likewise, there are critics that impugn the content contained in these batteries (e.g., Sternberg, 1999). Whatever the nature of method-specific effects may be, they are controlled when auditory and visual tests differ only in terms of sensory modality. Both the correlational approach and the method of demonstrating modality-specific effects should be pursued, as convergent results would greatly increase the plausibility of conclusions. However, from a clinical context, demonstrating modality specificity may be the preferred method because it is simpler and more efficient to implement in individual cases.

TREATMENT OF CAPD

A number of different treatment or management strategies for CAPD have been proposed. Among the formal methods suggested are auditory integration training (Musiek et al., 1999), Earobics (Musiek et al., 1999; Wertz et al., 2002), and Fast ForWord® (Keith, 1999; Musiek et al., 1999; Wertz et al., 2002). Informal methods, such as vocabulary building, signal enhancement strategies, and background noise reduction procedures (e.g., use of personal FM systems, controlling for room acoustics), have also been advocated (e.g., Musiek et al., 1999; Rosenberg, 2002). Conspicuously absent from these recommendations are discussions of the evidence and documentation that support the efficacy of these proposals.

Musiek et al. (1999) have suggested that habilitation techniques should be matched with specific test-related deficits. This is a reasonable approach, as the ultimate purpose of testing is to identify the appropriate course for treatment and remediation. However, matching of test results with therapy should be based on reliable and valid tests as well as treatments that have been shown to work. In addition, the appropriate matching of deficit to treatment should be empirically validated. To date, Musiek et al. (1999) have not addressed these issues.

The need for empirical evaluation of treatments has been emphasized in a variety of fields including speech and hearing services (Meline & Paradiso, 2003), medicine (Lohr et al., 1998), and clinical psychology (Kettlewell, 2004). Meline and Paradiso (2003) argued that evidence-based practice helps overcome the propensity toward confirmation bias (i.e., the tendency to notice and remember evidence that confirms one's beliefs and forget discrepant evidence). It is also noteworthy that recent health care policy analyses have placed greater weight on "scientific evidence" and less weight on "expert opinion" (Lohr et al., 1998). Evidence-based medicine emphasizes randomized clinical trials. Randomized clinical trials help to promote effective innovations and delay the spread of unproven interventions. This occurs because randomized clinical trials can provide conclusive evidence that one treatment is better than another or that a particular treatment is better than no treatment at all. In recent years, clinical psychologists have debated the role of science in clinical practice. Peterson (2004) argued that the complexity of problems facing practitioners limits the use of therapies based exclusively on scientific knowledge. At the same time, Peterson argued that science is necessary because it produces reliable knowledge due to its dependence on observation rather than authority. Kettlewell (2004) suggested that the scientific approach is the best way to advance knowledge and provide cost-effective therapies.

Auditory integration therapy involves listening to music that is altered by filtering selective frequency bands. Yencer (1998) conducted an evaluation of auditory integration training in three groups of children who had poor performance on tests of auditory processing. One group received standard auditory integration training, a second group was exposed to unaltered music, and a third group did not receive treatment. Yencer found no clear evidence of a treatment effect on a battery of tests although all three groups showed improvement on several of the tests. Dawson and Watling (2000) reviewed five studies examining auditory integration training and concluded that these studies "provided no, or at best equivocal, support for the use of auditory integration training in autism." At present, auditory integration training is lacking a rational theory and empirical support.

Also relevant to CAPD are computer programs used to enhance language abilities of children that have problems in basic language skills thought to be linked to deficits in processing rapid auditory information. Fast ForWord® consists of a group of computer programs, distributed by the Scientific Learning Corporation, that focus on phonological awareness, listening comprehension, language comprehension, and sustained attention. Initial evaluations in a small group of children showed pre–post differences on tests of auditory processing (Merzenich et al., 1996; Tallal et al., 1996). In a subsequent study, researchers affiliated with Scientific Learning Corporation showed normalization of fMRI effects (i.e., cerebral blood flow changes) in dyslexic children following Fast ForWord® training (e.g., Temple et al., 2003).

Fast ForWord® training has also been evaluated in a larger sample of children by a group of researchers not associated with Scientific Learning Corporation (Rouse & Krueger, 2004). They found increases in several measures of language and reading in the group receiving Fast ForWord® training from pre-to-post testing. However, a control group showed similar gains. The size of the change was significantly different between treatment and control groups only for performance with Reading Edge (a computer program distributed by Scientific Learning Corporation that measures skills similar to those trained with Fast ForWord®). Treatment with Fast ForWord® did not produce larger gains than those seen in controls based on standardized tests of language and reading. The authors concluded that Fast ForWord® may improve some specific aspects of students' language skills, but it does not appear to improve broader measures of language or reading skills. Hook et al. (2001) compared Fast ForWord® training to a traditional approach (i.e., the Orton-Gillingham method). They found that both Fast ForWord® and the Orton-Gillingham method showed immediate gains in phonemic awareness, but only the Orton-Gillingham method showed gains in word attack scores.

Hartley et al. (2003) questioned the voracity of the temporal processing hypothesis. Their study evaluated whether temporal processing versus a competing hypothesis termed "processing efficiency" could account for performance on forward, backward, and simultaneous masking studies of language-impaired children using the four-stage model of temporal resolution proposed by Moore et al. (1988). They argued that the processing efficiency hypothesis can provide an equally compelling explanation for a deficit in temporal resolution when attention, cognition, and motivational factors (alterations in the decision device) are accounted for during stimulus detection. Heath and Hogben (2004) suggested that studies by Merzenich et al. (1996) and Tallal et al. (1996) "confound training on nonverbal and synthesized speech stimuli, which means it is not clear that training on (perception of rapid sequences) PRS was the critical factor responsible for improvements (p. 1276)" These authors also make the appeal for better psychometric practices in this area. Additionally, as the results obtained by Watson and colleagues (2003) did not find that an auditory processing factor accounted for academic or linguistic performance of first-grade schoolchildren, they questioned the need to apply programs such as Fast ForWord® on a wide-scale basis. Similarly, Gillam et al. (2001) also questioned whether improvements in language abilities after Fast ForWord® training were caused by changes in temporal processing. Agnew et al. (2004) assessed temporal processing (judgment of relative durations) of auditory and visual stimuli before and after training on Fast ForWord® in seven children. Although improvements were found in auditory and not visual duration judgment performance, these improvements did *not* generalize to reading skills.

These results raise several issues concerning methodology for evaluating of treatment effects. Rosenberg (2002) suggested that clinicians should evaluate individual cases to provide evidence for efficacy of treatment. However, well-controlled studies demonstrate that change is to be expected both in treatment groups and in controls. Unambiguous documentation of treatment effects requires the use of methodologies that are capable of isolating treatment effects. Treatment outcomes may also depend on the outcome measures employed. Treatment effects are most likely to occur when assessment involves measures that are similar to the materials used in training. Whether or not training generalizes to broader, more ecologically relevant outcomes is an important issue. Finally, new treatments should be compared to standard treatments. As noted by Rouse and Krueger (2004), use of programs such as Fast ForWord® in schools often involves removing children from regular classroom instruction. Thus, it is important to ensure that students make optimal use of their time. This means that treatments must not only work, but also that they should be at least as good, if not better, than possible alternatives.

Although empirical support for treatments such as Fast ForWord® is limited, the companies that produce these products are marketing them to school systems. For example, the entire Philadelphia school system will be using Fast ForWord® in the 2004–2005 school year (Editorial, 2004). Because such decisions can potentially affect large numbers of students, the need for randomized clinical trials to evaluate the validity of treatment effects is self-evident (Gillam et al., 2001). It is our view that evidence-based research methlogy, such as randomized clinical trials, should be a precondition before implementing educationally relevant devices on a wide-scale basis. Whereas Heath and Hogben (2004) have been concerned with related issues in disordered populations of children, they also advocate a shift from a purely psychophysical assessment to one dealing with psychometric issues, such as those described herein (reliability, discriminant, and construct validity). When all is said and done, cogent practical advice by Reid Lyon, director of research in learning disabilities at the National Institute of Child Health and Human Development, may be most apropos to treatment devices like Fast ForWord®,— "if the computer game works, play it" (Barinaga, 1996). If not, then the best advice may be to shelve it, although this remains to be determined.

SUMMARY

Tests of and treatments for CAPD have been suggested over the years. However, evidence for the reliability and validity of tests and the efficacy of treatments are generally lacking. As a result of this state of affairs, very little can be concluded about the real benefit of using these tests and treatments. Therefore, more emphasis on science and less emphasis on "expert opinion" is required in order for this field to advance in a meaningful way.

REFERENCES

Agnew, J. A., Dorn, C., & Eden, G. F. (2004). Effect of intensive training on auditory processing and reading skills. *Brain and Language, 88*, 21–25.

Amos, N. E., & Humes, L. E. (1998). SCAN test-reliability for first- and third-grade children. *Journal of Speech, Language, and Hearing Research, 41*, 834–845.

ASHA. (1996). Central auditory processing: Current status of research and implications for practice. *American Journal of Audiology, 5*, 41–53.

Barinaga, M. (1996). Giving language skills a boost. *Science, 271*, 27–28.

Bates, T. C. (2005). Auditory inspection time and intelligence. *Personality and Individual Differences, 38*, 115–127.

Bates, T. C., & Eysenk, H. J. (1993). Intelligence, inspection time, and decision time. *Intelligence, 17*, 523–531.

Bellis, T. J., & Ferre, J. M. Multidimensional approach to the differential diagnosis of central auditory processing disorders in children. *Journal of the American Academy of Audiology, 10*, 319–328.

Boring, E. G. (1923). Intelligence as the tests test it. *New Republic, 35*, 35–37.

Bradshaw, J. L., Burden, V., & Nettleton, N. C. (1986). Dichotic and dichhaptic techniques. *Neuropsychologia, 24*, 79–90.

Burton, D. B., Ryan, J. J., Axelrod, B. N., & Schellenberger, T. (2002). A confirmatory factor analysis of WAIS-III in a clinical sample with cross-validation in the standardization sample. *Archives of Clinical Neuropsychology, 17*, 371–387.

Cacace, A. T., McFarland, D. J., Emrich, J. F., & Haller, J. S. (1992). Assessing short-term recognition memory with forced-choice psychophysical methods. *Journal of Neuroscience Methods, 44*, 145–155.

Cacace, A. T., & McFarland, D. J. (1995). Opening Pandora's box: The reliability of CAPD tests. *American Journal of Audiology, 4*, 61–62.

Cacace, A. T., & McFarland, D. J. (1998). Central auditory processing disorder in school-aged children: A critical review. *Journal of Speech, Language and Hearing Research, 41*, 355–373.

Cacace, A. T., McFarland, D. J., Ouimet, J. R., Schrieber, E. J., & Marro. P. (2000). Temporal processing deficits in remediation-resistant reading-impaired children. Audiology and *Neurootology, 5*, 83–97.

Campbell, D. T., & Fisk, D. W. (1959). Convergent and discriminant validation by the multitrait–multimethod matrix. *Psychological Bulletin, 56*, 1–21.

Carroll, J. B. (1993). *Human cognitive abilities: A survey of factor-analytical studies.* New York: Cambridge University Press.

Chermak, G. G. (2002). Deciphering auditory processing disorders in children. *Otolaryngol. Clin. North Am. 35*(4), 733–749.

Christopherson, L. A., & Humes, L. E. (1992). Some psychometric properties of the Test of Vasic Auditory Capabilities. *Journal of Speech and Hearing Research, 35*, 929–935.

Dawson, G., & Watling, R. (2000). Interventions to facilitate auditory, visual, and motor integration in autism: A review of the evidence. *Journal of Autism and Developmental Disorders, 30*, 415–421.

Deary, I. J., Bell, P. J., Bell, A. J., Campbell, M. L., & Fazal, N. D. (2004). Sensory discrimination and intelligence: Testing Spearman's other hypothesis. *American Journal of Psychology, 117*, 1–18.

Deary, I. J., & Stough, C. (1996). Intelligence and inspection time: Achievements, prospects, and problems. *American Psychologist, 51*, 599–608.

Delb, W., Strauss, D. J., Hohenberg, G., & Plinkert, P. (2002). The binaural interaction component (BIC) in children with central auditory processing disorder (CAPD). *International Journal of Audiology, 42*, 401–412.

Editorial. (2004). Better reading through brain research. *Nature Neuroscience, 7*, 1.

Eid, M., Lischetzke, T., Nussbeck, F. W., & Trierweiler, L. I. (2003). Separating trait effects from trait-specific method effects in multitrait–multimethod models: A multiple indicator CT-C(M-1) model. *Psychological Methods, 8,* 38–60.

Emanuel, D. C. (2002). The auditory processing battery: Survey of common practices. *Journal of the American Academy of Audiology, 13,* 93–117.

Evarts, E. V. (1952). Effects of auditory cortex ablation on frequency discrimination in monkey. *Journal of Neurophysiology, 15,* 443–448.

Friel-Patti, S. (1999). Clinical decision-making in the assessment and intervention of central auditory processing disorders. *Language, Speech, and Hearing in Schools, 30,* 345–352.

Gillam, R. B. (1999). Computer-assisted language intervention using Fast ForWord®: Theoretical and empirical considerations for clinical decision-making. *Language, Speech, and Hearing in Schools, 30,* 363–370.

Gillam, R. B., Loeb, D. F., & Friel-Patti, S. (2001). Looking back: A summary of five exploratory studies of Fast ForWord. *American Journal of Speech-Language Pathology, 10,* 269–273.

Green, D. M., & Sweets, J. A. (1966). *Signal detection theory and psychophysics.* New York: Wiley.

Hartley, E. H., Hill, P. R., & Moore, D. R. (2003). The auditory basis of language impairments: Temporal processing versus processing efficiency hypotheses. *International Journal of Pediatric Otorhinolaryngology, 67S1,* S137–S142.

Heath, S. M., & Hogben, J. H. (2004). The reliability and validity of tasks measuring perception of rapid sequences in children with dyslexia. *Journal of Child Psychology and Psychiatry, 45,* 1275–1287.

Hook, P. E., Macaruso, P., & Jones, S. (2001). Efficacy of Fast ForWord training on facilitating acquisition of reading skills by children with reading difficulties—a longitudinal study. *Annals of Dyslexia, 51,* 75–96.

Hulslander, J., Talcott, J., Witton, C., DeFries, J., Pennington, B., Wadsworth, S., Willcutt, E., & Olson, R. (2004). Sensory processing, reading, IQ, and attention. *Journal of Experimental Child Psychology, 88,* 274–295.

Jerger, J. (1998). Controversial issues in central auditory processing disorders. *Seminars in Hearing, 19,* 393–398.

Jerger, J., & Musiek, F. (2000). Report of the consensus conference on the diagnosis of auditory processing disorders in school-aged children. *Journal of the American Academy of Audiology, 11,* 467–474.

Jerger, J., Weikers N. J., Sharbrough, F. W., 3rd, & Jerger, S. (1969). Bilateral lesions of the temporal lobe. A case study. *Acta Otolaryngologica, Supplement, 258,* 1–51.

Kamhi, A. G. (2004). A meme's eye view of speech-language pathology. *Language, Speech and Hearing Services in Schools, 35,* 105–111.

Keith, R. W. (1999). Clinical issues in central auditory processing disorders. *Language, Speech, and Hearing Services in the Schools, 30,* 339–344.

Kettlewell, P. W. (2004). Development, dissemination, and implementation of evidence-based treatments: Commentary. *Clinical Psychology: Science and Practice, 11,* 190–195.

Livingston, R. B., Jennings, E., Reynolds, C. R., & Gray, R. M. (2003). Multivariate analyses of the profile stability of intelligence tests: High for IQs, low to very low for subtest analyses. *Archives of Clinical Neuropsychology, 18,* 487–507.

Lohr, K. N., Eleazer, K., & Mauskopf, J. (1998). Health policy issues and applications for evidence-based medicine and clinical practice guidelines. Health Policy, 46, 1–19.

Lynn, G. E., & Gilroy, J. (1977). Evaluation of central auditory dysfunction in patients with neurological disorders. In R. W. Keith (Ed.), Central auditory dysfunction (pp. 177–221). New York: Grune & Stratton.

McFarland, D. J., & Cacace, A. T. (1995). Modality specificity as a criterion for diagnosing central auditory processing disorders. *American Journal of Audiology, 4,* 36–48.

Medwetsky, L. (2002). Central auditory processing testing: A battery approach. In J. Katz, R. F. Burkard, & L. Medwetsky (Eds.), *Handbook of clinical audiology,* (5th ed., pp. 510–524). Philadelphia: Lippincott Williams & Wilkens.

Meline, T., & Paradiso, T. (2003). Evidence-based practice in schools: Evaluating research and reducing barriers. *Language, Speech, and Hearing Services in Schools, 34,* 273–283.

Merz, W. R. (1998). Review of SCAN-A: A test for auditory processing disorders in adolescents and adults. In J. C. Impara & B. S. Plake (Eds.), *The thirteenth mental measurements yearbook, Buros Institute of Mental Measurements* (pp. 870–871). Lincoln: University of Nebraska Press.

Merzenich, M. M., Jenkins, W. M., Johnston, P., Schreiner, C., Miller, S., & Tallal, P. (1996). Temporal processing deficits of language-impaired children ameliorated by training. *Science, 271,* 77–80.

Moore, B. C. J., Glasberg, B. R., Plack, C. J., & Biswass, A. K. (1988). The shape of the ears temporal window. *Journal of the Acoustical Society of America, 83,* 1102–1116.

Mudford, O. C., Cross, B. A., Breen, S., Cillen, C., Reeves, D., Gould, J., & Douglas, J. (2000). Auditory integration training for children with autism: No behavioral benefits detected. *American Journal of Mental Retardation, 105,* 118–129.

Musiek, F. E., Baran, J. A., & Schochat, E. (1999). Selected management approaches to central auditory processing disorders. *Scandinavian Audiology, Supplement, 28,* 63–76.

Olsson, H., Bjorkman, C., Haag, K., & Juslin, P. (1998). Auditory inspection time: On the importance of selecting the appropriate sensory continuum. *Personality and Individual Differences, 25,* 627–634.

Oyler, R., Rosenhagen, K., & Michal, M. (1998). Sensitivity and specificity of Keith's auditory continuous performance test. *Language, Speech and Hearing Services in the Schools, 29,* 180–185.

Peterson, D. R. (2004). Science, scientism, and professional responsibility. *Clinical Psychology: Science and Practice, 11,* 196–210.

The Psychological Corporation. (1997). *WAIS-III, updated: Technical manual.* San Antonio, Texas: The Psychological Corporation.

Rees, N. S. (1973). Auditory processing factors in language disorders: The view from Procrustes' bed. *Journal of Speech and Hearing Disorders, 38,* 304–315.

Rees, N. S. (1981). Saying more than we know: Is auditory processing disorder a useful concept? In R. W. Keith (Ed.), *Central auditory and language disorders in children* (pp. 94–120). San Diego: College Hill Press.

Rosenberg, G. G. (2002). Classroom acoustics and personal FM technology in management of auditory processing disorder. *Seminars in Hearing, 23,* 309–317.

Rouse, C. E., & Krueger, A. B. (2004). Putting computerized instruction to the test: A randomized evaluation of a "scientifically based" reading program. *Economics of Education Review, 23,* 323–338.

Schmidt, F. L., & Hunter, J. E. (1999). Theory, Testing, and Measurement Error. *Intelligence, 27,* 183–198.

Schow, R. L., Seikel, J. A., Chermak, G. D., & Berent, M. (2000). Central auditory processes and test measures: ASHA 1996 revised. *American Journal of Audiology, 9,* 63–68.

Sternberg, R. J. (1999). Successful intelligence: Finding a balance. *Trends in Cognitive Science, 3,* 436–442.

Swets, J. A. (1988). Measuring the accuracy of diagnostic systems. *Science, 240,* 1285–1293.

Tallal, P., Miller, S., Bedi, G., Byma, G., Wang, X., Nagarajan, S. S., Schreiner, C., Jenkins, W. M., & Merzenich, M. M. (1996). Language comprehension in language-learning impaired children improved with acoustically modified speech. *Science, 271,* 81–84.

Temple, E., Deutsch, G. K., Poldrack, R. A., Miller, S. L., Tallal, P., & Merzenich, M. M. (2003). Neural deficits in children with dyslexia ameliorated by behavioral remediation: Evidence from functional MRI. *Science, 100,* 2860–2865.

Tyler, L. E. (1965). *The psychology of Human Differences,* Appleton-Century-Crofts, New York 3rd ed.

Verbaten, M. N., Kemner, C., Buitelaar, J. K., van Ree, J. M., van Beijsterveld, C. E. M., & van Engeland, H. (1996). Effects of ORG-2766 on brain event-related potentials of autistic children. *Psychiatry Research, 63,* 33–45.

Voyer, D. (2003). Reliability and Magnitude of Perceptual Asymmetries in a Dichotic Word Recognition Task. *Neuropsychology, 17,* 393-401.

Watson, C. S. (1994). How does psychoacoustics show that central auditory processing is critical to audition? The view from psychoacoustics. In *Proceedings of Consensus Development Conference on Central Auditory Processing* (pp. 1–21). Rockville, MD: American Speech-Language and Hearing Association.

Watson, C. S., Kidd, G. R., Horner, D. G., Connell, P. J., Lowther, A., Eddins, D. A., Krueger, G., Goss, D. A., Rainey, B. B., Gospel, M. D., & Watson, B. U. (2003). Sensory, cognitive, and linguistic factors in the early academic performance of elementary school children: The Benton-IU Project. *Journal of Learning Disabilities, 36,* 165–197.

Wertz, D., Hall, J. W., & Davis, W. (2002). Auditory processing disorders: Management approaches past to present. *Seminars in Hearing, 23,* 277–285.

Yencer, K. A. (1998). The effects of auditory integration training for children with central auditory processing disorders. *American Journal of Audiology, 7,* 1–13.

Author Index

Subject Index

Note: Figures and Tables are denoted in the index by *f* and *t*, respectively.